Dominique Haensell
Making Black History

Buchreihe der Anglia/ ANGLIA Book Series

Edited by
Lucia Kornexl, Ursula Lenker, Martin Middeke,
Gabriele Rippl, Daniel Stein

Advisory Board
Laurel Brinton, Philip Durkin, Olga Fischer, Susan Irvine,
Andrew James Johnston, Christopher A. Jones, Terttu Nevalainen,
Derek Attridge, Elisabeth Bronfen, Ursula K. Heise, Verena Lobsien,
Laura Marcus, J. Hillis Miller, Martin Puchner

Volume 73

Dominique Haensell

Making Black History

Diasporic Fiction in the Moment of Afropolitanism

DE GRUYTER

D 188

ISBN 978-3-11-126665-7
e-ISBN (PDF) 978-3-11-072209-3
e-ISBN (EPUB) 978-3-11-072214-7
ISSN 0340-5435
DOI https://doi.org/10.1515/9783110722093

This work is licensed under a Creative Commons Attribution-NonCommercia-NoDerivatives 4.0 International License. For details go to http://creativecommons.org/licenses/by-nc-nd/4.0/.

Library of Congress Control Number: 2021939336

Bibliographic information published by the Deutsche Nationalbibliothek
The Deutsche Nationalbibliothek lists this publication in the Deutsche Nationalbibliografie; detailed bibliographic data are available on the Internet at http://dnb.dnb.de.

© 2023 Dominique Haensell, published by Walter de Gruyter GmbH, Berlin/Boston
This volume is text- and page-identical with the hardback published in 2021.
This book is published with open access at www.degruyter.com
Printing and binding: CPI books GmbH, Leck

Contents

Acknowledgments —— VII

Chapter I
Introduction – Writing Race in the Moment of Afropolitanism —— 1
   1 Imagining Diaspora under the Sign of Africa —— 1
      1.1   The Moment of Blackness and the Discourse of Postness —— 7
      1.2   The Extranationality of African Literature —— 18
      1.3   The Dilemma of the Black Writer —— 21
      1.4   An African Atlantic: Provincializing the Middle Passage Epistemology —— 27
   2 Writing Race in/as History —— 39
      2.1   Raced Temporalities —— 40
      2.2   Diasporic Historicism or the Search for a Usable Past —— 44
      2.3   Timing Historical and Racial Trauma —— 49
   3 Conclusion: The Challenges of Afropolitan World Making —— 53

Chapter II
Going Through The Motions – Movement, Metahistory, and the Spectacle of Suffering in Teju Cole's *Open City* —— 57
   1 Introduction: Moving On or Being Moved? —— 57
   2 "To Trace Out a Story": Narrating Movement and the Movement of Narrative —— 60
   3 "To Experience the Pain Afresh": Metahistory and the Circling Movement of Melancholia —— 69
   4 "Voices Cut Out of the Past Into the Present": Blackness in Diaspora Time —— 81
   5 "In the Swirl of Other People's Stories": Toward an Ethics of Listening —— 89

Chapter III
(Post-)Independent Women – Romance, Return, and Pan-African Feminism in Chimamanda Ngozi Adichie's *Americanah* —— 100
   1 Introduction: Not That Kind of #BlackGirlMagic? —— 100
   2 "You Can't Write an Honest Novel About Race in This Country": Reading for Race —— 105

3 "True from Experience": Reception and the Realness of Racialization —— 110
  4 "A Bitter Americanizing": Gendered Violence in the Aftermath of Slavery —— 117
  5 "An American Pathology": Reading *Americanah* as Quest Romance —— 125
  6 "An Unapologetic Love Story": Adichie's Gendered Romance with Africa —— 131
  7 "This Shared Space of Africanness": The Hair Salon as Afropolitan Heterotopia —— 142

Chapter IV
A Painful Notion of Time – Conveying Black Temporality in Yaa Gyasi's *Homegoing* —— 150
  1 Introduction: Writing Diaspora Across the Middle Passage —— 150
  2 Historical Fiction Is "Having a Moment" —— 155
  3 The Problem of History: Historiography's Imperial Legacies —— 158
  4 The Other Problem of History: What Cannot Be Represented —— 166
  5 "An Accumulation of Time": Writing Time as History —— 175
  6 "The Gnarled Fingers of Fate": Curse Temporalities and the Question of Agency —— 184
  7 Forgive Your Mother? Memory, Redemption, and the Sense of an Ending —— 190

Chapter V
Conclusion – The Past Is Always Tense, the Future Perfect —— 204

Bibliography —— 217

Index —— 238

Acknowledgments

First of all, I want to thank the ANGB editors for including my book in the Anglia Book Series.

I would also like to thank my PhD advisors Ulla Haselstein and Sabine Schülting, as well as Yogita Goyal, for their invaluable feedback, encouragement, and mentorship.

Thank you to the GSNAS administration for their ceaseless assistance and especially to my cohort, GSNAS 2014. You're radical and you are what made this fun.

My gratitude goes also to Zeno Ackermann, Justus K.S. Makokha, and Jo Malt for saying the right things at the right time and making me see that this was possible.

And, of course, to my family: Thank you for everything.

Chapter I
Introduction – Writing Race in the Moment of Afropolitanism

> "We all know the truth: more connects us than separates us. But in times of crisis the wise build bridges, while the foolish build barriers. We must find a way to look after one another, as if we were one single tribe."
>
> T'Challa

> "Whatever of good may have come in these years of change, the shadow of a deep disappointment rests upon the Negro people."
>
> W.E.B. Du Bois

> "I have always felt like I want to change the course of history."
>
> Opal Tometi

1 Imagining Diaspora under the Sign of Africa

Afropolitanism, that much is certain, is a quintessentially 21st-century phenomenon. The term itself was popularized by Taiye Selasi in 2005 in "Bye-Bye Babar (or What is an Afropolitan)," an essay for the British magazine *The LIP*. While Selasi's coinage most prevalently served as a new identificatory label for an African-descendant bourgeoisie in Western metropolises, described as "the newest generation of African emigrants, coming soon or collected already at a law firm/chem lab/jazz lounge near you" (2013: 528), the concept also featured slightly earlier in the writings of Achille Mbembe, drawing attention to the fluidity, mobility, and cultural hybridity already proper to the African continent. As Justus K. S. Makokha and Jennifer Wawrzinek, the editors of the first academic publication on Afropolitanism, put it, both Selasi and Mbembe "describe a novel critical term, at whose core are questions of borders and spaces of new African identities" and which denotes "Africans at home and abroad who subscribe to anti-nativist and cosmopolitan interpretations of African identities" (2011: 17–18).[1] In its wider reception, Afropolitanism has sparked a myriad of de-

---

[1] In the following, when needed, I will distinguish the two notions of Afropolitanism as "diasporic" and "continental," even though my focus lies on the former. Keeping in mind that Africa itself, as Gikandi describes it, is a "shifting signifier" that means something different in South Africa than it does in Kenya, and therefore means something else in Brazil or in the USA, those distinctions are of course already very general (2016: 47–48).

bates, with reactions ranging from affirmative praise to critical skepticism, e.g. in Binyavanga Wainaina's 2012 speech "I am a Pan-Africanist, not an Afropolitan" or in Simon Gikandi's endorsing of the concept, framing it as a "new phenomenology of Africanness" and a "way of being African in the world" (2011a: 9). While there is a plethora of publications trying to discern the normative value of Afropolitanism as an identificatory concept, label, politics, ethics, or aesthetics,[2] the working definition of Afropolitanism adopted in this book comes closest to the one formulated by Ryan Thomas Skinner in "Why Afropolitanism Matters" (2017). Skinner also wishes to retain the idea of Afropolitanism as a "polysemous and [...] 'floating signifier'" that is less defined as a "good idea as it is [...] 'good to think with'" (3). Indeed, in order to neither fix nor blur the polysemy or multidirectedness of Afropolitanism, and in ways elaborated in the following, this book conceives of Afropolitanism first and foremost as a historical and cultural moment. More precisely, I investigate a selection of Afropolitan novels, which could mean literature written by authors deemed to be Afropolitan or featuring Afropolitan characters but is here defined as literature written and received in the moment of Afropolitanism, that is, a certain historical constellation that allows us to glimpse the shifting and multiple silhouettes which Africa, as signifier, as real and imagined locus, embodies in the globalized, yet predominantly Western, cultural landscape of the 21st century.[3] How does one capture a moment? In "Bye-Bye Babar" Selasi historicizes Afropolitanism through an often-quoted narrative, referencing the increased African emigration to the Global North since the mid-20th century: "It isn't hard to trace our genealogy. Starting in the 1960s, the young, gifted and broke left Africa in pursuit of higher education and happiness abroad" (2013a: 528). In the context of the United States, it is indeed the 1965 Hart-Celler Immigration Act that is most often cited as inaugurating the emergence of a "New African Diaspora," epitomized by Sam Robert's statement in the *New York Times* that "[f]or the first time, more blacks are coming to the United States from Africa than during the slave trade" (2005: section 1.1.).[4] Yet Selasi also offers another time frame, one marked by matters of cultural representation. Somewhere "between the 1988 release of *Coming to*

---

[2] See Dabiri 2014; Eze 2014: 234–247; Gehrmann 2015: 1–12; Balakrishnan 2017: 1–11; Knudsen and Rahbek 2016.

[3] Here, I lean only partly on the influential work by Valentin Mudimbe because, in a diasporic imaginary, the symbol of Africa is not first and foremost characterized by lack or deviance. For further discussion on the image of Africa, predominantly from a Western perspective, see Mudimbe 1988 and 1994; cf. also Mbembe and Nuttall 2004: 347–372.

[4] For more information on this demographic shift, see Kondadu-Agyemang et al. 2006; Shaw-Taylor and Tuch 2007; Falola et al. 2017.

America and the 2001 crowning of a Nigerian Miss World," she writes, "the general image of young Africans in the West transmorphed from goofy to gorgeous" (2013a: 529).

For the purpose of my argument, I would like to trace Selasi's timeline into the more recent past. Three years after Selasi published her essay, the Studio Museum in Harlem produced the show "Flow" that showcased young diasporic African artists. In 2011, the Houston Museum of African American Culture hosted a symposium with the title "Africans in America – The New Beat of Afropolitans," the same year in which the Victoria & Albert Museum in London organized the evening event "Friday Late: Afropolitans." In the following years, the global literary marketplace was flushed with narratives by young diasporic authors like Selasi herself, who were praised for their cosmopolitan, transnational outlook and for their post-melting pot sensibilities and were deliberately marketed under the slogan Afropolitanism. So far, this reads as a fairly impressionistic yet straightforward succession and success story for Selasi's young, hip, and artistically gifted Afropolitans. Yet I would extend this timeline by adding a few related snapshots: In 2013, Beyoncé sampled another one of these authors, Chimamanda Ngozi Adichie, further cementing Adichie's pop-cultural fame. Three years later, 2016, Kendrick Lamar closed a spectacular Grammy performance by showing a silhouette of Africa inscribed with the word "Compton." And in 2018, Ryan Coogler's Marvel franchise *Black Panther* became one of the most successful movies of all time. In this timeline, Selasi's historization of the Afropolitan moment comes full circle, as the emergence of Afropolitanism is bracketed with two Hollywood representations: from *Coming to America*'s garishly stereotypical, traditionalist kingdom of Zamunda to the equally monarchist yet Afrofuturistic kingdom of Wakanda.

By adding these elements, the narrative changes in two important ways. For one, it is no longer about individuals labeled as Afropolitans but frames Afropolitanism as a larger diasporic discourse or mode of signification. Conceived by Selasi as the result of complex historico-political trajectories made visible through cultural representations, it marks how, in a global yet US-dominated cultural imaginary, the African signifier has evolved into a hypervisible and highly valuable symbolic currency: from goofy to glamorous, backward to vanguard. Secondly, this narrative relays how the contemporary diasporic imaginary goes beyond issues of identification and othering but is instead marked by various degrees of projection, rejection, citation, sampling, and collaboration. Contrary to claims that Afropolitanism is first and foremost a renunciation of Black diasporic unity or solidarity and "instead seeks to reimagine an Africa apart from Blackness," I argue that, particularly in the US, it marks a moment of intense resignification of Blackness and diasporic solidarity (Balakrishnan 2018: 576).

While Teju Cole in "On the Blackness of the Panther," a thought-provoking meditation on Hollywood fantasies, Bandung-solidarity, and African complexity, has criticized how films like *Black Panther* rely on the image of Africa "as trope and trap, backdrop and background" (2018: para. 15), he can be credited with fashioning a similarly effective trope himself: Africa not only in, but as index of the entire world. In "At Home in Brooklyn," an article for an exhibition catalogue featuring the works of Wangechi Mutu and others, Cole describes these artists as various instances of "what happens when Africa meets Brooklyn" (2014a: 30). Pondering his NYC borough, a place characterized by the author's intimate sense of belonging, Cole frames his experience of feeling at home in the world with a reflection on the famous 1972 photograph taken by the Apollo 17 space shuttle, showing, for the first time, our "blue marble." He writes:

> Just one continent is visible from the angle at which that photograph was taken. It was as though the earth presented itself with an indexical representation of all it contained. The planet puts its best face forward for its first formal portrait, and one continent happens to be visible in its entirety: Africa. (Cole 2014a: para. 12)

Like many other protagonists of the Afropolitan moment, Cole is actively inscribing Africa into a Black diasporic imaginary by claiming an (at least) two-tier type of belonging, in his case to a traditionally Black neighborhood like Brooklyn and the continent of Africa. At the same time, he identifies the substantial "energy flows" between the physically mismatched pair of Africa and Brooklyn as an indexical "picture of the world right now" (ibid.). If anything, *Black Panther* signals a similar will to (re)imagine the contemporary diaspora – or global humanity for that matter – unfolding in and across differences and under the sign of Africa. As King T'Challa's voiceover during the film's final scenes implores: "We all know the truth: more connects us than separates us. But in times of crisis the wise build bridges, while the foolish build barriers. We must find a way to look after one another, as if we were one single tribe."

The rubric of Afropolitan literature is as flexible as it is expansive, ranging from generational definitions to questions of genre, setting, or subject matter. Among the Anglophone novels and short story collections that usually make these ever extending lists are Taiye Selasi's *Ghana Must Go* (2013), NoViolet Bulawayo's *We Need New Names* (2013), Chris Abani's *The Virgin of Flames* (2007), Chinelo Okparanta's *Happiness, Like Water* (2013), Dinaw Mengestu's *The Beautiful Things That Heaven Bears* (2007), Sefi Atta's *A Bit of Difference* (2013), Chika Unigwe's *On Black Sisters' Street* (2007), and Brian Chikwava's *Harare North* (2009). For this study, a selection of three major Afropolitan novels has been made – major in that each of them has become an international bestseller –

which, to my mind, best capture what is both popular with and popularized by these literatures. Teju Cole's *Open City* (2011), Chimamanda Ngozi Adichie's *Americanah* (2013), and Yaa Gyasi's *Homegoing* (2016) are all deliberate investigations of the US, exploring the questions of Blackness and diaspora from, at minimum, bifocal and, as I will argue, pronouncedly metahistorical perspectives. Incidentally, these authors also represent the full spectrum of contemporary African/US-American relations, at least in respect to citizenship and positionality. Teju Cole, who was born in the US in 1975 yet grew up in Nigeria and returned to the US as a teenager, holds both citizenships and has referred to this duality as being "not 100 percent at home in either of them" (2017: para. 7). Chimamanda Ngozi Adichie was born in Nigeria in 1977 and moved to the US for university education. She is Nigerian, staunchly and outspokenly so, but has permanent resident status in the US, traveling back and forth. Yaa Gyasi was born in Ghana (1989) but raised in the US from the age of two, thoroughly undergoing what is commonly understood as the 'immigrant experience.'

Afropolitan literatures pose different sets of questions, some transnational, some intra-continental, some intradiasporic, and the following study is most interested in the latter. Rather than distinguishing merely between "Western-facing" and continental-facing literatures, as some commentators have, it is useful to differentiate further and acknowledge that the Afropolitan moment is also characterized by an Americanization of African fiction. An important and, due to this study's focus, overlooked role in this development is, of course, played by international publishing industries, which also mirrors the shift from Europe to North America. For example, the renowned Heinemann African Writers Series (later Penguin African Writer's Series) began in 1962 and was finally discontinued in 2003 after dwindling sales and diminished relevance over the prior two decades (its last publication was Ike Oguine's *A Squatter's Tale*, incidentally a novel about a Nigerian immigrant in the US). Yet all of the authors discussed here, and many others of their moment, have been picked up and promoted by US-American publishing houses. Regardless of the fact that African literatures have always had a bifurcated publishing history (with Heinemann based not only in London, but also Ibadan and Nairobi), the debate about the major role of Western publishing houses is usually flanked by references to a vibrant, if commercially limited, publishing scene on the continent, e. g. Chimurenga or Kwani Trust (which was also 'exposed' for being 'Western-funded'). More recent publishing companies like Cassava Republic, hailed as "the first African publisher to open a subsidiary outside the continent," complicate matters further by straddling multiple markets with impressive aplomb (Fick 2016: para 5).⁵

The US-American backdrop of the novels discussed here already adds a particularly defining and indeed 'new' spin to the émigré, exilic, or immigrant African novel of prior generations, which usually detailed African sojourns in Europe. While the protagonists in Buchi Emecheta's *In the Ditch* (1972) or Ama Ata Aidoo's *Our Sister Killjoy* (1977) would often encounter members of diasporic communities – hailing from other parts of Africa or the Caribbean, thus illustrating the fact that the Black Diaspora⁶ is made up of multiple diasporas – a US context shifts the framing of these different diasporic trajectories from the geographical to the temporal, rendering the contemporary diasporic imaginary primarily a conversation between the old and the new. Consequently, within the Afropolitan moment it is also possible to speak of an Africanization of (African) American fiction. In this sense, Afropolitan literature describes what Stephanie Li, in an *American Literary History* issue on contemporary African American writing, describes as one of its most salient features: "the impact of a generation of African-born or -identified authors like Chimamanda Ngozi Adichie, Teju Cole, and Mfoniso Udofia, who all bring a contemporary diasporic perspective to US race relations" (2017: 632). Of course, the impact of this conversation is not limited to the diaspora, not only because "the shape of diaspora is the shape of the globe" (Wright 2013: 15). By rebranding and simultaneously complicating the "lazy but necessary signifier" that is Africa (Hall 2003: 32), Afropolitan negotiations of Blackness embody yet another instance of Stuart Hall's notion of Black popular culture as a globally effective "site of strategic contestation" (Hall 1993: 108). Yet, as the following discussion will show, it is in the context of the US that shifting significations of Blackness develop the strongest ripple effect and the moment of Afropolitanism manifests as a particularly crucial historical constel-

---

5 See also Clarke 2003; Adesokan 2012; Nwaubani 2017.
6 While this study uses the terms African Diaspora and Black Diaspora sometimes interchangeably, a few clarifications are in order. Generally, my focus is on the Black Diaspora, precisely because it links Afropolitanism to various discourses on Blackness. At the same time, the notion of an African Diaspora can be helpful to emphasize the centrality of the African signifier as opposed to a distinct and ultimately severed notion of New World diasporic Blackness. It is also helpful when relating to the so-called newness and oldness of Black American groups hailing from Africa, as well as stressing the pivotal role of Africa in a global Black imaginary. However, the usage of African Diaspora occurs in the full knowledge that African does not exclusively signify Black and that an African Diaspora may subsume different racial groups. Because of this, and because I am also wary of terms that may obscure the specificities of anti-Blackness, this study generally favors the usage of Black Diaspora and, when referring to the African Diaspora, implicitly means Black African Diaspora.

lation. While the Afropolitan moment can surely be characterized as a symbolic and representational shift that has bestowed these hugely successful literatures with cultural currency, I conceive of it as mode or moment in which the shifting role of Africa in the global imaginary is part of an ongoing diasporic conversation determining the sometimes uneasy negotiations of race, nationality, and Black identity between the so-called old and new diaspora. In this, I follow Yogita Goyal's assertion that "now the new diaspora writes back," as well as her call that we need new diasporas, meaning we need new concepts and understandings of how Africa and its global dispersion may signify in the 21st century (Goyal 2017c: 659).

1.1 The Moment of Blackness and the Discourse of Postness

As these works are predominantly set, produced, and received in a US context, the supposed "newness" of the perspectives of a "Non-American Black" (Adichie 2013) or "Newly Black" (Chude-Sokei 2014) generation of artists needs to be questioned, contrasted, and related to more established diasporic epistemologies. Afropolitan writing, engaged in US-American racial discourses and championing a Black subjectivity that forgoes the formative trauma of slavery, thus runs the risk of being mobilized in opposition to African American subjectivity or as stand-in or proof of a post-racial paradigm. Thus, one of my key concerns is to find a nuanced and productive way to illuminate the notion of (historical) change symbolized and addressed by these novels while remaining wary of the rhetoric of postness, newness, turns or paradigm shifts. The Afropolitan moment, as a lens or tool that is "good to think with," allows me to reflect on history and temporality in a manner that traces the various entry points, origins, futures, and trajectories but also limits of Blackness in the contemporary diasporic imaginary. As these texts foreground different epistemic positionalities toward the Black Diaspora and its generic conventions through their respective treatment of temporality, historiography, and the transnational imaginary, I intend to frame them as articulations of a particular moment without neglecting that these novels are in continuous conversation with earlier or other traditions and epistemologies.

The aspect of *newness* that is often ascribed to the Afropolitan as another variant of postness, introduces another important framework for this study and one that is equally dependent on the notion of Afropolitanism as a moment. Why should one want to capture a moment if not to signal or indicate change? And who, in the course of this young century, has embodied the notion of change and the historical constellation of the Afropolitan better than Barack

Obama, the American son of a Kenyan immigrant? As scholar Paul Tiyambe Zeleza asserted, Obama's "multiple racial, religious, cultural, spatial, and social identities and affiliations make him the quintessential subject and sign, signifier and signified of a 21st century transnational African consciousness and solidarity" (2011: 37). Zeleza, who has elsewhere developed a system of "flows" when writing about the linkages between Africa and its diasporas (2019), identified the "age of Obama" as one of potentiality, a chance to regroup and refocus Pan-Africanism by seriously engaging the "overlapping diasporas in the US" and examining how they relate to their respective homelands and Africa as a whole (2011: 37). More or less independent from the fact that Obama would never implement a radical politics "committed to profound social change" (2011: 34), Zeleza predicted that the symbolic value of Obama's presidency, his impact on a Pan-African or larger diasporic imaginary would remain profound. As the son of a Kenyan immigrant and symbol "of black citizenship and African globality, who projects a new image of the African arrival and presence in America," Zeleza notes, "Obama reconnects the old diaspora to Africa and vice-versa in more immediate, intimate, and innovative ways" (2011: 38). Generally, Obama's presidency had a particularly galvanizing effect not only in (Black) American contexts, but throughout the diaspora and the African continent, symbolizing euphoric hope as well as intense disappointment.

In *Seeing Through Race* (2012), W.J.T. Mitchell develops the notion of the 'teachable moment' apropos Barack Obama's attempt to contain the controversy around the arrest of Professor Henry Louis Gates in 2009. Mitchell uses the pedagogical notion of the teachable moment and his interpretation of race as a medium to see through rather than look at, in order to pose "the more general notion of race as a global issue in our time – our 'moment' as it were" (2012: 2). In this, he is particularly wary of the rhetoric of postness, which he describes as "temporal substitutes for a positive historical description that has not yet found its proper name" (45). At the same time, he notes that our contemporary moment is marked by a "post-racial consensus" (60) that has allowed many white Americans to ignore these issues – at least until, through violent spectacles of police violence, "anti-Black racism becomes *visible*" (54).

Arguably, 2020 provided a tragic abundance of such spectacles. In particular, the brutal killing of George Floyd seems to have engendered a level of awareness that – if not in quality, then perhaps in quantity – seems to have broadly refuted the prevailing "post-racial consensus" that Mitchell identifies. Yet, if anything, the enhanced visibility of racist violence and its political responses, such as the US Movement for Black Lives, have highlighted the tenacity of post-racial claims amidst a pandemic that – contrary to the levelling effect of an ostensibly universal threat – has disproportionately affected African American communities

(Jean-Baptiste and Green 2020). The pervasiveness of post-racial thinking should not be surprising – given the complex ways in which race and racism structure contemporary societies. Even where it is not deliberately harnessed in favor of white supremacy, post-racialism acts as a cognitive shorthand, blanketing these often thorny complexities in lieu of lofty egalitarian or universalist ideals.

In a similar vein, the tendency to resolve and dissolve racial difference in claims of universality is also proper to Afropolitanism, which, as a concept, has always been embedded in theories of cosmopolitanism. This semantic kinship has triggered negative responses by critics who see in it not only a premature invocation of post-racialism but also warn against the uncritical appropriation of Enlightenment concepts relying on Eurocentric notions of exclusion. An outspoken critic of Afropolitanism, scholar Cheryl Sterling argues that the necessity to push back biological race concepts does not "eradicate racism or the history of racialism" that undergirds a concept like cosmopolitanism (2015: 121). In the wake of an increasingly globalized and demographically intertwined 21st century, she notes, "the continued sublation of the Black subject" persists, thus calling for a persistent reminding of the world that Black lives matter (ibid.).[7]

Notably, in terms of racial politics, the years of Obama's presidency – and their aftermath – have become more emblematic of stagnation or backlash than transcendence or advancement. Rather than prematurely signaling progress, then, one could still consider the 'moment of Obama' as ushering in a renewed and intensified discussion on race and racism, a 'teachable moment' one could say, that markedly affected Afropolitanism. Because Afropolitanism gains the most symbolic currency within this historical period, it is perhaps also unsurprising that its discourses mirror the affective economies triggered by Obama's presidency. The novels under discussion were all published post-2008, precisely because the Afropolitan moment dovetails with and derives sub-

---

[7] Sterling also points toward the discrepancy between the political actuality that has transpired through the Black Lives Matter movement in the US and the prevalent academic insistence on the virtuality and constructedness of race, indicating a post-racial paradigm shift that sees race identification or race-based theorizing as outdated modes of thinking (2015: 120). Having argued earlier against Paul Gilroy's positionality in *Against Race* (2000), Sterling turns to the concept of Kwame Anthony Appiah's rooted cosmopolitanism, which, she notes, is exemplary of the way "such work is used in academe as a key articulation of an idealized post-race trajectory" (ibid.). Sterling identifies both Appiah's and Gilroy's critiques of racialized discourse as theoretical positionalities that argue against the viability of race as "a paradigm in modern day constructs" (ibid.), rather than as critiques of the detrimental, and very real, effect of racism around the globe. For Sterling, these positions seem representative of a distinct, and perhaps even hegemonic, academic stance that shuns race-based theorizing as a defunct remnant of the past.

stantial momentum from the so-called post-racial moment, allegedly sealed by the advent of US America's first Black president. Equally premature, I argue, are initial interpretations of Afropolitan writers and fictions as being beyond race or about divesting Africanity from Blackness. The tensions arising from the conundrum of post-Black African cosmopolitanism is reflected in the literature, as well as in its criticism.

In 2011, in the wake of much enthusiasm around Afropolitanism, Gikandi hailed this "new phenomenology of Africanness" as a way to "embrace and celebrate a state of cultural hybridity – to be of Africa and of other worlds at the same time (2011a: 9). Five years later, Gikandi's assessment of literary Afropolitanism struck a notably minor key. In an interview with the authors of *In Search of the Afropolitan*, he observes that "this elite group of Afro-cosmopolitans has adopted Afropolitanism, not as a celebration of living a global life, but as anxiety" (2016: 49). Interpreting this affective change as a response to what he calls "the incomplete project of transnationalism, or of globalization," Gikandi notes his surprise at the persistency of identifications and the fraught need for cultural affiliations in these literatures (ibid. 51). For him, the most interesting question is why "these identifications do not disappear and coalesce into a certain cosmopolitan prose?" (ibid. 50). Works by Teju Cole, Sefi Atta, and particularly Tayie Selasi's *Ghana Must Go*, the first novel that was prominently marketed under the notion of Afropolitanism, express for Gikandi less of the term's confident global belonging but indeed "a constant failure to live in that world" (ibid. 49). Likewise, and particularly for the US-American contexts that these novels fictionalize, Louis Chude-Sokei detects "a sense of loss, of transformation and decline" in the literary texts of these newly Black American authors (2014: 53). Ascribing this to the complicated intradiasporic relationship, the unanswered questions and uneasy negotiations of racial solidarity and diasporic unity, he concludes: "These palpitating moments of discontinuity and Pan-African brokenness draw attention to the great width and depth of difference, of arguably different diasporas that assume the intimacy of a shared name but which can no longer assume a shared experience, much less shared politics" (55).

Adopting a similar, yet ultimately less bleak view, I would contend that the questions of race and Blackness are still too vexing to "coalesce" into cosmopolitanism. However, I agree that complicated intradiasporic conversations on these matters do play out in these texts, and that these often uneasy conversations defy the comforting notions of hybridity or Pan-African unity of prior decades. In particular, Afropolitanism challenges received notions of Blackness in the US. While the idea of post-racialism has been at least identified as a dangerous myth, Afropolitanism often hypostatizes in a post-Black discourse signaling a reconfiguration and regrouping of US-American Blackness rather than its overcoming. In many ways, the notion of post-Blackness in public discourse similarly retains and reconfigures its subject matter – like the other discourses on postness constituting Afropolitanism, e.g. the postcolonial or postmodern. Rather than disappearing, then, established modes of Black signification, both within the US and in the global context of the Black Diaspora, have mutated and differentiated in a way that cannot be captured by the temporal category of posteriority, at least not if one understands Blackness as a complex intersection of identities that cannot be neatly mapped onto a necessarily limited, national narrative of linear progress but is much better grasped though the elasticity of a moment. Indeed, elaborating on his definition of a moment as a more productive tool to preserve and see through, rather than censor, the issue at hand, Mitchell writes: "Ranging between the expansiveness of an epoch, a period, or an era, and the singular, decisive character of an event, the moment is arguably the most elastic term in the lexicons of time and history" (2012: 2). It is precisely this temporal elasticity that lends itself so well to the project at hand. In order to illuminate the complex negotiations of Blackness and the African signifier in the Afropolitan novel, a temporal metaphor seems most apt to encompass both historical and experiential configurations of Blackness without erasing and substituting one for the other or re-installing hierarchies that privilege narratives of authenticity.

In order to trace this development more closely, it is worthwhile to return to the "foundational" text of Afropolitanism, Taiye Selasi's "Bye-Bye Babar (or What is an Afropolitan)." Critics who consider the rejection of Blackness one of Afropolitanism's most salient features, often refer to the following passage from Selasi's essay:

> [T]he way we see our race – whether black or biracial or none of the above – is a question of politics, rather than pigment; not all of us claim to be black. Often this relates to the way we were raised, whether proximate to other brown people (e.g. black Americans) or removed. Finally, how we conceive of race will accord with where we locate ourselves in the history that produced "blackness" and the political processes that continue to shape it. (2013a: 530)

For those inclined to perceive Afropolitanism as a "willingness to break from received racial molds," this paragraph indicates "the need to reconfigure African identity outside of Blackness" – as if that were a prerequisite for the true "worlding" of the African subject (Balakrishnan 2018: 577). Indeed, the crucial sentiments behind Selasi's otherwise rather matter-of-fact definition of Blackness as a social, historical, and political construct seem to be the notions of agency and choice. She posits "the way *we see* our race" (emphasis added), defying the heteronomy of racialization, and also "not all of us claim to be black," meaning not all of us *choose* to be Black. Underlying the question of choice is the possibility of rejection, the "I prefer not to" and "I'd rather not" that suggest the disavowal of racism and the negation of solidarity and add to the perceived snobbery and slight that many associate with Afropolitanism.[8] However, while the observation that for many members of the new diaspora racial solidarity or Black identification is not given but negotiated surely holds true, Selasi's utterances must also be understood as part of a cultural and political discourse in which the notion of what constitutes 'authentic' Blackness is unstable, even, or especially, for African Americans. Rather than taking the willed divestment of Blackness as an Afropolitan *a priori*, I would argue that Selasi's hyperbolic and polemic text from 2005 signals not only the 'will' and 'need' of its performative agency, but also a profound insecurity and apprehension around the category of Blackness. More than a decade later, it becomes clear that this ambiguity is proper to the Afropolitan moment, particularly to how it pans out in the United States.

In 2001, Harlem Studio museum director Thelma Golden defined "Post-Black" as "characterized by artists who were adamant about not being labeled 'black' artists, though their work was steeped, in fact deeply interested, in redefining complex notions of blackness" (2001: 14).[9] The post-racial declarations of the Obama era were primed by this discourse of post-Blackness. As a figure, Obama crystallized several different yet related trajectories, all coalescing around the 21st-century version of Du Bois's inquiry into "the strange meaning of being black here in the dawning of the Twentieth Century" (*Souls* 3). Not only the demographic fact of overlapping diasporas, but also debates around post-Soul aesthetics or post-Civil Rights-politics were bundled by the symbol of Obama, creating highly charged nodes of interpretations.[10] The debates around Obama's racial identity were particularly indicative of these shifts, illuminating the overarching discourse of post-Blackness.In the most controversial piece, Debra Dickerson's "Colorblind," the author put it bluntly:

---

[8] Implied, too, in the notion of "choice" is the most crucial difference between the African diasporas of old and new, the element of choosing to come to America, albeit for oftentimes pressing reasons, rather than being abducted.

[9] The coining of the term "Post-Blackness" is usually ascribed to Thelma Golden and artist Glenn Ligon, who developed it in relation to "Freestyle," a show curated by Golden in 2001. Incidentally, "Freestyle" is also the forerunner for the above-mentioned "Flow," focusing on new diasporic African artists. See Campbell 2007: 317–330.

[10] The question whether Obama's presidency signaled an end or shift from Civil Rights politics informed countless political commentaries, which seamlessly connected with the realm of cultural politics and aesthetics, for example when Obama's memoir, *Dreams from My Father*, was associated with post-Soul aesthetics. See Ashe 2010: 103–15.

> Obama isn't black. "Black," in our political and social reality, means those descended from West African slaves. Voluntary immigrants of African descent (even those descended from West Indian slaves) are just that, voluntary immigrants of African descent with markedly different outlooks on the role of race in their lives and in politics. At a minimum, it can't be assumed that a Nigerian cabdriver and a third-generation Harlemite have more in common than the fact a cop won't bother to make the distinction. They're both "black" as a matter of skin color and DNA, but only the Harlemite, for better or worse, is politically and culturally black, as we use the term. (2007: para. 10)

Already the immediate reactions to this, however, conveyed the true complexity of this issue, namely that the debate was very much imbedded in a general reevaluation and questioning of the American category of "Blackness." As a *Poplicks* blogger named O.W. writes:

> I hear what she's saying here but does that mean that a third-generation Harlemite shares the same perspectives as every other African American (of slave-descent) in every other part of the country? Does the Blackness experienced or internalized by said Harlemite equal that of a Black person from Baldwin Hills? Or Chicago's Southside? Or Hunter's Point? The point here is that you can't have it both ways: either Blackness is a fixed identity (a philosophy that plays all too well into racist hands) or it's broad enough to include a range of Blackness beyond just the authenticating force of slavery's legacy. (2007: para. 7)

Hence, without even having to take up the issue of his Kenyan heritage or his biracial background, journalist Touré was able to state: "Post-Black means we are like Obama: rooted in but not restricted by Blackness" (2011: 12). Notably, the optimism signaled by the earlier instances of Post-Blackness soon made way for more critical assessments of that discourse's cultural and political merits. And this, in turn, also affected Afropolitan literatures. In his glum analysis of how the protagonists of novels like Ike Oguine's *A Squatter's Tale,* Teju Cole's *Open City,* or Adichie's *Americanah* intersect, or rather fail to intersect with Black American culture, Chude-Sokei argues that the aforementioned "sense of loss, of transformation and decline" is in fact "paradigmatic, not only of contemporary African writing and the waves of immigration that impel it, but for the wider context of the new cultural politics of a black America that is deeply in the throes of what theorist Judith Butler would call a 'category crisis'" (2014: 53–54).

It is possible to interpret the novels selected for my analysis as various responses to the 21st-century failures epitomized by the US – which was seen as a driving force of an incomplete project of globalization – and particularly those shortcomings associated with the figure of Obama: the extension of the color line into the foreseeable future and the incessant demotion of Africa's role in global and diasporic relations. For those who ever believed in it, Obama's notion of change, his vision of a "more perfect union," has fallen flat in the light of a violent and seemingly unchanging status quo. To many ears, then, Du Bois's description of post-Emancipation America in *The Souls of Black Folk*, that "[w]hatever of good may have come in these years of change, the shadow of a deep disappointment rests upon the Negro people," sounds strangely familiar (2007: 10). The disappointments born from that hopeful moment, its impact on how the US, the Black Diaspora, or the world narrates its notions of political progress, often translates into pronouncedly pessimist metahistorical positions that equally play out in the Afropolitan novel – already impacted by the pessimist outlook of post-independence African literatures. Seen from the more austere of these perspectives, the notion of progressive historical change has been fatally undermined, if not inverted, as the contemporary political moment is characterized not by progress, but by a sense of endless repetition and constant return, marked by what Aliyyah Abdur-Rahman describes as the "perpetuity of crisis" (2017: 687) and haunted by what Saidiya Hartman has coined the "afterlife of slavery" (2007: 6).

Yet, as Vinson Cunningham writes in *The New Yorker*, "Obama's truest political gift, perhaps, was the ability to let a thousand flowers of expectation, born of history, bloom" (para. 5).[11] The same moment that allowed Obama to signify and thwart the prefigured fulfillment of a promise – marking the final success of Black liberation, its telos and icon – also made way for Black Lives Matter, "the most significant political uprising since the Civil Rights era" (Li 2017: 633). As a digital movement, Black Lives Matter has effortlessly transcended borders; morphing from an online hashtag to galvanizing grassroots activism around the globe. The anti-racist protests occurring around the globe in the summer of 2020 were driven in large and significant parts by the concerted efforts of various local Black Lives Matter groups, many of which had formed amidst the wave of global demonstrations following the deaths of Michael Brown and Eric Garner in 2014, and who had since worked often independently but determinedly for racial justice.

In an article titled "The Changing Same," referencing the term coined by Amiri Baraka, George Lipsitz places the recent decade, along with its premature promise of a post-racial society, on an anti-progressive, static timeline that he calls the "Katrina-Ferguson-Conjuncture":

> A decade that began with the organized abandonment and yet punitive confinement of impoverished Black residents of New Orleans in the wake of Hurricane Katrina in 2005 culminated with the manipulation of the Grand Jury process to make sure that no charges would be brought against the killer of Michael Brown in Ferguson in 2014. Along the way, a racial-

---

11 For longer discussions of Obama's presidency, see Dyson 2016 and Coates 2017.

ly orchestrated economic crisis produced the greatest loss of assets in history for Black and brown people. Vehement rhetoric, violent acts, and vile policies have targeted immigrants of color, producing mass deportations and detentions. [...] In popular culture and political discourse, online and in the streets, in private acts of discrimination and in public policies [...] racism continues to be learned, legitimated and legislated. (2018: 16–17)

While Lipsitz accedes that the Katrina-Ferguson-Conjuncture is also an oppositional conjuncture, carrying the seed for change, he identifies the present as a time of uncanny returns: "Words uttered decades ago could just as easily have been spoken yesterday. The #BlackLivesMatter and #SayHerName movements of today are new, but their core concerns eerily echo James Baldwin's observations from 1963" (ibid. 16). Critical voices like Lipsitz often describe the political present as a reiteration of the Civil Rights movement to highlight the continuity of racism that underlies what Joseph R. Winters has called the "agony of progress." Yet there are crucial differences that may also affect the way one thinks about notions of historical change, repetition, and continuity. While it is not a secret, it is often overlooked that one of the three female founders of Black Lives Matter, Opal Tometi, is a Nigerian-American who understands anti-Black racism as a global problem and has made immigration a core issue of BLM's political work.[12] Conscious of how her experiences intersect with those of African Americans, she has repeatedly emphasized how "black immigrant experience in the U.S. must be understood not in contrast to the African American experience but as an integral part of it" (Noel 2016: para. 24). Surely, Black Lives Matter is already a feminist intervention into a narrative told and retold by the kind of singular men that Hazel Carby identifies as race men – men like Du Bois, Obama, or even the fictional T'Challa, who reiterate what Wright terms the "heteropatriarchal" stakes in Black counterdiscourses – but it is also an Africanist intervention, a repetition with a difference.[13]

All of the authors discussed in this book have, in one way or another, reflected on the ways in which their Blackness intersects with American notions of Blackness, as well as their Africanness. For example, in "On the Blackness of the Panther," Cole describes how, after moving to the US, he was often forced to abandon his ethnic or national modes of narrating the self in favor of a subsuming, and eternally 'othered,' Africanness (2018: para. 10–12). Cole names three stages of becoming: the first notion of being 'African' interpellated him as a strange "other," followed by a Pan-African sensibility engendered by inhab-

---

[12] For an excellent discussion and political contextualization of Black Lives Matter, see Taylor 2016.
[13] See Carby 2018; Wright 2005: 10–13; 229–231.

iting "mutual spaces with Africans" who had equally been placed in this category and who shared the "still fresh" experience of colonialism: "African, whatever else it was, was about collectively undoing this assault." Concomitant with this awakened political consciousness was the journey of becoming Black, which, however, proved "more complex":

> "Black" was something else. It was in a sense more inclusive. [...] [I]t took in all that colonial hangover and added to it the American experiences of slavery, slave rebellion, Jim Crow, and contemporary racism, as well as the connective tissue that bound the Black Atlantic into a single territory of pain – which brought all of the Caribbean into its orbit – as well as European, Latin American, and global diasporic blackness.

Yet the connective properties of the vast and multifaceted spatio-temporal network of the Black Diaspora could also be undermined by narrow conceptions of the category 'black.' Cole continues:

> But "black" was also more restrictive because, in everyday language, "black" (or "Black") was American black, and "American black" meant slave-descended American black. [...] To be black in America, that localized tenor of "black" had to be learned, it had to be learned and loved. [...] We learned black and loved black – knowing all the while, though, that it wasn't the only black.

Generally, the negative assessment of both the cultural context and the affective range of Afropolitan literatures holds only partially true, as especially more recent artworks by these newly Black Americans offer complex and self-confident explorations of the category of Blackness. Apprehending American racial formations through the moment of Afropolitanism, it becomes apparent that the scope of Blackness has expanded and continues to expand and that many artists, rather than signaling intradiasporic breaks and rifts, have grappled with this "category crisis" in an ultimately reconciliatory manner.

In an article on Yaa Gyasi and the artist Toyin Ojih Odutola from 2017, Selasi observes a very similar process. Here, she revisits precisely her statements on race and Blackness from "Bye-Bye Babar." She writes:

> In 2005 I wrote an essay describing an Afropolitan experience: the decidedly transcultural upbringing of many Africans at home and abroad. How such Afropolitans negotiate that second divide – not between black and white, but between black and African – often depends on where they are raised, whether among or apart from African-Americans. Gyasi and Ojih Odutola typify the distinction. (2017: para. 5)

In this text, Selasi sets out to investigate not only these artists' shared West-African backgrounds, but particularly their Southern upbringing in Alabama, depicting Blackness as an intersection of multiple lines of identification. Selasi asserts how both artists offer particularly astute observations on race in America:

> This, perhaps, is the answer to my second query: how two young African artists came to articulate America's racial complexities so beautifully. Gyasi and Ojih Odutola consider themselves black but have not always. In order to feel at home in that identity they've had to study, understand, expand it. Finally, their work insists that we "just look" – and expand our vision too. (para. 15)

What Selasi is saying here thoroughly undermines the notion of Afropolitanism being primarily about a divestment of Blackness or a transcending of race in favor of a global and/or neoliberal African identity. Rather, we begin to understand how this moment is also marked by complex and ever-changing significations of racial identity. Afropolitanism, thus contextualized, is not overdetermined by a rejection, but rather by an investigation and negotiation of Blackness. The complex ambiguities of Afropolitan novels articulate this distinction quite elegantly. Even a novel like *Ghana Must Go* that undoubtedly de-emphasizes the importance or race and foregrounds the dimension of class cannot ignore how racial formations structure social reality but rather interrogates an authenticating understanding of Blackness. *Ghana Must Go*, along with Selasi's essay from 2005, signals an important element and a stage of Afropolitanism that is important to investigate yet should not statically fix the temporal transience and dynamism of this moment. As Selasi concedes in her article on Odutola and Gyasi, not only have these two African-born artists bridged the "representational chasm" in which this immigrant group was largely absent from popular culture, but they have sublimated the attaining "story of unbelonging, an account not of double consciousness but triple" into becoming "two of the finest observers of race in America" (Selasi 2017: para. 1–3). I argue that all Afropolitan novels discussed in *Making Black History* can be understood as performing this kind of labor: studying, understanding, and expanding Blackness in order to "feel at home in that identity."[14] Considering how heavily overdetermined

---

[14] Rather than identity, however, which functions via exclusions and always threatens to reintroduce what this discourse seeks to challenge, it might be more apt to envision Blackness as a 'networked set of identifications,' and diaspora as a 'space' in which Afropolitanism (re-)inscribes Africa as a something other than a site of lack and separation. As James Clifford (1994: 302–338), expanding on Gilroy's *The Black Atlantic*, writes in his seminal essay "Diaspora": "Identifications not identities, acts of relationship rather than pre-given forms: this tradition is a network of partially connected histories, a persistently displaced and reinvented time/space of crossings" (1994: 321). For further discussion of diaspora space, see Brah's

these issues are, this is certainly not an easy or comfortable conversation to have – a balancing act that clearly shows in these carefully constructed novels, which appear highly aware of how the texts and authors have circulated and signified in public discourse. What follows is a brief overview over two distinct yet closely connected discourses impacting Afropolitan literatures.

1.2 The Extranationality of African Literature

African literature has often been defined in terms of national or nationalist literature and interpreted as a response to either colonialism, nation-building, post-independence disillusionment, or globalization. A lasting theoretical contribution to this mode of thinking is Fredric Jameson's much debated "Third-World Literature in the Era of Multinational Capitalism" (1986) and his reading of African fictions as "national allegories." Notably, these kinds of nationalist readings were almost always folded back or lumped into a greater whole – as African, internationalist, third-world, or postcolonial literature. In many cases, and even after the passing of Cold War world-mapping, dominant Africanist scholarship often interpreted African literature's transnational dimensions as extensions or projections of purportedly Western influence and ideologies. So much so that – in another widely influential, as well as contentious, analysis of African literature – scholar Eileen Julien explained the popularity or canonizations of one set of African novels over the other with the former's so called "extroversion," which is "characterized above all by its intertextuality with hegemonic or global discourses and its appeal across borders" (2006: 681).

Yet, when viewed differently, the interpretation of African literatures as transnational or extroverted rather than static and nation-bound is neither merely the result of influence or projection nor an arbitrary effect of history, but kind of its point. In *Globalectics* (2012), a slim volume synthesizing a few of his lectures, Ngũgĩ wa Thiong'o theorizes what he calls the "globalectic imagination" of African writing. Ngũgĩ traces the genealogy of the African novel through the impact of colonial education, decolonial movements, and key events such as the 1962 African Writers Conference at Makerere University in Kampala or the 1956 First Congress of Black Artists and Writers in Paris – where Fanon inaugurated the transnational thrust of what would later become 'third world' or 'post-

---

Cartographies of Diaspora, which formulates diaspora space as a concept that "foregrounds the entanglement of genealogies of dispersion with those of 'staying put'" (2005: 16).

colonial literature' by outlining the notion of 'Negro literature.'[15] Generally, this genesis narrative of the African novel has been similarly described by most Africanist scholars.[16] Bypassing the various origins and founding myths of the African imaginary tradition prior to the colonial experience, and focusing on what Irele has called the "*africanization* of the novel as a form of narrative," the African novel emerges during the era of independence and indeed as a particular genre, molded to fit a huge variety of different national backgrounds and experiences, yet recognizable in its main ideological thrust (Irele 2009: 8). Irele identifies the beginning of this process as one marked by the dialectic relation of Africa and Europe and aligns this with Jameson's notion of the "national allegory," as the critical consciousness reflected in the novels of the post-independence era transpires through what he calls "new realism" and a notably pessimist, often dystopian representation of 'failed' African states (2009: 10). Since the 1990s, however, Irele and other commentators have observed a creative burst and renewal of the form, through novels addressing urban milieus, the notion of global Africa and African diasporas. Faced with the vast scope of the African novel, Irele asserts that it "seems legitimate to propose the label 'African novel' as a generic term, covering written works in all the languages [...] that have enabled and continue to sustain the narration of the African experience as it continues to unfold in all its multiple dimensions" (ibid.). In *Globalectics*, Ngũgĩ also concedes the synthetic nature of African literatures, at least from a linguistic and geographical perspective. He also emphasizes the binding force of an inherent transculturalism, which echoes Fanon's assertion that it "is at the heart of national consciousness that international consciousness lives and grows" (Fanon 2001: 199). Ngũgĩ writes:

> Outside the fact of language, writers from the colonial world always assumed an extranational dimension. We talk of African literatures, for instance without batting an eyelid. [...] In terms of nations, Africa has more than fifty. But African literature always saw itself as

---

15 In *The Wretched of the Earth*, Fanon later formulated: "Colonialism did not dream of wasting its time in denying the existence of one national culture after another. Therefore, the reply of the colonized peoples will be straight away continental in its breadth. In Africa, the native literature of the last twenty years is not a national literature but a Negro literature" (2001: 212).

16 While Ngũgĩ' is acutely aware of the politics of English in the African novel, as shown by his seminal "On the Abolition of the English Department" (1972), it is his son Mukoma wa Ngũgĩ, who, in *The Rise of the African Novel* (2018), formulates an important intervention into the established genealogy by revisiting the complexities of its founding moments, particular the linguistic diversity of South African fiction at the time, and thus documenting the historical contingency of Anglophone dominance in African writing.

beyond the national territorial state, assuming, at the minimum, the continent for its theater of relevance and application. (2012: 54)

Ngũgĩ adds historical depth and continuity to the global impetus of what many have described as watershed moment in African literatures, assigning the latest wave of contemporary diasporic writing variably to a third, fourth, fifth, or Afropolitan generation of African writers. Ngũgĩ frames the global orientation of African literatures as an intrinsic feature and not merely a contingent, historical development born from Western influence or global forces. Describing his early work at the Nairobi literature department, he notes how "[f]or us, the point of departure was East Africa, radiating outward to Africa, the Caribbean, and African America, Latin America, Asia, Europe, and the rest. The organizing principle was one of from here to there. Hereness and thereness are mutually contained" (2012: 58).

These positions also counter what some critics fear to be a dilution of the concept of African literature. In "Bursting at the Seams: New Dimensions for African Literature in the 21st Century," Thomas A. Hale proclaims that the "21st century will be the century of African literature" (2006: 19), yet he also warns:

> One can argue that these writers are invigorating, reshaping, and renewing the literatures of Europe and North America as they extend the range of African literature today. It is not clear, however, to what extent these writers will fall into a no-writers-land that is neither African nor European. One wonders if they will be co-opted into a new literary context, or simply become pioneers in a new global village of world literature. (18)

Writing about the difficulty to account for the global aspect of African literature, Madhu Krishnan notes how the "idea of Africa" in predominant scholarship "remains caught in a critical schism between authenticity and cosmopolitan attachment" (2014: 4). Concomitant with this, she notes, is the tendency to analyze these literary works as either aesthetic or political, reifying the kind of critical compartmentalization that not only reproduces an oftentimes dated image of Africa in crisis but also fails to account for the ways that form, content, and context co-constitutively affect "the creation and dissemination of a global Africa" (2014: 5–6). Krishnan's study, therefore, reads contemporary African fictions as global texts, drawing not only on textual analysis, but also on the discursive and material circuits surrounding and shaping these works, in order to illuminate what she calls a "geopolitical aesthetic" of Africa.

An integrative view of African literature's in-built extranationality proves a helpful framework for today's increased visibility of global or diasporic African literatures. Most importantly, it is a framing that avoids outdated and often paternalistic indictments of African literature as mostly externally controlled, extroverted or subjected to market forces – and thus befits the self-confidence of the Afropolitan moment. The global orientation of African literature thus fulfills a function that goes beyond being "recognized" by the West and expresses its Afropolitan – read: fluid, transcultural, modern – reality. Along those lines, Eileen Julien has also recently revisited her notion of the extroverted novel:

> If writing to the world is not the only or the primary function of contemporary African novels and texts, I believe it is nonetheless a critical one. From the years of colonization to the present, modern African writers, particularly novelists, have indeed had transcontinental publics. It could be argued that these writers, like those of Asia, Latin America, and the periphery of Europe, were and are *necessarily* more worldly than Northern counterparts of one or two centuries back and even those of today [...] And while I should not like the world to mistake a subset of narratives with particular themes and features as the sum total of what the African imaginary is and has to say, I would not want African authors to turn a blind eye to global audiences and hegemonic power to which African realities and stories are intimately bound. (2018: 9)

Yet whether one frames Afropolitan literature as an expression of African literature's "globalectics" or "geopolitical aesthetics," the contentious notion of global literature, its appendix of audiences, markets, and appetites, looms large. While a detailed engagement with the scholarship on world or global literature exceeds the scope of my analyses, there are a few basic aspects to keep in mind when considering the complex positioning of Black African writers on a global stage.

1.3 The Dilemma of the Black Writer

There are certain critiques of the global novel, such as the one issued by the editors of *n+1* in "World Lite," that maintain an unabashed nostalgia for the "programmatically *internationalist* literature of the revolutionary left" (Saval and Tortorici 2013: 13). This kind of comparison reads romantic at best, and, as Krishnan reminds us, tends to perpetuate a stereotypical image of Africa in crisis. For critics of an apparently de-politicized, middlebrow global fiction, the culprits are easy to be found: Not only corporate publishers, but also universities – and in particular creative writing programs – become ready vessels for neoliberalism, peddling the "tastes of an international middlebrow audience" (Saval and Tortorici 2013: 14) and training a "global elite" (8). Combining the insights of Mark McGurl's widely discussed *The Program Era* (2009) with Graham Huggan's "The Postcolonial Exotic" (2001), Kalyan Nadiminti argues that "the influence of the American MFA program" has led to the evolution of a "a new realist style, one that is deeply inflected by both global capitalism and programmatic writing" (2018: 376). The MFA writing program, according to Nadiminti, becomes "not merely a networking agent but a crucial training ground of American globalism in a post–Cold War literary world" (2018: 377).

Surely, such analyses expose some of the most insidious, neo-imperialist mechanisms behind, as Huggan put it, "the globalisation of cultural production" (2001: 4). However, this kind of criticism, although heavily relying on a materialist critique of globalism, often loses sight of other, equally troubling sides to the argument. Much contempt for the perceived dominance – and aesthetic inferiority – of the global novel, as well as the complaint that writing programs are 'producing' what some regard as 'too many' minority authors, should be eyed with enough suspicion to account for the fact that this might also be part of a reactionary effort to maintain a social status quo. Consequently, these efforts are often coded in aesthetic terms and invested in discussions of artistic value, thinly veiling elitist claims to cultural hegemony. To some degree, this also concerns leftist Western intellectuals pining for the kind of revolutionary subject that remains ever subjugated, but it most certainly plays out when, for example, a white British critic huffily declares the end of the Booker prize because the shortlist's "superficial multicultural aspect conceal[s] a specifically North American taste" (Hensher 2013: para. 1).

Contrary to this, author and creative writing professor Aminatta Forna notes that "as the centre in literature begins to shift away from the Anglo-American writer towards writers with different backgrounds we are witnessing a backlash" (Flood 2014: para. 7). In "MFA vs. POC," a much-noted article from 2014, Junot Díaz provides a glimpse into the ways in which the hegemonic status quo has long since been maintained. Writing about the "unbearable too-whiteness" of MFA programs, he explains:

> Too white as in Cornell had almost no POC – no people of color – in it. Too white as in the MFA had no faculty of color in the fiction program [...] Too white as in my workshop reproduced exactly the dominant culture's blind spots and assumptions around race and racism (and sexism and heteronormativity, etc).
>
> In my workshop there was an almost lunatical belief that race was no longer a major social force (it's class!). In my workshop we never explored our racial identities or how they impacted our writing – at all. Never got any kind of instruction in that area – at all. Shit, in my workshop we never talked about race except on the rare occasion someone wanted to argue that "race discussions" were exactly the discussion a serious writer should *not* be having. (para. 3)

While Díaz' text mostly deals with memories of his own writing program of the 1990s, very similar concerns were raised by Claudia Rankine in her AWP (Associations of Writers and Writing Programs) keynote in 2016, where she noted how, in these programs, "certain life experiences are said to belong to sociology and not to poetry. To write beyond the white imagination's notion of normality and normality's traumas is to write 'political poetry,' 'sociology,' 'identity politics poetry,' 'protest poetry' – many labels but none of them Poetry" (Rankine 2016: para. 11).

Apart from structural shifts creating new areas of friction, these debates also point to the often-documented dilemma of the Black or minority writer who, in return for her admission into the illustrious circle of published literature, is faced with having to perform the status of 'otherness' – a process which often enough results in the repudiation of that status. In the context of the US, the pressure to 'represent the race' as well as the question of whether Black literature constitutes 'art or propaganda' is usually linked to the debate between Alain Locke and W.E.B. Du Bois. While both Locke and Du Bois converged on the social significance of literature and literary representation, Locke proposed a literature that was more in tune with his notion of the term "New Negro" and which, through "artistic self-expression," or what he later calls "purely artistic expression," aspired to universal values rather than denoting what was commonly understood as "the Negro problem" (Locke 1992: xxvi). Du Bois, on the other hand, argued for the necessary political situatedness of any illocution, pointing toward the very concrete constrictions of publishing. Most famously, Du Bois maintained that "all Art is propaganda and ever must be" (1926: 296).

This "great debate," as Leonard Harris calls it, around the social role of literature is often used to signpost the two most dominant theoretical strands of early 20th-century Black aesthetics, in particular during the Harlem Renaissance, but it extends well into the 21st century, notably through Kenneth Warren's proposition of the end of African American literature. In *What Was African American Literature* (2011), Warren claims that "African American literature was a postemancipation phenomenon that gained its coherence as an undertaking in the social world defined by the system of Jim Crow segregation" (107). Controversially discussed and often quickly dismissed, Warren's intervention nevertheless cuts to the core of an ongoing "debate over the efficacy of a racially grounded solidarity as a basis for resistance to injustice" (Hayman 2015: 128). This debate and its implications for literature actually transcend the realm of African American cultural production and thereby mark a historical continuity.

The Harlem Renaissance was, of course, also part of a "'new' black internationalism" (Edwards 2003: 2). Throughout history, the notion of the Black international, Pan-African, or African writer's role was likewise never without contestation. In 1956, at the First Congress of Black Artists and Writers in Paris, Alioune Diop, Léopold Senghor, Aimé Césaire, Richard Wright, Frantz Fanon, and others had anything but singular views on what constituted national or international culture, and consequently the role of the Black writer, even as the opening statement by Senghor insisted that "African Negro Literature and art" were "functional and collective" and thus necessarily "committed" (1956: 56). The various critiques leveled at the essentializing tendencies of the concept of "Négritude," particularly by figures like Fanon and Wright, have been well documented.[17] Wole Soyinka most famously transferred these debates into the context of Anglophone African literature, when, at the Makerere conference in 1962, he declared: "I don't think a tiger has to go around proclaiming his 'tigritude.'" Later, Soyinka clarified that he wanted to distinguish between propaganda and "true poetic creativity" (Jahn 1968: 266). Likewise, Nigerian writer Christopher Okigbo declared: "There is no such thing as African writing. There is only good writing and bad writing." On the same grounds, Okigbo later declined a prize by the Festival of Negro Art (Nwakanma 2010: 182). And Zimbabwean author Dambudzo Marechera put the sentiment quite simply: "If you are a writer for a specific nation or a specific race, then fuck you" (Ashcroft 2013: 79). Of course, these kinds of polemics are first and foremost leveled at external ascriptions and the specific heteronomous demands on Black and/or African art. The variously polemic or remedial responses triggered by these conscriptions, however, reveal a particularly insidious double bind, as Mbembe writes in *On the Postcolony:*

> The uncompromising nature of the Western self and its active negation of anything not itself had the countereffect of reducing African discourse to a simple polemical reaffirmation of black humanity. However, both the asserted denial and the *reaffirmation* of that humanity now look like the two sterile sides of the same coin. (2001: 12)

Relating these debates back to the current situation of Black and minority writers in Western institutions and literary markets, it becomes clear how fraught the issue of 'writing or not writing race' continues to be. In a way, there is 'no way out', or at least no easy way. Even though race, racialization, and identity make for not only valid but important and complex literary topoi, the structures of institutions which, following Sara Ahmed (2012: 43), often allow "an act of inclusion to maintain the form of exclusion" continue to conscript writers of color into the double role of not merely exploring, but performing these themes as the embodiment of 'a problem.' In this sense, admission into these spaces is predicated on the performance of difference rather than on the realization of actual change. Acknowledging this aporia however, may translate into its transference

---

[17] See M'Baye 2009: 29–42; Rabaka 2015; Bernasconi 2002: 69–83.

rather than incorporation, by wielding it as a tool rather than a burden. Thus, Ahmed's solution is to defiantly own the status of "killjoy" and continue to disrupt and unsettle. Rankine suggests a similar approach, noting that writing is "is and should be an arena full of discomfort as we try to keep present the differences that keep us in relation" (2016: para. 43).[18] And it is possible to interpret Wole Soyinka's addendum to his notorious "tigritude" comment – a tiger doesn't proclaim, "he pounces" – in a similar vein. Rather than declaring difference – qua existence, or rather, admittance – writers can try to affect change through actions, and the choice of 'improperly' political topics as a literary subject may well be one of them. In "The Writer in the African State," Soyinka thus explicitly advises writers to address their political realities. "[T]here can be," he writes, "no further distractions with universal concerns whose balms are spread on abstract wounds, not on the gaping yaws of black inhumanity" (1967: 356).

Facing these "gaping yaws" and occupying an "arena of discomfort" while still being heard is a difficult task for any writer. It is worth carefully examining how it affects these widely popular authors, who are granted a wider platform than many and appear to self-consciously navigate the representation of Blackness. The following analyses will attend mostly to the textual representation of Blackness and to the ways in which the representation of race is itself thematized. There are, however, also important extratextual angles to this. One is the way the authors self-define; another is how the texts and authors are read or appropriated. As mentioned above, many of these novels were received as proof or sign of a post-racial age and described with the still young terminology of a post-racial aesthetics. While each of the novels indeed investigates and questions received notions of a particularly US-American episteme of Blackness and a somewhat outdated notion of Pan-African solidarity, it is striking how often their nuanced explorations were first stripped of their ambiguity and then folded back on to their authors, reducing them to post-racial taking heads. More than once, for example, *Americanah*'s often satirist description of an esoteric American race discourse was mobilized for articles running some version of 'race is over' or 'even minorities are tired of talking about it' or indeed showcasing Adichie's smiling face under the headline "Race doesn't occur to me." The fact that Adichie had applied this comment to Nigeria, or, often in the same context, put it in past tense and declared that she now considers herself "happily black," was omitted by the kind of sensationalist media representations feeding into the no-

---

18 Rankine, most notably through her *Racial Imaginary Institute*, also specifically advocates the exploration of whiteness, thus echoing what Mitchell describes as an unquestioned "time of 'White Mythology'" posing as a post-racial moment (2012: 5).

tion that the new visibility of Africans signaled not only a distraction from African Americans but an end to race politics. This narrative, as Goyal notes, framed the diaspora as "some kind of zero-sum game, where only one community could assume center stage in a kind of Darwinian free-for-all" (2017c: 643).

I would argue that, paradoxically, the literature of these African-born or identified authors was thus framed as an instance of the "New Negro" paradigm, even and precisely when they were dis-identified with US-American Blackness. In "Afro-Modernity," Michael Hanchard traces several trajectories of the "New Negro" discourse in the Americas, concluding how "the New Negro's evidenced discomfort with forms of behavior that could have been – and often were – negatively associated with slavery by white and black alike would become the basis for a key dilemma of black aesthetics and cultural production throughout the diaspora" (1999: 259). Read as a paradoxical iteration of the "New Negro," one that had not only left behind the painful memories of slavery but simply lacked them and thus signaled not only a change but an end to its very category, Afropolitan authors were indeed conscripted into a variety of related discourses, some political or cultural, others socio-economic. Noticeable in discussions that framed the African story as somehow distracting from the African American story, Goyal writes, are the fears of commentators "as African immigrants become the US' latest model minority" (2017c: 643). Read in this way, their "entrepreneurship, habits of industry, and cultural values of hard work and discipline seem only to rebuke African Americans and blame them for their continuing subordination or malaise" (ibid.). These scenarios, reminiscent of how other Black immigrant groups have historically been pitted against African Americans, capture and enlarge only one aspect of diaspora identification, namely its uneasy articulations of unity, fraught negotiations of identity, and, most of all, its vast socioeconomic and cultural diversity.

While I generally regard Afropolitanism not as a secession but as part of a long tradition of transatlantic, intradiasporic entanglements, it is true that this moment challenges the most intensively theorized constituent of both African American and Black Atlantic consciousness: the centrality of the Middle Passage. In order to further contextualize this, the following section provides an overview of the two most prominent theorizations of Blackness relying on that centrality, Paul Gilroy's seminal *The Black Atlantic* (1993) and US-American Afro-pessimism, one of the most prominent correctives to post-racialism in contemporary academia. Though the two intellectual frameworks differ greatly, both share a distinct form of historicism that prioritizes the epistemological effect of slavery and the Middle Passage.

1.4 An African Atlantic: Provincializing the Middle Passage Epistemology

Highlighting the ways in which the events of African American past formations speak to or are entangled with current-day migration, Roderick A. Ferguson has called for a decentering of African American history and a repurposing of African American studies (2011: 113–131). For him, a more lateralized African American studies could be a tool for questioning the hegemonic valences and ideological implications behind these concepts – despite the danger of being co-opted or subsumed under the broad academic rubrics of transnationalism, globalization, or cosmopolitanism. Other scholars like Simon Gikandi, Natasha Barnes, and Michelle M. Wright have also argued against a conception of diasporic unity grounded in the experience of slavery alone.[19] Afropolitanism certainly enacts a necessary intervention into what Wright has called the "Middle Passage Epistemology" by exhibiting diasporic Black experiences that do not draw their main cues or epistemic origins from the transatlantic slave trade (alone) but narrate their specific histories in relation to colonialism and/or socioeconomic changes like globalization. Yet this kind of dialogue remains highly charged and contested, both outside and inside the academy. The uneasy relation between Afro-pessimist theorizing and Afropolitanism often appears unresolvable, as particularly the optimism associated with the early Afropolitan moment seems thoroughly antithetical to it.

Neither encompassed by the notion of a coherent school of thought or political movement but a self-described "project" or "enterprise," Afro-pessimism as a whole strongly diverges from the reparative rhetoric that, according to Afro-pessimist theorist Jared Sexton, often buttresses Black cultural and historical scholarship. For example, the same global imperative of the Afropolitan moment that Ferguson views as a chance for African American Studies, signals danger for Sexton. Whereas Ferguson writes that the "contours of globalization, generally, and global migration, specifically, provide an opportunity to fashion an African American studies organized around heterogeneity and radical non-identity of black racial formations" (2011: 116), Sexton warns against a latent global didacticism toward African American studies, and Black Americans in general, which he interprets as a barely concealed imperative to 'get over oneself,' to transcend and graduate in order to become "truly worldly and cosmopolitan" (2011: 8). While not entirely denying the existence of Black (social) life, Sexton notes, Afro-pessimism insists that this sociality is excluded from the modern world sys-

---

[19] See Gikandi 1996: 1–6; Barnes 1996: 106–107; Wright 2015.

tem: "Black life is not lived in the world that the world lives in, but is lived underground, in outer space. This is agreed" (2011: 28).[20]

Crucially, from an Afro-pessimist perspective, a more inclusive repurposing of African American studies is easily co-opted by a post-racial argument that signals not only a "fresh perspective" on American racial politics but, most importantly, severs its constitutive ties to the past. In the field of African American studies especially, the posting, shelving away, and neatly categorizing of past epochs proves problematic in light of ongoing racial violence. Yet it is not only in these violent spectacles but also in the everyday and the mundane that scholars like Sexton, Saidiya Hartman, or Frank B. Wilderson identify an "afterlife of slavery" that bars all periodization but rather intimates the continuation of a century-old "racial calculus and political arithmetic" that "has yet to be undone" (Hartman 2007: 6). Here, it is neither the "antiquarian obsession with bygone days [n]or the burden of a too-long memory" that keeps the past alive and well understood, but a sense of permanence or even simultaneity of past and present (ibid.). Theorizing this state of permanence, Afro-pessimist scholars often draw on the work of sociologist Orlando Patterson, who, in *Slavery and Social Death*, develops the concepts of "social death" and "natal alienation." Patterson describes the slave as a "socially dead person" that is isolated from "all 'rights' or claims of birth" and without any "right to any legitimate social order" (1982: 5). For Afro-pessimist thinkers, the "highly symbolized domain of human experience" that Patterson sees embodied by slavery exceeds the historical event and continues to condition the Black body (1982: 38).

In the blurring of historical demarcations and the assertion of not only history's inevitable return but its ongoing presence, Afro-pessimist theorizing can be linked to broader concerns in both African American and Black Atlantic studies. The inclination to excavate and actualize the past's hauntings, as well as the theoretical centrality of the Middle Passage, embed Afro-pessimist critique in the ongoing effect of an 'archival turn' in literary studies in general, and diaspora studies in particular – albeit under a different, decidedly pessimist sign. In *Archives of the Black Atlantic*, Wendy Walters describes the archival turn as having engendered a "reading of the past for which we may have either no evidence or compromised evidence, and yet which must be imagined as possibility" (2013: 2). This imaginative attachment to a traumatic past and the recurrent revisiting thereof affects a wide range of contemporary Black studies. In "On Failing to

---

[20] Extending the Afro-pessimist project beyond his own moment, Sexton also claims that to read Du Bois – properly, that is – is to understand how, contrary to what is widely accepted as his cosmopolitan or Pan-Africanist stance, there actually is "no place like home" (2011: 8).

Make the Past Present," Stephen Best has termed this particular historiographical mode "melancholic historicism," and traced its ur-moment to Toni Morrison's *Beloved* (1987) and Gilroy's *The Black Atlantic*. Best argues that this mode has become somewhat paradigmatic, and he criticizes its "promotion of a feeling to an axiom" (2012: 464). In a 2017 issue of *American Literary History*, Patricia Stuelke warns against what she calls the "American antiblack tragedy trap: a double bind that locks black subjects into the infinitely recursive roles of universal tragic martyrs or pathological tragic victims" (755). In the same issue, Margo Natalie Crawford historicizes in the tried and tested rhetoric of "turns," by describing similar developments as "The Twenty-First-Century Black Studies Turn to Melancholy" (2017: 799–807). Crawford, who after the publication of Best's essay had already begun to theorize "postmelancholy," now concedes that 21st-century African American theory and literary criticism are indeed characterized by a recurring or continuous turn to melancholy. Commenting on Jermaine Singelton's *Cultural Melancholy: Readings of Race, Impossible Mourning, and African American Ritual* (2015) and Joseph R. Winters's *Hope Draped in Black: Race, Melancholy, and the Agony of Progress* (2016), Crawford writes: "How does it feel to *move on* with unresolved grief? [...] These recent texts signal that we are now, in black studies, developing the new frames – and new grammar – that can make legible the 'jam-full of contradictions' of black life in the afterlife of slavery in the twenty-first century" (2017: 805).

The 21st-century "turn to melancholy" in Black Atlantic studies constitutes less a turn than a continuation – given that the inaugural scholarly text on the Black Atlantic also formulates a distinct "reading of the past [...] which must be imagined as possibility" through the notion of a 'slave sublime' that becomes knowable only through the experience of the Middle Passage. At the heart of Gilroy's *The Black Atlantic* lies the focus on rhizomatic maps of entanglements rather than singular roots, as a push back against definitions of Blackness that threaten to recede into cultural parochialism or racial essentialism. Yet its extraordinary scope and poststructuralist unmooring notwithstanding, the main coordinates of Gilroy's *Black Atlantic* are clearly located and demarcated. While wary of the ways in which Blackness is easily submerged under "the smooth flow of African American exceptionalism" (2002: 120), Gilroy offers no different provenance or alternative technique for locating Black consciousness, other than perhaps digging deeper – meaning, he too prioritizes African American (male) Blackness by centering figures like W.E.B. Du Bois, Frederick Douglass, Martin Delany, and Richard Wright and predominantly tracing the concentric spreading of Black American culture. Framing his inquiry into a Black British identity that exceeds both nationality and nationalism, he concedes that he first needed to make "an intellectual journey across the Atlantic." In "black America's histories of cultural and political debate and organization" he finds "another, second perspective" – the "lure of ethnic particularism and nationalism" notwithstanding – which helps him orient his own position (ibid. 4).

Gilroy's *The Black Atlantic* remains an influential and highly important text, despite drawing criticism for its narrow Euro-Atlantic and Anglophone focus and its centering of predominantly male, modernist intellectuals. Various scholars, Yogita Goyal, Simon Gikandi, and Michelle M. Wright among them, have pointed out how the Black Atlantic framework eclipses the African continent.[21] By conceiving of Blackness as a quintessential New World identity, characterized by the epistemic rupture of the Middle Passage, Africa necessarily recedes or "figures as an object of retrospective rediscovery, rather than as an active agent" (Law and Mann 1999: 308). Arguing against essentialist and Afrocentric notions of Blackness that rely on genealogical and traditional ties or biological 'roots,' Gilroy fashions Black Atlantic culture as a kind of counterculture of modernity, following Zygmunt Bauman, that actually better embodies the 'true' claims of modernity. This fundamental understanding of the modernist potential derives from the experience, or memory, of slavery. Gilroy notes how, despite or particularly because of the "racial terror" of slavery inherent to Western civilization and thought,

> blacks in the west eavesdropped on and then took over a fundamental question from the intellectual obsessions of their enlightened rulers. Their progress from the status of slave to the status of citizens led them to enquire into what the best possible forms of social and political existence might be. (2002: 39)

Black Atlantic culture, necessarily blurring the boundary between the aesthetic and the political, is thus either adamant in bringing the enlightened claims of modernity to their logical conclusion, what Gilroy terms a discursive "politics of fulfillment," or, in seizing modernity's inherent and violent contradictions, aims to expressively limn its utopian overcoming through what he calls the "politics of transfiguration" (ibid. 37).

Throughout *The Black Atlantic*, Gilroy attempts to redefine the meaning of tradition, prying it from the hands of those who value it as a culturalist, meaning racially essentialist, link to African origins. This "wrench[ing] open" of tradition, as James Clifford describes it in his discussion of the book, allows Gilroy to con-

---

[21] See, for example, a special issue of *Research in African Literatures* from 1996, edited by Simon Gikandi and featuring contributions by Natasha Barnes, Colin (Joan) Dayan, and Ntongela Masilela that specifically tackle the incompatibility of Gilroy's Black Atlantic and African modernity (Gikandi 1996).

struct a notion of Black Atlantic culture that is fluid rather than fixed, self-generating and self-referential rather than derivational or estranged from its source (Clifford 1994: 321). At the same time, the terms tradition and memory are again limited because memory first and foremost pertains to the "ineffable, sublime terror" of slavery (Gilroy 2002: 215) that is then "actively preserved as a living intellectual resource" through the "expressive political culture" that marks the Black Atlantic tradition (ibid. 39). Gilroy's privileging of the Middle Passage Epistemology in the making of Black culture certainly disrupts Afrocentrist romanticizing of pre-modern Africa. However, as Goyal notes, it does not "provide any alternative way of thinking about Africa" and instead reifies its role in Atlantic culture as static and passive (Goyal 2014: v).

Framing Africa as passive witness is surely not mandatory to thinking about the horrors of the Middle Passage, but it might be a tacit continuation of that conceptualization of Africa as helpless victim or abject non-place that Mbembe (2001: 4) describes: "More than any other region, Africa thus stands out as the supreme receptacle of the West's obsession with, and circular discourse about, the facts of 'absence,' 'lack,' and 'non-being,' of identity and difference, of negativeness – in short, of nothingness." It is precisely this brand of Afropessimism, as a globally mediated discourse on the African continent as hopeless heart of darkness, that Mbembe sees confronted by Afropolitanism as a "way of being in the world, refusing on principle any sort of victim identity" (Mbembe 2005: 28–29).[22] However, as Mbembe adds, this "does not mean that it is not aware of the injustices and violence inflicted on the continent and its people by the law of the world" – and this awareness certainly also pertains to the transatlantic slave trade (ibid 30). Mbembe's later work *The Critique of Black Reason* (2017) is thus a conscious attempt at rereading the African American history of Blackness from a continental perspective and expanding a myopic vision of the Middle Passage Epistemology. In a conversation with Theo David Goldberg, Mbembe elaborates on how he wanted to "take seriously the idea that Black, or blackness, is not so much a matter of ontology as it is a matter of historicity or even contingency" as well as "contest those lineages of blackness that use memories of trauma to develop discourses of blackness as ontology" (Mbembe 2018: para. 4). What is being contested here, are Afro-pessimist perspectives in which Blackness is not only an ontological, socially and philosophically pre-determined and political category, but the kind of political ontology from which a

---

[22] See Ebanda De B'Beri and Louw (2011: 335–346) for a discussion of Afropessimism as it relates to the continent. Here, the term denotes a certain skeptical and/or hopeless attitude toward Africa's political and economic developments, particular in comparison with other 'developing' regions. The hyphenated Afro-pessimism denotes the US-American school of thought.

global civil society derives its notions of lack and non-being by "dividing the Slave from the world of the Human in a constitutive way" (Sexton 2011: 23). By emphasizing, instead, the effect of "historicity or even contingency" in the making of Blackness, Mbembe draws a sharp distinction between his own and Afro-pessimist theorizing.[23]

While it is important to distinguish between continental Afropessimism that paints a derelict picture of post-independence Africa (particularly through media coverage) and American Afro-pessimism as an umbrella term for contemporary political, historical, aesthetic, and theoretical approaches that radically problematize anti-Blackness and the afterlife of slavery, both instances converge on the point of African agency – or the lack thereof. The self-described "unflinching paradigmatic analysis" of Afro-pessimist theories tends to negate the historical and political agency, or even the existence, of Black subjects in general, including African agency.[24] Elaborating on the incompatibility of Africa as a "homeland" for its diaspora, Frank Wilderson notes:

> But the fact of the matter is that captivity and social death are the essential dynamics which everyone in this place called Africa stands in relation to [...] [W]hat Afro-pessimism is saying is that a Black African diaspora is fundamentally different from any other diaspora, because any other diaspora has actually been dispersed from a place that has sovereign integrity. And Africa has never had sovereign integrity; since it has gained conceptual coherence as Africa. [...] Africa has always been a big slave estate. That has been and still is the global consensus. (2016: 9)

The demographic fact of those very visible and active African diasporas in the US that carry with them very concrete and coherent notions of their respective homelands challenges this sentiment. But it also reveals the particular myopia on which it relies. I would argue that Wilderson's, and by extension Afro-pessimism's, rendering of a Black ontology as lack and non-being is just as reliant upon the 'emptiness' of the African signifier as the racist epistemologies that

---

[23] It is important to note that, these crucial differences and a few intellectual skittles aside, Mbembe's writings, in particular his notion of "necropolitics" and his bleak assessment of the "Postcolony," have actually proven a fertile intellectual ground for the US-American brand of Afro-pessimism. In *Red, White, & Black*, Wilderson explicitly lists him as an Afro-pessimist, among Hortense Spillers, Ronald Judy, David Marriott, Saidiya Hartman, Frantz Fanon, Kara Keeling, Jared Sexton, Joy James, Lewis Gordon, George Yancey, and Orlando Patterson (Wilderson 2010: 79).

[24] To be fair, even though there is a utopian dimension to Afro-pessimist thinking, a certain "knowledge of freedom" that is discernable only through the crucible of slavery, it also offers no agent of change in the figure of the New World subject.

rendered Africa "the supreme receptacle" of the West (Mbembe 2001: 4). However, this process of projection is fundamentally challenged by a contemporary African diaspora that fills this blank or negative space with its very own, if often conflicting, presence. This issue is now particularly charged as many members of the new African diaspora in the US, and most certainly the majority of Afropolitan writers, hail from West African countries, e.g. those areas from which most enslaved African were taken and which, with the exception of Ethiopia, figure most prominently in Afrocentric notions of the 'motherland.'[25] At first glance, this West-African kinship would suggest a distinct reckoning with the common history of slavery and enslavement, probing issues like lineage, tradition or complicity and perhaps triggering feelings of guilt, avowal, or forgiveness. Despite, or perhaps precisely because of, these loaded issues, the topic of slavery has structured the cultural encounters between old and new diasporic communities in the US much less overtly, or at least differently, than former (intra-)diasporic or transnational Black discourses. An example that is more recent than 19th-and early- to mid-20th-century Pan-Africanism would be the long and fruitful linkage between South African and African American cultural production. As scholar Neville Choonoo notes, the 20th-century dialogue between South Africa and Black America has been characterized by "interplay" or even "kinship," founded on notions of diasporic solidarity and commonality (2015: 30). The crucial difference between South Africa and Nigeria is, of course, the former's history of Apartheid and settler colonialism, but I would argue that this circumstance also profoundly implicates the semantics of slavery and Blackness transmitted within this exchange. Here, slavery is much more than a historical fact or experience. It actually represents the same system or effect of white supremacy that is implemented by Apartheid. And in this sense, American Blackness comes to be defined as a product or response to this racist order and is able to travel outside of its national framework. This is part of the "moment of Blackness," as Mitchell describes it in *Seeing Through Race*, that was "never exclusively confined to the African American population of the United States" but was "disseminated most notably in the apartheid struggle in South Africa, which was accelerated by the example of the Civil Rights Movement in the United States" (2012: 60).

---

[25] Akinbi (2017) cites Okun Uya's estimation that the highest number of African slaves came from West Africa, particularly Nigeria and Ghana. He also notes that "the twentieth century migration of Nigerian immigrants [...] to the United States has been unprecedented" (98). According to the United State Bureau census (2008–2012), Nigerians and Ghanaians (West African) now constitute the largest African immigrant group in the US, followed by Ethiopians and Kenyans (East African) and Egyptians (North African). See Falola and Oyebade 2017: 3.

While various anticolonial independence movements were also implicated in that moment of Blackness, South Africa provided a much more durable ground for political recognition, even in the decades following 'the wind of change' on the continent – precisely because slavery had transmuted from a historical, discreet event to a mutable and mutating system. "African Americans," Choonoo writes, "saw in South Africa a common Black experience under White hegemony" (2015: 30). The political situation of South Africa under Apartheid, together with its status as a settler colonial nation, allowed for "spontaneous and mutual" intradiasporic recognition, particularly during the 1960s and onwards (ibid. 36).

Obviously, one could even further investigate how the gulf of the imaginary, the effect of the mythical idea Africa, implicates today's diasporic encounters. A generation removed from the internationalist, Pan-African ambitions of Du Bois, the Black American search for African roots was mostly characterized by what Choonoo calls a "naive interest in African culture" (2015: 38). This is also why South Africa offered an "easy access" for interconnectedness, allowing many intellectuals to forge concrete political linkages (ibid.). These concrete political ties were less prone to implode the mythical ideas of the motherland, simply for lack of direct confrontation. This confrontation, however, is now occurring with the heightened influx of West African immigrants to the US. Yet confrontations are mutually constituted. A recurring Afropolitan narrative recounts African immigrants' indignation at being conscripted into the racial hierarchies of US society – usually upon realizing that "black is at the bottom of America's race ladder" (*Americanah* 105). Consequently, African immigrants often adopt the model minority narrative ascribed to them, emphasizing their distinctness from African Americans. Culturally however, and the pervasiveness of white supremacy and institutional racism notwithstanding, Africans in America are also benefactors of the Black Power movement and the symbolic shifts brought about by African Americans who, as Paula Moya notes, have done "important decolonizing work through their sustained efforts to delink African ancestry from notions of biological inferiority" (2015: 128). Yet at the same time, these symbolic acts have often remained just that: symbolic and steeped in Afro-centric mythology. As Africans position themselves apropos and within systems of signification that alternately (de)value or (mis)recognize them, this creates a complex environment marked by different and often ambiguous modes of rejection, adoption, and appropriation. In sum, both the limited framework of Gilroy's *Black Atlantic* and the singular focus on South African similarities have, despite their productivity, done little to complicate the naïve or reductionist role that Africa often plays in the diasporic imaginary.

Perhaps it is unsurprising then, that Frank Wilderson has little to no use for Africa in his theorizations, *except* for South Africa, where he spent five years as one of only two American ANC members and about which he extensively wrote in his memoir *Incognegro* (2018). In the case of South Africa, Afro-pessimist thinking is able to extend its Middle Passage Epistemology through an understanding of apartheid as a mutation and extension of the logic of enslavement. For Wilderson, it is evident that "slavery is and connotes an ontological status for Blackness; and that the constituent elements of slavery are not exploitation and alienation but accumulation and fungibility" (2010: 23). Today, with the intensified diasporic encounters between West-Africans and African Americans, I argue that it may be precisely the historico-geographical proximity of these groups that renders slavery a somewhat blatant, mutually constitutive historical fact, rather than a system or effect of white supremacy. In this context, slavery might present itself as a shared trauma, a history of exploitation, or even a system of labor that implicates but not exclusively defines what it means to be Black.

It becomes clear that for theorizations centering on the Middle Passage, like Afro-pessimism or Gilroy's Black Atlantic mapping, slavery really is a way of thinking, an epistemology, and particularly a way of thinking about (and constituting) Blackness. As Colin Dayan wrote in response to *The Black Atlantic*, the Middle Passage thus becomes a "metaphor, anchored somewhere in a vanishing history" rather than locating a complex node of global history (1996: 8). In relation to Blackness, the effect of this is twofold. For one, subjects who do not refer to or regard themselves through this epistemology may not be considered or consider themselves Black. Secondly, it installs a certain hierarchy or primacy of experience that sidelines all other modes of Blackness and submerges alternate histories. Conversely, however, Afropolitan narratives that insist on their own routes to becoming Black automatically counter the hegemony of the Middle Passage Epistemology and provincialize it as merely one of multiple modes, metaphors, and histories of Blackness.

In many ways, Afropolitanism seems incompatible with the tenets of Afro-pessimism. However, as my readings of the novels aim to show, their relation isn't simply reducible to antagonism or irreconcilableness but rather an uneasy negotiation of sometimes similar, and oftentimes diverging conceptualizations of Blackness. In short, the Afropolitan moment – as it plays out in the US and in the novels selected here – both challenges and reconfigures the distinct tradition of diasporic cosmopolitanism that is often referred to as Black Atlantic culture. Afropolitan narratives intervene in the Middle Passage Epistemology in ways that need not refute Afro-Pessimist concepts of fungibility or social death as much as challenge or lateralize their singular mode of plotting African American racial formations in linear rather than rhizomatic ways. As Ferguson asserts: "Contemporary black migrations productively derail the project of African American history. [...] [N]ew African American subjects question the utility of grounding African American history within a line of descent that starts with the middle passage, moves to slavery, proceeds to Emancipation, stops briefly at Reconstruction, passes through Jim Crow segregation, and arrives at civil rights" (2011: 115). While Afro-pessimist theories certainly denounce the notion of a linear progress in the afterlife of slavery, they still rely on linearity as they propose instead "a reverse linear narrative indicating that no *Black* progress has been made" (Wright 2015: 8).

Instead, a synchronistic exploration of Blackness in the moment of Afropolitanism allows me to approximate Wright's theorizations of Blackness as both construct and phenomenology. In *Physics of Blackness*, Wright develops the concept of "spacetime," where historical constructs of Blackness and progress are associated with temporal linearity and the interpretative moment of non-linear experience is linked to the phenomenological manifestations of Blackness (2015: 4). In light of demographic shifts she identifies as belonging to a post-WWII moment, Wright notes that the "question of defining Blackness has become more urgent as the collectives that perceive themselves though these multiple histories find themselves encountering each other more frequently" (ibid.). She proposes that

> the only way to produce a definition of Blackness that is wholly inclusive and nonhierarchical is to understand Blackness as the *intersection* of constructs that locate the Black collective in *history* and in the *specific moment* in which Blackness is being imagined – the 'now' through which all imaginings of Blackness will be mediated. (18)

The Afropolitan moment may help explore what Crawford terms the contradictions of "black life in the afterlife of slavery in the twenty-first century" by relating it to the larger framework of the global Black Diaspora, highlighting not only the disparate socioeconomic and epistemic subject positions of a Black imaginary but also the subordination of narratives that are *not* routed through the Middle Passage or rooted in Gilroy's notion of the slave sublime. Read in this way, the literatures under discussion shift rather than replace the centrality of the Middle Passage Epistemology, countering what Adichie, in a famous TEDtalk, described as the "danger of a single story" (Adichie 2009a).[26] One example of this would be

---

[26] Here, Adichie used the phrase in relation to dominant stereotypes about Africans, immigrants, or 'others' in general, which become hegemonic and suppress alternative narratives.

their exploration of (post-)colonial traumas, highlighting how these traumas are just as intrinsic to global and diasporic history. Rather than identifying Afropolitan literatures with a distinct break with the kind of literatures which, following Toni Morrison's *Beloved*, actualize the (re-)memory or afterlife of slavery, these literatures could be read as a reminder that there are other historical traumas that also speak to the diasporic imaginary. As Goyal notes, reading a novel like Mengestu's *The Beautiful Things That Heaven Bears* in posttraumatic terms, like some critics have, is only possible "if the only traumatic template allowed to a black writer is that of slavery and its afterlife" (2017c: 646). Whether plotted as linear progress narrative or as Afro-pessimist reversal, it becomes clear that the Middle Passage Epistemology has long determined not only the centrality of historicism in Black and diasporic writing but also whose history is conducive to African American and Black Atlantic racial formations. Despite the fact that many 20th-century literary and intellectual movements such as Négritude or the Harlem Renaissance have been described as a "cycle of reciprocities" (Irele 2001: 72) between Africa and New World diasporas, evoking the image of call and response, most models have ultimately prioritized the concerns of diasporic communities or reinstated US-American hegemony. With the Afropolitan reconfiguration, an *African* Atlantic imaginary transpires in which Gilroy's notion of a "living memory" of slavery (2002: 198) gives way to the active presence of Africa.

Even in this configuration, it is important to take the notion of diasporic reciprocity seriously, rather than pitting one model against each other. If painted in broad and decidedly binary strokes, Afropolitanism is often conceived as a futuristic, race-less cosmopolitanism and mobilized in opposition to a racially inflected African American or Black Atlantic parochialism centered on the memory of slavery.[27] In many ways, this perspective simply reiterates the spatial separation

---

This sentiment has often been linked to the so-called "poverty porn" debate, launched in particular by Helon Habila's critique of NoViolet Bulawayo's *We Need New Names*.

[27] For example, in scholarship that focuses on Afropolitanism as a continental phenomenon, the waning importance of racial signification as a binding element for African cultural integrity is read as an effect of the cosmopolitan turn in African studies that "presented Africa's multiracial societies as harbingers of a futuristic post-racial order" (Balakrishnan 2017: 8). However, this interpretation conceives of similar discourses in diasporic Afropolitanism as a mere consequence of this disassociation of "African identity from Blackness" rather than relating these debates to their immediate contexts, e.g. the post-racial discourses that accompanied Obama's presidency in United States (Balakrishnan 2018: 579). If used as a lens to investigate intradiasporic race discourses, it becomes clear that the discourse of post- and newness impacts the moment of Afropolitanism on all sides of the Atlantic. What this also reveals is that the moment of Afropolitanism encompasses both continental and diasporic dimensions, that these dis-

of the Middle Passage in temporal terms. The focus on rifts and disassociations, however, is not only a somewhat limiting, if tried and tested, way of conceptualizing the Black Diaspora, it also fails to recognize precisely how the legacy of slavery figures in these narratives. While it is obvious how the primacy of the Middle Passage threatens to trump the traumatic role of colonialism in the making of modern Blackness, the Afropolitan moment does not only provide counterweight to the damaging effect of a "single story" by presenting new or neglected narratives, but also by inverting the perspective on slavery itself. While the history of slavery has affected Africa and the diaspora unevenly, this does not mean that they aren't *both* affected. One particular pitfall of emphasizing the unequal positionings toward the history of transatlantic slavery is a latent disregard for the traumas that the slave trade wrought on the African side of the Atlantic. Already, the absence of institutionalized memory culture around the slave trade has created an epistemological lacuna that is directly taken up by Yaa Gyasi's novel *Homegoing*. It is also addressed by the narrator of Teju Cole's *Every Day Is for the Thief*, who, during his visit to Lagos, muses about the "chain of corpses" forging a "secret twinship" between Lagos, the former largest slave port, and New Orleans, "the largest market for human chattel in the New World" (112). Consequently, he criticizes that this "history is missing from Lagos. There is no monument to the great wound" (Cole 2014b: 114). This aspect is very much part of the labor that these Afropolitan works and authors are performing: a thorough reckoning with history, an investigation of how it implicates and involves them, as the history of Blackness. In this sense, Afropolitanism is indeed motivated by the vision of a better, more perfect union, marked by mutual recognition and historical culpability. I describe this motivation as the novels' diasporic desire.

In "Afropolitanism and the End of Pan-Africanism," Balakrishnan accredits the shortcomings of Afropolitanism as an African philosophy of history to its inability "to reckon with the agency of Africans in the dispersion of diaspora: the betrayal at the heart of the symbol 'Black'" (2018: 581). She claims that what might have served as a "powerful point of reflection: a reckoning in the form of unity," has "not occurred" (ibid.). Yet the literary explorations discussed in this book – cautious of and attentive to its dilemmas and mobilized by a deep-seated diasporic desire – certainly belie this pessimist statement. Indeed, all three novels convey what British-Sierra Leonean writer Aminatta Forna described in an interview: a nuanced understanding of how "the legacy of slavery

---

courses affect each other reciprocally, and that the diasporic discourse of Afropolitanism is not a byproduct of its continental counterpart, just as the diaspora is not a mere byproduct of Africa.

breaks differently on each side of the Atlantic." Moving to the US, Forna elaborates, allowed her to discover a "sharp distinction in how she claims her past and how others view that history through skin color" (Otosirieze 2017: para. 12). We find this realization in all three texts, along with the same willingness or desire to explore and perhaps blunt the sharpness of this distinction through reckoning with that history, formally and thematically.

As such, the Black Diaspora reveals itself as a geographical space, mutually constituted by both homeland and diaspora, as well as a distinctly temporal community that is both imagined and probed by these texts. Acknowledging reciprocity thus also means understanding that the Black Diaspora is in fact this Janus-faced entity, mobilized by the push and pull of homeland and diaspora, past and future. What I aim to show in my readings of Afropolitan fictions is that while the shift toward imagining diaspora under the sign of Africa certainly correlates with post-racial discourses, these processes aren't necessarily mutually defined and much less causally related. Newly Black Americans may question the category of Blackness, but they are nevertheless Black. Afropolitan fictions may reverse the perspective on the Middle Passage, but they are not revisionist. Diasporic desire is marked by the hope for an antiracist future, but it does not renounce racist pasts and presents. Hence, what connects these novels apart from emerging in the moment of Afropolitanism is their respective investigation of "history through skin color," or what I propose to call race in/as history.

2 Writing Race in/as History

By 'making Black history', Cole, Adichie, and Gyasi investigate the historicity of Blackness and the ways in which it implicates them, rather than treating Blackness as a specific condition that automatically includes or excludes them or an ontological fact that is inherited or rejected. In this, and rather than primarily signaling the shifts and turns of post- and newness, these fictions are just as attentive to notions of stasis, repetition, and tradition as an accumulation of certain 'structures of feeling.'[28] As such, the novels are responding to these struc-

---

[28] In *The Long Revolution* (1961), Raymond Williams elaborates on a given culture's "structures of feeling" in respect to selective ancestry. He writes: "In a society as a whole, and in all its particular activities, the cultural tradition can be seen as a continual selection and re-selection of ancestors. Particular lines will be drawn, often for as long as a century, and then suddenly with some new stage in growth these will be cancelled or weakened, and new lines drawn. In the analysis of contemporary culture, the existing state of the selective tradition is of vital importance, for it is often true that some change in this tradition – establishing new lines with the

tures selectively, if not necessarily consciously. As expressions of diasporic desire, however, they appear to employ this knowledge strategically, wielding time as the medium with which Blackness is negotiated. Like time, race can be made malleable in literature, it can be condensed, extended, or repeated, it can be foregrounded or surreptitiously rendered, but neither race nor time can be simply explained away. Because race, as Mitchell writes, is a "*time-based* medium that both has a history and itself narrates history," it becomes a particular interesting topos for narrative fiction (2012: 21).

2.1 Raced Temporalities

I have chosen to describe these contemporary diasporic texts as belonging to or emerging in the historical moment of Afropolitanism not only as a way to bypass the open debate on whether the Afropolitan denotes a useful or problematic mode of identification, but also because I want to draw attention to the central role of time and temporality in these novels. The moment thus becomes another descriptor of the 'race and time' of any social articulation, defining Afropolitan discourse as a historical constellation and an investigation of what Stallings has called a "race-time continuum," reminding us that race and time are both "basic social discourses that reverberate off each other" (2013: 194). In her discussion of "CP-Time," colored or conscious people's time, in Paul Beatty's *Slumberland*, Stallings argues that Black culture and identity have been quite thoroughly investigated in spatial terms, focusing on notions such as dispersal and displacement in national or geographical frameworks. However, she notes, "little work has been done to examine the impetus to create the temporal placement and displacement of black identity and culture, as well as its intersections with diaspora and transnationalism" (Stallings 2013: 194). The issue of temporality has been extensively explored in postcolonial theorizations of diaspora and race, most famously in Homi K. Bhabha's *Location of Culture* (1994). Bhabha elaborates on the post-colonial time lag and other discourses of disjunct temporality in order to display "the *problem of the ambivalent temporality of modernity* that is often overlooked in the more 'spatial' traditions of some aspects of post-modern theory" (2004: 342). In a similar vein, Gilroy identifies the protagonists of *The Black Atlantic* as belonging to "non-synchronous communities" (2002: 174), marked by a "syncopated temporality" (202). Hanchard defines the notion of "racial time"

---

past, breaking or re-drawing existing lines – is a radical kind of contemporary change" (Williams 2001: 69).

as "the inequalities of temporality that result from power relations between racially dominant and subordinate groups" (1999: 253).

This focus on temporality, in particular in relation to Blackness, is already inherent in Fanon's most infamous 'primal scene': the instance of racial interpellation in "The Fact of Blackness" from *Black Skin White Masks* where Fanon details the effect of a child's public exclamation: "'Look, a Negro [...] I'm frightened!" He recounts how being hailed a frightening thing, an "object in the midst of other objects" when all he desired was to be "a man among other men," causes him to substitute Merleau-Ponty's corporeal schema with a racial epidermal schema, which is in turn constituted by a "historico-racial schema" (2008: 82–84). Confronted with this initial interpellation in a white environment, Fanon discovers his "blackness, [his] ethnic characteristics" (84–85).

Fanon's "The Fact of Blackness" is a dense text, exploring notions of (non-)recognition and visibility, ontology and metaphysics, which have acquired a certain universality in postcolonial theories but take on a heightened significance in relation to Critical Race and Black Studies.[29] Questions of temporality and historicity, however, are just as central to these disciplines. History, in most cases, is a problem. Regardless of whether the word denotes lived experience, academic discipline, or dominant episteme – it is either fraught with painful memories, complicit with exploitative structures or the principal author of race, "our deadliest fiction" (Spillers 2003: 379). The history *of* race denotes a periodization that obscures its contingency and projected finitude by claiming the eternity of myth or the timelessness of science. The history *in* race is first of all an accumulation, Fanon's historico-racial schema made up of "legends, stories, history, and above all, historicity" (2008: 84).

Both the history in race and the history of race inform the "historical, instrumental hypothesis" that constitutes the fact of Blackness and that triggers in Fanon only two kinds of responses: Either radically freeing oneself from the prison of history, rejecting any claims made by the past and becoming one's "own foundation" (2008: 180), or, when the colonized intellectual decides to use the past for "his people" [sic], he should do so only "with the intention of opening up the future, of spurring them into action and fostering hope," while, most importantly, also supplementing his efforts through political action (2001: 187). This defiant position toward history emerges from a distinct temporal position, what Bhabha calls the "time lag of cultural difference" that is born from a "temporal

---

[29] Fanon scholar Lewis Gordon organizes what he calls "several stages" of academic engagement with Fanon as moving "from that of ideological critique to postcolonial anxiety to engagement with his thought" (2007: 5).

break" or "caesura" in the "continuist, progressivist myth of Man" (2004: 341). Relating Fanonian temporality to the notion of postcolonial and subaltern agency in general, he writes:

> Fanon destroys two time schemes in which the historicity of the human is thought. He rejects the "belatedness" of the black man because it is only the opposite of the framing of the white man as universal, normative – the white sky all around me: the black man refuses to occupy the past of which the white man is the future. But Fanon also refuses the Hegelian-Marxist dialectical schema whereby the black man is part of a transcendental sublation: a minor term in a dialectic that will emerge into a more equitable universality. Fanon, I believe, suggests another time, another space. (ibid.)

For Bhabha, Fanon resists rather than deplores the heteronomous temporal ordering by the West, gaining agency by occupying and speaking from the interstices of time and history. It is noteworthy that for Bhabha, Fanon anticipates an alternative time of Blackness that also conditions a different spatial scheme or space, or perhaps even a different world, indicating what he describes as the shift of the cultural location of modernity "to the postcolonial site" (Bhabha 2004: 360). This process, which he also identifies in the temporal strategies of Toni Morrison's *Beloved*, is marked by the "translation of the meaning of time into the discourse of space." Bhabha describes this as an active and willed performance, a "catachrestic seizure of the signifying 'caesura' of modernity's presence and *present*," which insists simultaneously on an analysis of power that thinks through both sexuality and race, a critique of the nation's inherent imperialism, and the reconfiguration of teleological class-consciousness through the "doubling and splitting" of race (ibid.). While Bhabha's high hopes for postcolonial narratives align with the "writing back" paradigm that has become somewhat synonymous with certain definitions of postcolonial literature, Afropolitan narratives don't quite map onto his paradigm as neatly. They do, however, also translate the "meaning of time into the discourse of space" by voicing what Bhabha describes as a "vernacular cosmopolitanism which measures global progress from the minoritarian perspective" (2004: xvi).

At least in the sense of these texts being (post-)postcolonial novels, one could thus state that – without suggesting that the two can ever be fully pried apart – the centrality of temporality has somewhat replaced spatiality. The importance of issues such as (involuntary) exile and displacement or the interplay between center and periphery largely recedes for a generation characterized by a global, and surely privileged, ease of mobility. What increases is a textual mobility through time, yet not as reenactment of history, the conjuring of a 'pre-modern' idyll or the countering of alleged African ahistoricity. These writers are not mainly writing back to some colonial center, and neither are they merely reflecting on their respective African homelands from a diasporic distance, even though both modes inform their texts. In the aftermath of what Mbembe and others have identified as the "planetary turn of African predicament," theirs are attempts of writing themselves into the world as global citizen, as African *and* as Black cosmopolitan (Mbembe 2016: 31). Via the "epistemological proposition" of Afropolitanism, they draw attention to their own privileged perspective on the world (ibid.) However, due to their intimate experience with hegemonic epistemologies, they are simultaneously acceding to the impossibility of theorizing globally. The distance they have gained is not necessarily geographical but temporal; they are drawing on the multiangular shape of history, both exhibiting and occupying discrete vantage points, specific relations with and toward the past. Indeed, deliberate Afropolitan movements through history limn a particularly transnational vantage point, the ability of relating oneself in and as the planetary. This perspective also resembles Wai Chee Dimock's understanding of the particular scale enlargement of *deep time*, which draws on a notion of planetary entanglement that exceeds the chronology of an individual nation. As Dimock writes: "[T]he concept of a global civil society, by its very nature, invites us to think of the planet as a plausible whole, a whole that ... needs to be mapped along the temporal axis as well as the spatial, its membership open not only to contemporaries but also to those centuries apart" (2007: 5). Shunning the inherent spatial hierarchization of a single elevated viewpoint, these texts do not only rely on a transnational or multilocal perspective but limn the planetary configuration of the Black Diaspora along a temporal axis and through specific chronotopes.

Of course, as Mikhail Bakhtin's seminal work on the literary chronotope shows, temporality is an intrinsic element of literature. While time, as topos and formal element, represents a fundamental building block and major preoccupation particularly of modernist writings, it is indeed noteworthy how these contemporary literatures explore the deceivingly blunt realization that both "time and race are social discourses reverberating off each other." An example of how the dimensions of race and time relate would be the notion of hair in *Americanah*, the novel's "third protagonist," as Rask Knudsen and Rahbeck (2016: 243) write, or, as I describe it, the Proustian cookie that triggers Ifemelu's childhood memories. As such, however, it is not just a temporal device to structure the narrative but also indexes both psychological and social temporality. Arguably, Black hair carries broader historical and collective significance than Proust's very personal, yet ostensibly universal, memory of his aunt. *Homegoing*, on the other hand, investigates Black temporality on multiple levels and, quite literally, through fragmentation and repetition, while *Open City* echoes Fanonian moments of interpellation and, through its pronounced dialogism, offers contrapuntal readings of history that simultaneously comment on diasporic metahistoricism. While these raced temporalities are formally woven into the fabric of these texts – through topos, trope, or syntax – notions of history or historicism seem to play out much more discursively, as extra- or contextual referent. In fact, however, these topics are so overdetermined that it might be better to speak of a certain diasporic meta-historicism that also profoundly – and formally – affects these literatures.

2.2 Diasporic Historicism or the Search for a Usable Past

Generally, I argue that the 21st-century vantage point of Afropolitan literature is particularly metahistorical insofar as it already encompasses and reflects on the role of temporality and history in earlier diasporic writing, both fictional and academic. Diasporic literature in the moment of Afropolitanism is thus able to draw on these notions, as both intertext and direct referent. It is noteworthy that most academic theorizations of Black cosmopolitanism are occupied with historical formations, most notably in *The Black Atlantic*, but also, for example, in Ifeoma Kiddoe Nwankwo's *Black Cosmopolitanism* (2014) or Brent Hayes Edwards's *The Practice of Diaspora* (2003). The growing scholarship on Afropolitanism allows for a much-needed update of these concepts, developing a contemporary model of diaspora while drawing on the historical depth prompted by a comparative reading with concepts such as Black Internationalism or Pan-Africanism. On a smaller scale, I aim to integrate these concerns by showing the significance of temporality in contemporary diasporic literature and the impact of decades of diasporic historiography.

For scholar Markus Nehl, the influence of 20th-century historiography is a distinguishing feature of contemporary diasporic fiction. In *Transnational Black Dialogues* (2016), Nehl identifies a "second generation neo-slave narrative" in novels like Toni Morrison's *A Mercy* (2008), Yvette Christiansë's *Unconfessed* (2006), or Marlon James's *The Book of Night Women* (2009). These texts, he argues, draw on antebellum slave narratives and 20th-century neo-slave narratives but are also influenced by the cultural politics of the Black Power era and the adjacent "radical reconceptualization of the historiography of slavery" (24). Nehl suggests that, through this dense intertextuality, these neo-slave narratives "not only try to fill in the gaps of the historical record but also self-reflexively comment on the dangers and limits inherent in their attempt to reconstruct the history of slavery from today's perspective" (32). The novels under discussion are also characterized by this heightened self-reflexivity and intertextuality, mobilized by an acute awareness of the ongoing legacy of slavery and colonialism and the necessity of inscribing these counter-histories into the present. However, in Afropolitan literatures, slavery becomes merely one of a cast of diasporic cornerstones, albeit an important one. Generally, and perhaps more so than other literary fields, the literatures of the Black Diaspora are implicated by the quest for 'usable pasts' as well as the discursive struggles surrounding them. The notion of a 'usable past' itself has a complex and divergent history, taking on slightly different connotations in different contexts. What follows is a brief glimpse into the two contexts that most affect Afropolitan fictions, e.g. the US-American and the postcolonial African.

In its many iterations within academic and public discourse, the notion of a 'usable past' has always been linked to issues of cultural values, norms, and identities. In the context of the US in particular, the process of consciously selecting and appropriating the past was motivated by an inquiry into 'what it means to be American' and also aimed to indicate 'what America *should* be,' thereby designating so-called usable and unusable pasts. First schematized during the Progressive era – yet clearly already informing the creation of a white Anglo-Saxon racial imaginary – the quest for America's usable pasts spawned numerous debates throughout the 20th century, often feeding into discussions about (literary) canons or other debates generally subsumed under the so-called culture wars, by raising questions of inclusivity and diversity.[30] In the 1990s, David Thelen and Roy Rosenzweig conducted a large survey that focused on personal relations with and attitudes toward history, published as *The Presence of the Past: Popular Uses of History in American Life* (1998). The survey of more than 1,450 individuals revealed, among other things, a strikingly diverse appropriation and function of history among different racial and ethnic groups. Accordingly, the notion of distinctive African American pasts has been explored both in terms of their reciprocal relation to a wider, normative idea of American history and identity and, in accordance with popular culture theories á la John Fiske or Stuart Hall, as an actively employed toolkit for the creation of personal and collective identity.

The term 'usable past' also gained importance in the context of Africanist historiography, albeit with different connotations. While Progressive era historian Brooks lamented a "sterile" past and argued for lending it "living value" (1918: 338–339), the colonial context provided a much more vexed notion of

---

[30] For the earliest mention of the "usable past," see Brooks 1918. Here, the pragmatic and didactic function of history is stressed in opposition to an idealized Puritan heritage. Mid-century discussions of the term reflect the increased influence of cultural studies, e.g. Susman 1964. For its use in literary studies, see Reising 1986. For more recent overviews on its contested applications, see Nash et al. 2000; Launius 2013.

the historical archive and its impact on lived experience. The impact of imperial historiography installed a particularly sharp distinction between 'official' and 'popular' or 'recorded' and 'lived.' As J.M. Coetzee put it in *Waiting for the Barbarians*, "[e]mpire" and its creation of "the time of history" made it impossible for Africans to "live in time like fish in water" (1983: 133). A similar sentiment resonates in Ousmane Sembène's denouncing of Western historiographers as "chronophages," eaters of time (Murphy 2000: 177). As a consequence of this contested relation to the colonial archive, as well as the epistemic gaps it produced, post-independent national historiographers were often quick to emphasize unwanted 'unusable pasts,' in the same way that the national instrumentalization of history often overrode the personal or experiential one. As Cooper (2015) writes:

> African and African-American intellectuals long sought to counter primitivizing ideologies of their times by pointing to narratives of African state building. The real breakthrough in writing African history occurred as colonial rule was crumbling and the quest for a usable past – notably a usable national past – attracted young scholars in Africa and beyond (286).

This project, however, soon created its own forms of discontent. The nationalism inherent in those early quests for usable pasts is even more significant if one follows scholar Bogumil Jewsiewicki's contention that "the post-colonial state is an extension of the colonial state model," hence also sidelines popular historiography and eclipses historical narratives of anti-nationalist insurgence (1989: 4). This sentiment is echoed by Ngũgĩ wa Thiong'o, who, wary of all kinds of official Kenyan historiography, deplores the "state historians, whose role it is to give rational legitimacy to the traditions of loyalism and collaboration with imperialism" (1993: 98). Ngũgĩ also contends that the "people's real history of struggle and resistance" has produced its own historians – unofficial historians like himself, but also those unwilling to further corroborate the state-sanctioned, sanitary narrative of nation building (ibid.). Indeed, as Falola writes, by the 1980s, the "confident tone in nationalist historiography began to change to one of despair" (2011: 410). As a countermeasure, scholar Terence Ranger had already advocated a somewhat depoliticized notion of a "usable past for Africa," one that more closely resembled a definition of the term as lived experience and pragmatic social tool (1976). In accordance with the idea of the "invented tradition," which Ranger later developed in his eponymous work with Eric Hobsbawm, Ranger sought to de-mystify African historiography and wrench it out of the hands of corrupt political elites, who had in turn inherited it from racist colonial rulers.

There are a few aspects in these discourses that can help illuminate the notion of Afropolitanism as diasporic iteration, particularly within the US. For one, the shift from passive consumption to active appropriation matters here, as well as the attention to societal hierarchies and cultural hegemonies. Secondly, the fact that negotiations of usable pasts are almost always national projects needs to be carefully parsed. Deeply enmeshed in American mythologies of purity and plurality, the question of usable/unusable pasts determines the often subtle but crucial shifts between narratives of assimilation, hybridity, or difference.[31] In the Unites States, the so-called new African Diaspora symbolized by Afropolitanism is thus thrice conscripted by – while notably pushing against – nationalist narratives.[32] Afropolitanism marks the moment when the old narratives of Black Nationalist solidarity but also the national framing of assimilationist immigrant fiction and that of the exilic or émigré novel are questioned.[33] These diasporic fictions are not singularly marked by aspirational melting pot narratives or, in its reversal, by anti-aspirationalist narratives of return. Rather, they are characterized by a complication of either of these paradigms, often combining both. A good example is Imbolo Mbue's *Behold the Dreamers* (2016), a novel that was celebrated precisely for its renunciation of the American Dream, purportedly showing its collision with "immigrant reality" (PBS 2017). Yet where that novel's ending, the protagonists' return to Cameroon, merely truncates rather than questions its fairly straight-forward assimilationist story line,[34] others, like Adichie's *Americanah*, Sefi Atta's *A Bit of Difference* (2012), or Akwaeke Emezi's *Freshwater* (2018), offer protagonists who are not primarily preoccupied with mapping onto the progressive linearity of national time – a change that is not solely ascribable to these characters' financial privilege but also a willed change in perspective.

In the same way that the "era of disillusionment" and its links to contemporaneous historiography affected African fiction, Afropolitan literature conveys a

---

31 See, for example, Paul 2014, particularly chapter 5.
32 Nationalism, here, includes the nationalism of post-independence African states, American civic nationalism, and the cultural nationalism of a Black Power movement that threatens to misrecognize and conscript African immigrants into a mythologized and monolithic notion of Africa. For a deeper discussion of the relationship between the latter two, see Singh 2004.
33 As Balakrishnan notes, the repudiation of nationalism is not only a distinguishing feature of Afropolitanism, but one that may also serve as a binding function for its diverse iterations: "And thus, in the end, it may be said that Afropolitanism's symbolic potency – of these disparate elements – reduces to one: its abdication of nationalism as a political project" (2018: 578).
34 In its historicizing of national time, here the banking crisis of 2008, the novel's plotting suggests an extreme form of cultural assimilation, as it explores the economic ascension and financial crash of an aspirational Cameroonian couple and their WASP employers in a strangely unproblematized analogy.

specific historicism.[35] Neither disappointedly shunning political history nor glorifying narratives of national progress, the novels under discussion nevertheless heavily historicize the moment of Afropolitanism. *Homegoing*, for example, traces over two hundred years of diasporic history into the early 2000s, while *Americanah* historicizes Nigerian military rule, 'multicultural' Britain, and Obama's election. *Open City* navigates the tense post-9/11 climate of New York and Brussels. Other contemporary fictions like Esi Edugyan's *Half-Blood Blues* (2011), Yvonne Adhiambo Owour's *Dust* (2013), Jennifer Nansubuga Makumbi's *Kintu* (2014), Novuyo Rosa Tshuma's *House of Stone* (2018), and Namwali Serpell's *The Old Drift* (2019) also revisit crucial moments of African and diasporic history, often illuminating the more hidden paths that have led to the present. Identifying Afropolitanism as space, analogous to Avtar Brah's definition of diaspora space as a conceptual category, the author and blogger Minna Salami notes how the imaginative "glocal" space of Afropolitanism is equally characterized by its pronounced historical anachronisms (Rask Knudsen and Rahbeck 2016: 157). And it is not only because "the internet is Afropolitan" – the fact that a wealth of information is literally at their fingertips – that Afropolitan writers and artists move so frequently in and out of time (Mbembe 2015). Their revisiting of the past occurs in and with the full knowledge of how today's political presents are shaped by past trajectories and how these pasts have ultimately timed and positioned themselves. To paraphrase Martin Luther King Jr., these anachronisms inquire into many arcs of history, subtly interrogating if and how they may have bent toward justice.

While these novels cannot be neatly aligned with or co-opted by earlier nationalist or internationalist projects, the notion of a 'usable/unusable past' has not disappeared. Through active negotiation rather than passive consumption, the novels under discussion probe if and how history bears upon the present and whose pasts may actively constitute the contemporary diasporic imaginary. The latent distinction between the usable and unusable already affects what could otherwise be interpreted as arbitrary or self-sufficient metafictional play. Moreover, the deliberate and earnest exploration of pasts, both usable and unusable, counters what Ella Shohat has critiqued as the "ambiguous spatio-temporality" of the postcolonial (1992: 102). Arguing against certain "ahistorical and universalizing" (ibid. 99) tendencies in postcolonial theorizing, Shohat writes: "The term "post-colonial" carries with it the implication that colonialism is

---

[35] Key texts that fall into the period of post-independence and deal with the appending notions of arrested development and disillusionment are, for example: Ayi Kwei Armah, *The Beautyful Ones Are Not Yet Born* (1968); Ngũgĩ wa Thiong'o, *Devil on the Cross* (1980); or Chinua Achebe, *A Man of the People* (1966).

now a matter of the past, undermining colonialism's economic, political, and cultural deformative-traces in the present" (ibid. 105).

The notion that the past has left its "deformative-traces" in the present also resonates with Anne McClintock's critique that much of post-colonial theory may feign to dismantle "the imperial idea of linear time" yet reintroduces it through the term's emphasis on posteriority (1992: 85). As such, the "post-colonial scene" emerges "in an entranced suspension of history, as if the definitive historical events have preceded us, and are not now in the making" (ibid. 86). These auto-critiques of the postcolonial correspond with an important aspect of these novels' pronounced (meta)-historicisms, anachronisms and explorations of asynchronous or repetitive temporalities. It exposes the simple fact that "trauma doesn't care about time." That sentence, uttered by the contemporary psychiatrist Paul Conti on a popular medical podcast, relays how Freud's theories, despite generally having lost much of their clinical significance, continue to inform the study of trauma temporality.

2.3 Timing Historical and Racial Trauma

The timelessness of trauma is central to Freud's model of psychic representation. What Freud observed in the shell-shocked WWI soldier's constant reliving of painful experiences led to his development of the death drive and also confirmed his belief that "unconscious mental processes are in themselves 'timeless'" (1955: 28). The "'daemonic' force" of the death drive notwithstanding, Freud interpreted the compulsion to repeat as an attempt at mastering the original trauma. Yet he also understood this as a temporally indefinite endeavor given the fact that, regarding unconscious mental processes, "time alters nothing in them, nor can the idea of time be applied to them" (ibid.).

In literature, one form of mastery is indeed form itself. Hence, yet another way that these texts can be read as meditations on race and time is through their metafictional play on genre. Following Goyal's notion of "genre as the presence of the past in the present," all three readings explore how these contemporary texts navigate the generic conventions of diasporic literature (2010: 10). In many ways, if not all, these explorations also illuminate questions of race and racialization as they sometimes navigate, sometimes strain at not only the ghostly presence of violent diasporic pasts, but also their textual conventions. Considering the traumatic nature of these pasts, it is unsurprising that this kind of metafiction rarely takes an ironic or self-parodic stance. At times, however, the novels' use of metafiction does provide a metacommentary that questions the critical purchase or ethico-political value of specific modes of writing trauma.

Conditioned by the abovementioned impetus of determining usable pasts in a contested discursive arena, both the historical novel and so-called trauma fiction are common genres in Black Diasporic writing.

Historically, literary and cultural approaches to trauma theories are rooted in Holocaust studies, yet numerous scholars have endeavored to widen trauma theory's analytical framework or productively relate it to racial and colonial violence.[36] Michael Rothberg, whose *Traumatic Realism* (2000) forms one of the key texts of trauma studies (among them Elaine Scarry's *The Body in Pain* from 1985 and Cathy Caruth's *Unclaimed Experience* from 1996), has also added his critical heft to the call for decolonizing and globalizing trauma studies. Among some of the core issues at stake in "Postcolonial Trauma Novels," he lists "the articulation of race and space; the uncanny historicity of colonial (and other forms of) violence; the intergenerational transmission of trauma; and the problem of unequal recognition of disparate traumatic histories" (2008: 226).

Many of these different theorizations converge on a critique of Caruth's notion that "trauma itself may provide the very link between cultures," by revealing how Eurocentric notions of trauma aren't actually always transferable (1995: 11). In fact, prevalent models such as PTSD or processes such as acting out, moving through or witnessing trauma may not be universally applicable or differently achieved. Trauma theory, as Craps writes in *Postcolonial Witnessing*, should thus always "take account of the specific social and historical contexts in which trauma narratives are produced and received, and be open and attentive to the diverse strategies of representation and resistance which these contexts invite or necessitate" (2013: 43). For example, in "The Question of 'Solidarity' in Postcolonial Trauma Fiction: Beyond the Recognition Principle," Hamish Dalley questions whether contemporary postcolonial literature's revisiting of traumatic historical events can really be understood as attempts at achieving recognition, or even solidarity.[37] As Dalley observes, not only do postcolonial and trauma studies appear to complement each other, exemplified by the emergent field of postcolonial trauma studies, but the very terminology of trauma theory – its focus on metaphors of invasion, disturbance or assimilation – already lends itself to narrativizing the traumas of colonialism and slavery. Further-

---

36 See Ifowodo 2013; Visser 2011; Craps 2012; Borzaga 2012.
37 Aware of the abovementioned auto-critiques of (postcolonial) trauma theory, particularly in relation to potentially Eurocentric theoretical lenses that are treated as trans-human universals, Dalley's article identifies as particularly limiting literary approaches the focus on individualized recognition, as well as the anxious apprehension of literary modernism, as a non-linear and intentionally estranging, privileged aesthetic form of trauma representation (Dalley 2015: 369–392).

more, most trauma theories implicitly or explicitly develop a trajectory that moves "from pain to recognition to solidarity," thus privileging what Dalley considers the most productive, albeit ambiguously demarcated, convergence of trauma and postcolonialism (2015: 373). That said, contemporary postcolonial texts seem to draw on these convergences in unexpected ways, as they offer a range of different, and often conflicting, subject positions. Among the vast range of literary traumas in fictions like Adichie's *Americanah* or Okey Ndibe's *Foreign Gods, Inc.*, Dalley identifies those of the colonized, colonizers, and what he calls transnational proletarians (2015: 372). By conducting a comparative analysis of ostensibly incomparable sites of trauma, Dalley aims to reveal a fundamental ambivalence of contemporary postcolonial literature regarding the ethico-political purchase of prevalent trauma discourses.

This ambiguity certainly informs the Afropolitan novels selected here, as all works appear to dramatize the realization that – not only with regards to the disparate members of the contemporary African diaspora but also in terms of addressing differently positioned audiences – "recognition is more complex than it may appear and that, even when it seems unquestionably desirable, it does not necessarily lead to solidarity" (Dalley 2015: 372). Hence, these novels draw attention to the limits of an empathetic recognition that is not grounded in a critical reckoning with historical and material circumstance. Solidarity, they suggest, cannot be grounded in the realization of an other's humanity and vulnerability alone, but must come replete with a deeper understanding of – and desire to change – the conditions that make traumatizing structures possible.

Apart from various historical traumas that are metafictionally commented upon or revisited, there is also the more insidious, and less distant, trauma of racialization that repeatedly surfaces in these novels. The notion of racial trauma is already apparent in Fanon's primal scene in "The Fact of Blackness," where, following the initial event, his sense of self appears to be disintegrating, disassembled by the transfixing gaze, the awareness of his body splitting into dizzying, nauseating multitudes. He writes: "My body was given back to me sprawled out, distorted, recolored, clad in mourning in that white winter day" (2008: 86). Here, racialization is immediately equated with trauma, as the scene threatens his physical and psychological integrity and is also 'compulsively' repeated throughout the essay. Generally, it is important to distinguish between historical traumas and traumas of racialization in these fictions. Compared to other traumas, the temporality of racial trauma is often marked by the move from the historical to the transhistorical, thus approximating the 'timelessness' of trauma temporality. While this move diminishes the facticity or historicity of the event – a central concern of much of historical trauma fiction – it does reveal Black temporality as an effect of the conflicting poles between which Black subjects hover: having no history and, simultaneously, too much of it.

Rather than striving for the kind of historicity that is suitable for contesting 'official' historiography, traumatic scenes of racialization suffer from the weight of a historicity assuming the guise of the eternal. This distinction also roughly corresponds with the difference between a (postcolonial) historicist investment in subaltern or contested historiography and that of (Black American) melancholic historicism. The latter cares much less about the facticity of the past – the horrors of slavery have been well documented and, with few exceptions, are institutionally recognized – than about its effect on or extension into the present; or put differently: it is less about the past not *being* the past, than about it not *having* passed.[38] Here, repetition really is inevitable, if not eternal, as the present is gripped by the afterlife of slavery and its appendant "racial calculus and political arithmetic" that "has yet to be undone" (Hartman 2007: 6). Positioned amid these sometimes closely related diasporic historicisms, the selected novels represent the temporal communities of the Black Diaspora in unique ways. Apart from historicizing rather than ontologizing Blackness, these texts remain both attentive and resistant to the concept of race in/as history. Resistance, while sometimes analogously structured, it is not the same as rejection. In the following literary analysis, another aspect of the complex node of race and history transpires, something much more elusive that may also take the form of an opening, a wedge with which to uncouple this fateful schema. These openings are unable or simply cannot dare to imagine a time- and race-less future and translate instead into a call for stopping time, for brushing history against the grain, if not even ending it. In continuation of the heavy Benjaminian influence on diasporic writing via the work of Gilroy and others, this call is mobilized by the desire "to stay, awaken the dead, and make whole what has been smashed" (Benjamin 2003: 392). And, as I argue, it is the historical constellation of Afropolitanism, marked as it is as a repetition with a difference, that allows these texts to appropriate the past as it "flashes up in a moment of danger" (ibid. 391).

In this sense, there is another dimension to repetition that is neither blind to the effect of its original trauma nor invested in a futile undoing or reversing of time but endeavors to recognize, through repetition, what happened and what

---

[38] This is of course a rather sweeping statement with regards to how the former category corresponds with (postcolonial) historical trauma fiction. As Dalley argues, it would be equally reductive to read these novels' treatment of historical events merely as "struggles over discursive power," as this position "misses crucial dimensions of its realist epistemology." Complicating this would mean understanding their knowledge claims as "neither naively mimetic nor comprehensible as a play of ungrounded signifiers" (2014: 10–11).

might have changed. From this perspective, all of the novels can be read as earnest explorations of other people's pasts that, through emphatic transference and historical awareness, inscribe and implicate a range of diasporic positionalities. Far from signaling rifts and fissures, their often distanced and distancing metahistoricist stance is employed in order to understand others and oneself in relation to them. The Afropolitan moment thus emerges as a historical constellation through which the Black Diaspora is able to refract and reflect itself. In reading and interpreting the texts accordingly, the term race in/as history attempts to convey how race can be curiously situated in the past and firmly envelope the 'now' through which that past is imagined.

3 Conclusion: The Challenges of Afropolitan World Making

Objectively, the global moment of Afropolitanism affords a greater visibility to people of African descent, be it in the world of visual arts, media, literature, or business.[39] Yet parallel to what commentators have described as a positive rendering of what is usually a negative 'African exceptionalism,' Afro-pessimist thinkers like Wilderson have contended that the "ruse of analogy erroneously locates the Black in the world – a place where s/he has not been since the dawning of Blackness" (2010: 50). While especially the irreducible antagonism at the heart of Afro-pessimist arguments nullifies Afropolitanism as an attempt to locate a Black positionality in the world, particularly as an analogous appropriation of a humanist concept such as cosmopolitanism, *Making Black History* argues that the Afropolitan moment is ambiguously constituted by optimism *and* pessimism, hope *and* anxiety, and that much of its negative affect is already apparent in the uneasy negotiations of Afropolitanism as a label. As scholar Chielozona Eze has noted, the fusing of African and cosmopolitan suggests that the African cannot "just be cosmopolitan" (2014: 240). A reading of *Ghana Must Go* and other novels as profoundly anxious expressions of transnationalism suggests the same: Why is it so hard to live in the world as an African? Are Africans not of this world?

I want to argue that this uneasy 'worlding' indeed helps situate the moment of Afropolitanism apropos contemporary notions of critical race theory. For Afro-pessimist thinkers, the world is defined by anti-Blackness in such a way that al-

---

[39] This visibility is multicausal but often variably linked to market forces, an exoticizing appetite for 'otherness,' colonial guilt, and political progress (after all, 2015 to 2024 is the UN International Decade for People of African Descent), or an emphasis on the exemplary agency of African actors (cue "Africa rising" or model minority narratives).

lows only one conclusion: the end of the world. As Wilderson asserts in an interview: "We're trying to destroy the world" (2014: 20). Yet how does this worlding or unworlding occur in the Afropolitan novel? Rather than unequivocally asserting global social belonging, Afropolitanism has always conveyed more ambiguity than certainty, echoing concerns that are not entirely unlike Afro-pessimist concerns. However, rather than rendering Blackness an ontological position overdetermined by the social death of the slave, these novels investigate Blackness as a mutually imbricating history. Stretching and probing the global Black imaginary, they also interrogate the historicity of anti-Blackness, bringing together Hegel's eclipsing of African agency, the social death of the slave, as well as the neocolonial and anti-Black carceral state.

William David Hart, in a survey of the most important trajectories of critical race studies from W.E.B. Du Bois to Hortense Spillers, distinguishes broadly between two modes of theorizing anti-Black racism. One is a strictly materialist conceptualizing that renders racism either an effect or an enabler of capitalism. The other trajectory understands Blackness (also) as an ontological position of Western metaphysics. For the latter thinkers, Afro-pessimists chiefly among them, the "ideological needs of capitalism do not explain the perdurance of antiblack racism, its virtually limitless scope, its metastatic reproduction, and the depths of its pathological animosity" (Hart 2018: 14). By highlighting not only the historicity of race and Blackness but also its actual equation with or mutual imbrication with the idea of history and temporality, the novels under discussion strike a particular balance. Relying neither primarily on transhistorical metaphysics nor on historical materialism, they reveal how the fictions of race and racism, of whiteness and Blackness, are indeed constituted by both. Similar to the way that, for many, capitalism seems inextricably bound up with very idea of national time and global history, allowing for a 'no alternative' mode of imagining, so are our common narratives of capital H history and national progress deeply invested in the endless reproduction of race and racism.[40] Yet by making 'Black'

---

40 For an investigation of the linkage of "progress," "national time," and "race struggle," see Michel Foucault's fourth lecture in *Society Must Be Defended*. Here, Foucault distinguishes between a "struggle between races," the discourse of races (or popular struggles), which is anti-hegemonic, revolutionary and the "discourse of race," which is biological or medical and requires state sovereignty to preserve the notion of purity. Viewed as discrete discourse, however, the historical discourse of race marked the movement from the temporal narratives of antiquity and "introduced us into a form of history, a form of time that can be both dreamed of and known, both dreamed of and understood, and in which the question of power can no longer be dissociated from that of servitude, liberation, and emancipation" (2003: 84). Foucault defines the discourse of race struggle as a polyvalent, mobile discourse that can morph from an oppositional or revolutionary – and often eschatological or biblical – discourse that struggles against history rather than ontology, they highlight how temporality and historicism carry a heightened significance for the Black Diaspora as a whole, but also, ultimately, how they express the hope that the shackles of the current world ordering *can* be broken and, along with anti-Blackness, may actually recede into history. Unequivocally, if to varying degrees, these novels do not simply project into the future but also attend to the particularly urgent manner in which race in/as history manifests itself in the contemporary context of the US. In addressing and reflecting this urgency, they signal the very solidarity they are accused of lacking – even though this solidarity takes a different guise than the assumed sameness of old.

The following readings are predominantly invested in how these novels negate or negotiate ethico-political belonging – to various worlds, yet particularly the Black Diaspora – through their often-metafictional play and engagement with temporality and historicity. As such, they are investigations into these novels' intradiasporic world making. "In its multispatial and multitemporal dimensions," Ngũgĩ writes, "the novel literally can bring all spaces and times within itself" (2016: 8). But how do these novels speak to, dismiss, or actualize Black Diaspora legacies, presents, and futures? These questions need to be carefully parsed, since all three novels employ these elements to varying degrees and effects. As Cole's *Open City* probes both the generic confinements and the limitations of a (diasporic) solidarity grounded in the recognition of trauma – or, rather, the limited empathic transference engendered by an aesthetic sublimation of trauma – diasporic histories appear almost hopelessly gripped by the kind of historicism that conditions a melancholic response as much as it bars an actual engagement with the present. The gleam of hope merely anticipated in *Open City* is hyperbolically realized in Adichie's *Americanah*, as genre-induced, libidinal attachments to a rosy, perhaps even race-less, future wrest its protagonists from the overdetermining reach of history and back to the mother country. Gyasi's *Homegoing*, on the other hand, employs both the forward push of futurity and the backward pull of historicity as a novel that flashes the hopeful potential of restoration and connection across the rupture of the Middle Passage, without trivializing the long-lasting effects of slavery and its aftermath.

These subtle renderings of diasporic temporalities accrue specific meaning if one acknowledges that Afropolitanism emerges in a moment when both the

---

oppressive forms of power, for example in the 19th-century post-revolutionary project of writing a history of "the people," to using that same eschatological or biblical discourse in order to disqualify "colonized subraces" (2003: 77).

promise of a post-racial US-America and that of Black diasporic unity are called into question. Against this discursive background, I argue that Blackness – like time – is not only investigated, probed, stretched, and made malleable by these novels. It is also employed, purposefully, as a form of truce and as earnest endeavor signaling diasporic desire, hope for unity, and imagined collectivity.

At the same time, it is fair to say that the extraordinary critical acclaim and commercial success of these novels was at least partly fueled by an iteration of the "New Negro" paradigm. Authors and works were, sometimes, peddled as spokespersons for a version of Blackness that has not only surpassed, but even bypassed the disgraceful history of slavery. Their contested position within the cultural landscape, as well as an acute awareness thereof, is reflected in Teju Cole's laconic statement: "I'm an Afropolitan, a pan-African, an Afro-pessimist, depending on who hates me on any given day" (Bady 2015: para. 36). Surely, these authors were conscious of how their success could be mobilized and pitted against African Americans and often went to great lengths to assert that they were "happily black" (Adichie), "black on all sides" (Cole), or that slavery "affects us still" (Gyasi).[41]

Should we read their perspectives on slavery, their investigation of US race relations, and their employment of race in/as history as an act of duty? That would be too easy and most likely unconvincing. Could it, then, be an act of love? While they are marked by a diasporic desire that indeed strives toward "a more perfect union," infusing the space of diaspora with a renewed, multilateral sense of kinship, this is not an entirely selfless act. They are expanding Blackness in order to insert their positionality, amplifying their voices and their perspectives. Their giving shape to the sign of Africa in the moment of Afropolitanism is also a conscious inscribing, not only into the US, or the world, but into the time and space of diaspora *as* the world. Particularly within the political and cultural context of the US, however, it is a precarious balancing act to do both: to challenge but not to undermine. My readings attempt to trace this balancing act, and to show how these novels are carefully constructed narratives that, in one way or another, help us acknowledge that there can never be a single narrative on anything – and certainly not on Blackness. Rather than supplanting or making Blackness disappear, these texts purposefully probe and navigate race in/as history. By actively (re-)inscribing Africa into the diasporic imaginary, they alter and make Black history.

---

41 See Segal 2013; Adeleye 2016; Gyasi 2017.

Chapter II
Going Through The Motions – Movement, Metahistory, and the Spectacle of Suffering in Teju Cole's *Open City*

> "[L]iterature, like psychoanalysis, is interested in the complex relation between knowing and not knowing."
>
> Cathy Caruth

> "And above all beware, my body and my soul too, beware of crossing your arms in the sterile attitude of a spectator, because life is not a spectacle, a sea of sorrows is not a proscenium, because a man who screams is not a dancing bear."
>
> Aimé Césaire

1 Introduction: Moving On or Being Moved?

It is with the first paragraph of Teju Cole's *Open City*[42] that we not only gain a concrete sense of this peculiar novel's set and setting, but also a crucial insight into its entire structure, mode, and tone: "And so when I began to go on evening walks last fall, I found Morningside Heights an easy place from which to set out into the city" (3). It is from this precise localization that the novel's ulterior narration sets out, mapping the distances between fixed points like Morningside Park or Central Park in units measured by "walking pace" (ibid.). In the course of the narrative, spanning the "final year" of his psychiatric fellowship, New York City "work[s] itself into" the life of the first-person narrator Julius (ibid.). The sense of temporality maintained here is deictic: later we will discover that the story is set in the period from the fall of 2005 to that of 2006. The opening composition of a specific place in a somewhat fixed yet unsure time, however, will structure the way that Julius experiences the city. It marks a sense of time as something to be decoded, linked to the experience of space yet also independent of it. Throughout the novel, unhinged temporalities present themselves as a narrative force, as something imbued with an agency of its own, altering urban space and affecting the narrated "I," as Julius finds himself "gripped by [...]

Note: This chapter is derived in part from an article published in *Atlantic Studies: Global Currents. Critical Perspectives on Teju Cole*, edited by Isabel Soto and Paula von Gleich.

[42] Herafter cited as *OC*.

a commotion from an earlier time" (74), feeling as if he had "stumbled into a kink in time and space" (191) or caught in the kind of temporal limbo in which "it could have been any day from the last fifteen hundred years" (165).

For all its temporal suspensions and historical excursions, *Open City* is very much concerned with the fleeting present moment, and – especially in light of both the author and the novel's reception – also with the arguably even more elusive, contemporary moment of Afropolitanism. As such, both author and protagonist have often been read as embodiments of a new African or Black cosmopolitanism. Identifying Teju Cole as "one of a talented generation of global writers, at home in the world" (Kunzru), whose debut novel opens up, amongst others, "new vistas [...] on race, identity" (*The Economist*) allows a reading of *Open City* as the fictionalized account of a distinct experience of New York. This experience is mediated trough the perspective of a highly educated, cosmopolitan man of German/Nigerian descent whose complex past and present intermingle with the city's historical and contemporary challenges; while establishing a multilayered form of 'being Black' in New York City – and the world.

Yet *Open City* does not simply mark a novel phenomenology of global Blackness by providing "new vistas" on the world. Rather than merely reading Julius's position as exemplary of a new African or diasporic identity, it is important to resist taking the novel's realism at face value. With regards to any of its themes, and, crucially, to the way it employs race in/as history, *Open City* must be understood not simply as exemplifying a novel social formation but in its distinct novel form. Or, as Malcom Bradbury put it in a different context, it is important to remain attentive both to "the novel's propensity toward realism, social documentation and interrelation with historical events and movements," and to "its propensity toward form, fictionality, and reflexive self-examination" (1977: 8).[43] Despite the ostensibly mundane action it details, *Open City* provides less documentary realism than a highly formalized rendering of time and history as subjective experience. Skillfully, it brings in dialogic relation both subaltern and hegemonic, contrapuntal and dominant readings of history, foregrounding metahistorical positionalities that are seldom actively reflected upon. By detailing how individuals, collectives, communities, and even nations, move away from and/or through past trauma, it probes how exactly a conjunctural relation with history is established, as well as the various modes of being, ethical and

---

[43] Giles Foden, also citing Bradbury in his review of *Open City*, writes that the novel "recommences a process of synthesis" between these two often contested aspects of the novel (2011: para. 6). I agree that the novel dramatizes this, and that most careful readings of the novel acknowledge it – except when it comes to notions of race and racism, which are either ignored or not afforded this kind of hermeneutic nuance.

otherwise, that each positionality may entail. *Open City* thus embodies an important aspect of the Afropolitan moment, yet one that is less interested in making history through novelty but rather investigates the subjective and affective *poesis* of history, or how history is made, and the hermeneutics of history, how history can be read.

The evidently modernist motifs in *Open City* have led critics to align Julius with the figure of the *flâneur*, whose putatively aimless wandering, erudite cosmopolitan sensibility, and "acute, sympathetic eye" invite the reader to "see interesting things in the city, and to notice them well" (Wood 2012: para. 6). The same review, by James Wood, while noting an "interesting combination of confession and reticence about Julius," nevertheless sees the narrative motivation of *Open City* thus exhausted (para. 5). However, the narrative flow of *Open City* is clearly not aimless, yet it is also not causally driven – at least not in the common sense of action and reaction, event and idea. There are lapses, there is meandering, there is the cautious revolving around a theme that remains largely unresolved. This chapter illuminates how the formal structure of *Open City* bespeaks its narrative motivation, while being attentive to the novel's carefully constructed ambiguity. Its thematic complexity and ostensibly motiveless protagonist and story resist a totalizing interpretation and prompt remarkably varied reader responses.[44] An important premise of the following investigation is the assumption that the diversity of readings and their respective emotional responses mirror the extent and potential of *Open City*'s protagonist Julius to move in and out of, and be moved by, the stories he records. Reading the novel through the polysemic trope of movement makes it paramount to relate its affective and chronotopic configurations to the Black Diaspora – as a political movement predicated on historical imbrications and contemporary solidarity. Hence, this chapter argues that it is precisely through the exploration of spatiotemporal movement that the novel also stages the (im)possibility of emotional transference – of being moved to feel – and establishes an ethical relation to the past.

---

[44] While popular reviews of the novel hail it as an "exhilarating post-melting pot" and a "hopeful, affirming book", or laud its cosmopolitan and liberal sensibility, other, mainly scholarly, interpretations tend to focus on the novel's more foreboding and pessimist tones. See Liu 2012; Hallemeier 2013.

2 "To Trace Out a Story": Narrating Movement and the Movement of Narrative

With its vast array of historico-ontological and metaphorical connotations, movement can easily be identified as a master trope of the Black Diaspora, be it the forced movements and removals of colonialism and transatlantic enslavement, the northbound movements of the Underground Railroad, the Great Migration, Post-war emigration from the colonies, or the complex flows of contemporary migration. Theoretically, too, some hugely productive conceptualizations of Black or postcolonial culture have relied on notions of movement; from the ambivalent vacillation behind Homi K. Bhabha's idea of liminality (2004: 5) to the "vertiginous movement" underlying the cultural practice Henry Louis Gates has identified as signifyin' (1988: 55). In Gilroy's *The Black Atlantic*, the connection is made particularly explicit when he centers his exploration on the image of "ships in motion," calling this particular chronotope of passage the "central organising symbol" of the diaspora (2002: 4). Apprehending *Open City* through the trope of movement, it appears as if it is movement in and of itself, rather than its aim, origin, or directedness that seems to determine its overall narrative structure. The protagonist Julius, repeatedly emphasizing the aimlessness of his urban strolls, could thus be interpreted as an embodiment of the most prevalent image of the Afropolitan – sophisticated, unfettered, and monied. Yet it is rather difficult to align this complicated protagonist with the glossy surfaces of that consumerist notion of Afropolitanism, showcasing a shiny and new generation of African immigrants who move swiftly and elegantly from country to country, cultural sphere to cultural sphere, seemingly at ease and carrying no grudges, creating no friction. The leisurely movements of Julius are indeed marked by the kind of agency, nonchalance, and self-possession that are not commonly afforded to the global movements of Black bodies, who have historically been imagined as either economically trafficked, externally driven, or coerced itinerant objects. What drives the following investigation, however, is how 'unmotivated' and 'free' any form of movement – particularly Black movement – can ever be.

While *Open City* variedly explores movement, its most obvious instance is the physical movement of the narrator, which allows for the unfolding of most of the action, while also determining the narrative pace, temporality, and structure of the novel. In order to distinguish the temporalities of these levels, I operate with Gérard Genette's narratological model of *histoire*, *récit*, and *narration*, or story, plot, and narrating, as well as duration, mood, and voice. Looking at the way that spatiotemporal configurations evoke formal conventions or constraints, I draw on Mikhail Bakhtin's notion of the chronotope, as developed in *The Dialogic Imagination*.

2 "To Trace Out a Story": Narrating Movement and the Movement of Narrative — 61

Open City's first-person narrator Julius is a young psychiatrist who roams the city like a restless *flâneur*, measuring its lengths and depths, an isolated and distant observer winding down after long days at the hospital. Apart from a trip abroad and a short visit to an immigration detention center in Queens, Julius traces out a map of Manhattan, staying true both in spirit and scope to the vastness of this "sea in the middle of the sea," the "urban island" evoked in French historian Michel de Certeau's much cited essay "Walking in the City" (2008: 91). The narrative momentum of *Open City* unfolds in a pedestrian rather than panoptic way, slow and subtle. Yet this is not to say that there is no action, no drive, no emplotment – or elevated viewpoint, for that matter. The particular movement of his purportedly "aimless wandering" (3) dictates a narrative rhythm that is somewhat monotonous, a lulling pace accompanied by his distanced and sophisticated musings on predominantly Western history, art, philosophy, and psychology. This rather cool and detached surface reading is punctured by violent intrusions that seem to force themselves upon the narrator, as he strolls through, or perhaps flees from, his own past and part in history.

The novel comprises twenty-one chapters and is divided into two parts. The epigraph to the first part reads "*Death is a perfection of the eye*" (1); the second part is themed "*I have searched myself*" (147). Part one spans the beginning of Julius's evening walks until the end of his visit to Brussels, Belgium – a trip of several weeks intended to bring about a reunion with his maternal German grandmother that is marked by extensive rain, more walking, a chance sexual encounter, as well as an engagement with Europe's colonial heritage and post 9/11 islamophobia. In the chapters leading up to Julius's lonely Christmas in Brussels, we learn that he is an avid listener of classical music, an eclectic reader, and an occasional birdwatcher, that he has few friends, one of them an 89-year old Japanese-American professor of Early English Literature, and that he has recently broken up with his girlfriend, Nadège. These biographical details are woven into his autodiegetic narrative in a piecemeal fashion; everything is filtered through reflection, little is shown in action, everything is told in retrospect. The telling, however, is intimate, often casual, omitting and passing over information in a mode more akin to that of a diary or internal monologue than that of a memoir or autobiography. The overall effect, however, maintains the impression of the narrator as author. In this sense, the intradiegetic world of Julius's narrating takes on mimetic qualities. We learn that Julius is not white through the incidental observation that "[i]n the Harlem night, there were no whites" on page 18. We gather that he is African when he thinks back to his childhood memories of watching a movie about Idi Amin's atrocities, and we find out that he is Nigerian when he recalls an uncomfortable situation in the house of a medical professor, an East African Indian who had been expelled by Idi Amin and who speaks with disdain and disgust of all Africans, "sidestep[ing] the specific" (31).

Apart from numerous passages that indulge in erudite soliloquies on urban and art history and, in their ostensibly calm and collected objectivity, resemble the style of historiography, frequent excursions into Julius's recent and more distant past accompany his narration. Curiously, they appear to be both central and accidental to character and plot motivation. When the narrating comes to an end, a year later, it seems as though not much has 'happened,' at least on the surface. Julius has completed his fellowship at the clinic and taken up an opening in a private practice in Manhattan. We have reached the present tense of the narrative; he is organizing his new office (248). His final memory ventures only so far as the previous night, a visit to the opera to see one of "Mahler's final works – *Das Lied von der Erde*" (250). Following the memory of getting locked out on the fire staircase of Carnegie Hall, gazing at the starry skies and evoking strong notions of futurity, he recounts the unexpected experience of a boat trip on the Hudson River later that night. Moving onto the Upper Bay, the boat comes close to the Statue of Liberty, triggering in Julius a train of thought on the statue's history as a lighthouse and the fatal danger it presented to migrating birds. This passage appears to be embedded in the frame of remembering the "[l]ast night" to Julius's present, yet, unlike countless other historical digressions, this one closes the narrating and narrative as a whole:

> A large number of birds met their death in this manner. In 1888, for instance, on the morning after one particularly stormy night, more than fourteen hundred dead birds were recovered from the crown, the balcony of the torch, and the pedestal of the statue. [...] On October 1 of that year, for example, the colonel's report indicated that fifty rails had died, as had eleven wrens, two catbirds, and one whip-poor-will. The following day, the record showed two dead wrens; the day after that, eight wrens. [...] On the morning of October 13, for example, 175 wrens had been gathered in, all dead of the impact, although the night just past hadn't been particularly windy or dark. (258–259)

With this cumulative account of the generic names and numbers of birds that perished, disoriented by the Statue of Liberty's gleaming light, the novel ends not merely in the intradiegetic past tense of recent memory but also in the distanced authorial mode of historiography – and a strangely inverted invocation of a bird's eye perspective. Again, recalling de Certeau's distinction between the panoptic overview of a city, in his case initiated by the view from the World Trade Center, and the street-level perspective of the pedestrian or *flâneur*, this particular instance of another iconic New York City building and the interesting blurring of perspectives functions as a peculiar coda to the novel. Without actually leaving the street or, in this case, sea level of the narration, without being offered an untroubled, totalizing overview of Julius's account, we are still left with a somewhat elevated perspective and narrative voice that is not one or no one's and could thus be ours. This perspective also questions the kind of narrative situation invoked in *Open City*, and the ground the narrating actually attempts to cover. Modeled on the ambling movement of the pedestrian, Julius's narrating forecloses a final interpretation for himself in the same way that de Certeau asserts that the bodies of urban *Wandersmänner* "follow the thicks and thins of an urban 'text' they write without being able to read it" (2008: 93).

Yet who is the receiver or interpreter of this text and what is the motivation for it being written? In the very first chapter, Professor Saito evokes the spatial dimension of a text in a striking reversal of de Certeau's notion of the "long poem of walking" (2008: 101), alluding to it as "the environment created by the poems" (*OC* 14). Julius also affirms this notion, along with the unintelligibility of a textspace with regard to the body that produces it: "I told him a little about my walks, and wanted to tell him more but didn't have quite the right purchase on what it was I was trying to say about the solitary territory my mind had been crisscrossing" (12). This passage is also interesting in that it casts Julius in the role of reader or interpreter in a way that might signify an interpretative model for his own narrative. From listening to the memories of his former mentor, Julius notes, he has "learned the art of listening [...] and the ability to trace out a story from what was omitted" (9). Throughout the entire narration, Julius places subtle and not so subtle reminders that his narrative, too, is built on lapses and omissions that might be central to reading it as a whole. Only two paragraphs in, he already admits that he "couldn't trust his memory" (4), but it is finally through the rape accusation made by his childhood friend's sister, Moji, that we realize with more clarity that Julius is an unreliable narrator. In an interview with scholar Aaron Bady, Cole sheds light on Julius's particular unreliability: "I wasn't going for regular unreliability: "I was thinking more in terms of a formalized testimony, of the kind that might happen on a psychiatrist's couch. In other words, a plausible framing device for *Open City* is a series of visits by Julius to his psychiatrist" (2015: para. 11).

If we are to take this kind of framing seriously, we will have to adapt both the aim of Julius's purportedly unmotivated meandering and the narrative situation to that of a serialized confession, resting on the pivotal axis of Moji's disclosure. Thus, while most readers might experience the revelation as happening close to the end, it is in truth the end, at least the end of Julius's intradiegetic narrating. It is the culmination of a recollected story and occurs just before we reach the present tense of the narrating instance, in the final chapter. Furthermore, the temporal intervals between the two bracketing ulterior narrations and the narrating instance render the latter not merely a subsequent, but an interpolated narrative instance. Julius is telling this story as "a series of visits" and, as he cannot trust his memory, he also remembers it in a way that will influence the story. Genette describes this narrating instance as particularly complex, because "the story and the narrating can become entangled in such a way that the latter has an effect on the former" (1980: 217). In addition, Julius performs the narrating in a particularly cunning manner; he is a psychiatrist, after all. Asked by Bady if a therapist would not push him toward exploring the issues he is avoiding, Cole answers:

> Not in psychoanalysis. They'd let him unfold. They'd let him circle and digress. All the pushing will come from within himself. And since the patient is also a psychiatrist, he's naturally going to brood over questions like whether he has a blind spot, or come up with a statement like "I have searched myself." He would present with that kind of self-deceiving self-awareness. (2015: para. 15)

This temporal structure of *Open City*, organized around the disavowed rape of Moji, reveals a narrating instance that takes on crucial importance for interpreting the story as a scene of confessing or confiding and, on the part of the narratee, witnessing and constructing. Even though Julius never explicitly acknowledges his guilt, the novel's narrative structure renders his confession if not the story's 'point' or 'purpose' then at least the fundamental moment that motivates its telling. The implicit reader of *Open City*, as a psychotherapist, would, of course, be able to anticipate or trace this kind of pivotal moment through the narration's momentum and structure, as well as the following clues.

Moji enters Julius's story at the beginning of *Open City*'s second part, whereas the revelation appears at the very end. In-between these brackets we gain a very restrained sense of agitation, a subtle acceleration moving toward a climactic break, not only when Julius observes that he "had the ulcerous sensation of too many things happening at once" (184), but also in the form of a denser succession of action. Following the chapter in which Julius runs into Moji, we learn that his favorite patient V. has died, quickly followed by the death of Professor Saito, spanning two chapters. After a brief, and, as we will later see, illusory moment of leisure, Julius is robbed and injured by a group of teenage boys. The next externally motivated plot point is already Moji's telephone call, inviting him to a party at her boyfriend's apartment and leading up to the scene where she will confront him.

Instances that anticipate Moji's accusation and Julius's disavowal are especially poignant in the scene of their reencounter in New York, as well as in Julius's delayed reaction to it in the following chapter. Here, Julius's attachment to a self-contained, coherent – and innocent – sense of self not only barely conceals, but actually highlights his own sense of lack and fear of disintegration.

2 "To Trace Out a Story": Narrating Movement and the Movement of Narrative — 65

The passage opens with a reflection on one's relation toward the past and the deceptive integrity of a coherent life story:

> We experience life as a continuity, and only after it falls away, after it becomes the past, do we see its discontinuities. The past, if there is such a thing, is mostly empty space, great expanses of nothing, in which significant persons and events float. Nigeria was like that for me: mostly forgotten, except for those few things that I remembered with an outsize intensity. (155)

The ensuing evocation of a singular, isolated present is contrasted with a different kind of temporality, one that questions the former's disjuncture and contingency by providing the kind of continuity that is neither simply coherent nor convenient, but in its estranged familiarity, is uncanny and repetitive, and invested in the "reiteration" of things "that recurred in dreams and daily thoughts":

> But there was another, irruptive sense of things past. The sudden reencounter, in the present, of something or someone long forgotten, some part of myself I had relegated to childhood and to Africa. [...] She appeared (apparition was precisely what came into mind) to me in a grocery store in Union Square late in January. I didn't recognize her [...]. At the same moment that I confessed to having blanked out on who she was, she accused me of just that, a serious accusation, but jocularly expressed. (156)

Julius reacts politely, lightheartedly, "mask[ing] the irritation" he "suddenly" feels (156). Yet his actual response will work its way out only a few pages later, in the following chapter. Here, Julius experiences an explicit bout of amnesia. Trying to withdraw money at an ATM machine, he is unable to remember the correct four-digit code and is deeply disturbed by this "sudden mental weakness" (161). He detects an "unsuspected area of fragility" in himself that poses a threat to his sense of integrity and wholeness, rendering him "incomplete" in the same way that walking would be "suddenly lessened" by "a broken leg" (ibid.). After repeated, unsuccessful attempts, he gives up and eventually returns home. There, he tries to find the code amongst his documents and then, he claims, "forg[ets] all about the incident" (166). The following day, a call from his bank causes the embarrassing failure "to become fresh again, and this time more heavily, and this time without witnesses or an official record" (ibid.). When he repeats, only a few lines down, that he "had forgotten the incident," this creates an uncanny resonance within the paragraph and also, in its conspicuous tautology, echoes both the memory lapse of the previous day and another uncomfortable and equally inevitable return. In repetition, Julius links this incident to others like it, to the disavowed rape, Moji's "serious accusation" (156). An event that is part of his past, and that is not really forgotten, but merely "hovering [...] out of reach" (167).

We find two notions of coherence established in these passages that are both threatened by disintegration. The first is a sense of the past or history that is particularly interesting in its spatial qualification as "empty space" in which people or events "float" (155). This notion of history, echoing Walter Benjamin's "homogenous, empty time" of progress (2003: 395), is penetrated by "another, irruptive sense" of the past, in the form of Moji's ghostly "apparition" (156). The second illusory coherence is that of the psyche as a governable realm, of an imagined ideal ego, threatened by the irreversible blow of an uncontrollable memory lapse. By comparing this to the effect of a broken leg to a body's movement (161), Julius is recapitulating the idea of memory, or personal history, as a text-space, traversed by an abled body, moving freely. Both the movements of walking in the city, and the "fixtures in [his] mental landscape" (19) are spatiotemporally mapped and subject to the differing models of linearity and progress or recursiveness and gridlock.

Even though the disavowed rape of his childhood friend's sister renders the narrator of *Open City* as unreliable as any narrative of unfettered progress, this discrepancy is not part of the immediate telling and generic structuring of the novel, where he presents himself as the hero of his story, albeit mediated through reflection and self-awareness. In the passage ushering in the story's climax, Julius reflects on this:

> Each person must, on some level, take himself as the calibration point for normalcy, must assume that the room of his own mind is not, cannot be, entirely opaque to him. Perhaps this is what we mean by sanity: that, whatever our self-admitted eccentricities might be, we are not the villains of our own stories. In fact, it is quite the contrary: we play, and only play, the hero, and in the swirl of other people's stories, insofar as those stories concern us at all, we are never less than heroic. (243)

Writing about the journal and the epistolary confidence as the genres that are also characterized by *Open City's* interpolated narrative instance of "quasi-interior monologue and the account after the event," Genette asserts:

> Here, the narrator is at one and the same time still the hero and already someone else: the events of the day are already in the past, and the "point of view" may have been modified since then; the feelings of the evening or the next day are fully of the present and here focalization through the narrator is at the same time focalization through the hero. (1980: 218)

This kind of focalization can also be analyzed by looking at the dominant chronotope of Julius's narration. Following Mikhail Bakhtin's understanding of the chronotope, literally "timespace," as a prerequisite unit of any narrative and also "a formally constitutive category of literature," we may align at least

2 "To Trace Out a Story": Narrating Movement and the Movement of Narrative — 67

some aspects of Julius's narration with a distinct generic convention (1986: 84). Especially certain temporal indeterminacies of Julius's wanderings and his pedestrian recording of interchangeable, temporally reversible vignettes on everyday life in New York City, do in fact echo the "simplest time" chronotope of "adventure time." Bakhtin identifies this particular spatiotemporal configuration with certain forms of classical Greek romance. This chronotope exhibits a "sharp hiatus between two moments of biographical time, a hiatus that leaves no trace in the life of the heroes or in their personalities" (ibid.: 90) and is predominantly marked by an *"enforced movement through space"* (ibid.: 105). Action, thus, is characterized simply by "a change in spatial location" (ibid.). Here, the lack of initiative or motivation on behalf of the character opens up room for fate, for chance encounters (as with Moji), or failures to meet (as in his trip to Brussels). We can sense in the ostensible aimlessness of Julius's walks, his pronounced alienation and unmoored, billiard-ball like passivity, an echoing of the "random contingency" that marks the chronotope of "adventure time" as an ancient narrative form (Bakhtin 1986: 101). This is emphasized even more so by Julius's avowed understanding of life as a series of disjunctures, of linear amnesia, rather than that of recursivity, continuity, or historical and social embeddedness. However, folding in the overarching structure of the narrative as serial confiding, the particular world-making of Julius's confession can perhaps better be described with the Bakhtinian notion of an "adventure time of everyday life." Here, time and space do in fact leave traces and bear significance on the development of the character, precisely through the pivotal moment we can identify as confession, if not even retroactive redemption. Elaborating on this particular chronotope, Bakhtin writes:

> In this everyday maelstrom of personal life, time is deprived of its unity and wholeness – it is chopped up into separate segments, each encompassing a single episode from everyday life. The separate episodes [...] are rounded-off and complete, but at the same time are isolated and self-sufficient. The everyday world is scattered, fragmented, deprived of essential connections. [...] These temporal segments of episodes from everyday life are [...] arranged, as it were, perpendicular to the pivotal axis of the novel, which is the sequence guilt → punishment → redemption → purification → blessedness (precisely at the moment of punishment–redemption). (1986: 128)

In thinking about the effect of Julius's story as a whole, it is important to register that different chronotopic modes – the simple chronology of "adventure time" and the vignette-like yet cathartic structure of the "adventure time of everyday life" that revolves around the pivotal axis of Moji's accusation – are contrasted, conflated, and questioned in a way that essentially foregrounds their function as modes of storytelling. Moreover, we can now understand Julius as the author of a particular kind of narrative, one that ostensibly develops and invests in a narrative movement akin to a "pedestrian unfolding of the stories accumulated in a place" but also follows a particular generic logic and motivation that is betrayed by its narrative levels (de Certeau 2008: 110).

Open City is, as Cole asserts in the aforementioned interview with Bady, "a narrative troubled from beginning to end by Julius's origin in Africa" (2015: para. 7). The sudden "apparition" of Moji causes Julius to encounter "some part of myself I had relegated to childhood and to Africa" (156). Hence, Africa, as the repository of childhood memories, dreams, and distant traumas, plays hardly any role outside of Julius's past and is relegated to his understanding of immaturity, origin, and youth.[45] At the same time, his linear, progressive movement away from Africa is troubled by Moji's presence, who confronts his capacity to forget, to simply move on and maintain his "secure version of the past," with the encumbering spell that his acts have cast on her own evolvement (156). While Julius had acted like he

> knew nothing about it, had even forgotten her, to the point of not recognizing her when [they] met again [...], it hadn't been like that for her [...] the luxury of denial had not been possible for her. Indeed, I had been ever-present in her life, like a stain or a scar, and she had thought of me, either fleetingly or in extended agonies, for almost every day of her adult life. (244)

In the same way that Julius's luxury of forgetting is related to Moji's curse of remembering, various diasporic encounters throughout the novel highlight how Julius's purportedly autonomous motions correspond to other, more conflicted and obstructed movements. The fact that his narrative, too, is "troubled from beginning to end by Julius's origin in Africa" belies the motivelessness of his ambulation and renders these encounters particularly significant. It is possible, as many critics have, to read Julius's *flânerie* as a failed performance of cosmopolitanism, highlighting instead how his hyper-individualism is fundamentally, and fatefully, connected to others.[46] Having established the crucial role that Moji's disclosure plays in relation to narrative progress, it is possible to link this postlapsarian allegory to a more general, metahistorical notion of trauma, which situates

---

[45] This sentiment echoes of course Hegel's description of Africa as "the land of childhood" or *Kinderland* (2011: 109).
[46] See Vermeulen 2013; Hallemeier 2013; Hartwiger 2016; and Krishnan 2015. Krishnan writes: "Like the memory of rape, Africa, for Julius, becomes a site of radical disconnection, a landscape to which he claims allegiance and whose memory severs, erased under a bland cosmopolitanism which seeks to eradicate the traces of its violent cleaving" (2015: 690).

particularly African American and postcolonial discourses within a wider debate about literary criticism.

3 "To Experience the Pain Afresh": Metahistory and the Circling Movement of Melancholia

Compared to the other novels I discuss in this book, *Open City* addresses the notion of race much less overtly. To a large extent, this is due to Julius's self-fashioning as a "rooted cosmopolitan" apropos Anthony Kwame Appiah, as we see him repeatedly wrestle with and bristle at various racial and ethnic conscriptions.[47] Yet apart from these mostly unwanted interpellations, the aspect of race does not seem to play a hugely significant role. However, I conceive of Afropolitanism less as a cosmopolitan identity with African roots and more as a temporal mode of inquiry or 'tool' to think with. I suggest that the most interesting way *Open City* negotiates the subject of race and the politics of Blackness is not by explicitly referencing these topoi but through its juxtaposing of metahistoricist modes, or readings of history. This orientation toward questions of history and historicism rather than (merely) experience and ontology allows a reading of *Open City* that reconciles what may be indeed post-racial in its aesthetic with a rebuttal of the charge that it may not be concerned with race at all. Instead, the novel's focus on issues like history, historicism, trauma, melancholy and recognition provides a very sophisticated metaliterary commentary on the post-racial moment and the temporal crux of such notions as post-critique and postmelancholy.

Even if one were to describe the novel's overall aesthetic as post-racial, the term would not necessarily foreclose its engagement of race. As Ramón Saldívar points out, the undoing of and moving away from seemingly eternal, essentialist racial identities is not a process of forgetting but rather marked by a thorough engagement with history or, in his particular example, literary history. He notes that the term "postrace" should therefore always be used "under erasure

---

[47] Appiah, who subscribes to an understanding of racism as a "moral error" (1992: 18–19), fashions his notion of a "rooted cosmopolitan" in explicit opposition to ethnic, racial, or otherwise ascriptive identities. While cognizant of cultural difference, Appiah instead develops an ethics of individual affiliations where a liberal individualization compels one to grant precisely this liberty to others, especially other communities. See Appiah's *The Ethics of Identity* (2005) and *Cosmopolitanism – Ethics in a World of Strangers* (1992), of which Julius incidentally also posts a copy to Moroccan shopkeeper Farouq. For a discussion of Julius as a thinly veiled version of Appiah himself, see Sollors 2018.

and with full ironic force" (2) – an irony, which can only become fully effective through the expansive historical knowledge of its source material. In a similar vein, Kenneth Warren's polarizing *What Was African American Literature?* symbolizes anything but a clean cut with the past but, in its historicizing effort, an assessment of the current moment as one that is characterized by a move from the prospective to the retrospective (2011: 42). Before the legal and juridical achievements of the Voting Rights Act of 1964, Warren argues, African American literature typically projected into the future. He notes that, while the "past was indeed important," it was primarily explored "as a way of refuting charges of black inferiority and only secondarily as a source and guide for ongoing creative activity" (42–43). Of course, this kind of neat categorizing is particularly antithetical to Afro-pessimist scholars, who are less interested in the shelving away of periods, but rather invested in the blurring of historical demarcations and the assertion of the past's inevitable, constant return. Contrary to Warren, many scholars question the seismic effects of the Civil Rights movement. As Abdur-Rahman writes: "In the twenty-first century, the logics and implications of race have supposedly shifted, yet ongoing state violence and systemic exclusion expose racism as a lethal apparatus of psychosocial and material asymmetry superseding the legal remedy of recognition politics" (2017: 699). What Warren rightly exposes is the shift and turn toward the past, yet he errs in his interpretation of this shift's affective components. Rather than being a "source and guide for ongoing creativity," the past often figures much more problematically in contemporary African American writing. As Abdur-Rahman's analysis of recent Black writing conveys, such novels rather express a profound "skepticism about accretive racial progress" (2017: 699), instead revisiting "histories that haunt and hurt" (695).

By having these violent histories come back and haunt the present, this kind of retrospective perspective reveals itself less as a self-congratulatory taking stock of historical milestones than as a deliberate abandonment of what one might call the cruel optimism of emancipation. Thus viewed, the political depression of Black America arises in large parts from what Lauren Berlant has called a "relation of attachment to compromised conditions of possibility" (2006: 21). Accordingly, looking back and dwelling on a history of racist compromise, backlash, and continuity sustains rather than heals the "open wound" of melancholia, and prompts a "refusal of nourishment" in the form of past achievements (Freud 1989: 587–589). Indeed, the term "melancholic historicism," coined by Stephen Best in "On Failing to Make the Past Present," seems apt in describing what Best similarly identifies as an "affective conception of history" (2012: 464). Framed as an auto-critique of what he sees as concomitant with his own "ethical imperatives and political commitments," Best queries the paradigmatic dominance of this affect as well as its metahistoricist usefulness (ibid.). With regards to confronting the predicaments of the present as well as assessing the past, he asks: "Why must we predicate having an ethical relation to the past on the idea that there is continuity between that past and our present? What kind of history would permit one not only "to stay" with the dead but to rouse them from their sleep?" (ibid. 464–465). Answering with Leo Bersani's tackling of criticism's theological latency, exposing its "will-to-redemption" (2015: 465), Best concludes that this "kind of history," focusing on the 'healing powers' of repetition, springs from the "inability to reckon with the true alterity of the past." He argues that, in order to treat historical experience aptly, one must forego or short-circuit the redemptive function (ibid.).

On an even broader level, these debates can also be placed on a continuum responding to the humanities' turn from historicist, suspicious readings to reparative or surface analyses that question both mood and method of a form of critique that has, as Bruno Latour opts, supposedly "run out of steam" (2004). Questions of historiography become paramount when scholars like Rita Felski circumscribe this turn, emphasizing that "[t]he trick is to think temporal interdependency without telos, movement without supersession: pastness is part of who we are, not an archaic residue, a regressive force, a source of nostalgia, or a return of the repressed" (2011: 578). While the turn from suspicious to surface reading appeared tangible enough for the editors of *Representations* to dedicate an entire issue to "the way we read now," the definition of the critic's proper or improper historicism is fairly unclear. Similar to Best's critique of melancholic historicism, he and Sharon Marcus argue against an ideologically inflected historicism à la Jameson and advocate for "a clearer view of the past" (2009: 19). Yet at the very point where "the way we read now" perhaps promotes too clean a break with Jameson's "moral imperative" to "always historicize," Jennifer Fleissner detects an implicit hyperbolization of the concept, a claim to actually historicize more "rigorously" (2013: 700–701). That the purging of historicism seems rather futile, given the elusive nature of its aim, ties in with her observation that "[e]very time we believe we have made [history] our focus […] it slips once again from our grasp." Equally persistent seems to be the historian's tendency to oscillate between a "fetishization of the archive" and a somewhat supercilious presentism (700). These debates throw into sharp relief how no positionality toward history can be conceptualized in a way that is not susceptible to methodological changes and critique. One way to circumvent this difficulty may be to change the conversation in the manner pointed out by Felski and also Fleissner, who wonders why, "if literary texts are to be neatly shelved as exempla of historical formations, we still place value on the moment of repeated *reading*" (2013: 703).

Open City actually always contrasts at least two ways of reading. One is indeed the archeological, deeply historicizing and unearthing of, for example, urban history, the other is accumulative, descriptive, and often engaged in the aesthetic experience of surfaces. These modes, however, are often so self-consciously enmeshed and conflated that none of them gains the epistemological upper hand, let alone moral authority. Interestingly, this process extends to the very notion of referentiality and reading itself. *Open City* is a markedly metafictional text, it is "a reader's writing" (Bady 2015). It recurrently addresses reading and aesthetic consumption and is brimming with high literary and cultural references – to the point of a hyper-referentiality that has led Giles Foden to call Julius an "intellectual show-off" (2011: para. 9). Perhaps in respect to frequency, this device may function as an end-in-itself, but in terms of content, the selection of quoted artworks is far from arbitrary. In many ways, the various references present themselves as keys to unlock or as mirrors to reflect and contrast Julius's state of mind. They are offered up as props, in every sense of the word, to support certain, perhaps even pathologizing, analyses, as well as functioning as theoretical prostheses that fetishistically direct to and conceal Julius's psychological wounds. On the level of character, if not also of form, the novel ostentatiously indicates its autopoiesis and intertextual moorings via this referential density. Julius, who is estranged from his mother and appears to be a lover of photography, reads Roland Barthes's *Camera Lucida* on various occasions. Frequent mention of Coetzee's *Elizabeth Costello* evokes the concept of sympathetic imagination and echoes the centrality of rape in Coetzee's *Disgrace*. A mention of Bruegel's *Landscape with Falling Icarus* recalls W.H. Auden's and William Carlos Williams's poetic treatment of the same, lamenting humanity's indifference to suffering. Without suggesting that the intertextual and metafictional references are thus exhausted and are not in most parts and many ways much subtler and covert, it is one incident of name dropping that most distinctly indicates a blueprint for *Open City's* play with temporalities, while shedding light on Julius's own concept of history. On the day Julius and the Brussels shopkeeper Farouq engage in conversation for the first time, Farouq is reading "a secondary text on Walter Benjamin's *On the Concept of History*" (103).[48]

The distinctly Benjaminian frame adopted in *Open City* is remarkable in its scope. The treatment of mobility in a metropolitan environment immediately connects Julius's ambling movements to Benjamin's understanding of Charles

---

[48] It is in fact interesting that – perhaps because it is so obvious, perhaps because it is actually so close to the narrator that he is unable to distance himself from it in critical contemplation – Walter Benjamin is never referenced by him directly, never offered as analytical shortcut. Even in the mention of Farouq's reading of him, he appears as citable text only in secondary instance.

Baudelaire's figure of the *flâneur*. In Julius's melancholic gaze, his pronounced alienation even, or especially, among the urban crowd and his weaving of urban space into the "long poem of walking" (de Certeau 2008: 101), we hear a distinct echo of Benjamin praising Baudelaire's allegorical genius in *The Arcades Project*. Instead of narrating a sense of national or local belonging, the "gaze which the allegorical genius turns on the city betrays, instead, a profound alienation. It is the gaze of the *flâneur*, whose way of life conceals behind a beneficent mirage the anxiety of the future inhabitants of our metropolises" (Benjamin 1999: 20). In *Open City*, Julius's observation of urban masses mirrors the disenchanting "shock experience"[49] Benjamin identifies in Baudelaire's irritation at being jostled by the crowd, turning the dazzling luster of a "crowd with soul and movement" (Benjamin 2003: 343) into a somber, threatening occurrence:

> The sight of large masses of people hurrying down into underground chambers was perpetually strange to me, and I felt that all of the human race were rushing, pushed by a counterinstinctive death drive, into movable catacombs. Aboveground I was with thousands of others in their solitude, but in the subway, standing close to strangers, jostling them and being jostled by them for space and breathing room, all of us reenacting unacknowledged traumas, the solitude intensified. (*OC* 7)

Interspersed with Julius's documentation of contemporary urban life are also numerous passages like this that link his concept of history to the bleak accumulation of tragedy evoked by Benjamin's Angel of History. In "On the Concept of History," Benjamin develops this figure apropos a painting by Paul Klee, showing an "angel who seems to move away from something he stares at," hurled backwards by the irresistible pull of a storm blowing in paradise. Before his eyes, the seemingly teleological chain of events that one might call moments in history transforms into "one single catastrophe." Benjamin's Angel desires to stay with and "awaken the dead," to "make whole what has been smashed" (Benjamin 2003: 392). With this image, Benjamin develops a historical materialist view of history that, instead of relating the past only to itself by rigorously containing each moment within its epoch, instead thinks in the "tradition of the oppressed" and understands how the current state of emergency "is not the exception but the rule" (ibid.). Looking out the window on the drive from Brussels

---

49 Benjamin's distinction of *Erfahrung*, experience over time, and *Erlebnis*, as the isolated experience of an isolated moment, as well as their respective functions in literary composition seem noteworthy here. Similarly, Benjamin's treatment of *durée*, as it occurs in Henri Bergson's *Matter and Memory*, allows for a supplementary investigation of movement as spatiotemporal rhythm in *Open City*.

airport, Julius recalls the on-flight conversation with Dr. Maillotte of the previous night. In the mode of Benjamin's Angel, Julius concentrates on the historical trajectory of one moment in 1944, the single tragedy of human history:

> I saw her at fifteen, in September 1944, sitting on a rampart in the Brussels sun, delirious with happiness at the invaders' retreat. I saw Junichiro Saito on the same day, aged thirty-one or thirty-two, unhappy, in internment, in an arid room in a fenced compound in Idaho, far away from his books. Out there on that day, also, were all four of my own grandparents: the Nigerians, the Germans. Three were by now gone, for sure. But what of the fourth, my oma? I saw them all, even the ones I had never seen in real life, saw all of them in the middle of that day in September sixty-two years ago, with their eyes open as if shut, mercifully seeing nothing of the brutal half century ahead and, better yet, hardly anything at all of all that was happening in their world, the corpse-filled cities, camps, beaches, and fields, the unspeakable worldwide disorder of that very moment. (96)

While *Open City*'s adoption of a Benjaminian reading of history also coincides with the novel's decidedly modernist motifs,[50] this particular text has been related to diasporic theories of history and trauma in profound and lasting ways.

In his discussion of Benjamin's Angel of History, Stephen Best credits this notion of redemption apropos the "theater of the historical situation" (2012: 464) for constituting the prevailing mode of melancholic historicism in African American and Black Atlantic studies. Throughout *Open City*, we encounter this specific mode on several occasions, often related through the pathologizing eyes of Julius's profession. Initially, it is the mention of Julius's patient V., a historian and member of the Delaware tribe, that most explicitly transports Faulkner's notion that "the past is never dead – it's not even past."[51] V. has written a historical biography of a particularly brutal colonizer of Manhattan Island, chronicling gruesome torture and genocide in the "calm and pious language that presented mass murder as little more than the regrettable side effect of colonizing the land" (26). Julius makes clear that V.'s depressive condition is in part

---

50 Apart from linking Julius's ambling movements to Benjamin's understanding of Baudelaire's figure of the *flaneur*, other literary modernist antecedents to this kind of urban movement include James Joyce's *Ulysses* and Walt Whitman's wanderings in New York, while various motifs taken from William Carlos Williams to Ezra Pound permeate the novel.
51 In Cole's *Every Day Is for the Thief*, a short novel published prior to *Open City* by the Nigerian Cassava Republic Press and later republished with minor changes by Random House and Faber & Faber, this quote is actually directly referenced. Here, the unnamed narrator who, due not only to similar biographical details but also a strikingly similar tone, can be read as being the same as in *Open City*, ponders the memory of slavery in Lagos, Nigeria: "This history is missing from Lagos. There is no monument to the great wound. ... Faulkner said: 'The past is never dead. It's not even past.' But in Lagos we sleep dreamlessly, the sleep of innocents" (Cole 2014: 114).

a product of the psychological toll these studies take on her, a work she describes, according to Julius, as "looking out across a river on a day of heavy rain, so that she couldn't be sure whether the activity on the opposite bank had anything to do with her, or whether, in fact, there was any activity there at all" (26–27). In a similar way that Benjamin's "On the Concept of History" from 1940 warns that *"even the dead* will not be safe" (2003: 391), V. verbalizes her fear of historical erasure: "I can't pretend it isn't about my life, she said to me once, it is my life. It's a difficult thing to live in a country that has erased your past. [...] And it's not in the past, it is still with us today; at least, it's still with me" (27). Later in the narrative, Julius's mention of V.'s death suggests that she has committed suicide (165).

While V. clearly suffers from her particular form of melancholy, it is important to note that the presentation of her case allows for an interpretation that locates the source of her anguish not in the inability to let go of the past, but in the academically prescribed constraint to treat the past as past. This constraint entails writing about it in the form of a "strict historical record" (*OC 27*) rather than voicing the simultaneity of past and present and perhaps even working through this trauma, in a subjective, repetitive mode recalling the "affective conception of history" that Best criticizes (2012: 464). Because Julius empathizes with V. more than with other patients, his own position toward her case remains unclear. Equally ambiguous is his attitude toward his patient M., who, like V., is one of the rare patients whose problems "were not relegated to the back of [his] mind when [he] stepped out onto the street" (44). Both V.'s and M.'s cases inflect and tinge Julius's experience of walking in the city and thus resonate in the way he conceptualizes history and memory. His thoughts on M's case punctuate the entire course of his longest urban excursion in chapter 4, where, instead of heading home at nightfall, he takes a train to lower Manhattan and spontaneously gets off at Wall Street. From the moment he passes the "ancient wall" hemming in the graveyard of Trinity Church, it appears as though he somehow enters an older, historical version of New York, echoing the way Walter Benjamin excavates the ancient Paris that literally underlies the surface of the modern metropolis in his *Arcades Project*. Here, Benjamin conjures an underworld that surfaces at night, ushering the nocturnal pedestrian through dream-like narrow passages into a darker, older realm of urban consciousness. After reflecting on the US-American forefathers buried in the graveyard, Julius enters an alley on his way toward the waterfront:

> When I crossed the street and entered the small alley opposite, it was as though the entire world had fallen away. I was strangely comforted to find myself alone in this way in the

heart of the city. The alley, no one's preferred route to any destination, was all brick walls and shut-up doors, across which shadows fell as crisply as in an engraving. (52)

As he passes the ruins of the World Trade Center, Julius's preceding thoughts on New York's early beginnings as a trading post intersect with his encounter of contemporary memorials, again recapitulating the sense of pastness in the present. Interspersed with this literal and metaphorical meandering between past and present are the thoughts on his patient M., "thirty-two, recently divorced, and delusional," and, as Julius asserts, "completely in the grip of the delirium" (48). M. repeatedly recounts to Julius the painful story of his divorce, each time crying and experiencing "the pain afresh" (56). Julius naturally pathologizes his patient in a way that would seem innocuous, were it not for the fact that he himself has recently split up with his girlfriend and seems unable to confront his grief directly. Thus, while thinking about M.'s compulsion to repeat, Julius experiences an "unexpected pang" of his own: "a sudden urgency and sorrow, but the image of the one I was thinking of flitted past quickly" (56). Quickly too, does he assert himself: "It had been only a few weeks, but time had begun to dull even that wound" (56). Yet this professed equilibrium is belied by his unexplained behavior in the chapter's opening passage, where he feels compelled to lie underneath a rock in Central Park, "as though led by an invisible hand" (42). Only the unpremeditated mention of his breath returning to normal, quieting the "bellowing" in his ribs, suggests, by omission, the turmoil behind his calm and collected persona. His obsessing with M.'s case, then, allows us to doubt the emotionally flat tone Julius deploys in respect to his recent break-up as well as his professionally distanced attitude toward the dangerous, delirious grip of a traumatic past.

Generally, Julius puts some emphasis on the line that separates his avowed melancholic disposition, his "heavy mood" (43), from the pathological conditions of his patients. In many ways, this endeavor is so overdetermined that we can sense the degree of self-deception that is taking place. This does not mean, however, that Julius's attitude does not generally express a level of ambiguity that forecloses unequivocal diagnoses. In a section that opens with Julius's thoughts on Freud's "Mourning and Melancholia," he affirms the grip of melancholia cloaking New York City, its inability to internalize the dead and complete the process of mourning, by drawing too neat a line "around the catastrophic events of 2001" (209). This sectioning off, he claims, has rather resulted in the incorporation of loss, creating an atmosphere of anxiety. He then goes on to discuss the memory of another patient of his, setting against "this bigger picture, the many smaller ones." Mr. F., an eighty-five-year-old veteran of the Second World War, had been diagnosed with depression late in life, after showing symptoms of appetite loss, low moods, and experiencing, as Julius recounts, "a racing of his thoughts that he described, with great difficulty – he was a reticent man – as an effort to keep from drowning." Mr. F. soon moved on to psychotherapy, and on one of the few occasions Julius had met with him, he had interrupted his medical assessment and spoken with "sudden emotion" in his voice: "Doctor, I just want to tell you how proud I am to come here, and see a young black man like yourself in that white coat, because things haven't ever been easy for us, and no one has ever given us nothing without a struggle" (210). This memory is presented without Julius's reaction to it, concluding the chapter. As far as we know, Julius may have never corrected Mr. F.'s reading of him as African American. It remains equally unclear whether Mr. F. actually misinterprets Julius's German-Nigerian ancestry or if he extends this redemptive moment to Julius nonetheless. The way that his comment is framed, however, how Julius describes him as someone bearing the "faraway look of those who had somehow gotten locked inside their sadness," suggests that he considers Mr. F.'s vision to be clouded, in the grip of repetition.

In these passages, Julius expresses a critique of melancholic historicism akin to Stephen Best's, for whom the emphasis on repetition results in a failure to treat the past adequately "as it falls away, as that which falls away – a separateness resistant to being either held or read in melancholic terms" (2012: 466). While Jennifer Fleissner points out that simply adhering to such a model may reinstate "the neatly periodized version of history [...] which these depictions of repetition legitimately critique" (2013: 706), she identifies in Best's account an important exposure of how that mode of criticism's assumptions have been relying on the transferability of past and present to such a degree that they may now even resemble the historicist ideology critique they set out to oppose. Even more importantly, she notes how this "twinning of past and present" (ibid.) also generates a certain affective mood through its flattening of history that may be claustrophobic but, in its repetitive sameness, perhaps equally *reassuring*. Fleissner quotes Eve Sedgwick's illustration of that particular Gothic sameness across history: "it happened to my father's father, it happened to my father, it is happening to me" (2013: 706). Extrapolating and reading the scene of Mr. F. as him reducing Julius to his version of repetitive history, Mr. F.'s historical conceptualization would seem to be both limiting and self-assuring. At least in Julius's interpretation, his presence and present denote for Mr. F. a Benjaminian constellation or struggle that is actually different and that he fails to recognize in its difference. On the other hand, a Benjaminian concept of history that alternates between the messianic moment of redemption and the repetition of sameness would only recognize redemption as repetition with a change. In this reading, Mr. F. has seen Julius quite clearly.

Nevertheless, the framing of this incident and Julius's emphasis on melancholy as an incomplete process of mourning suggests the latter, as Julius's reaction excludes the possibility for redemption, aligning Mr. F's concept of history with Best's understanding of melancholic historicism. Here, Benjamin's replaying of a historical moment is stripped of its messianic intention, as what is repeated is not necessarily the memory of a revolutionary moment, flashing up "in a moment of danger," but rather that of a trauma, accompanied by the kind of circling and lingering movement ascribed to Freud's pathologically melancholic person (Benjamin 2003: 391). In *Open City*, Julius gives us no clear perspective but again embodies ambiguity, moving swiftly on a continuum comprising the position of Benjamin's positivist *and* materialist historian, the simultaneity of present and past *and* their radical difference.

While Julius also attempts to adopt a melancholic mode, voicing the bleak critique of modernity that "atrocity is nothing new [...]. The difference is that in our time it is uniquely well-organized" (*OC* 58), his often distinctly objective, historiographical mustering of traumatic data ostensibly bars a meaningful reckoning with it in the present. Here, his concept of history resembles that of a positivist accumulation of historical events. Yet at the same time, Julius longs to savor the mood and atmosphere of a given period. More often than not, Benjamin's dialectical image is reversed when Julius's nostalgic gaze, emulating the sensitivities of the modernist *flâneur*, has to adapt the historical aura of an urban space to the lively complexity of the current moment. Upon entering a Portuguese restaurant in Brussels, Julius renders its contemporary international immigrant scene into a 19th-century *tableau vivant*, "an exact Cézannesque tableau [...] accurate even down to the detail of one man's thick mustache" (116). At other times, Julius is so transfixed by his meditations on history that he notes his surprise at how "the past had suddenly transformed into the present" (233). Generally, even though he frequently uses a Benjaminian perspective that is rooted in remembrance or mourning, he seemingly distances himself from it as a method to work through trauma in the present.

In a passage in which Julius switches from the usual soliloquy of his historical excursions to a conversation with friends, he holds forth at length on the absence of loss and atrocities in the present, compared to preceding histories. He elaborates on his theory with the historical example of the city of Leiden, which, during the time of the plague, "lost thirty-five percent of its population in a five-year period in the 1630s" (200). Julius asserts the relative luxury of living in the contemporary moment: Leiden, German for suffering, is of the past. That this contention only holds true for Julius's particularly periodizing view on history becomes clear when his African American friend adds: "What you said about Leiden, well, in a way, my family was Leiden" (202). He goes on to recount the details of, as Julius describes it, "the appalling family background my friend had had to overcome to go to university and to graduate school, and to become an assistant professor in the Ivy League," ending the brief synopsis of a tragedy marked by harsh violence and loss with "a peaceful expression on his face" (203). Julius notes that he has heard this story before. This situation is different from the scene with Mr. F, as he cannot so easily diagnose his friend with the unhealthy repetition of traumatic events. In the absence of his scientific toolbox, he is asked to make sense of the social realities expressed by his friend, rather than attest a pathological behavior.

In grappling with the ubiquity and effect of racism, diagnosing his friend with melancholia would attribute the effect of trauma to his melancholic attachment to loss instead of the circumstances engendering it. Julius is uncomfortable and appears to find this situation embarrassing, and this is also shown by his reaction to Moji's emphatic yet clear-sighted remark on how, for Black people who have lived in the United States for generations, the racist structures must be "crazy-making" (203). When his friend's white girlfriend tries to smooth over the situation by joking: "Oh, man, [...] don't give him excuses!" Julius feels relief and an instant liking toward her. Moji, however, he finds abrasive, and he is "struck" by her "brittleness" (ibid.). The fact that Moji is willing to be moved by a past that is not hers, while Julius endeavors to treat the past only in relation to itself speaks to their complicated mutual history but is also indicative of Julius's conflicted attitude toward a traumatic diasporic past and present. While being attentive to and knowledgeable of history, he finds it difficult to concretely connect present grievances with their violent pasts. That this kind of preemptive emotional transference might indeed have its limits is shown by a particular noteworthy scene from the latter part of the book.

Shortly after being robbed and injured, Julius stumbles upon the memorial for the African Burial Ground, marked by a solitary monument in the midst of Manhattan. Due to renovation, Julius is unable to approach it directly, standing instead "a few yards" away (220). It is no coincidence that Julius finds himself cordoned off from the burial site, having, as he states, "no purchase on who these people were" (ibid.). The distance, marked here by a physical barrier, signals Julius's desire to treat the past as past, maintaining his aloofness and rooting his position in the notion that the past remains citable, yet unobtainable. However, instead of interpreting his inability to engage with the continuing presence of the past as an obstacle to understanding the present, one could also interpret this moment differently. Not having access to the past here might signal a vital necessity because its aims, ambitions, and futures need to be reformulated through the present moment. In *Conscripts of Modernity*, David Scott calls for this kind of adaption in respect to narrative modes, proposing a turn from the teleological agenda of romanticist anti-colonialism, which seamlessly merges a fixed past with an equally fixed future, toward a certain "tragic sensibility" that is more "apt and timely" to register the complexities of the current moment in decolonial and antiracist struggles (2004: 210). For Scott, a reiterated historical argument may not "have the same usefulness, the same salience, the same critical purchase, when the historical conjuncture that originally gave that argument point and purchase has passed" (2004: 50).

At the monument, Julius finds himself "steeped in [...] the echo across centuries, of slavery in New York" (*OC* 221). Slavery, here, is a legible trace or reflection of things past. Julius recounts the physical "traces of suffering" found on excavated bodies, "blunt trauma, grievous bodily harm," but he finds it "difficult [...] from the point of view of the twenty-first century, to fully believe that these people [...] were truly people" (220). As he tries to overcome this distance, to bridge time, by stepping across the cordon, bending down and lifting up a stone, pain shoots through his injured left hand, rooting him firmly, instantly, in the present. This could be read as another reversal of Benjamin's dialectical image, where instead of the past flashing up in the present, the complexities of a charged present assert themselves and arrest the "flow" of transference into the past. Instead of reading this passage as another instance of Julius's chronic aloofness, one could thus interpret this detached curiosity as a clear demarcation and starting point from which to transfer an 'archeological' endeavor of excavating the past to one revolving around "the question of desire in relation to the dead [...] rather than the dead (or buried) themselves" (Ranjana Khanna qtd. in Fleissner 2013: 716).

These complex historicist configurations of *Open City* may be best understood as meta-historicist commentary that probes rather than definitively evaluates specific relations with and perspectives on the past. As such, the novel contextualizes a moment of calibration, in which the extent to which historical atrocities may bear on the present is measured apropos its own brand of melancholic retrospective – a nostalgia for the safety of an alleged ideological common ground, perhaps, or the redemptive promises of an archeological working through trauma. As Goyal notes, *Open City* "may easily be read as writing in the wake of the desire to connect or to believe, a work in synchrony with our post-critical times" (2017b: 66).

As such, the novel mirrors important debates in the humanities concerning the value or effect of a specific hermeneutics of history, while remaining skeptical and impartial toward either. Not entirely embracing a Benjaminian or messianic view of history by questioning its melancholic revolving around the originary site of loss and proclivity to conflating past and present, the novel equally reveals the danger of a positivist, linear or additive, mere mustering of history that severs the present's ties to painful pasts – while remaining wary of the ideological implications of either mode. While the call for replacing suspicious with surface readings may challenge the moral safe ground and performative mastery of ideology critique, it doesn't exempt that way of reading from similar mistakes. "[I]n the cool distance it assumes from the past," as Fleissner notes, such a model "no less attempts to deny its implicatedness in the issues it studies than do the more morally charged distancing gestures of ideology critique" (2013: 708).

4 "Voices Cut Out of the Past Into the Present": Blackness in Diaspora Time

The ambiguity of its metahistorical purport notwithstanding, *Open City* provides a staunch critique of totalizing aspirations of mastery, whether in relation to historical discourse, temporality, space, or through these theme's metaphorical amalgamation: movement. Repeatedly, Julius is shown as failing in his attempts at mastery, feigning a sense of coherence he cannot quite maintain. The dissolution of linear movement becomes particularly striking in relation to the space-time of Blackness, both in its physical, bodily dimension and its temporal mediation of race in/as history.

While Julius's long walks construct a sense of duration, albeit interspersed with the chronicling of personal and urban history, there are moments when the phenomenological experience of time is substantially altered. These moments are almost always connected to a distorted concept of physical integrity, movement, and the body. The moment when Julius is attacked and beaten, is particularly explicit: "We find it convenient to describe time as a material, we 'waste' time, we 'take' our time. As I lay there, time became material in a strange new way: fragmented, torn into incoherent tufts, and at the same time spreading, like something spilled, like a stain" (219). Here, the physical threat of disintegration is coupled with the dissolution of linear time, throwing into sharp relief the privilege and precariousness of Julius's ambling, unfettered movements through time and space. But is also serves as an invocation of a different, fragmented temporality that is marked by the 'human stain' of race. Opening the scene, Julius sees two young men at a crossing and overhears some of their talk, marked by the kind of vernacular that suggests they are Black. Julius further observes: "They walked effortlessly, lazily, like athletes, and I marveled at their prodigious profanity for a moment, then forgot about them" (212). Julius had exchanged a glance, a nod with them, interpreting this "gesture of mutual respect [as] based on our being young, black, male; based, in other words, on our being 'brothers'" (212). A few moments later, they pass him again and fail to acknowledge him, causing Julius to be "unnerved" at this misrecognition (212). Seconds later, they attack him, steal his phone, and kick his curled-up body. In truth, Julius is the one who has misrecognized, has failed to see the tenuousness of that purported, superficial solidarity, made porous by economic and class disparities. He has not only misread the age of these boys, who turn out to be "no older than fifteen" (213), but also their "profanity" and the effortlessness of their movements. When they later "melt [...] away" to somewhere "deep in Harlem" (214), it becomes clear how the limits of their environment will affect and most likely curb their movements in the world, athletic bodies or not.

Later, when Julius examines his wounds, he seems astonished at the fact that he had never acknowledged the privilege of an intact body: "How could I have been less than completely aware of how good it was to be injury-free?" (215), he wonders. Physical integrity and its relation to movement as such is a particular preoccupation of Julius. While getting on a subway in chapter 2, he notices "a cripple" (24) moving onto the carriage, triggering thoughts on the Yoruba deity Obatala, associated with physical infirmity and blamed for the making of "dwarfs, cripples, people missing limbs, and those burdened with debilitating illness" (25). That Julius is able to move freely in New York City, more freely than many others perhaps, is also indicated by a prior passage, where he observes a crowd of women from his apartment window, marching through the nocturnal streets, chanting, beating drums, and blowing whistles. At first, Julius cannot make out what they are saying, but soon it becomes clear that he is witnessing New York City's "Take-Back-The-Night" movement: "We have the power, we have the might, the solitary voice called. The answer came: The streets are ours, take back the night" (23). Yet the very moment that the women shout "*Women's bodies, women's lives, we will not be terrorized*" (ibid.), Julius shuts the window, distancing himself from his role in and contingency upon the precariousness of other bodies.

Julius feigns a sense of coherence, metaphorically likened to his free and autonomous walking through New York City, in order to make legible the particular textspace that is his story. At certain points of conjuncture, the nodes where his adopted mode threatens to disintegrate, we gain a glimpse of other, underlying (hi)stories. In this sense, *Open City* employs the structural equivalence to the kind of Benjamin-influenced reading of diasporic narratives that, as Goyal writes, releases "the alternatives that a single line of narrative has to suppress in order to constitute itself as dominant" (2010: 16). Moreover, and not only in form but also in content, the novel stages the contrast between the isolated temporal moment and hero of the "adventure time" chronotope, and the specific historicizing mode of what Goyal terms "diaspora time" – a time which, instead of being defined by "the 'homogenous, empty time' of progress" is more appropriately understood as "a time that is characterized by rupture but also by various kinds of imagined or projected simultaneities" (Goyal 2010: 15). A particularly dense exposition of "diaspora time" can be found in chapter 5, which is worth looking at in more detail.

The chapter opens with a memory inserted into the linear progression of the narrative. Julius remembers the day that he and his girlfriend Nadège visited a detention center in Queens. The visit, we learn, is erotically motivated. Julius distances himself from "that beatific, slightly unfocused expression" he identifies with the "do-gooders" organizing the visit (62). Instead, he fantasizes how Nadège might fall in love with the idea of him acting as "the listener, the compassionate African who paid attention to the details of someone else's life and struggle" (70). At the facility, Julius is assigned to a selected inmate, a young man from Liberia named Saidu, who tells him in great detail about the stunted movements of his arduous journey to the United States. Saidu, Julius notes, is "well educated," showing "no hesitation in his English," and Julius lets him speak "without interrupting" (64). His story begins roughly 10 years earlier in 1994, in the midst of Liberia's first civil war, with the bombing of his school – the same school in which "he had been taught about the special relationship between Liberia and America, which was like the relationship between an uncle and a favorite nephew" (64). He recounts the tragic losses of his family members and various confrontations with different military groups, some more fortuitous than others, interspersed with the itinerary details of his year-long flight. Hitching a ride with Nigerian ECOMOG soldiers, walking "on foot to Guinea, a journey of many days," and crossing the Sahara on a truck full of multinational refugees, he reaches Tangier. Here, he notices "the way the black Africans moved around, under constant police surveillance" (67). Saidu manages to enter European soil on a rowing boat to Ceuta, continues on a ferry to Spain, and then makes his way to Lisbon, where he spends two years working as a butcher's assistant and then as a barber, sharing a room "with ten other Africans" until he has saved up enough money to fly into JFK airport with a fake ID.

As Julius recounts Saidu's story in the manner of an extradiegetic narrator, the flow of the story is interrupted by Julius's doubts: "I wondered, naturally, as Saidu told this story, whether I believed him or not, whether it wasn't more likely that he had been a soldier. He had, after all, had months to embellish the details, to perfect his claim of being an innocent refugee" (67). This play on the reliability of the narrator is complicated even further by the second part of the chapter, set again during the course of Julius's primary narration. Here, Julius is confronted with another diasporic narrative, this time presented in the unmarked direct speech that is characteristic of Julius's encounters with other urban dwellers.

In the "underground catacombs of Penn station," he meets a Haitian, a shoeshine named Pierre, so old-fashioned that the "older term" bootblack seems more appropriate. He tells Julius how he "came from Haiti, when things got bad there," when both black and whites were killed (70 – 71).

Pierre's story spans many decades in New York, is marked by a religious rhetoric, and focuses at length on his life in the service of the Bérards, with whom he had come from Haiti. Even after the death of Mr. Bérard, a "cold man at times" but with a heart, who taught him "to read and write," Pierre stays in the service of his wife because "Service to Mrs. Bérard was service to God" (73). Pierre is able to work as a hairdresser outside of the house and earn "enough to purchase freedom for [his] sister Rosalie" (72). Only after the death of Mrs. Bérard does he seek "the freedom without," finally marrying his sweetheart Juliette at age forty-one and building a school for Black children (74).

While this kind of rhetoric is already peculiar, it is the specific dates and historical events around which his story is built that reveal what an unusual narrator Pierre actually is. The killings, under the "terror of Boukman," he notes, were as bad as under "the terror of Bonaparte," indicating the era of the Haitian revolution from 1791 to 1804, namely the slave revolt led by Dutty Boukman and the previous French rule under Napoleon Bonaparte (72). Pierre also mentions the difficult years of yellow fever in New York City, taking the lives of many, including his sister Rosalie. The last record of yellow fever in New York is dated to 1822 – more than 40 years before the 13th Amendment officially ended slavery in the United States. Set against the hard facts of history, Pierre's story is not a strange narrative, it is a slave narrative.[52]

The presentation of this story leaves no doubt about it being anchored in Julius's narrated present. What is missing is Julius's direct reaction to the telling, leaving the temporal plausibility of the story entirely uncommented. When he leaves and steps outside, he merely remarks upon how his "shoes gleamed, but the polish revealed only that they were old and in need of replacing" (74). Julius, it seems, has encountered a walking and talking ghost in Penn Station. Then, however, something remarkable happens to his perception of the city. Julius sees an overturned police barrier and perceives some kind of "silent commotion" (74). The following passage concludes the chapter:

---

[52] In fact, the historical details allow one to identify Pierre as the historical figure Pierre Toussaint, (born 1766 in Saint-Domingue, died 1853 in New York City) a former slave who was brought to New York, became a famous hairdresser and Catholic philanthropist, and named himself Toussaint after the leader of the Haitian revolution. See Sontag 1992.

> That afternoon, during which I flitted in and out of myself, when time became elastic and voices cut out of the past into the present, the heart of the city was gripped by what seemed to be a commotion from earlier time. I feared being caught up in what, it seemed to me, were draft riots. [...] What I saw next gave me a fright: in the farther distance, beyond the listless crowd, the body of a lynched man dangling from a tree. The figure was slender, dressed from head to toe in black, reflecting no light. It soon resolved itself, however, into a less ominous thing: dark canvas sheeting on a construction scaffold, twirling in the wind. (74–75)

Julius imagines a violent scene from New York City's racist draft riots of 1863. More accurately, he experiences the simultaneity of "diaspora time," in which, as Goyal writes, the Benjaminian "'time of the now' is shot through with the memory of the Middle Passage" (2010: 15). While Julius may be able to distance his biography from the unfortunate story of Saidu or the anachronistic narrative of Pierre, the history of place simply overwhelms his present and momentarily arrests his linear movement, frightening him and flooding his ostensibly safe and removed 'now' with the knowledge of past continuities.

Apart from illuminating the intricate temporal layering of *Open City*, the chapter under discussion is also extraordinary in its metafictional purport. The way that Pierre's story is inserted into the narrative, complete with the register and rhetoric of the slave narrative, but at the same time part of Julius's intradiegetic world-making, introduces a postmodern play with genre while complicating the generic status of this ostensibly realist novel as a whole. In juxtaposing the generic conventions of Pierre's slave narrative with those of Saidu's refugee story, Cole draws attention to the implicit claims of autobiographical authenticity inherent in both stories – and in the overarching frame of *Open City* itself.

Broadly looking at the generic conventions of the slave narrative, one could call the claim to authenticity both its major concern and formative constraint. As the authorship of these narratives was routinely questioned, the narrative would almost always address the question of literacy, stressing the way that the author had been taught "to read and write" (*OC* 72), often by his or her master, thus proving to be "well educated" (64) enough to be the author of their own story. In one of the most renowned slave narratives, *The Interesting Narrative of the Life of Olaudah Equiano* (1789), the author is particularly aware of these pitfalls, including several self-reflexive passages addressing the conventions of the memoir and stressing the authenticity of his tale. In its wider reception, especially in the 20th century, the question of this authenticity was further extended to the accuracy of the historical details. Many scholars doubted whether he could have really been born in the "part of Africa known by the name of Guinea" in 1745 or whether he had gained the necessary information on this area and the Middle

Passage while growing up in the Americas (Equiano et al. 1969: 1).[53] Commenting on this debate, Paul E. Lovejoy writes: "Despite the existence of documentation that refutes his claim to an African birth [...] *The Interesting Narrative* is reasonably accurate in its details, although, of course, subject to the same criticisms of selectivity and self-interested distortion that characterize the genre of autobiography" (2006: 318). Elaborating on the function and origin of these debates, he adds:

> The issue is clear: are his descriptions of his experiences of Africa and the notorious "Middle Passage" fabricated or are they derived from his personal experience? It might be argued that it does not matter that much in terms of Vassa's impact on the abolition movement, which was profound, because a fictionalized account of his childhood might have been just as effective for political purposes to garner support for the abolitionist cause as an account that was in fact the truth. (2006: 319)

Distinguishing fact from fiction and the claim to authenticity became crucial questions in the time of abolition and they remain equally crucial questions for an African refugee like Saidu. The gruesome details of Liberia's civil wars are told to an effect and, as Julius notes, might be embellished "to perfect his claim of being an innocent refugee" (67). Read as fiction, and not merely an appeal to a legal status, Saidu's story might also be considered effective for political purposes, even, or perhaps especially, if he had been a child soldier in Liberia. One is reminded of certain generic conventions in postcolonial literature, for example the purportedly rallying effect of Dave Eggers ventriloquizing a Sudanese child soldier in *What Is the What* (2006) or the open debate amongst contemporary African authors on whether bleak depictions of the African continent are "performing Africa" in a way that may be meant to evoke "pity and fear" but merely succeeds in producing "poverty-porn" (Habila 2013: para. 1). We may read this chapter as Cole's meta-fictional commentary on these debates, and on the generic constrains of diasporic writing. Identifying two examples of narratives that wittingly adhere to their respective genre conventions, we are invited to interrogate the way we actually read Julius's story, questioning what kind of expectations we bring to the narrative of a young, bourgeois, and cosmopolitan Nigerian. Especially, one might add, if he shares these characteristics with the actual author.

---

[53] Most notable among these scholars is Vincent Carretta, who maintains that Equiano was a literary figure, conceived by the author Gustavus Vassa, actually born in South Carolina. The published narrative did indeed bear two names, his birth name Equiano and his slave name Vassa, by which the author went publicly. For Carretta, this distinction is crucial, as it reveals the difference between literary figure and author. See, for example, Carretta 1999 and 2005.

While the generic issues of autobiography naturally dovetail with notions of accuracy and authenticity, the impetus of these questions arises from their convergence at the point of history. This, at least, is what Paul de Man suggests in "Autobiography as De-Facement," where he notes that since "the concept of genre designates an aesthetic as well as a historical function, what is at stake is not only the distance that shelters the author of autobiography from his [sic] experience but the possible convergence of aesthetics and of history" (1979: 919). Here, de Man also problematizes the notion of the author's identity verifying the authenticity of an autobiographical text and proposes an understanding of autobiography as mode of reading or understanding that in fact pertains to all texts and all readings. Instead of the life or the subject matter determining the genre, he notes "that the autobiographical project may itself produce and determine the life and that whatever the writer does is in fact [...] determined, in all its aspects, by the resources of his medium" (1979: 920). For de Man, the notion of writing determining life is fundamentally a function of language folding back unto the subject.

The complex blurring of fictionalized historiographic and fictionalized autobiographical writing in *Open City* is thus a particular apt illustration of the historical function of genre and also stages the tensions arising from so-called autoethnographic writing. Exposing how we bring certain expectations to these generic forms, as well as positing Goyal's notion of "genre as the presence of the past in the present," we may think about the continuation of certain claims read into the narratives of the Black Diaspora (2010: 10). In the case of Julius's story, or *Open City* as an Afropolitan narrative, the claim here may not be to the status as a human being, as in the slave narrative, nor the claim to legal protection and citizenship, as in a refugee's or immigrant's tale. Its quasi-autobiographical mode can, however, be read as a claim nonetheless, an appeal perhaps to the status of world citizenship, or more accurately to liberal cosmopolitanism. Bringing Julius's narrative in conversation with two other diasporic narrative modes exposes the way that liberal Western cosmopolitanism, as it is widely understood, functions as a neo-nationalism that diasporic subjects are generically and legally expected to appeal to. The way that Julius embodies and complicates these claims is an important critique of this kind of surreptitious yet prescribed functionalism of autoethnography and problematizes the ontological status of Black cosmopolitanism.

In a way, the fugitive movements of Liberian Saidu, manumitted Haitian slave Pierre, and ambling Julius are brought into conversation and presented as a single form of Black movement. Through this juxtaposition, the reader is again reminded of how contemporary Black movements are anything but free and continue to be shaped by various kinds of bordering. What may be read as post-racial in the novel's aesthetics, the rendering of a protagonist author who rejects recognizable racial scripts, is actually a nuanced investigation of how the difficulties of Black movement aren't always as obvious as the often visible race lines that run through a city or along global borders. These lines sometimes also present a question posed internally, as Julius moves and asserts himself along those visible lines and others, less visible but all the more intransigent. Thus viewed, *Open City*'s coveys a notion of fugitivity as a response to or escape from the discursive reach of a liberal hegemony commanding very distinct modes of recognition and subjecthood. It may also reveal the author's desire to slip through the net of any single ascription, including narrow conceptions of Blackness. In "On the Blackness of the Panther," Cole writes:

> Escape! I would rather be in the wild. I would rather be in a civilization of my own making, bizarre, contrary, as vain as the whites, exterior to their logic. I'm always scoping the exits. Drapetomania, they called it, in *Diseases and Peculiarities of the Negro Race* (1851), the irrepressible desire in certain slaves to run away. (2018: para. 21)

In this chapter of *Open City*, Julius experiences a simultaneity that transports him through the arduous routes of the Sahara, and the slave ship, to the catacombs of New York City. Embedded in this triadic encounter is not only the acknowledgment of how race in/as history has positioned each of these men in a particular constellation, but also the anticipation of a certain fugitive movement. How indeed might we think of a Black diasporic encounter that operates outside the theater of representation, and that might have escaped the logic of legitimization and recognition? What if these encounters, what if the dialogism of this novel occurred outside of history or at least outside that model of time which, following Bergson, can only ever account for and measure the moment as that which has passed?[54] A model which, at the same time, is also the mechanical, progressive clock-time that sought to mechanize the enslaved and that their fugitive movements seek to resist? As a Boston emissary observed in 1865, the year of emancipation, the "sole ambition of the freedman" appears to be to "cultivate" and "plant" what and when he wishes: "to be able to do *that* free from any outside control, in one word to be *free*, to control his own time and efforts without

---

[54] Distinguishing between the "lived time" and the "clock time" of experience, Bergson develops the notion of duration (*durée*) as "the very stuff of our existence and of all things" (1965: 62). Rather than measuring time spatially, in closed-off units, the "duration lived by our consciousness is a duration with its own determined rhythm, a duration very different from the time of the physicist, which can store up, in a given interval, as great a number of phenomena as we please" (1991: 205).

anything that can remind him of his past sufferings in bondage. This is their idea, their desire and their hope" (qtd in Foner 1994: 459). The freedom to experience 'now' in its duration, as a state of being in which the past touches present and future in a continuous yet open-ended flow, may be the ultimate utopian horizon limned here.

5 "In the Swirl of Other People's Stories": Toward an Ethics of Listening

Benjamin develops his Angel of History – the historical materialist view of history – apropos the dominant historicism of his time, which not only claims to understand the past "the way it really was" but naturally sympathizes with the victor's story (2003: 391). Notably, while often being attentive to the histories of the oppressed and marginalized, there are also those crucial moments in *Open City* that remind us how Julius is the hero of his own story. For Benjamin, the "process of empathy" with a historical epoch is already suspect because the historicist inevitably sympathizes with history's victors and thus becomes complicit in the lineage of rulers stepping "over those who are lying prostrate." Knowing this, the perspective of the historical materialist should be characterized by a "cautious detachment" (Benjamin 2003: 391–392). Considering Benjamin's wariness of emotional transference, and echoing Stephen Best's concerns with melancholic historicism, an important question arises: To which degree does an ethical relation to the past actually predicate an emotional response?

As noted above, Julius's capacity for moving and thus writing and weaving this urban text relies on his sense of integrity, and his progress appears to be contingent on others' arrested development. Furthermore, his authorial distance from the stories of others is purportedly engendered by the fact that he has no place in them, or at least that his connection is not legible to him (59). Julius wanders through New York like an Isherwoodian camera, simply recording the city's everyday life, passing little or no judgment whatsoever. In conceptualizing chapter 5 even further, one might ask what it means to hear ghostly voices, to simply record and not comment on them, as if they were present. Julius, in many ways, is a chronicler, if not a storyteller, confronted with the loss experienced by others. One might even go so far as to consider the entire narrative as being motivated by the recording of loss. *Open City* is not what Goyal has termed a "comforting narrative of hybridity and redemption." Most established notions of collectivity are, if not negated, at least questioned by the atomized diasporic model embodied by Julius (2010: 208). Moreover, while stressing the pervasiveness of individual and collective trauma, the model of subjectivity proposed here also foregrounds the predicament of rooting one's sense of individual and group coherence in a fetishized notion of loss, or, in Julius's case, the fetishistic disavowal of loss. The notion of fetishism is important here because of its ethnographic connotations and allusion to the linkage between primitivism and the avant-garde, but also because it introduces the aspect of visibility and the danger of transmuting violence into a reified and aestheticized spectacle of suffering.

At this point, it may be helpful to briefly recollect the concept of fetishism in the writings of Karl Marx, Sigmund Freud, and Walter Benjamin. In *Capital Vol. 1*, Marx draws attention to the strange faculty of commodities to denote value in the "fantastic form of a relation between things," thus substituting relations between people and masking the actual constitution of their value through largely exploitative social relations and modes of production (165). [55] With reference to the religious origin of the word, Marx called the curious quality that attaches itself to commodities fetishism. The concept of the sexual fetish developed by Freud in the eponymous essay of 1927 is a result of the (male) child's disavowal of what is fantasized as the mother's castration, in which both perceived lack and denial are mingled and transferred onto another, fetishized object.[56] Laura Mulvey notes that despite raising different issues – Marx being concerned with the want of indexical value, Freud with an excessive inscription of value – both use the term to explain "a refusal, or blockage, of the mind, or a phobic inability of the psyche, to understand a symbolic system of value, one within the social and the other within the psychoanalytic sphere" (1996: 2). It is this aspect that informs my use of the term here. Both notions of the fetish conceal a labo-

---

55 As cannot go unnoted here, the slave as not only virtually "speaking" commodity presented a peculiar riddle to Marx, who was indeed well aware of how capitalism relied on the "primitive accumulation" of colonial exploitation. As he writes: "The discovery of gold and silver in America, the extirpation, enslavement and entombment in mines of the aboriginal population of that continent, the beginning of the conquest and plunder of India, and the conversion of Africa into a preserve for the commercial hunting of blackskins, are all things which characterize the dawn of the era of capitalist production" (1976: 915). In the section on the "The Fetishism of the Commodity," Marx invites the reader to imagine commodities speaking about their fictitious value, ventriloquizing, as Fred Moten writes in "Resistance of the Object," the commodity's "impossible speech" (2003: 9). In this much-cited chapter of *In the Break*, Moten traces "the historical reality of commodities who spoke – of laborers who were commodities before, as it were, the abstraction of labor power from their bodies and who continue to pass on this material heritage across the divide that separates slavery and 'freedom'" (ibid. 6).
56 Here, too, a crucial qualification must be made. As Moten writes: "It is important to note in this regard that black castration is not just to be seen as *prospective* figure and *symbolic* inability, since for the black tradition, castration is not just phantasmic possibility or introjection based on a fleeting glance at that which is read as sexual difference, but is also the proper name of an oft-repeated literal, historical, material event" (2003: 177).

rious or traumatic condition with a glossy surface; they both stand in for and suppress a violent history.

Open City, adopting what many commentators describe as a Sebaldian tone, foregrounds a general preoccupation with historical trauma that corresponds with what Roger Luckhurst has dubbed our "contemporary trauma culture" (2008: 2). Yet it also appears to subtly critique the very pervasiveness of this fascination, its fetishization of the archive and memory and perhaps also the melancholic circularity, claustrophobic reassurance, and potential reification that may result from this. It does so by routinely uncovering and recording violent and marginalized histories – yet refracted through the lens of an unreliable and most likely morally reprehensible narrator.[57]

This in turn raises the question of what might ensue if everything is rooted in loss, everyone is guilty, every people's history marked by trauma. Does this notion not promote the very blurring of distinction, the kind of pervasive, flattening fascination with history and trauma that arouses in scholars like Andreas Huyssen the urge to properly "discriminate among memory practices"? (2003: 10). While this would appear to be a rather fruitless endeavor, one might ask instead how the hard backdrop of the systemic becomes visible apropos such fleeting yet particular concepts like experience, memory, and culture. In many ways, the ectoplasmic traces of past violence have congealed into grooves that not only shape certain ways of thinking, seeing, and doing. They also channel flows of wealth and stratify societies in manners so rigorous that the imaginative act of tracing back their originary moments will hardly undo them. As Goyal notes, when diasporic subjects are linked by "feelings of shame, guilt, and loss, rather than by skin color, or a political identification [...] the historical specificity of slavery as a transnational system of labor disappears from view" (2010: 208).

While a central concern of *Open City* seems to be the possibility of understanding both the insight and the blindness of a given perspective on history – and indeed Paul de Man's *Blindness and Insight* is directly referenced – it seems as though the novel refrains from presenting the past as a transformative key to unlock the problems of the present or provide a different future. Especially, one might add, if this transformation relies on the process of uncovering, witnessing, and working through trauma in a way that attaches surplus value or excess desire to the past's open wounds. Although Julius's meandering narrative seems to be motivated by the acknowledgment of his guilt, this retroactive real-

---

57 At the heart of the novel, as Kappel and Neumann write, lies this "performative paradox of a weighty historical narrative that asks readers to think about historical atrocities through the use of an ethically unreliable narrator who abuses the privileges afforded by his hegemonic position as a male, intellectual American" (2019: 57).

ization neither changes the course of history nor necessarily informs his present. "I don't think you've changed at all, Julius," Moji finally says to him, "[a]nd maybe it is not something you would do today, but then again, I didn't think it was something you would do back then either. It only needs to happen once" (245).

When Julius appears almost entirely unmoved by Moji's accusation, it becomes apparent that there are other important forms of movement that are mostly lacking, and conspicuously so, from this spatiotemporally invested novel. In *Ugly Feelings*, Sianne Ngai offers a definition of the category of "tone" as "a literary or cultural artifact's feeling tone: its global or organizing affect, its general disposition or orientation toward its audience and the world" (2005: 28). Looking at *Open City*'s tone, it is striking how the effect of the lulling, pedestrian rhythm of Julius's recounting could be best described as atonal or lacking affect, similar to the way that Julius himself relates to the world. Especially, but not only, in his reaction to Moji, Julius shows barely any immediate signs of emotional investment, displaying instead the very same "flat affect" (244) or "affective disorder" (7) he ascribes to Moji's accusation or researches in his clinical study on the elderly. While the additional qualification of Moji's delivery as being "emotional in its total lack of inflection" perhaps belies his own emotional equilibrium, his manner throughout the narrative is one of distance and detachment (244). Only the individuals whose stories he records are emotionally invested; loss and "irrational" attachment are to be found in others. At one point, Julius reflects on the Moroccan shopkeeper Farouq and the dangerous pull of political vehemence on young people: "It seemed as if the only way this lure of violence could be avoided was by having no causes, by being magnificently isolated from all loyalties. But was that not an ethical lapse graver than rage itself?" (107).

A key to interpreting Julius's pronounced solipsism and his ostensible lack of affective transference lies perhaps in *Open City*'s particularly dense descriptions of aesthetic experiences, as well as the manner in which Julius aestheticizes moments of commonality and potential understanding. Transference does occur in the novel, repeatedly, yet it is the kind of emotional transference engendered by an aesthetic experience, converting even uncomfortable and painful emotions into an aesthetic spectacle and potential source for consumption. In "Flights of Memory: Teju Cole's Open City and the Limits of Aesthetic Cosmopolitanism," Pieter Vermeulen further discusses the scene of Moji's revelation. He notes: "Julius's response, when it comes, is startling in its inadequacy. Rather than speaking, he imaginatively converts the river, at which Moji had been staring during her monologue, into an aesthetic spectacle: "the river gleamed like aluminum roofing" (2013: 53). Julius bars the possibility of understanding by actively digressing and invoking the notion of solipsistic, aesthetic pleasure. Overall, *Open City* is marked by thick, often exaggerated descriptions of Julius's aesthetic experiences. It is interesting how movement is employed here, too, when Julius professes that he is "rapt" by the opening movement of Mahler's *Das Lied von der Erde* or when the meditation on John Brewster's paintings, "outside the elite tradition" but imbued with "soul" (36), causes Julius to leave the museum "with the feeling of someone who had returned to the earth from a great distance" (40). Overall, the effect of *Open City*'s extensive use of ekphrasis is markedly not that of communal experience, stressing instead the sense of isolation inherent in Julius's aesthetic consumption.[58] There are instances when that communality is evoked, it seems, only to provide a contrast to his pronounced solipsism. For example, when he remembers his visit to the opera: "And a few minutes before this, I had been in God's arms, and in the company of many hundreds of others, as the orchestra had sailed toward the coda, and brought us all to an impossible elation. Now, I faced solitude of a rare purity" (255). This emphasis on solitary spectatorship also harks back to the figure of Benjamin's alienated *flâneur* and is particularly evident at the points where this modernist sentiment is employed to aestheticize everyday experience, instances where the narrator appears to enter into a cathartic moment of commonality.

The opening scene of chapter 17 is such an instant. It is set in spring, at a "picnic in Central park with friends." From the narrative distance of retrospection, Julius notes how the burgeoning sunlight makes him more sociable, actively seeking out the company of others. He is, for the first time in the narrative, part of a 'we' that is not the anemic, heteronomous 'we' of pensive abstraction but denotes an active, concrete collective. Reclining on a blanket in a group of four and watching the happy scenes of family life around him, Julius merges not only with his group, but with the entire city around him. "We were part of a crowd of city dwellers in a carefully orchestrated fantasy of country life" (194), he notes, playing on the illusiveness of this idyllic urban moment and his own performance in it. While this passage harnesses certain modernist sensibilities in its aestheticized consumption of a colorful, vibrant mass, those moments are also interspersed with acute feelings of isolation and separateness, the kind of cosmological loneliness that perhaps only occurs among large groups of people. This peculiar mélange of sensations, and the modernist blueprint to this urban experience, is skillfully signposted by the opening paragraph to this serene scene, which evokes Ezra Pound's *In A Station of the Metro*. Lying in the grass, gazing through the "petals of the cherry blossom," Julius becomes aware of "a sudden apparition of three circles, three white circles against the

---

58 For further elaboration, see Neumann and Rippl 2017, or Rippl 2018.

sky." The circles turn out to be parachutists, illegally landing in Central Park. While watching them descend, Julius feels "the blood race inside [his] veins" and is suddenly transported back to a childhood memory of rescuing another boy from drowning. Even though the occasion is one of a positive, altruistic connection, Julius dwells on the sensation of being "all alone in the water, that feeling of genuine isolation, as though [he] had been cast without preparation into some immense, and not unpleasant, blue chamber, far from humanity" (196).

In a scene during Julius's time in Brussels – a trip which could be read as a reverse journey into the heart of darkness[59] in its listing of European barbarisms – Julius enters a church and is mesmerized by the sound of Baroque music: He is soon startled, however, by "distinct fugitive notes that shot through the musical texture" (138). The "unsettling half step of a tritone" he perceives is in fact the sound of a cleaning woman's vacuum, intermingled with the sound of recorded organ music (ibid.). The woman, he assumes, is most likely part of the African immigrant communities he has encountered in Brussels. Julius wonders whether her "presence in the church might doubly be a means of escape: a refuge from the demands of family life and a hiding place from what she might have seen in the Cameroons or in the Congo, or maybe even in Rwanda" (140). While Julius identifies the "fugitive" (138) blues notes of her presence and perceives them in their tension and dissonance with a "European" idea of harmony, it is only later, during his lunch with Dr. Maillotte that the echo of the tritone, or the flattened fifth, morphs into the commodified pleasure of jazz. Sophisticated Maillotte, brimming with life stories featuring royals and millionaires, may be an outspoken connoisseur of jazz, but she is not particularly fond of difference and dissonance in society. When Julius confronts her previous assessment of a colorblind Europe with Farouq's experience in Belgium, she brushes him off:

> Our society has made itself open for such people, but when they come in, all you hear is complaints. Why would you want to move somewhere only to prove how different you are? And why would a society like that want to welcome you? But if you live as long as I do, you will see that there is an endless variety of difficulties in the world. It's difficult for everybody. (143)

Julius launches into a feeble attempt to convince her otherwise, but finally succumbs, sinking into the comforts of refinement, "the smell of food and wine, interesting conversation, daylight falling weakly on the polished cherry-wood of the tables" (142). This bleak vision of an open society is rarely lifted, as Julius's ability to record difference never suggests an engagement with it. Yet, as Theodor

---

59 Isabel Soto in conversation with the author.

Adorno notes in relation to the social role of art, "what does not exist, by appearing, is promised" (1999: 233). And perhaps this is how we can read the prospects evoked by Farouq, who, for all his shortcomings, wants to understand "the historical structure that makes difference possible" (114) and for whom the telephone shop functions as "the test case" of how "people can live together but still keep their own values intact" (112). In Julius's eyes, however, this minor cosmopolitan space still looks "like fiction" (ibid.).

These explicit musings on the fugitive notes created by contrapuntal presences encapsulates much of *Open City*'s particularly dire sense of hope, including the sliver of hope embodied by literature and its simultaneous inclination toward commodification. These scenes project yet another notion of fugitivity that transcends an understanding of Julius as a suspect *fugueur* fleeing from a shameful history but limns the promise of Black life as a different kind of life, Black ways of living as alternatives to the way life is commonly ordered, and as something that can be glimpsed in fiction. Viewed temporally, or musically, the diasporic master trope of 'movement' thus acquires additional meaning. In "Fugitive Justice," Best and Hartman examine the distinct mélange of hope and resignation in Ottobah Cugoano's slave narrative "from the retrospective glance of our political present" (2005: 3). Thus viewed, fugitivity, the "master trope of black political discourse," transpires "in the interval between the no longer and the not yet, between the destruction of the old world and the awaited hour of deliverance" (Best and Hartman 2005: 3). Here, they write, "we find the mutual imbrication of pragmatic political advance with a long history of failure; in it, too, we find a representation in miniature of fugitive justice" (ibid. 3). Or, as Fred Moten writes in "The Case of Blackness": "Black [...] is the victory of the unfinished, the lonesome fugitive; the victory of finding things out, of questioning; the victorious rhythm of the broken system. Black(ness), which is to say black social life, is an undiscovered country" (2008: 202).

In Farouq, Julius encounters someone who wills this undiscovered country into existence with a perhaps too literal vehemence, and he finds in the character of Maillotte someone who is simply unable (and unwilling) to listen, to discern the alternative order from the commodified chaos of jazz. In its general emphasis on art and aesthetic pleasure, *Open City* could perhaps be read as an exaltation of cultural and aesthetic refinement, yet one that self-consciously confronts the limits of aesthetic consumption by contrasting it with (the lack of) an ethical understanding that comes to fruition through listening and responding. In a way, the novel also foregrounds its own commodity form, its proclivity toward a fetishistic distraction from and reification of suffering, without entirely undermining the utopian potential of art.

Open City, one could say, stages the tense conversation of postmodernity by bringing various historicist modes and ways of being in dialogic relation while suspending the finite judgement of a totalizing viewpoint. Tracing its genealogy as a literary or linguistic concept back to Bakhtin's *Dialogic Imagination*, the dialogic primarily describes the way that a literary work is in open exchange with other discourses. Grounded, however, in the understanding that "[e]very utterance participates in the 'unitary language' [...] and at the same time partakes of social and historical heteroglossia" (1986: 217), the dialogic extends well beyond the communication between two parties, or discourses, but denotes the socially stratified orientation of all words or utterances. According to Bakhtin, dialogism thus accounts for the diversity of voices in a novel, rendering it a particularly "distinguishing feature of the novel as a genre" (ibid. 300). The dialogic in a novel may describe the relationship between the author and the narrator's story, the double-voiced discourse inhabited by character speech and also the social embeddedness of the novel's heteroglot background. Moreover, dialogism is encountered in the very condition of language, as any "object is always entangled in someone else's discourse about it, it is already present with qualifications" (ibid. 330). Rather than begetting monolithic or monologic conceptualizations, the spectral dispersion of the artistic "image" creates an "atmosphere filled with [...] alien words, value judgments and accents," allowing the "social atmosphere of the word" to sparkle (ibid. 277). Such open-endedness and complexity is necessarily opposed to the closedness of value judgements.

Understanding how the narrative situation of the novel informs the way that information is presented reveals the dialogic nature of *Open City*. Read as a series of sessions with a therapist revolving around the pivotal moment of confession, the role of the implicit reader of Julius's account is that of a purportedly neutral witness or patient listener rather than that of a judge afforded with the morally invested, elevated, and totalizing bird's eye perspective that is both evoked and rebuked in the novel's coda. This patient-therapist relationship is mirrored in, or rather transferred onto, Julius's numerous encounters with other people's stories that cast him in the role of witness or chronicler, rather than passer of moral judgments. In his review of *Open City* in *The New Yorker*, Wood conflates these differing modes, interpreting Julius's neutral detachment as an ethical mode of being. Highlighting the passage in which Julius verbalizes his confusion at Moji's accusation, its threat to conceiving himself as "never less than heroic," Wood applauds the novel's display of "ordinary solipsism," but does not take the subsequent revelation into account (2011: para. 18). He thus identifies the narrative stance of *Open City* as one that showcases the somewhat necessary "limits of sympathy." He further praises the way this "lucky, privileged equilibrium of the soul" is portrayed as admittedly sometimes being an "obstacle to understanding other people" but as not reducing the value of this kind of "solitary liberalism" as an enabler of comprehension (ibid.).⁶⁰

That there is not merely a certain plurality of readings taking place, but something that may be better understood as a kind of conscious disavowal, is apparent in the way the novel's more sinister notes can so easily be overheard or appear understated. The character of Julius allows for these contrary readings: his own ambiguousness not only permits, but actually *conditions* ambiguous interpretations. As Bakhtin argues, all rhetorical forms are "oriented toward the listener and his answer" (280). He notes that the orientation of the speaker "toward the listener is an orientation toward a specific conceptual horizon, toward the specific world of the listener," and "[u]nderstanding comes to fruition only in response" (282). Equipped with the knowledge of multiple worlds, and poised at the metahistoricist vantage point of Afropolitanism, *Open City* knowingly orients itself toward conflicting histories and horizons. While the historical and present-day atrocities he records may provoke an emotional reaction in readers, they could, however, also easily be registered as a mere mustering of information or even, in the case of Moji's rape accusation, be completely overlooked.

Julius's movement does not enact an ethical response but actually evokes that question. Most important, his movement creates the textspace that allows for a response to happen. Under every narrative move of this novel at large lies the open question of how people are moved to feel, to develop an ethical and emotive relation toward the world. Readers are invited to register Julius's passivity and complacency despite his selective focalization. If they can see beyond the manner in which he either sexualizes or demeans Moji, they can recognize how she is altogether more perceptive and cognizant of the way her Blackness intersects with other collective identities – while acknowledging that her

---

60 Two individual academic articles on *Open City* both reference this popular review by Wood, only to depart strongly from his interpretation of Julius's detachedness as "selfish normality." Pieter Vermeulen identifies Wood's review as trying to bring the novel in line "with the dialectic figure of flaneur" (52). He contrasts this with his own interpretation of the novel as substituting the *flâneur* with the *fugueur*, a figure identified by Ian Hacking as the dark counterpoint to the exalted, celebratory movements of the modernist *flâneur*, characterized by vagabundry and "ambulatory automatism" (Vermeulen 2013: 54). For Vermeulen, this crucial difference prohibits a reading of *Open City* as a prime example of "literature's enabling role in fostering cosmopolitan feeling and understanding" (41). Similarly, Katherine Hallemeier's essay develops a more critical argument against the backdrop of Wood's endorsement of Julius's cosmopolitan liberalism. Highlighting the way Wood foregrounds how this kind of liberalism is engendered by erudite, "bookish" types like Julius, she argues that both *Open City* and the preceding *Every Day Is for the Thief* "self-consciously embrace and critique the literariness that is integral to the protagonists' cosmopolitan identities" (2013: 240).

investment banker job at Lehman Brothers in 2007 implodes an all too simplistic articulation of solidarity or complicity. Readers can, however, also choose not to see this.

The ambiguous reading responses engendered by the counter-narrative of Moji's accusation could also be related to the varying impact made by challenges to hegemonic histories – particularly from decolonial and diasporic perspectives. Thus, Julius's detached observations of the world still provide the necessary clues to perform what Edward Said has called a contrapuntal reading as an alternative to a "linear and subsuming" historiography (1994: xxv). Whether this moves one to emotions and to action, if not to activism itself, is yet another issue.[61] In walking, encountering, and recording, Julius becomes the dialogic textspace of the novel. Merely witnessing these voices, however, does not generate an ethical relation to them in the same way that an ethical relation to the present is not necessarily predicated on the ability to "stay with the dead" and actualize the past in the present. Instead of merely pathologizing Julius's attitude toward others or imbuing it with an ethical purport, one could also read his uninvolved staging of other people's stories in correspondence with the novel's negating of totalizing unity, especially the kind that is promised by the aesthetic consumption of an art work. The function of Julius's isolated and unresponsive observation might best be understood as the staging of heteroglossia and otherness that allows equally for the recognition of collectivity, the emotional thrust of an ethical positionality, or the celebration of solipsistic liberalism.

Open City highlights the cynicism and privilege behind the kind of flat affect that poses as liberal imagination, yet it also explores the limits of grounding collective identity in transhistorical feelings of guilt, anger, or melancholia. Neither formulating a moral directive nor offering a totalizing viewpoint, it nevertheless raises the question of how attentive we want to be toward the world and its different voices, of how we want to live our lives among them. The novel also points toward the complicated and conscientious labor behind this seemingly innocuous ethics of listening, as an already complex and cacophonic present is shot through with contrapuntal fugue notes, as well as past voices vying for the attention of patient listeners. As an instance of the Afropolitan moment, the novel thus knowingly historicizes a moment in which the making of history itself be-

---

[61] Thinking about "animatedness" as a most basic form of affect and its racialization apropos the genre of the propaganda novel, Ngai writes: "In this manner, the racialization of animatedness converts a way of moving others to political action ('agitation') into the passive state of being moved or vocalized by others for their amusement" (2005: 32). Perhaps Julius's pronounced unwillingness to portray this causal sense of agitation could be related to an understanding of *Open City* as the polar opposite of a didactic novel.

comes the lens through which to view the complexities of a contemporary diasporic imaginary. It utilizes this moment as an opportunity to reflect on the aestheticization, or even fetishization, of loss and the limits of an archeological working through trauma, without entirely undermining the importance of documenting and witnessing historical violence. As such, it performs a balancing act that questions rather than displaces certain modes of recognition. Similarly, while configuring a post-Black aesthetic as that which moves away from monolithic conscriptions and hollowed appeals to racial solidarity, it still employs race in/as history by inscribing its own purportedly cosmopolitan or Afropolitan movements into a tradition of Black fugitivity.

Chapter III
(Post-)Independent Women – Romance, Return, and Pan-African Feminism in Chimamanda Ngozi Adichie's *Americanah*

> "Since I must not all the same allow you to look at the future through rose coloured glasses, you should know that what is arising, what one has not yet seen to its final consequences [...] is racism, about which you have yet to hear the last word. Voilà!"
>
> Jacques Lacan

> "The desire of the text (the desire of reading) is hence desire for the end, but desire for the end reached only through the at least minimally complicated detour, the intentional deviance, in tension, which is the plot of narrative."
>
> Peter Brooks

1 Introduction: Not That Kind of #BlackGirlMagic?

What presents itself as a subtle balancing act in *Open City* emerges more formally and overtly in Chimamanda Ngozi Adichie's best-selling novel *Americanah* (2013). Here, the ability or desire to voice the different ways in which members of the Black Diaspora view "history through skin color" (Forna) extends well beyond the novel's themes and also manifests itself in the manner in which the novel appears to straddle two ostensibly opposed genres at once, rendering it a soothingly utopian romance that also aspires to "gritty," real-life realism. *Americanah* spans three continents and is set at various locations in Nigeria, England, and the US. It follows the lives of high school sweethearts Ifemelu and Obinze, who, unsatisfied with the dismal situation under Nigerian military rule, make their way to the American East Coast and London, respectively. After undergoing quite different immigrant experiences, both eventually return to Lagos. Told predominantly from the perspective of Ifemelu, who has only recently made the decision to return and nurtures the hope of reuniting with the now estranged Obinze, most of the novel's seven parts are told in flashbacks that trace her initial difficulties and then steady success in the US. Inserted into the otherwise plot-driven and decidedly romantic narrative are several short passages that tackle the subject of US-American racism from the perspective of an African immigrant and are taken from Ifemelu's successful blog *Raceteenth – or Various Observations About American Blacks (Those formerly Known as Negroes) by a Non-American Black*.

This chapter argues that Adichie's novel is highly conscious of how these different positionalities may be pitted against each other and that its depictions of uneasy intradiasporic encounters in deeply racist US-America are ultimately offset by its Pan-African aspirations. While most commentators have read *Americanah* as a contemporary realist novel, it also historicizes several impactful periods, such as a post-independence Nigeria under military rule, the postcolonial melancholia of pre-Brexit Britain, and, crucially, Barack Obama's election in the US. The novel paints the Afropolitan moment as precisely this split or potential turn, and it does so by deftly handling temporal devices such as memory, foreshadowing, and the nostalgic yet future-oriented thrust of romance, while reflecting on the multitemporality and historicity of race and racialization. Likewise, I would argue that much of the novel's ambivalence – and its success – lies in the way that it aims to be both gritty and real, and fancifully romantic. Couching realism in romance allows the novel to signify doubly, as in contradictorily, and to signify both, as in the 'absent-presence' or 'not yet' of utopia.

The novel's peculiar, double-faced nature also crucially affects the level of reception, as it effectively addresses particularly broad yet differently positioned audiences. By far the most popular novel discussed in this study, the key to its success may lie in its ability to signify strongly – if multiply.[62] Like any text, the novel does not allow unequivocal readings, even though it offers the right amount of accessibility for readers to engage easily, and the right amount of ambiguity to address many. While inseparably linked, these attributes may equally befit its author, who has developed an almost brand-like persona in public discourse. Prior to *Americanah*'s publication, Adichie had already received numerous accolades with her novels *Purple Hibiscus* (2003) and *Half of a Yellow Sun* (2006), as well as regularly publishing short stories in publications such as *Granta* or the *New York Times Magazine*, many of which were collected in *The Thing Around Your Neck* (2009). Following the publication of *Americanah*, and ever since Beyoncé sampled parts of Adichie's TED Talk *We Should All Be Feminists* on her eponymous album later that year, Adichie morphed from popular writer to pop icon.

---

62 The website chimamanda.com notes that the novel has been licensed for publication in 29 languages. It has won the 2013 National Book Critics Circle Award for Fiction and *The Chicago Tribune* Heartland Prize for Fiction of the same year, was named an NPR "Great reads" Book, a *Washington Post* Notable Book, a *Seattle Times* Best Book, an *Entertainment Weekly* Top Fiction Book, a *Newsday* Top 10 Book, and a Goodreads Best of the Year pick. It was also listed among the *New York Times Book Review*'s "Ten Best Books of 2013" and won the "One Book, One New York" campaign in 2017. Its film rights were acquired in 2014 by Brad Pitt's production company Plan B, and the production is said to star David Oyelowo and Lupita Nyong'o.

Today, it seems as though she has organically grown into the role of the world-famous writer of whom many people might have heard (even if they have never read her), who is both asked to comment on international politics and lauded for her fashion sense, and whose whimsically illustrated quotes circulate the web in meme-like manner. Yet, without discrediting any of her literary and/or cultural achievements, there is certainly more to her fast ascent and fame than mere merits. Many, if not all of these commentaries and quotes relate to issues of race and gender, and this also reveals the discursive realm in which both her status as literary writer and her role as a public intellectual most strongly overlap.

It is probably safe to say that, particularly among a younger demographic, Adichie is the most popular African writer living today. And this is probably not due to the fact that she is repeatedly dubbed as Chinua Achebe's heir, but because she is actually *not* like him, that she embodies a new, female, and glamourous generation of African writers apart from eminent forefathers like Soyinka, Achebe, Ngũgĩ, or Farrah. In a way, Adichie is the poster child of the agency and autonomy associated with both Afropolitanism and what some call either third-wave pop-feminism or neoliberal post-feminism; she is the perfect (post-)independent woman writer. While, as Sisonke Msimang writes in "All Your Faves are Problematic," Adichie occupied "a unique place in contemporary black women's thought and literature for at least a decade before the phrase black girl magic was coined as a hashtag," her rise to celebrity cannot be tethered from an era in which this hashtag has become "the motto for a new generation's struggle for recognition and self-love" (2017: para. 6).

As a popular representation of #BlackGirlMagic, Adichie has become a spokesperson for a range of contemporary feminist issues, along with the potential pitfalls that accompany such discourses. When Adichie attracted heavy criticism for her comments on trans women, Msimang wrote a takedown not necessarily of her, but of what she called the "trap of #blackgirlmagic." For the purpose of my argument, articles like "All Your Faves are Problematic" are less instructive on the specific dynamics of fan idealization or call-out-culture but indeed reveal how much Adichie has become not only a global or African, but a specifically Black feminist icon. As Msimang writes:

> Adichie is African of course, but because she began writing in a world that was more global than it had ever been, because she traveled so frequently between Nigeria and America, she was easily claimed as a member of a much larger global African diaspora. She may technically belong to two countries, but she is collectively seen as a daughter or a sister to Black people in a broader sense. (2017: para. 7)

Yet Adichie was able to simultaneously signify something entirely different, too, allowing for multiple projections, as all highly visible figures do. While, on the one hand, Adichie's achievements were tagged with #BlackGirlMagic and her novels filed under "Black Woman Writers" reading lists, she was also able to signify as not Black, or at least as not *that* Black, and as disassociated from Blackness.[63] How was she able to signify both? For one, Adichie's coming to fame in the moment of Afropolitanism is marked by this moment's ambiguity, signaling both an alleged post-racialism and an intense re-signifcation of political Blackness. As such, the novel must be placed within a literary context that functions "as a space to explore the contradictions and paradoxes of race in a putatively 'post-racial' age" (Schur 2013: 252).

On the other hand, Adichie's novel demonstrates what Goyal calls "a new discourse about race being conducted in African novels" – yet an additional or supplementary one, rather than one that advances a usurping or disassociated kind of Blackness (Goyal 2014: xvii). Placing this discourse "alongside the frame of the black Atlantic" rather than above it means being attentive to the manner Adichie conducts her investigations of intradiasporic difference or intra-racial divides in *Americanah*. It means asking for a level of nuance that is usually not employed by post-racial pundits or those inclined to stress diasporic rifts, fissures, or an Afropolitan divestment of Blackness.

With her protagonist Ifemelu, Adichie shares the often-quoted narrative of becoming Black in America, of not considering herself Black in her home country Nigeria and 'not getting' the concept of race. Yet if one views the novel through the lens of its popular reception, particularly in respect to how the author and protagonist tend to be conflated, that narrative is surprisingly often truncated in editorials on *Americanah* and interviews with the author, rendering it a static truism rather than the dynamic process Adichie goes on to describe. While Adichie in fact historicizes and 'provincializes' a hegemonic, Euro-Atlantic notion of Blackness, many commentators ignore the latter part of the narrative and somewhat eagerly latch onto the notion of Adichie simply rejecting an overblown American race discourse.

In one of her earliest non-fiction texts on race in the US, a *Washington Times* opinion piece from 2008, Adichie describes her unease at being called "sister" in

---

[63] The German weekly *Die Zeit* and a public radio feature, *radioWissen* on BR2, titled "Ich bin nicht schwarz!" for its discussion of *Americanah*; an interview on *Salon.com* had the quote "Race doesn't occur to me" as its title. The German *Frankfurter Allgemeine* went as far as deeming the novel a "caesura" that finally voiced how even minorities themselves are weary of anti-discrimination discourses and political correctness. See Mangold 2014; Bayerischer Rundfunk 2019; Bady 2013; Spiegel 2014.

a Brooklyn store. Having recently come from Nigeria, a country that may have been colonialized, but, as Adichie quips, thanks to its mosquitos never experienced the racial hierarchy of a settler colony, race had remained an "exotic abstraction" to her, something of a fiction: "It was Kunta Kinte," Adichie writes, followed by the candid reflection: "To be called 'sister' was to be black, and blackness was the very bottom of America's pecking order. I did not want to be black" (2008: para. 2). She then goes on to recount an almost Fanonian moment of being interpellated by a little white boy: "'She's black,' he said to his mother and stared silently at me before going back upstairs. I laughed stupidly, perhaps to deflate the tension, but I was angry" (Adichie 2008: para. 3). Following this personal exposition, Adichie snidely dissects the different deflecting attitudes toward racism that represent "how mainstream America talks about blackness" (para. 5).

However, in the same way that Adichie's narrative of 'coming to America' goes beyond the mere bewilderment at an obtusely coded racial discourse or the 'foreignness' of race as outdated ideology, so does *Americanah* reflect a much more complex coming to terms with, rejecting, and embracing of different notions of Blackness. Like Ifemelu, Adichie has eventually *learned* to be Black. This 'learning of Blackness,' however, is represented quite differently in the novel. For one, it is book knowledge, such as Ifemelu devouring *The Fire This Time* and then "every James Baldwin title on the shelf" (*Americanah* 135). At other times, it is lived, and actually quite intensely felt experience, angering or frustrating Ifemelu in a similar way to Adichie's memory of the little boy – a truly primal scene. In a 2013 interview, Adichie expands on how, eventually, her "resentment turned to acceptance":

> I read a lot of African American history. And if I had to choose a group of people whose collective story I most admire today, then it would be African Americans. The resilience and grace that many African Americans brought to a brutal and dehumanizing history is very moving to me. Sometimes race enrages me, sometimes it amuses me, sometimes it puzzles me. I'm now happily black and now don't mind being called a sister, but I do think that there are many ways of being black. (Segal 2013: para. 25)

In *Americanah,* the journey from rejection to nuanced celebration of Black consciousness is spurred by a certain diasporic desire, a Pan-African subtext marked by varying degrees of over- and dis-identification. Generally, while *Americanah* offers plenty of scenes that illustrate the irritating and harmful effects of racism in a majority-white society, there are just as many that highlight the uneasy negotiations between diasporic identities of old and new, where racial solidarity and imagined community are measured with the finely calibrated scales of class and gender. Ifemelu feels hurt when she is accused of not feeling "the stuff she's writing about," and she senses disdain toward her "Africanness," apparently rendering her "not sufficiently furious" (345). And, when confronted with the earnest zeal of her Black American partner Blaine, she drifts toward a francophone African scholar named Boubacar, with whom she shares a playful condescension for American culture, while sensing Blaine's resentment at "this mutuality, something primally African from which he felt excluded" (340). However, as a self-identified Non-American Black, Ifemelu does employ Blackness as grounds for solidarity, even though she eschews both the somewhat outdated Pan-African scripts of old and the linear spatiotemporal trajectory of a Middle Passage that eclipses Africa.

Instead, the novel develops the notion of denaturalized, historically contingent Black identities – in Ifemelu's case an African *and* Black identity – that are more akin to Stuart Hall's notion of cultural identity as a "matter of 'becoming' as well as of 'being.'" In "Cultural Identity and Diaspora," Hall famously stresses the necessary historicity of cultural identities while drawing attention to the way they are articulated and developed apropos historical constellations (1994: 394). This dynamic process is performed both by Adichie and *Americanah*, but because it is mediated differently, it is also important to distinguish the levels and modes through which this "continuous 'play' of history, culture, and power" is articulated in the historical constellation of Afropolitanism (Hall 1994: 394).

2 "You Can't Write an Honest Novel About Race in This Country": Reading for Race

Both in terms of style and content, the *Washington Times* opinion piece resembles Ifemelu's successful race blog in *Americanah*. Here, Ifemelu satirizes her initiation into America's racial order in a blog post titled "To My Fellow Non-American Blacks: In America, You Are Black, Baby" (220). She recounts her bewilderment at an almost indecipherable code – where being asked whether one likes watermelon becomes a covert insult – while admitting to the difficulties of either representing race for Black Americans or talking about race with white liberals or white conservatives. "If possible, make it funny," she advises the reader (221). This tongue-in-cheek pitch of Ifemelu's witty blog posts, her equal puzzlement at the notion of offensiveness, liberal sensitivities, and conservative aggression, is perhaps what commentators have often lauded as being so "refreshing," "eye opening," and "non-didactic" about the novel – as if *Americanah* were in fact a humorous blog or a sociological study on race relations in the US. Eva Rask Knudsen and Ulla Rahbek's interpretation of *Americanah*, "A Complex

Weave," draws much of its critical content from reading the blog as performed authorship. The authors posit that both Adichie's and the character Ifemelu's "pose and prose" can be identified as characteristic of "an Afropolitan demeanour [...] that takes a point of departure in the human rather that the ideological aspects of the twenty-first-century African experience in the diaspora" (Knudsen and Rahbeck 2016: 240). This leap of first conflating author and protagonist and then deducting the ontological status of Afropolitanism from these authors' textual engagements is meant to stress the political and potentially radical purport of digital Afropolitanism. Their claim is that, while Adichie's novel is inherently political (the authors point out the political dimensions of its major themes hair and love), the novel's blog is explicitly so, and thus merely a smaller, fictionalized version of Adichie's self-avowed desire to write a "gritty, taken-from-real-life book [...] about race" (Mesure 2013: para. 10).

It is surely a delicate act to read *Americanah* through this lens without reducing it to the 'race novel' as which it has been hailed. Indeed, more so than her earlier novels, *Americanah* partakes in a global conversation on race and the African signifier. In terms of geographical scope, there is an obvious shift from her decidedly national fiction to this transnational novel, even though her short stories and her earlier novels set in Nigeria already signify the Black Diaspora.[64] Thinking through both the significance and the limitations of reading *Americanah* through race, Goyal writes: "[N]ovels like *Americanah* are often held to a different standard and required to be ethnography or a sign of resistance, and aesthetic questions are too easily suppressed in favor of expected modes of reading through a rather simple political lens" (2014: xvii). Generally, although race and diaspora are predominant topoi in *Americanah*, we cannot for example read the blog as sociological testimony to this. This is what Goyal suggests when she notes that, in order to "assess the novel's realism as a craft, and not simply a given," it is imperative to distinguish "between the claims of the race blog and those of the narrative itself" (2014: xiii). There is a certain compulsory bluntness, as well as a generic limitation to the blog that the novel both utilizes and navigates.

---

[64] Despite being repeatedly described as a literary 'heir' to Chinua Achebe and the more national focus of her previous novels, links between the US and Nigeria have certainly played a role in Adichie's writing, most markedly in the immigrant's perspectives of her short story collection, but also through migratory characters such as Aunty Ifeoma in *Purple Hibiscus*, or via the Pan-Africanism of Odenigbo in *Half of a Yellow Sun*. Here, tentative links are also established between the freedom dreams and nationalist plight of Biafra and the Birmingham bombing in US America's segregated South. For a discussion of Adichie's rewriting of and positioning toward Achebe, see Eisenberg 2013: 8–24.

The blog posts are inserted at various points in the narrative, sometimes complementing the action, at other times appearing more random. They are set apart from the main narrative not only typographically, but also in terms of style, embodying the *"irreverent, hectoring, funny and thought-provoking voice"* her readers have praised. While the function of the race blog's accompanying and oftentimes commenting on her life could perhaps be compared to that of a choir, the blog is also theatrical in another sense. There is an unequivocal element of performativity to the blog posts, with their frequent use of *ad spectatores*, rhetorical questions, and an acute awareness of the audience, that culminates in Ifemelu's feelings of paranoid stage fright and nakedness, of identity layers peeling away. The blog's most vocal critic is surely Blaine, who accuses it of lacking depth and political zeal (345). But already with the opening chapter, the reader is told how Ifemelu herself is unsatisfied with the way her celebrated race blog has developed. At this point, she has already sold it and remembers how, anxious to impress her ever-growing readership, she had "began, over time, to feel like a vulture hacking into the carcasses of people's stories for something she could use. Sometimes making fragile links to race. Sometimes not believing herself. The more she wrote, the less sure she became. Each post scraped off yet one more scale of self until she felt naked and false" (5).

Where the blog only feigns self-assuredness, the novel's tone is notably poised and confident in its straight-forward realism, displaying an emphatically clear style, an impression heightened by the fact that the main protagonists Ifemelu and Obinze repeatedly fret about misinterpreted, one-sided, or otherwise warped communication, particularly via technology. While mulling over a love interest's email or text message certainly makes for a good romantic plot device, this kind of exploration of the limits and levels of written communication is noteworthy in a novel whose prose, according to the author, aspires to Orwell's dictum of being "like a windowpane" and whose main protagonist and author hold a degree in communications (Smith 2014: 00:14:54).

I would argue that Ifemelu's self-conscious doubts concerning the performativity of the race blog are negotiated through recourse to other, ostensibly more 'authentic' or meaningful literary genres. The various notions of literariness exercised in *Americanah* are striking, as pronounced distinctions are made in respect to newer communicative forms such as the blog post, the email, the text message and the either more enduring or simply more personal reading experience of novels and poetry. An example of this self-reflective meditation on authenticity, literary genre, and form is the scene of Ifemelu and Blaine's initial encounter. Having only just decided "to stop faking an American accent" (173), Ifemelu feels confident and "truly" like herself when she meets the handsome African American Yale professor on a short train ride to Massachusetts. They instantly lapse into a mild flirtation, with Ifemelu holding forth, somewhat flippantly, about academese-speaking academics "who don't really know what's happening in the real world" and Blaine replying: "That's a pretty strong opinion." "I don't know how to have any other kind", Ifemelu retorts (179). During their brief encounter, she also experiences a bout of self-consciousness when she watches him reading a hardcover and the *New York Times*, while she is reading a glossy women's magazine. Suddenly, she feels the "unreasonable urge to tell him how much she loved the poetry of Yusef Komunyakaa" (178).

Although the novel offers much critique of the kind of intellectual sparring and cultural cachet that attaches itself to some texts and not others, poetry does play a significant role in Ifemelu's coming of age narrative. While the course of the narrative suggests that Ifemelu is also evolving as a writer, the final incarnation of her blog garners the highest praise when someone, possibly Obinze, comments that a blog post reads *"like poetry"* (474). Apropos the deliberate forthrightness of the blog, the bluntness of strong opinions, and the ostensive immediacy and authenticity of realist prose, *Americanah*, it seems, also advocates for the circumspectness of poetry. The poet Komunyakaa himself has commented on the necessary indirectness of his work: "Poetry is a kind of distilled insinuation. It's a way of expanding and talking around an idea or a question. Sometimes, more actually gets said through such a technique than a full-frontal assault" (2000: 135). Like Ifemelu reading a women's magazine while actually thinking about and eventually writing like poetry, the novel also somewhat defiantly adopts the libidinal economy and glossy surface of romantic genre fiction while suggesting that there is some kind of 'real' poetic truth beneath the surface.

Accordingly, I would also argue that *Americanah*'s most profound meditations on race do not occur through the bluntness of the blog, but through the medium of genre. Or, more accurately, the key to understanding the novel's treatment of the Black Diaspora lies in the way these themes are embedded in, or strategically deployed through, genre. In this approach, I follow Goyal's reminder that to "assume that genre is not pertinent to the study of race is to suppose that the minority text exists as itself, without institutional identity or pressures" (2010: 11). As such, it is important to contextualize the vexed question of authenticity and the dialectic relation to literary realism for African as well as African American fiction. One need only recall Jameson's national allegory argument, according to which the third world text necessarily expresses "daily reality" because, even if it assumes genres distinct from "traditional realism," it "must be situational and materialist despite itself" (1986: 85–86). As Gikandi notes, "Adichie is certainly engaged in the production of the realistic cultural narrative, but at the same time she wants to do this without necessarily confirming our desire for a certain kind of Africa" (2016: 56). In the historical context of African American fiction, as scholar Gene Andrew Jarret notes, the relation between race and authenticity has often been negotiated via the genre of "racial realism,", a term that, he writes,

> pertains to a long history in which authors have sought to re-create a lived or living world according to prevailing ideologies of race or racial difference. Intellectuals in the past seldom used the term to describe African American literature, though [...] Alain Locke came closest in 1928, when he called 'modernist' black authors 'race-realists.' Rather, they employed other words to measure the degree to which literary representations of the race gravitated toward public expectations of realism. The words included 'real,' 'true,' 'authentic,' 'objective,' 'bona-fide,' 'genuine,' 'original,' 'creative,' 'curious,' 'novel,' 'spontaneous,' and 'vigorous.' (Jarrett 2011: 8)

Notably, rather than employing a modernist or postmodernist aesthetic, or modes of estrangement that foreground its literary rather than its documentary purport, *Americanah* displays a pronounced skepticism toward these kinds of literatures, or, more accurately, toward the people excessively valuing such forms over all others. Upon meeting a journalist and former English major at a party, Obinze notes with regret that, for him, "a book did not qualify as literature unless it had polysyllabic words and incomprehensible passages" (31). Ifemelu, reflecting on her failed relationship with Blaine, notes his predilection for "novels written by young and youngish men and packed with *things*, a fascinating, confounding accumulation of brands and music and comic books and icons, with emotions skimmed over, and each sentence stylishly aware of its own stylishness" (12). Neither skimming emotions nor dumbfounding readers with opaque prose, *Americanah* appears to embody its own gold standard. Yet despite its confident narrative poise, the novel expresses an ambiguity toward its realist status, self-consciously foregrounding "its own reception as a new kind of black novel," as well as expounding the difficulties in writing about race (Goyal 2014: xiv). As Blaine's sister Shan notes:

> If you write about how people are really affected by race, it'll be too *obvious* [...]. So if you're going to write about race, you have to make sure it's so lyrical and subtle that the reader who doesn't read between the lines won't even know it's about race. You know, a Proustian meditation, all watery and fuzzy, that at the end just leaves you feeling watery and fuzzy. (335–336)

Squared with the novel's critique of the blog, this statement appears to be arguing for a somewhat circumspect nuance and a direct simplicity that need not complicate or obscure race. This ambiguity may also be discernible through its recourse to other, notably gendered and less obviously racialized genres such as 'chick lit' or romantic genre fiction. Indeed, the novel may wittingly announce its own, inevitable failure through the character of Shan: "You can't write an honest novel about race in this country" (335). At the same time, rather than fully accepting this defeat, the novel's accentuated realism leaves just enough room for believing that it might be up for the challenge, that it may indeed be that "honest" and authentic representation of American race relations. Perhaps, this openness may also account for its particularly wide appeal. As Gikandi argues, "part of the realism of her works emerges from the assumption that she is just presenting people as they are. *Americanah* has great moments of ordinariness, but there are also moments where it seems to want to be going out of its way to attract a certain kind of readership" (2016: 59). Without suggesting that the different generic forms structuring *Americanah* can be neatly separated and mapped, the following sections explore when and to what effect the novel employs realism or romance, and what the stakes may be in prioritizing one over the other.

3 "True from Experience": Reception and the Realness of Racialization

Writing about the 19th-century realist novel in *The Bourgeois*, Franco Moretti argues that "description *as a form* was not neutral at all: its effect was to inscribe the present so deeply in the past that alternatives became simply unimaginable" (93). One could argue that *Americanah* employs realism in an effort to document the facticity and pervasiveness of race in/as history and counters its grip by resorting to romantic flights of fancy. Yet this neat binary would obscure the novel's self-aware acknowledgment that realism, like reality or history, is far from neutral but always preordains a certain viewpoint or positionality. Clearly, serious tensions arise when this kind of relativism rubs against the hard realities of racism. That this is a central concern for the novel can be seen in two distinct scenes, one set in supposedly Cool Britannia, the other in the US at the cusp of the Obama era.

Shortly before he will be deported, *Americanah*'s second protagonist Obinze experiences a moment of racial splitting, or double consciousness, that interpellates him as an index of the causal course of history and, at the same time, conscripts him into the ontological timelessness of the racialized, eternal 'other.' On a train to Essex, Obinze finds himself travelling in, but not part of, a group of Nigerians. All of a sudden and only "for a moment," he perceives the "unfettered non-white foreignness of this scene through the suspicious eyes of the white woman on the tube" (259).

As an instance of racialization, this scene recalls the often-quoted passage in Fanon's "The Fact of Blackness," where he discovers his "blackness, [his] ethnic characteristics" and "above all *historicity*," becoming "responsible at the same time for my body, for my race, for my ancestors [...]. [B]attered down by tom-toms, cannibalism, intellectual deficiency, fetishism, racial defects, slave-ships, and above all else, above all: 'Sho' good eatin'" (2008: 84–85). As Bhabha describes it in *The Location of Culture*, Fanon's phenomenological performance illustrates what it means: "To be amongst those whose very presence is both 'overlooked' – in the double sense of social surveillance and psychic disavowal – and, at the same time, overdetermined – psychically projected, made stereotypical and symptomatic" (2004: 339). Obinze's realization in *Americanah* is ominously contextualized with a reflection on how a xenophobic headline in the woman's evening newspaper is "echoed" not only by so many others like it, but also by "the radio and television, even the chatter of some of the men in the warehouse":

> The wind blowing across the British Isles was odorous with fear of asylum seekers [...], as though the writers lived *in a world in which the present was unconnected to the past*, and they had never considered this to be the normal course of history: the influx into Britain of black and brown people from countries created by Britain. (258–259, emphasis added)

Seeing himself through the eyes of a woman who most likely perceives him as a threat, Obinze becomes a marker of "non-white foreignness," his identity reduced to both a group and a historical moment that are, curiously so, overdetermined by history and at the same time not historicized at all. Obinze knows that the influx of Black and brown people, if not even the very existence of these racialized others, is a historical fact made by Britain. Yet what appears to be a simple fact of history, indeed its "normal course," is a disruptive anomaly to those who seem to live "in a world in which the present was unconnected to the past." As Gilroy writes in *Postcolonial Melancholia* (also published as *After Empire*):

> The immigrant is now here because Britain, Europe, was once out there; that basic fact of global history is not usually deniable. And yet its grudging recognition provides a stimulus for forms of hostility rooted in the associated realization that today's unwanted settlers carry all the ambivalence of empire with them. [...] Indeed, the incomers may be unwanted and feared precisely because they are the unwitting bearers of the imperial and colonial past. (2005: 100)

This strange coupling of known unknowns, of conscious disavowal, or active forgetting, is not easily parsed. Yet it speaks to exactly the temporal conscription that Obinze experiences, who is an "unwitting bearer" of both too much and not enough history. For Gilroy, that sense of historical disruption rather than continuity, and the manner in which this is connected to the immigrant body, bespeaks Britain's "inability to disentangle the disruptive results supposedly produced by an immigrant presence from the residual but potent effects of lingering but usually unspoken colonial relationships and imperial fantasies (Gilroy 2005: 100). Attached instead to a fantasy of lost imperial greatness, expressed by postcolonial melancholia, Britain is unable to connect the causal effects of this complicated past to the present moment. Rather than work through the complexities and ambiguities of Britain's colonial past, as Gilroy notes, "that unsettling history was diminished, denied, and then, if possible, actively forgotten" (2005: 90).

This scene also conveys that there are two incompatible metahistorical views on Britain's present and that Obinze is able to glimpse both by seeing himself through the eyes of the white woman – a classic example of double consciousness. The notion of fundamentally different, yet parallel historical timelines – one a liberal notion of history as progress that may also entail an active forgetting, the other a more pessimist notion of deadlock or constant return – is also encapsulated in the novel's rendering of the Obama election. Here, the novel's particular use of realism also comes to the fore. In a 2017 article, scholar Alexander Manshel invokes the genre of the "recent historical novel," describing it as a "literary phenomenon invested in the very near-term process of making historical memory" (2017: 1). Among the most conventional historical events recently fictionalized, he lists "9/11 and its aftermath, [...] the 2008 financial crisis [...], and even the early career, election, and inauguration of Barack Obama," citing *Americanah* as an example for the latter (ibid.). One distinct feature of the recent historical novel, according to Manshel, is its preoccupation with contemporary "news and its narrative" not merely as "mediating experience" but as actually "*constituting* experience entirely" (2017: 6). In contrast, albeit clearly indebted to literary postmodernism's concerns with mediation, these novels express neither "jest" nor "bemusement," but rather a "deep uncertainty about the limits of historical experience in the context of contemporary media saturation" (ibid.).

Americanah does reflect on contemporaneous news and media cycles in the context of Obama's election campaign. Here, it becomes particularly interesting how the novel relates its most prevalent example of mediality, its formal and thematic engagement with the blogosphere of the late 2000s, to the news coverage of more established, mainstream media. Analogous to her relationship with African American Yale professor Blaine, the protagonist Ifemelu's excitement over the post-racial promise of Obama's presidency eventually sours. His election is depicted as a highly mediated and communal event: MSNBC's live coverage interspersed with comments of Blaine's friends and a text message from Ifemelu's Cousin Dike: "*I can't believe it. My President is black like me*" (360). At this particular point in time, Ifemelu's romance with America and Blaine appears intact – we are told that "there was, at this moment, nothing that was more beautiful to her than America" (361). Yet her disenchantment with both is already anticipated when, leading up to the election, Ifemelu scours the internet "seeking information and reassurance" and inevitably finds the blunt racism of the chat rooms. The crude and violent comments on Obama, written "under monikers like SuburbanMom231 and NormanRockwellRocks" (354), upset Ifemelu to the point of tears and make her successful race blog "feel inconsequential, a comedy of manners, a mild satire about a world that was anything but mild" (354).

The parallel media world of the chat rooms entirely undermines the surface glamour of, for example, MSNBC's official news coverage, its "searing, sparkling liberal rage" (360), thus conveying another, uglier and ostensibly more realistic image of America.[65] In its representation of the mediation of Obama's election, the novel aspires to impart something of a realist truth about the US that differs from the "ironic nothingness" its characters find in "contemporary American fiction" (256). As Manshel distinguishes the recent historical novel's relation to postmodern fiction, "mediation here smacks less of simulacrum than of a particularly contemporary form of realism" (2017: 6).

In the context of the narrative, Obama's election, a symbol of hope and liberal progress not merely for the US but for a wider global and diasporic imaginary, becomes the lifeline for a relationship that is destined to fail. Thus, while Manshel cites "the narrative satisfaction of historical telos" (2017: 11) as a key feature of the recent historical novel, *Americanah* also employs the melancholic historicism tethered to Obama's presidency – the realization that it does not symbolize progress but stagnation and constant return. Here, realism really pertains to the realness of racism, as a true representation of a messy status quo too easily overlooked, glossed over, or disavowed.

---

65 Indeed, as an analysis of FBI hate crime statistics by *The Washington Post* shows: "There was a 21 percent increase in reported hate crimes the day after Barack Obama won his first election in 2008 (Williams 2018: para. 3). In his prior work as a lead analyst for homeland security, Daryl Johnson reported an almost instantaneous popularity spike for right wing movements during Obama's campaign and especially after he was elected (the website *Stormfront* had five times more traffic on election night). These findings are testament to the political backlash *Americanah* indicates in this scene, leading to more overt racism, such as the formation of the Tea Party movement that incidentally also spin-doctored Johnson's initial report and led to the disbanding and defunding of Johnson's homeland security team by substituting the term "right wing extremism" with "violent extremism" (Johnson 2012).

How does this connect to the novel's reception? In a widely cited *New York Magazine* review, Kathryn Schulz credits the novel's appeal to how, rather than serving as an "exotic" window into Nigeria or the immigrant experience, it "endotically" reflects back cultural idiosyncrasies to US-American readers (2013: para. 8). That being said, the novel clearly 'does' different things for differently positioned audiences. When Ifemelu tells her effusively sensitive white employer Kimberly, "You know, you can just say 'black.' Not every black person is beautiful," this frankness is described as "the moment they became, truly, friends" (*Americanah* 147). One wonders how much of the mainstream appeal of the novel relied on the perceived taboo breach of bluntly looking at US race relations from the perspective of a purportedly removed yet participating observer: A Non-American Black who doesn't take racism quite so personally. Or, as one character notes about Ifemelu: "She's writing from the outside. She doesn't feel all the stuff she's writing about" (336).

Another poignant example of the novel's self-conscious exploration of parallel worldviews is the scene of the dinner party that Ifemelu attends with Blaine, where she accuses another guest, a stylish Haitian poet, of merely professing colorblindness in order "to keep our nice liberal friends comfortable" (291). A little drunk, feeling "overpowered" by words tumbling out of her mouth, Ifemelu exposes the "lie that race is not an issue," sharing what she knows to be "true [...] from experience." The other dinner guests, of whom an aging white man had just confessed his belief that "Obama will end racism" in the US, appear to be strangely fascinated by Ifemelu's candor. Sensing the kind of contained taboo break that makes for unforgettable dinner parties, they keep "their eyes on Ifemelu as though she was about to give up a salacious secret that would both titillate and implicate them" (291). That this level of reception is already folded back into the narrative seems to speak to the fact that *Americanah* indeed is this carefully crafted genre picture of contemporary American society, and that Adichie is well aware of the potential effects its content may have on certain readerships. I would argue that the novel provides an informed glimpse into these parallel worldviews but also allows itself to be received as "a mild satire about a world that was anything but mild." It is able to hold a slightly satirical mirror to differently positioned audiences without seriously offending any one of them, while also offering somewhat cathartic moments that purportedly cut through the charade.

In this sense, the novel's performative labor of 'giving voice to' or 'unveiling' uncomfortable truths relays another function of its (race) realism. For example, in "The Strange Familiar: Structure, Infrastructure, and Adichie's *Americanah*," Caroline Levine focuses on the defamiliarizingly realist descriptions of structural racism and infrastructural electricity, showing how the novel utilizes "long-standing realist traditions" in order to render strange or noteworthy what is commonly taken for granted or disavowed (2015: 588). Here, she follows an understanding of realism as not only reaffirming and reifying (predominantly of bourgeois social structures), but as also potentially startling and alienating. She writes: "Does description confirm the old or introduce the new? At its best, I will argue, it does both: it asks us to perceive anew what we thought we already knew but did not perceive well enough" (Levine 2015: 589).

In order to analyze the intricate layering and complex relations of social structures and their straightforward and familiar ubiquity, Levine advocates "a descriptive and defamiliarizing alertness" and finds this in *Americanah*'s prose, its avowed dedication to render concrete and authentic what it sees elsewhere obscured. Certainly, the novel seems to foreground its opposition to obscurity – be it the opaqueness of academic jargon, the linguistic acrobatics of highbrow literature, religious bigotry, political correctness, or the moral bankruptcy of the postcolonial state – in the form of its outspoken and plainspoken protagonist Ifemelu.

Yet while conscious of the way privilege makes certain structures "easy to naturalize or take for granted to those who are benefiting from them" (2015: 600), Levine's argument – at least where it pertains to *Americanah*'s ability to render racism strange – seems to rest on very similar assumptions. Indeed, the entire premise of defamiliarization works only for those who can actually be startled into recognizing the ubiquity of racism, thus suggesting the privilege of considering oneself an unmarked norm. Interestingly, Levine draws on two passages from classical realist texts, Charles Dickens's *Bleak House* and George Eliot's *Middlemarch*, to show their alignment with *Americanah*'s prose, their particular rendering "unusual" and noteworthy of what is otherwise habitual. However, the passage Levine selects from *Bleak House* is striking in more ways than Levine suggests. For her, it exemplifies Dickens's interest in making "the ordinary feel shocking but also to make shocking the fact that it feels ordinary" (Levine 2015: 591). Levine quotes the passage in which the narrator presents the death of crossing-sweeper Jo as resulting from poverty. This poverty, in turn, is proffered as a wider effect of social neglect, embodied, in this case, by Mrs. Jellyby. While not commented upon by Levine, Mrs. Jellyby is satirized in *Bleak House* as an philanthropist wholly consumed with "Africa" and engaged in numerous charitable activities that channel her wealth and attention away from her immediate surroundings and into this "Telescopic Philanthropy."[66] The passage quoted by Levine, its musings on how Jo isn't "a genuine foreign-grown savage; he is the

---

[66] See Robbins 1990 for a different reading of *Bleak House*'s chapter "Telescopic Philanthropy."

ordinary home-made article," marked by filth, parasites, sores, and "native ignorance, the growth of English soil and climate," does not only code the "homely" as the overlooked habitual, as Levine claims (2015: 591). It also permits a fairly obvious, and much more troubling, double meaning.

To the reader intimately familiar with racialization, colonialism, or indeed with the not only Victorian habit of racializing the poor, this passage conveys more than a meditation on the ordinariness of tragedy and indeed communicates an all too familiar logic which – not despite, but precisely because of its ordinariness – never ceases to make "the ordinary feel shocking." As with Levine's notion of racism defamiliarized by *Americanah*, it begs the question of who is allowed to become habituated, willfully or ignorantly so, and who is forced to repeatedly experience the habitual return of the same old. But perhaps this is exactly Levine's point, as she lauds the way that "Ifemelu's bluntness about the ordinariness of race and racism repeatedly startles white Americans out of their usual responses" (594). Her reading of the novel indeed illuminates the way *Americanah* tackles the parochialism of American race discourse, "endotically" reflecting back to a white liberal audience. But in its blind spots, Levine's reading also reveals the very double-faced nature of the novel. Levine rightly notes how the novel sets out to voice uncomfortable truths, yet it is more or less up to the reader to determine which kind of notions are able to "jolt [...] us into a new alertness to a world we thought we knew" (603) and which represent blatantly obvious social facts, knowable to anyone, constantly endured by some. Put differently, what enables one to see the overt racism or blunt race talk engendered by the era of Obama as progressive change and who is left see a still ugly present, inseparably tethered to the past? Such is the ambiguity of these conflicting levels or ambitions in the novel that even Levine's nuanced appraisal of the novel's defamiliarizing realism may convey the very myopia that the novel purportedly heals.

It is important to understand that *Americanah* is not merely positioned toward a liberal, white audience – even though it seems to specifically touch a nerve here – but is also celebrated and claimed by a wider diasporic or Pan-African imaginary, for example when the indelible Binyavanga Wainaina blurbs *Americanah* as "the Africa of our future. Sublime, powerful and the most political of [Adichie's] novels." Perhaps it is the politics of voicing and thus confirming everyday racism that draws particularly Black audiences to the novel and that also feeds into the celebration of Adichie as an "intellectual rock star" (Msimang 2017: para. 12).[67] In this sense, the novel's 'truth telling' also appears to

---

[67] To offer a piece of anecdotal evidence, I myself was privy to this curiously divergent set of

hold a cathartic promise for Black audiences. Yet its positioning as a 'Black novel' for a Black audience can be best understood in its negotiation of the category of Blackness itself, as an account by a Non-American Black claiming a Blackness apart from a hegemonic American history.

4 "A Bitter Americanizing": Gendered Violence in the Aftermath of Slavery

Americanah is part of a discourse that diversifies notions of Blackness in the diaspora. This is what Goyal asserts when she notes that "the novel self-consciously foregrounds its own reception as a new kind of black novel, an exploration of blackness that does not highlight injury or trauma, but focuses on romantic love, hair, and nostalgia" (2014: xiv). It is, quite unequivocally, Adichie's counterweight to "a single story" of Blackness. However, this does not mean that Adichie is not fully aware of the narrative she sets herself apart from and, in parts, rewrites to make her own. Though the mapping of US America's racial landscape in *Americanah* never presents itself as an ahistorical inventory of a messy status quo, slavery appears as an irrelevant coordinate en route to Ifemelu's Blackness – particularly because she ultimately doesn't adopt an American Blackness but forges her own, confidently Pan-African Black identity. She nonetheless employs certain tropes and narrative strategies that suggest an engagement with the legacy of slavery. At second glance, and framed through the prominence of gender in *Americanah*, Ifemelu's racialization occurs with and through a notion of femininity that is inextricably bound to slavery. In this sense, the epistemological crucible of slavery still remains a central concern for *Americanah's* investigation of Blackness, albeit one that is negotiated and ultimately worked through and thus rendered a historical effect rather than an ontological conscription.

Americanah bears the traces of a particular tradition of female, or as Alice Walker would call it, womanist tradition of African-American writers. [68] In the

---

expectations at an Adichie reading in Berlin in 2014, where the author was indeed greeted like a pop star. The audience was comprised of quite a few Black activist groups who explicitly thanked the author for writing a book that might help breach the subject of everyday racism in Germany, a topic Adichie seemed open to talk about – until her increasingly nervous white publisher stipulated that all audience questions had to relate to the novel only.

[68] Adichie's often quoted TED Talk "The Danger of a Single Story" opens with her memory of being exposed to English and American literature as a child and not thinking that "people like [her] could exist in literature." This changes drastically when she discovers African writers. Adichie goes on to describe the detrimental effects of cultural stereotyping in various contexts and

same way that "the specter of lynching" haunts diasporic writing from Richard Wright to Teju Cole, so is rape and sexual exploitation a symbol for Black oppression primarily explored by African American women writers from Harriet Jacobs and Zora Neale Hurston to Toni Morrison and Ntozake Shange. In her study on this field of writers, *Reconstructing Womanhood* (1987), Hazel Carby plainly states that the "institution of slavery is now widely regarded as the source of stereotypes about the black woman" (20). During an interview at the *Washington Ideas Forum,* Adichie noted that: "I like to say I'm happily black. [...] But in this country I came to realize [...] that meant something, that it came with baggage and with all of these assumptions" (Norris 2014: 00:04:34). That this baggage is historically linked to slavery is not spelled out in *Americanah*, but it is circumscribed in the one thing that initially causes a traumatic break with her past, namely the blunt commodification and sexual exploitation Ifemelu experiences in her encounter with the tennis coach.

Leading up to this scene are several chapters chronicling Ifemelu's first months in the US, echoing common tropes of immigrant fiction such as culture shock, alienation, financial and legal insecurity. Ifemelu's later success dwarfs this kind of experience, yet we are forced to witness it with full brunt in Obinze's failed attempt at gaining a footing in the UK. His illegal residence status ultimately condemns him to a narrative path that runs directly from cleaning toilets to being forcefully deported, crushing his hopes and dreams on the way. Ifemelu, while afforded a more secured legal status, is in turn nearly crushed by the financial weight of living and studying in the US. Because she cannot work on her student visa, she attempts to find a job with another Nigerian woman's social security number. For fear of being found out, she then starts looking for jobs that pay cash in hand, like the job with the tennis coach and finally the babysitting employment that gets her through college. The enormous economic pressures weighing on Ifemelu cause an increasing sense of hopelessness and despair and determine her particularly precarious social position. Ifemelu's poverty makes her socially invisible and thus acutely vulnerable. Ironically, it is through the junk mail of a credit card preapproval – a predatory loan if there ever was one – that Ifemelu at one point is made to feel more present and "a little less invisible" (132).

The tennis coach is described as a short, muscly white man from the suburbs, who routinely has inner-city students travel out to him to provide sexual

---

ends on a quote by Alice Walker. Where, in other contexts, Adichie often supplements the "English and American" with Enid Blyton, and the "African writers" have often been equated with Chinua Achebe, I believe that the third touchstone in her writer's genesis is too easily overlooked.

favors for cash. While Ifemelu describes the encounter with him as "sordid" (154), it is particularly the ruthlessly commercial nature of their exchange, his "venal" and "corrupt" air that stands out for her (143). He is, as it turns out, not simply one of "those white men she had read about, with strange tastes, who wanted women to drag a feather over their back or urinate on them" (153). He isn't motivated by a perverse fetish, but by cold calculation, the type of man who doesn't like to waste time and says things like "So here's the deal," "It's a great gig," or "If you want the job you can have it" (143). It is not only because Ifemelu receives money that this encounter is framed by an absolute commodification, from his "mercilessly sizing her up" to the business-like dismissal afterwards. Ifemelu decides to take the job out of utter desperation yet is determined to enter into this transaction on her own terms, applying lipstick and contemplating her personal boundaries beforehand. Once Ifemelu enters his house, she senses that none of her self-determination will change the way that the system is set up against her:

> The power balance was tilted in his favor, had been tilted in his favor since she walked into his house. She should leave. She stood up. "I can't have sex," she said. Her voice felt squeaky, unsure of itself. "I can't have sex with you," she repeated.
> "Oh no, I don't expect you to," he said, too quickly. She moved slowly toward the door, wondering if it was locked, if he had locked it, and then she wondered if he had a gun. (153)

While fear definitely plays a role in Ifemelu's compliance, what ultimately breaks her is the man's complete assuredness about her acting in a certain way. It seems as though she has entered a ritualized transaction that forces her to comply with the rules of the game. While Ifemelu feels "defeated," he already seems to know "she would stay because she had come. She was already here, already tainted" (154). Afterwards, she feels most ashamed and repulsed by the fact that her body had responded automatically. While critic Seth Cosimini interprets this as a subtle investigation of the question of consent, the way it connects with both character and story development suggests otherwise. Ifemelu experiences a pronounced disconnect between her motive will and her body. Thrice announcing her dissent ("She did not want to be here, did not want his active finger between her legs, did not want his sigh-moans in her ear"), her body nevertheless responds with a "sickening arousal," as if it "no longer belonged to her" (154). Her body's 'mechanical' reaction leaves Ifemelu feeling dehumanized and thing-like.

While the scene is far from equivocal, the point is not whether her desire or consent are conflicted but that, in effect, Ifemelu suffers from this encounter. It becomes the most dehumanizing and scarring experience she makes in the US. Across the Atlantic, Obinze's utterly negative experience in the UK equally culminates in the objectifying experience of being "removed" from the country: "That word made Obinze feel inanimate. A thing to be removed. A thing without breath and mind. A thing" (279). Yet in Ifemelu's case, the dynamics of class, race, and gender converge in a very distinct form of objectification and vulnerability. Ifemelu finds herself in a situation where the simple fact of her body turns against her, where the commercial objectification of her body is directly linked to the way it is marked, the facade of equal transaction notwithstanding. In finding herself in the tennis coach's house, placed in and subjected to a particular network of power, she is "already tainted." This dynamic resembles the one Hartman describes in a discussion of a young Black girl's pornographic photograph in *Wayward Lives, Beautiful Experiments*: "[H]er body was already marked by a history of sexual defilement, already branded as a commodity. Its availability to be used, to be hurt, was foundational to the prevailing set of social arrangements, in which she was formally free and vulnerable to the triple jeopardy of economic, racial, and sexual violence" (2019: 29).

Ifemelu's enhanced vulnerability as a Black woman, her multiple entanglement in what Patricia Hill Collins has coined the "matrix of domination," leads to a complete commodification and dehumanization and poses a sustained threat to her sense of self (Hill Collins 2000: 18). While, in the larger context of Adichie's writing, objectifications, sexualized violence, and discrimination are seen as global issues, there is a level of "sordidness" to her utter dependency that pushes Ifemelu over the edge.[69] Her strange sense of complicity and powerlessness emphasizes how Ifemelu finds herself thrust into structures that vastly exceed her range of autonomy – economic and social structures disastrously interacting with a deep and entrenched repository of stereotypes about Black womanhood.

Throughout the novel, Ifemelu's experience as a Black woman in the US ranges from blunt objectification, oversexualization, and fetishization to not

---

[69] Looking at Adichie's earlier writing, sexual violence is not an unfamiliar theme. Her second novel *Half of a Yellow Sun* deals explicitly with the omnipresence of rape and violence against women during the Biafran War. Adichie's representations of sexual violence are, however, not limited to such spectacular settings but extend to everyday experience of contemporary Nigerian women – within the domestic space but also in its insidious coupling with the power dynamics of the workplace. In the short story "Jumping Monkey Hill," for example, a character experiences various forms of sexual harassment while trying to secure a job in Lagos. Ifemelu's experience with the tennis coach is therefore, thematically, not particularly exceptional. And while it frames their encounter in a distinct way, neither is his whiteness per se. Earlier on in her job search, Ifemelu encounters a Mexican who, lewdly staring at her chest, suggests that she may "work for him in another way" (145). What becomes clear then, is that Black women find themselves at the bottom rung of any social order.

being considered female at all. Various levels of visibility, invisibility, and hypervisibility combine with distinct stereotypes, all of which can be traced to "scientific" racism in general and slavery in particular. The sexualized transaction with the tennis coach most poignantly highlights the reverberations of what Adrienne Davis has termed the "sexual economy of slavery," where legal and political arrangements "systematically expropriated black women's sexuality and reproductive capacity for white pleasure and profit" (2002: 105). Writing about the emergence of the African American woman writer, Carby elaborates on the long lasting impact of sexualized violence under slavery. She notes that while "rape has always involved patriarchal notions of women being, at best, not entirely unwilling accomplices, if not outwardly inviting a sexual attack," the alleged complicity of Black women in the subordination of Black men has rendered institutionalized rape a less powerful symbol for racial oppression than the spectacle of lynching (1987: 39).

At the same time, the systemic rape of enslaved women occurred outside and against a notion of white Victorian womanhood, rendering these violations not only morally permissible but also literally unspeakable, as Harriet Jacob's *Incidents in the Life of a Slave Girl* and its contemporaneous circulation and instrumentalization illustrate. As Ulla Haselstein notes, it is precisely the glaring contradictions emerging from the moral charges of the sentimental novel and their inapplicability to its utterly vulnerable protagonist that render Jacob's narrative a potent indictment of slavery (2000: 133). Nevertheless, the text foregrounds its inability to adequately represent the trauma of slavery within the symbolic order of white culture by simultaneously veiling and unveiling the sexual economy of slavery (Haselstein 2000: 143). The only way that these extralegal violations could be framed, both by white women and antebellum courts, was through the perpetuation of what Saidiya Hartman identifies as the "discourse of seduction," further obscuring "the primacy and extremity of violence in master-slave relations and in the construction of the slave as both property and person" (1996: 538).

The "powerful ideological consequences" of these implicit accusations feed into common assumptions about the corruptible and corrupting sexuality of Black women, oscillating between images of lascivious Jezebels and emasculating matriarchs and reifying in studies like the infamous Moynihan report (Carby 1987: 39). It is the latter's attempt at pathologizing African American family relations that serves as the starting point of Hortense Spillers seminal essay "Mama's Baby, Papa's Maybe: An American Grammar Book" from 1987. Here, Spillers explores the impacts of an anti-Black discourse routed in slavery, particularly in regard to female subjectivity. From a discussion of the mid-60s report, Spillers moves on to discuss notions of gendering and ungendering as the prelude to a "bitter Americanizing for African persons" (2003: 216). While the "quintessential 'slave,'" she notes, "is *not* a male but a female" (215), Spillers focuses particularly on how the "zero degree of social conceptualization" (206) that accompanies enslavement effectively eradicates gender difference, severing "the captive body from its motive will, its active desire" and turning it into totally objectified, ungendered "flesh" (2003: 67). Afro-pessimist thinkers have extensively picked up on this notion of barred subject positions, arguing that slave subjectivity exists prior to or outside of the symbolic realm. Where Frank Wilderson specifically focuses on the process of ungendering through what he calls "gratuitous violence," I would hesitate to prematurely dispose of the category of gender in the context of racialization (Wilderson 2010: 34). Surely, Spillers' text requires one to recognize that slavery and its aftermath render the question of African-American womanhood more vexed than it is cursorily understood. The problematizing of gender in African American family relations, she concludes, mustn't result in the desire of "joining the ranks of gendered femaleness," but instead might allow one to imagine "a radically different text for female empowerment" (2003: 229).

In *The Melancholy of Race: Psychoanalysis, Assimilation, and Hidden Grief*, Anne Anlin Cheng notes how the "contemporary American attachment to progress and healing, eagerly anticipating a colorblind society, sidesteps the important examination of racialization: How is a racial identity secured?" (2001: 7). In many ways, *Americanah* is an exploration of precisely this process, and equally from the pronounced intersectional perspective that Cheng identifies in Toni Morrison's *The Bluest Eye* and Maxine Hong Kingston's *Woman Warrior*. In all of these texts, "reading race is a prerequisite to reading femininity [...]. [They] show how femininity (what it means to be a girl) comes to acquire its social and aesthetic values under the signs of racial difference" (Cheng 2001: 19). Of course, *Americanah* cannot be neatly placed within a genealogy of Black feminist thought. Rather, it signals Adichie's individual, post-independence African engagement with issues of race and gender. There is, Adichie acknowledges, a particular coming to being (or non-being, as Afro-pessimists like Wilderson would argue) of Blackness that cannot be unhinged from slavery, and that takes on a defining centrality in the US. Yet *Americanah* deftly illustrates how Blackness is also affected by issues of locality, class and, above all, gender. As such, the scene signals how it is one thing to become Black in America and another to become a Black woman. The novel's frank and realist description of Ifemelu's particular vulnerability could be read as Adichie's exploration of the historicity of racial and gendered scripts and the socio-economic structures keeping these histories alive.

The way that Ifemelu's experience of extreme poverty intersects with race, gender, and citizenship thus highlights the kind of distinction Nancy Fraser draws between exploitation and expropriation. Arguing against the infamous Marxist notion of "side contradictions," or, for that matter, any political proposition that neglects an anti-racist critique in favor of a purportedly more basal critique of economic structures, Fraser warns against obfuscating "capitalism's deep-seated entanglement with racial oppression." She proposes a three-tier model that expands the concept of exploitation, itself a corrective to a limited model of exchange, with the historically even more obfuscated aspect of expropriation (Fraser 2016: 166). While exploitation may still operate under the guise of contractual agreements, expropriation entirely dispenses with this legal tenet, substituting contracts with conscription and confiscation. Considering the historical roots of capitalism, such as the primitive accumulation of colonialism or the unwaged labor of New World slavery, Fraser points toward the close correlation between expropriation and racial subordination that leads her to schematize this relation not only historically, but also structurally. In an interview with George Yancy she summarizes her argument as such:

> Capitalism harbors a deep-structural distinction, at once economic and political, between exploitation and expropriation, a distinction that coincides with "the color line." I can also state the point in a different way: the racializing dynamics of capitalist society are crystalized in the "mark" that distinguishes free subjects of exploitation from dependent subjects of expropriation. (2016: 172)

Apart from its structural entrenchedness in capitalism, Fraser identifies the ongoing legacy of slavery and colonialism mostly through its institutionalized forms such as segregation or Jim Crow, or the unequal exchange with, and unjust "structural adjustments" demanded of, post-independent African states. Without entirely unraveling this complex node of history and lived experience, her usage of the term "mark" also points toward the insidious way racialization harks back to and inhabits the body, the skin, the self: Fanon's racial epidermal schema.

When Ifemelu 'becomes Black' in America, it is not only, but crucially so, through an experience that couples a distinct historical with a distinct physical configuration – an experience wrought by race in/as history. It is a situation that reveals the disproportionate viability of certain bodies to expropriation, and it also expounds the problematic historicity of Black American womanhood. In sum, *Americanah*'s narrative emphasis on the encounter with the tennis coach scene is anything but coincidental but marks an engagement with Black American racialization from a particularly gendered perspective. *Americanah*'s more or less subtle investigation of Black subjectivity, as a carefully constructed exercise in intersectionality, affirms how class, gender, sexuality, and nationality all play into Ifemelu's experience of Blackness.

Although I would not want to extend the analogy too far by comparing Ifemelu's experience to the rape of enslaved women, mapping her narrative onto Harriet Jacobs's or suggesting that this incident signals something akin to her personal Middle Passage, I would still contend that, within the logic of the romance narrative, it indeed operates as a violent, traumatic break with her past that engenders an initial loss of self through the circling movement of racial melancholia. Crucially, however, this moment is followed by an almost cathartic route to self-affirmation and rebirth as soon as she stops trying to assimilate and confidently voices her own Africanness. Toward the end of the novel, Ifemelu finally tells Obinze about her traumatic experience. She opens with, "'I hated myself. I really hated myself. I felt like I had, I don't know, betrayed myself'," and concludes with the words: "'I remember it, but I don't dwell on it,'" claiming that she has passed from melancholy to mourning (439).

Before this is allowed to happen, however, Ifemelu experiences this "bitter Americanizing," characterized by the loss of home, her sense of identity, and her voice. After the incident, she is unable to reach out to Obinze. In fact, Nigeria and Obinze conflate, leaving her utterly uprooted: "She no longer read the news on Nigeria.com because each headline, even the most unlikely ones, somehow reminded her of Obinze" (159). In a way, this conscious forgetting of Obinze mimics the Americanization of enslaved Africans in what Homi Bhabha has referred to as the "syntax of forgetting" inherent in nation building (2004: 160). It is precisely this traumatic break with her past that forces her to grapple with America in a way that is distinct from both the "lost" generation of immigrants, who are fighting "on the Internet over their mythologies of home, because home was now a blurred place between here and there" (117), and the flexible, young Nigerians like Dike or Ginika, who have 'mastered' American culture simply because it has "seeped into [their] skin" (125).

Directly following her experience with the tennis coach, Ifemelu experiences her first snow,[70] announcing her ensuing depression:

---

[70] It is not difficult to infer a certain symbolism to "That night, it snowed," signaling how Ifemelu is cloaked in a hostile culture of whiteness, truly far from home. To this effect, it is a fairly well-established trope, from the snowstorm in Richard Wright's *Native Son*, leading to Bigger's arrest, and the various qualities of snow in Ralph Ellison's *Invisible Man*'s eviction scene, to the recurrent postcolonial theme of "snow on the cane fields." It is also quite common in contemporary African writing, with NoViolet Bulawayo's *We Need New Names* (2013) relying heavily on the symbolic significance of snow. Fanon, too, concludes the description of racial interpellation with a reference to snow: "My body was given back to me sprawled out, distorted, recolored,

That night, it snowed, her first snow, and in the morning, she watched the world outside her window, the parked cars made lumpy, misshapen, by layered snow. She was bloodless, detached, floating in a world where darkness descended too soon and everyone walked around burdened by coats, and flattened by the absence of light. The days drained into one another, crisp air turning to freezing air, painful to inhale. Obinze called many times but she did not pick up her phone. She deleted his voice messages unheard and his e-mails unread, and she felt herself sinking, sinking quickly, and unable to pull herself up. (155)

When she emerges from this depression, two chapters on, she has found her voice. And it is on the same day she decides to "stop faking an American accent" that she meets Blaine. Even though their paths will not cross again for years to come, Ifemelu is sure of the "significance to her meeting this man on the day she returned her voice to herself" (180). At this point, she considers herself to be better at distinguishing African Americans from other American Blacks, claiming that she has learned to detect "the fine-grained mark that culture stamps on people." Right away, Ifemelu "knows" that Blaine is "a descendent of the black men and women who had been in America for hundreds of years" (176). Perhaps this knowledge is gained through a certain aloofness, the kind of outsider's perspective that is perhaps the most salient aspect of the Afropolitan, that is: a subject position unencumbered by the 'not white – not quite' impasse, the impossible assimilation of the postcolonial or immigrant subject, but characterized instead by her own, insular sense of self that is perhaps best described as a global, Pan-African identity, gloriously emerging from what would otherwise threaten to crush her.

5 "An American Pathology": Reading *Americanah* as Quest Romance

As Adichie remarked in an interview about the novel: "I am more or less expected, or maybe permitted, to write about African pathology, but I don't think I am expected to write about American pathology" (Sehgal 2013: para. 21). At this point, it may be useful to distinguish what the novel's turn toward realism accomplishes, and where it resorts to the form of romance that, as Goyal summa-

---

clad in mourning in that white winter day" (86). The snow in *Americanah* also indicates Ifemelu's winter of the soul, the onset of the depression anticipated by the reference to Robert Frost's "Nothing Gold Can Stay" at the beginning of the chapter (144). This kind of overdetermined symbolism is rare in *Americanah*, but it clearly marks the significance of this caesura, affecting not only Ifemelu's life, but also the overall narrative momentum of the novel.

rizes, marks a "shift outside of realism into the sphere of the marvelous rather than the mundane, often organized around the motif of a quest into unknown territories (both physical and the uncanny zone of the self)" (2010: 13). If racism is America's pathology, what is the function or effect of the novel's engagement with it? Is it a means of diagnosis or does it, in part, even suggest a cure? And as such, does it fashion its cure as an antidote or a miracle?

On the one hand, Adichie paints her story from a particularly complex angle of America's racial landscape, at a particularly complex moment in time. Set at the onset of a proclaimed post-racial age in the US, it is written at a time when this very same proclamation serves as foil to the true shape of American racism. While, from a certain point of view, the US appears to be caught in the lock of a history wrought by slavery, Blackness never stays the same. The narratives, models, and modes of being Black change and multiply, both globally and in the US. Ifemelu, a "Bourgie Nigerian" (177) predominantly moving through "Postbourgie" (414) Black America, nevertheless witnesses first-hand how a certain, most dehumanizing form of Blackness refuses to leave the equation.

Therefore, the novel's realist description of America's racial landscape renders Ifemelu's hard-won experience of becoming Black in the US an exercise in attaining the informed, self-consciously metahistorical positionality of Afropolitanism. Her perspective allows her, while not to transcend it, at least to distance herself enough to not only *see* Blackness in this country, but to *know its name*. Analogous to her increasing class privileges, this positionality does not make her immune to racism, but it enables her to disassociate herself from it, at least partially, in order to critique it.

In some ways, the distance Ifemelu has gained speaks to the "psychological distance" Richard Wright detects between African Americans and their country, directly resulting from the experience of violent subjugation and slavery (1995: 81). But Ifemelu's position is, of course, different from such established models of race consciousness. One could say that Ifemelu is behind the veil but not of it and that this may allow her to not "really feel what she is writing about," to ward off the pathological danger of American racialization. Neither (merely) 'second-sight,' nor 'double consciousness,' the insights Ifemelu has gained only structurally resemble those of African Americans.[71] Regarding her own, intensely felt in-

---

[71] Here, I refer to this much quoted passage in Du Bois's *The Souls of Black Folk:* "After the Egyptian and Indian, the Greek and Roman, the Teuton and Mongolian, the Negro is a sort of seventh son, born with a veil, and gifted with second-sight in this American world, – a world which yields him no true self-consciousness, but only lets him see himself through the revelation of the other world. It is a peculiar sensation, this double-consciousness, this sense of always

stance of racialized gendered objectification, Ifemelu has apparently worked through her grief and exited the circling movement of melancholia. As such, the realism of the novel presents racism as a problem to be solved, or cured, at least for a character like Ifemelu.

However, it is altogether possible to frame Ifemelu's transformation in less realist and more fantastical terms in the same way in which race and racism can be rendered both real and tangible, and magically abstract. Similarly, as Brent Hayes Edwards notes in the introduction to *The Souls of Black Folk*, Du Bois's usage of the term "veil" suggested a move away from race as a purely sociological category toward a more mythical, obfuscated presence better described in the "spiritual vocabulary of German Romanticism" (Du Bois and Hayes Edwards 2007: xiv). *Americanah* also foregrounds its literary rather than sociological purport by couching its diagnosis of American racism – and Ifemelu's realist *Bildung* – within a romantic gesture toward Pan-Africanism and the logic of a fantastic quest-romance. The latter becomes particularly apparent both in the way that the subject of racialization connects to the novel's narrative structure, and in what I would describe as the novel's tone, which assumes a particular naiveté in order to voice a more 'truthful' image of American racism.

Despite its ostensive realism, *Americanah* formally functions like a romance, not only in the sense of genre fiction, but also in terms of the particular romance paradigm described by Northrop Frye. Identifying romance as indeed the "structural core of all fiction" (1976: 15), Frye's entry in *The Harper Handbook to Literature* defines it as "a continuous narrative in which the emphasis is on what happens in the plot, rather than on what is reflected from ordinary life or experience" (1997: 403). Besides its plot-driven narrative, *Americanah* is also characterized by what Frye describes as the mode of romance in *Anatomy of Criticism* (1957). As Fredric Jameson notes, Frye understands romance as "a wish fulfillment or utopian fantasy, which aims at the transfiguration of the world of everyday reality" (1975: 138). Interpreting *Americanah* as not only popular romance, but also as quest-romance, the novel thus turns "our attention to those elements in the ordinary world which must be transformed, if the earthly paradise is to reveal its lineaments behind it" (Jameson 1975: 138).

Barbara Fuchs, in her concise monograph on the subject, also identifies romance as a fundamental stratum of narrative, not necessarily in the archetypical sense proposed by Frye, but as narratological device or strategy of form and content. In line with Peter Brooks's assertion that the meaning of narratives may

---

looking at one's self through the eyes of others, of measuring one's soul by the tape of a world that looks on in amused contempt and pity" (2007: 8).

only be discernible "because we read them in anticipation of the structuring power of those endings that will retrospectively give them the order and significance of plot" (1984:94), *Americanah*'s ending crucially informs its quest romance plot. Examining the implications of Americanah's romantic return to Nigeria in terms of narrative strategy, it is worthwhile to focus also on the detours that make such a resolve possible. As Fuchs notes, most critics of romance "emphasize its ultimate wish-fulfillment while disregarding the often complex picture of suffering and subjugation that precedes the resolution" (2004: 29). If we look at *Americanah*'s ending according to the logic of a realist *Bildungsroman* as well as that of a quest romance, Ifemelu emerges not only as romantically and intellectually matured heroine, but also as someone who has undergone the arduous social process of 'becoming Black' in a foreign land. Tried and tested, Ifemelu thence returns to Nigeria, where she is allowed to step "off the plane in Lagos and [stop] being black" (475). Rather than reading this only as a rekindling of redemptive diasporic return or a disassociation of Blackness, this perspective on the novel's ending might draw attention to the "suffering and subjugation" Ifemelu has undergone in the US: she has been racialized.

Like the hero of a classical romance adventure, *Americanah*'s protagonist ventures into the dangerous, dreamlike realm that is US America, only that instead of witches and ogres she encounters the particularly stupefying, spellbinding power of what Karen and Barbara Fields, in their eponymous essay compendium on US-American race relations, have coined "racecraft." Both witchcraft and racecraft, they write, "are imagined, acted upon, and re-imagined, the action and imagining inextricably intertwined" (2014: 19). Pointing toward the particular pervasiveness of racism, its stubborn "efficacy" beyond rational realizations of race constructedness, they draw attention to the analogous relation between the two concepts, their mutual reliance on "circular reasoning, prevalence of confirming rituals, barriers to disconfirming factual evidence, self-fulfilling prophecies, multiple and inconsistent causal ideas, and colorfully inventive folk genetics" (Fields and Fields 2014: 198). And so, in *Americanah*, the "pervasive belief" in and of racecraft becomes the "mental terrain" that Ifemelu too must learn to navigate (ibid. 18).

This also affects the novel's particular tone and, for some, allows a reading of Ifemelu as voicing purportedly unheard of and never-noticed truths. Applied to the novel and its generic conventions, Ifemelu's stance toward US race relations adheres to the narrative tropes of romance, where "the hero's dominant trait is naiveté or inexperience" and his "most characteristic posture is that of bewilderment" (Jameson 1975: 139). Furthermore, the pose of the naïve and bewildered outsider is of course predetermined by the novel's generic anchoring in romance. Like the hero of romance, who is at first more of "an observer, a moral spectator surprised by supernatural conflict," Ifemelu too is "gradually drawn in, to reap the rewards of victory" (Jameson 1975: 139).

The story line of Ifemelu's race blog is particularly instructive here. At first, the blog is presented as a positive force in her life, a literalized transformation of her observational quest that gives her financial independence and amplifies her voice. As a textual medium, it also foregrounds the utopian promise of generating a feminist or subaltern counterdiscourse. While, in this fast-paced digital word, there is something quite dated about a literary character whose livelihood subsists in writing a successful blog, during the mid-2000s the notion of blogging arguably marked the idea, or rather ideal, of a new public sphere along with the hope for a theretofore-unknown inclusion of marginalized voices. In its ostentatious presentation as a platform for disenfranchised or structurally silenced voices, online discourse in the novel thus embodies the "counterpublic" or "alternative public spheres" envisioned by feminist scholars such as Rita Felski (1989) or Nancy Fraser (1990). Embodying the feminist dictum that the private is political, Ifemelu's observations on matters of race and racism are, with few exceptions, drawn from everyday life and personal experience. Mimetically, the main narrative of *Americanah*, Ifemelu's life in America, relates to the blog in a manner that also reveals the former's status as quest romance. For example, when Ifemelu writes about her relationships, she presents her partners as cultural tropes, referring to Curt as "Hot White Ex" and Blaine as "Professor Hunk." In the 'real life' of *Americanah*'s diegesis, the names *Curt* for her *courteous*, rich, WASP and *Blaine* for her *black*, Jazz-loving, political-science-teaching boyfriend also read like cyphers. As each of her partners opens up a new window into American race relations, they function as formulaic figures in her 'racial adventure story.'

Encapsulated in the somewhat naïve claim that Ifemelu came "from a country where race was not an issue" is the assumption that she had to "come to America" to 'become Black' and also to become the acclaimed race blogger leading a charmed financial existence. Ironically, the ability to see and name race, while allowing her to monitor and measure racist aggressions, ultimately enables her to transcend her dismal economic situation and social dependency. Set in the gold-digging era of digital content, Ifemelu's blog signifies the promise that a Black woman, and a non-citizen as such, can add her voice to the choir of public discourse, be individually heard, and eventually join the ranks of America's intellectual elite. This particular riff on the American Dream obviously draws much impetus from the post-race era in which it is set, but it also draws on an established immigrant narrative. Ifemelu's almost mythical journey from impoverished African student, living in a moldy apartment, to Princeton fellow, traveling the country on speaking gigs and owning a condominium, is as unrealistic as it is economically aspirational. It also renders her decision to leave this life behind, to sell both her lucrative blog and her condo in the midst of an unfolding, and unmentioned, financial crisis and leave the US for Nigeria, all the more interesting.

If racial capitalism is also "the process of deriving social and economic value from racial identity," then, paradoxically, Ifemelu can generate capital from performing a certain kind of Black racial identity, one that slots into the context of corporate diversity trainings and neoliberal multiculturalism (Leong 2013: 2189). In a sense, Ifemelu's later career runs on the currency of what Gilroy has described as "racial *Americana*" – a mode of talking about and indeed marketing race that, while repeatedly provincializing itself, simultaneously asserts its global reach (Fisher 2014: 210).[72] Clearly, the blog's financial success and political impact are not enough to sustain Ifemelu's sense of victory, of having successfully countered the evils of racecraft. On the contrary, this racial performance eventually appears to stump her character development and forestall her quest. As noted above, her sense of accomplishment regarding the blog eventually sours, rendering it "inconsequential" (354), and leaving her feeling "naked and false" (5).

In addition, the novel's plot and structure preordain its happy ending in a particular way, necessarily eclipsing a hopeful romance with America. The break with Obinze, caused by Ifemelu's experience of sexual exploitation and signaling the 'darkest night' of her adventure, prompts the major detours in her romantic quest. It is the plot point the novel has anticipated and worked toward. Set within the novel's frame narrative, which promises the imminent reunion of these star-crossed lovers, everything following the event triggers the kind of genre-typical, libidinous reading pleasure that arises from knowing that each and every detour will only bring the narrative closer to the inevitable end – a romantic climax made even sweeter by its deferral. Concerning the novel's ambiguous straddling of different genres, it is worthwhile to consider what their employment enables and what kind of conclusions it predetermines. Fundamentally, *Americanah* is a tale about a female heroine's move toward self-knowledge; it's a classic romantic adventure with a happy ending. It is also, as Adichie herself has claimed, "a gritty, taken-from-real-life book [...] about race." How do these aspects go together? How can there ever be a happy ending in race? The answer is, obviously, by having race end. Asked whether she con-

---

[72] This reach follows from the global circulation of commodified cultural objects, where rampant consumption, for example of Black music, strips these objects of their moral and political dimensions. See also Gilroy 2010.

tinues to write about race in her Nigerian blog, Ifemelu replies: "'No, just about life. Race doesn't really work here. I feel like I got off the plane in Lagos and stopped being black" (476).

6 "An Unapologetic Love Story": Adichie's Gendered Romance with Africa

Adichie herself has called *Americanah* an "unapologetic" love story, and it is indeed remarkable how extensively it adheres to and inverts the narrative strategies of romantic genre fiction (Sehgal 2013: para. 15). To offer some anecdotal insight, I once overheard two women in a café discussing the book. While the first woman thoroughly enjoyed the novel and its protagonists, the other found it "unrealistic" how romantically popular Ifemelu was, with each successive boyfriend getting "better," all of them "worshipping the ground under her feet." I can see how the generic rendering of Ifemelu as a flawed, but nevertheless fairly idealized heroine can be grating to some and deeply pleasurable to others. Yet, as I have argued, the novel employs different generic forms to a political effect, and it is worth examining the function of romantic genre fiction in *Americanah* beyond questions of 'high' and 'low,' marketability, or popularity.

Where the protagonist Ifemelu may deem Mills & Boon romances "silly" while nevertheless conceding to a "small truth in those romances" (*Americanah* 58), Adichie is more candid about her early passion for romantic genre fiction, claiming that she must have read "every Mills & Boon romance published before [she] was sixteen" (2014: 10). Elsewhere, she has called *Americanah* an "anti-Mills & Boon" novel, and her knowledge of the genre transpires clearly (Smith 2014: 00:21:23). Even without the intertexual and contextual references to romantic fiction, the novel can be linked to the genre of romance simply on behalf of what may be cursorily described as the readerly pleasure it evokes, as well as its form. It is not difficult to see how the "anti" in "anti-Mills & Boon" applies, considering a genre notorious for its reinforcement of traditional, perhaps even antifeminist gender roles. According to some critics, 20th-century feminist updatings of Mills & Boon or Harlequin novels have proven difficult, if not impossible, due to the genre's rigid scripting of male-female relationships. For many, the bone of contention is these novels' emphasis on female dependency. In one study on Mills & Boons fiction, Sandra Engler observes that "[f]emale independence is presented as an extremely undesirable attribute for a woman which prevents her from achieving her ultimate goal – marriage" (2004: 33).

Cursorily viewed, *Americanah* employs a marriage plot while withholding the marriage. Ifemelu and Obinze are reunited only for a brief period, after which Obinze ends the extramarital affair out of a sense of responsibility to his wife and daughter. Despite the ensuing heartbreak, we are told that Ifemelu, at some point, has finally "spun herself fully into being" (475) by finding a way to connect with and write about Lagos. On the very last page of the novel, Obinze appears on Ifemelu's doorstep and begs her to "give this a chance," and Ifemelu finally allows him to come in. Arguably, *Americanah* forecloses the goal of marriage only in so far that it is projected into an unnarrated future. Yet compared to the preceding account of Ifemelu's self-knowing, emotional, and financial independence, the ending, while romantic, appears as an anticlimactic afterthought. Though I would suspect most readers to be relieved at Obinze's reappearance, inviting us to at least imagine their future union, the sense of closure preceding the actual ending does intimate that *Americanah* may follow the plotline of the conventional love story, yet the only 'marriage' that occurs is that of Ifemelu and her sense of self and home.

Simply applied to the script of romantic genre fiction, this sort of rewriting would seem to be a somewhat obvious, unconvincing choice. Deferring the actual marriage and presenting an independent, self-confident heroine in lieu of a dependent bride merely updates this kind of plotting with a similarly clichéd fairy tale ending, namely that of the headstrong, self-reliant woman who defies social conventions – and finds love after all. Yet much of *Americanah* suggests that not (only) the romantic love for Obinze, but a romantic desire for Africa and Nigeria function as prime motivators or stand-in goals on Ifemelu's path to self-knowledge.

At the core of the novel's carefully crafted realism and its quest-romance-like structure lies a romantic gesture that makes it "an unapologetic love story" and allows Adichie to write about Africa in unexpected ways. Told in the language of everyday life, *Americanah* is a romantic love story, but it is also a romance in the fanciful and marvelous way that renders the heroine Ifemelu's quest for self-knowledge pleasurably unrealistic. Ifemelu's already fairly charmed existence in the Unites States is surpassed even by the happy ending Nigeria provides, where Ifemelu is able to quit a safe but boring editor's position in favor of writing a blog that eventually reads *"like poetry."* Only utopian fantasy could equip a protagonist with the arguably least lucrative literary occupation and still suspend disbelief. The blog, as the sole vehicle of Ifemelu's success and independence, notably evolves from the engagé American race blog that threatened to strip Ifemelu of her identity, to a grounded and grounding, 'authentic' representation of life in Nigeria. The Nigerian incarnation of her blog, titled *The Small Redemptions of Lagos*, initially features posts that maintain her "provok[ing]" (415), "self-righteous" (435) style of social commentary. With time, she begins to write about Lagos as it presents itself to her. Still suffering from the breakup with Obinze, Ifemelu almost therapeutically writes her new self into existence.

The opening chapter of *Americanah* already highlights the significance of Nigerian soil for Ifemelu's sense of identity. Voicing her creeping dissatisfaction with American life, Ifemelu describes her homesickness as a "dull ache of loss" causing "amorphous longings, shapeless desires" (6). Indistinguishable from the fact that it is also where Obinze is, Nigeria becomes for her "where she was supposed to be, the only place she could sink her roots in without the constant urge to tug them out and shake off the soil" (ibid.). When Ifemelu returns after being away for over a decade, she needs time to adapt to the dazzling urbanity of Lagos, a place so overpowering and energetic that the US, particularly her former life in Princeton, seems bucolic in comparison. Yet whatever processes of maturity she has undergone in America, this is where her new self is truly hatched: "Here, she felt, anything could happen, a ripe tomato could burst out of solid stone. And so she had the dizzying sensation of falling, falling into the new person she had become, falling into the strange familiar" (385).

Lagos is shown to be a dynamic, ever changing place that is nevertheless home. It becomes the desired locus for a fluctuant self's need to be in touch with itself, know itself, and find an authentic voice. In this respect, the novel clearly rehashes a notion of Africa as rejuvenating and rooting and of diasporic return as an authenticating experience. However, by stressing the vibrancy of Lagos, along with the "dizzying" sensation of falling and "sp[inning] herself into being," Adichie is careful to distinguish this familiar diasporic trope from the kind that aligns Africa with the idea of a stable, traditional, and unchanging essence. Careful not to perpetuate a certain romantic desire for Africa, at this point in particular the realism of the narrative is asked to bear the weight of *Americanah*'s romantic thrust.

The change that Ifemelu has undergone, while rendering her more 'authentic,' mirrors Nigeria's pulsating and unpredictable potential, that of a literally young country on the cusp of a new era. Katherine Hallemeier reads the novel as a challenge to the assumption that the United States remains "at the center of economic and cultural geopolitics," because, for her, "*Americanah* presents an alternative, utopic vision of global power in which the United States stands as a foil to the promising future of late Nigerian capitalism" (2015: 231). While Adichie's careful observations of class relations in Euro-American and Nigerian contexts indeed point toward an image of Nigeria as a socioeconomically distinct, if not rivaling, hub of global capitalism, I would still want to retain the unavoidably hegemonic role the United States takes on in the racial discourse that structures *Americanah* in as many and perhaps more important ways than economic or class discourses.

Compared with vibrant and young Nigeria, America is represented as bucolic and sleepy and appears downright archaic in its tribalism and racist lore. For the novel's predominantly 'Western' reader, contemporary Nigeria thus appears as strange but familiar locus, driven by the creative destruction of capitalism rather than being pulled back by the feudal mythology of racism. Here, the novel employs the alleged "archaism and fantasy of racism" that Bhabha detects in prominent writings on modernity by Foucault and Anderson (2004: 358). Yet the novel moves it from the colonial site in which Anderson sees it being acted out to the alleged endpoint of Western progress itself – America. Reversing the script, Nigeria emerges as the supremely rational nation state, and the fateful ties of racism and capitalism appear consciously, and wishfully, uncoupled. Framed though the temporal discourse of race and progress, the novel's ending thus becomes even more crucial, relying heavily on the hopeful, futuristic thrust of romance and signifying a decidedly progressive, alternative historical arc.

From a diasporic perspective, one that addresses a diasporic audience and is located within the already alternative spatio-temporal mappings of the Black Atlantic, *Americanah*'s ending serves yet another purpose. Its invocation of the fantasy of return, along with the promise of rootedness and self-knowledge, performs a similarly "compensatory" function to that of the fantasy of unconditional love Janice Radway identifies in typical romantic genre fiction (1984: 88–95). Yet the gendered emphases of this genre also allow the novel to remove its rose-tinted glasses with regards to gender equality and sexism, showing instead the multiple ways in which Nigerian women from all rungs of society are stifled and stumped in their development. Read thus, Nigeria may be presented as the future, but it is far from perfect. Here, the novel employs a bleaker vision of post-independence and a similar critique of postcolonial progress to the one issued by McClintock:

> In a world where women do 2/3 of the world's work, earn 10% of the world's income, and own less than 1% of the world's property, the promise of "post-colonialism" has been a history of hopes postponed. It has generally gone unremarked that the national bourgeoisies and kleptocracies that stepped into the shoes of "post-colonial" "progress," and industrial "modernization" have been overwhelmingly and violently male. (1992: 92)

In sum, the novel's unequivocally gendered anchoring, the love story, becomes the most interesting lens through which to view Africa and its diaspora. This also corresponds with the fact that Adichie is an outspokenly feminist writer and, while her politics are of course distinct from its earlier incarnations, also a Pan-Africanist.

Alongside her literary works, Adichie has published two book-length essays, both on the matter of feminism. First an adapted version of her popular TED talk

We Should All Be Feminists in 2014, following in the slipstream of *Americanah*, and a second slim volume titled *Dear Ijeawele, or A Feminist Manifesto in Fifteen Suggestions* (2017). Subsequently, Adichie collaborated with high fashion brand Christian Dior, who printed the TED talk title turned pop sample turned bestselling essay on t-shirts and sent it down the run way. For all the ease with which Adichie literally wears the feminist label, she has repeatedly distanced herself from what she calls "academic feminism," criticizing it for being "too jargony" and "exclusive" and claiming that she has learned much more "about feminism from watching the women traders in the market in Nsukka [...] than from reading any seminal feminist text" (2015: para. 44). In a similar vein, she ends *We Should All Be Feminists* by describing her great-grandmother as a feminist *avant la lettre*, thus rejecting the notion of feminism as an exclusively Western concept.

While Adichie's concerns could be interpreted as a critique of institutionalized Western feminism's global validity and failure to incorporate different realities, she has equally distanced herself from Black feminist terms that have sought to do just that. Yet Adichie's own avowal that she is "angrier about sexism than [...] about racism" is better understood in the context of her Pan-Africanist feminism, signaling less a normative ranking of oppression than an unfaltering commitment to Nigeria and its immediate political matters (2017b: 23). Particularly her understanding of feminism as indigenous to African societies mirrors the concerns of African feminists before her. In defining African feminism, Nnaemeka stresses how "it is not to Western feminism but rather to the African environment that one must refer. African feminism is not reactive; it is proactive. It has a life of its own that is rooted in the African environment. Its uniqueness emanates from the cultural and philosophical specificity of its provenance" (1998: 9). Nnaemeka's position might also help to contextualize Adichie's skepticism toward feminist theory. While cautioning against an uncritical rejection of "theory per se" and a "stance that is so staunchly antitheory that it leaves no room for any engagement with theory" (2004: 358), Nnaemeka also asserts the practical, grassroots dimension of African feminism, or what she calls nego-feminism, meaning negotiation, "no ego" feminism (2004: 357–385).

Regarding other prominent African feminists, it is striking how similar many of Adichie's positions are to those of Ghanaian writer Ama Ata Aidoo. Aidoo, whom Adichie has repeatedly called a literary role model, has often pointed to the existence of feminist structures in African societies, prior to or outside of Western influence. Asked about the prominent role of outspoken female protagonists in her work, Aidoo insists: "If the women in my stories are articulate, it is because that is the only type of women I grew up among. And I learnt those first feminist lessons in Africa from African women" (Frías 2003: 27). Likewise, when Adichie distances herself from the term womanism, perhaps as a theoretical stand in for African American feminist theories, we can hear an echo of Aidoo distancing herself from the term in conversation with Alice Walker. And, the commonplaceness of the statement notwithstanding, even the title of Adichie's TED Talk seems to reiterate Aidoo's definition of feminism: "When people ask me bluntly every now and then whether I am a feminist, I not only answer yes, but I go on to insist that every woman and every man should be a feminist – especially if they believe that Africans should take charge of African land, wealth, African lives, and the burden of African development" (1998: 39). The latter half of this quote is an important qualification that further aligns the two author's political positionalities.

Having been intellectually raised during the vibrant era of African independences, Aidoo is very much a product of her time and an outspoken Pan-Africanist. In contrast to preceding intellectual movements such as Négritude, Aidoo eschews a "romanticisation of Africa's past as some exotic golden age," as Victor Odamtten notes in *The Art of Ama Ata Aidoo* (1994: 10). Instead, Aidoo dedicates herself to the concrete political advancement of her home country and continent – to the point of becoming Ghana's Minister of Education in 1982. Adichie too, has referred to herself as politically Pan-African, stating that, "for me, that means I care about what's happening in Kenya, I care about the people in Bahia, Brazil [...] I'm interested in Afro-Colombia [...] because there's a familiarity there to something I feel connected to" (2017a 00:38:27).

Aidoo's Pan-African politics are inseparable from her commitment to feminism, and Adichie's purportedly global feminism is also affected by Pan-African sensibilities. Yet it is in their fictional works that these concerns are most organically interwoven and the analogies between Adichie and Aidoo are particularly striking. Since the late 1960s, Aidoo has become one of the most renowned female African writers, with plays such as *Dilemma of a Ghost* (1965) and *Anowa* (1970) or short story collections such as *No Sweetness Here* (1995) or *Diplomatic Pounds* (2012); narratives that, similar to Adichie's work, focus almost exclusively on the lives of young African women. Her most read work to this date, however, remains *Our Sister Killjoy*, published in 1977.

The novel traces the European travels of its protagonist Sissie, who dissects the former colonial center with biting precision, reversing the gaze, as it were, through the particular optic of a "Black-eyed Squint." *Our Sister Killjoy*, written a decade before its publication, obviously denotes a different historical constellation. The waned importance of England as the colonial mother country – yielding to the increased cultural and economic allure of the US in *Americanah* – is only the most apparent marker for the passing of time. However, the structural and thematic similarities between *Americanah* and *Our Sister Killjoy* are ample. There is the notion of the inverted colonial travel narrative, as well as the rejection or reversal of racialization, where, as Cheryl Sterling notes, "Sissie's response realigns the specular burden, for now Africa looks back and finds that the Western world too is lacking" (2010: 136). Yet the two novels are equally critical of homespun ills, such as political mismanagement, corruption, or the effects of the African brain drain to the West. Where the term 'Americanah' mocks the haughtiness of a particular type of Nigerian returnee, *Our Sister Killjoy* exposes the phoniness of the "been-tos," who speak of the "wonders of being overseas, pretending their tongues craved for tasteless foods" (Aidoo 1977: 90).

Both novels also exhibit the kind of generic experimentation that has left critics unsure about the mimetic relation between its literary form, the novel's diegesis, and the authors' politics. Where *Americanah* clearly distinguishes blog posts from the main narrative, in *Our Sister Killjoy* the already fairly lyrical, third-person chronological account of Sissie's travels is interspersed with a highly poetic choric commentary. While Odamtten suggests that the text's heavily ironic inflections hinder the kind of reading that would allow for a conflation of author and text, Sterling interprets the multilayered narrative structure of *Our Sister Killjoy* as a self-conscious performance of political discourse, pitting itself "against constructions of subjectivity, primacy and power" (Sterling 2010: 134). Yet similar to the way that *Americanah*'s blog posts allow for an ambiguous reading of performed authorship, Sterling concedes that "we are left to wonder if the voice is an externalization of Sissie's interiority, a psychic venting of the colour-coded frustration generated in her journey or a device Aidoo improvises from the oral tradition [...] or even if Aidoo is blatantly embedding her own political position into the text" (Sterling 2010: 134).

Where the commentary of the chorus often puts Sissie's confident and sarcastic, and at times essentializing and condemning, voice into question, *Americanah* creates a similar effect by having the prose action displace the authority of the blog posts. In her reading of Aidoo's novel, Goyal explores the split between the two textual voices as an ambiguous and tense attitude toward Africa and its diaspora (*Romance* 2010: 188–92). While one denotes a historically linear trajectory that places (Pan-African) hope in the nation state and views diaspora as loss, the other expresses a more expansive and more pessimist view on the global effects of racism and colonialism and frames migration as transhistorical inevitability. In *Americanah* too, we find conflicting yet distinct attitudes toward the African Diaspora, the most obvious one represented by the novel's romantic arc. As I have argued, it is Ifemelu's return home and ability to see and write truthfully, past race and "like poetry" that functions as the novel's final *dénouement*. Not only Ifemelu's new blog, *The Small Redemptions of Lagos*, but also the narrative itself reads like a complicated but dedicated love letter to Africa. This is another aspect the novel shares with *Our Sister Killjoy*, the fourth and final section of which is titled "A Love Letter."

Here, the narrative voice changes from the previous, poetically punctuated travelogue to an epistolary farewell written by a finally returning Sissie and addressed to her African lover in Europe. While abounding with romantic terms of endearment, most of the letter's content revolves around various disagreements, in particular the scene of their first meeting, where Sissie engages in a lengthy argument with a group of expatriate Africans at a student union. Sissie chides them for their self-exile and urges that "instead of forever gathering together and victoriously spouting such beautiful radical analyses of the situation of home, we should simply hurry back" (121). While, as Goyal notes, at this point Sissie clearly holds a "cultural nationalist view of diaspora as betrayal" (2010: 199), we are also presented with her interlocutors' contrary positions, including that of her lover, as well as Sissie's own doubts and reservations.

This multiplicity of voices does not quite perform the same destabilizing role of the choir in the book's other parts, where the authority of Sissie's position is undercut by a broader view of history. When her lover attests her an "anti-western-neurosis" (119) or accuses her of being melancholically locked in time (113), these arguments are oftentimes echoed and countered by Sissie's self-reflective stream of consciousness. Sissie appears aware of the potential presumption of her "righteous anger" (121) and, when imagining a pre-colonial idyll where she and her lover could have met, she stops herself short of becoming lost in "nostalgia and sentimental nonsense" (115). The final iteration of Sissie's knowledge quest is thus characterized by the kind of commitment to Africa that requires her physical return. Interpreting *Our Sister Killjoy*'s ending as an unequivocal Pan-African celebration of return, Sterling notes that, "since her true love is Africa, Sissie is intertwined in its history and its destiny" (2010: 148).

However, Sissie's candid reflections on the conflicts shaping her romantic relationship represent a conflicted relation to Africa and the diaspora. Her love letter is framed by two short sections that further suggest that the actual addressee and subject matter of Sissie's love letter is Africa and that this message is also important for its diaspora. The opening passage reads like an anecdote, a common joke even in its vagueness, describing the encounter of a visiting African professor and a young African American student, eager to hear of Africa's, notably Egypt's, past glories in an attempt to refute what he must see as the root cause of racism: The Western denigration or conscious erasure of Africa's role in world history. Yet in his earnest desire to set records straight, he threatens to reduce Africa to a mere symbol once again, if not of lack then of monolithic essence. Hence, the professor's answer:

> My dear young man [...], to give you the decent answer your anxiety demands, I would have to tell you the detailed history of the African continent. And to do that, I would have to speak every day, twenty-four hours a day, for at least three thousand years. And I don't mean to be rude or anything, but who has that kind of time? (111)

As a prologue to Sissie's love letter, this exchange reads like a refusal to offer finite and limited positions in a nevertheless encompassing Pan-African stance, while setting the tone for a difficult intradiasporic conversation. The very last passage of the novel reverts to the previous third-person narrative and describes how Sissie, her plane approaching the continent of Africa, decides never to post the letter:

> There was no need to mail it. It was not necessary. [...] Besides, she was back in Africa. And that felt like fresh honey on the tongue: a mixture of complete sweetness and smoky roughage. Below was home with its unavoidable warmth and even after these thousands of years, its uncertainties. 'Oh, Africa. Crazy old continent [...].' (133)

Like Adichie, Aidoo is wary of perpetuating romantic notions of Africa. As Goyal notes, Sissie is "careful to articulate both her resistance to the West and her commitment to Africa without invoking a pre-colonial idyll" (2010: 202). At the same time, Sissie's bird's eye view of Africa, "huge [...], certainly warm and green" (*OSK* 133), evokes the mythic image of a pastoral, fertile African soil, the place where Ifemelu in *Americanah* longs to "sink her roots." Similarly, the strong sensory imagery in *Our Sister Killjoy*'s final paragraphs could easily collapse into the kind of romantic idealization that links Africa to physicality and affect and harks back to Négritude thinker Senghor's notion of the reciprocal relation between African soil and culture, resulting in the "physio-psychology of the Negro" that renders him [sic] "the man of Nature [...], sensual, a being with open senses" (1956: 52). Yet Aidoo counters such readings, which emphasize an eternal and essential "primacy of intuitive knowledge," with Sissie's understanding of the very unknowability of a vast continent in motion, the sheer potentiality of which surpasses, and perhaps even overwhelms, any attempt at sensual or intellectual mastery (ibid.).

The ending of *Our Sister Killjoy*, culminating in a romantic return that forecloses a romantic union with a lover, is notably similar to *Americanah*'s final part in Lagos. Equally similar are the protagonists' representations of Africa as a virtually unpredictable, vibrant space of possibilities that defies various historical scripts, not only the Eurocentric model of Africa's eternal backwardness, or the Afrocentric fixation with some form of pre-modern innocence, but also the pessimist gloom of the immediate post-independence era that equally locks the continent in a deterministic limbo. At the same time, Adichie and Aidoo are not in the business of rebranding Africa simply to up its market value, as their political love letters to Africa are engaged in complicating the continent while committing to its futures, not its predetermined destiny.

To this end, it is worthwhile to reconsider Ifemelu's description of Lagos: "Here, she felt, anything could happen, a ripe tomato could burst out of solid stone. And so she had the dizzying sensation of falling, falling into the new person she had become, falling into the strange familiar." On the one hand, the passage stresses the abovementioned dynamism and unpredictability of contemporary Nigeria in a defamiliarizing imagery that converges both stability and insecurity, newness and oldness. At the same time, the passage echoes another text by Aidoo, namely her 1970 play *Anowa*. The play centers on the eponymous heroine and her husband Kofi Ako and is set on the Gold Coast circa 1870, a period characterized by the effects of the Bond Treaty of 1844 that granted Britain exclusive trading rights in the area today known as Ghana and that fatally allied Fante slavers and British colonialists in the transatlantic slave trade. Anowa, who has married Kofi against her parents' will and was hence expelled from her family and community, becomes increasingly estranged from and dissatisfied with her husband and his role in the trade. She empathizes with the enslaved people he deals with, euphemistically referred to as "wayfarers." Using the term for herself, she asks Kofi: "What is the difference between any of your men and me? Except that they are men and I'm a woman? None of us belongs" (*Anowa*: 97).

As in her previous play, *The Dilemma of a Ghost*, Aidoo explores Ghana's role in the slave trade as a haunting and uncomfortable feature of diasporic estrangement. In *Anowa*'s most notable scene, the childless Anowa recounts having dreamed of being "a big big woman," out of whom "poured men, women and children" (106). In her dream, she embodies "Mama Africa" losing her children to the "boiling hot" sea and its pink-faced lobster people, who seize and violently destroy them. Finally, she concludes: "Any time there is mention of a slave, I see a woman who is me and a bursting of a ripe tomato or a swollen pod" (107).

Coincidently or not, the unusual imagery of the bursting tomato links both authors' aspirations to depict Africa in its defamiliarizing complexity, and to engage in a Pan-African or diasporic conversation that holds up to its conflicting contemporary and historical trajectories. To this effect, Aidoo's intentional usage and subtle reworking of the figure of the African mother is a pronounced feature of her writing, not only in *Anowa* but also in *Our Sister Killjoy*, where Sissie mocks the African self-exiles' sentimental mobilizing of "the mother thing" in order to justify their foreign stay (122).

No metaphor for Africa is more overused than that of the African mother, simultaneously standing in for the proverbial motherland and the genealogy of its people. *Our Sister Killjoy*'s protagonist Sissie equally makes use of this image when she angrily rebukes: "Of course she has suffered, the African mother [...]. Just look at what's happening to her children over the last couple of hundred years." She then recounts the ill fate of Africa's children on both sides of the Atlantic (123). In her discussion of the novel, Goyal comments on this passage as follows: "Sissie extends the particular, local situation to a broader, diasporic one, seeing black history as a global one. Invoking the global history of the diaspora, she recalls the pain of slavery, rape, poverty, service in colonial armies, and cultural alienation" (2010: 201). It is quite significant, Goyal notes, that Sissie ends her litany of historical atrocities with the image of the "been-to" grandchild, who is so alienated from Africa that it cannot even speak its (grand)mother tongue. This decidedly critical view of migration is not absent from *Americanah*, despite the novel's generally more migratory and cosmopolitan sensibilities.

While Ifemelu is, of course, herself an *Americanah*, a modern day 'been-to,' there is one character who firmly embodies both the critical stance and the maternal stereotype: Obinze's mother, a university professor and single parent. Ifemelu is not only impressed with her knowledge and independence but indeed with her African femininity. Upon their first meeting, her image and that of a popular Nigerian singer conflate in Ifemelu's imagination, causing Ifemelu to swoon at her "full-nosed, full-lipped beauty, her round face framed by a low Afro, her faultless complexion the deep brown of cocoa" (68). As a child, Ifemelu had already "guiltily fantasize[d]" about her father being married to the beautiful singer instead of her mother (69). Now, Obinze's mother becomes an equally idealized maternal figure, the kind of African mother who is deeply connected to her cultural heritage, who cooks *garri* and soup asks Ifemelu to translate her Igbo name, but who is also strongly committed to the future of her country, particularly the future of its girls. It is Obinze's mother who, similar to Aidoo's Sissie, repeatedly mourns the brain drain to the West and issues a particular warning to Ifemelu about not jeopardizing her education through an unwanted pregnancy.

Both critical and loyal toward the nation state, Obinze's mother also displays a Pan-African or diasporic commitment. When an old Jamaican woman in London calls Obinze "brother," he wants to call his mother and tell her about it (255). Similarly, in the US, when Ifemelu experiences conflicting processes of 'becoming Black,' she remembers watching *Roots* at Obinze's house, and also how "she had felt lacking, watching Obinze's mother, and wishing that she, too, could cry" (137). Almost to the point of cliché, Obinze's mother embodies Mother Africa weeping for the loss of her children, now and then. Yet it is her matured sense of solidarity in a global Black imaginary that also inspires Ifemelu's own process of maturity.

7 "This Shared Space of Africanness": The Hair Salon as Afropolitan Heterotopia

Americanah is a diasporic novel that explicitly negotiates different Black epistemologies. While acceding to the constitutive force of an afterlife of slavery, the novel also investigates other moments of race in/as history, and it proffers other forms of Blackness: communal, diverse, Pan-African. At times, we can detect a strained but nevertheless existent notion of a feminist Pan-African solidarity, in the continental sense of the term, as well as the glimpses of a global frame for Blackness that is contingent upon the contradictory multiplicity of the diaspora. To this effect, it is worth revisiting the first chapter. Opening with the line, "Princeton, in the summer, smelled of nothing," Ifemelu travels, imaginatively, to various other places on the East Coast, comparing their various odors to the unmarkedness of Princeton. She is making her way to Trenton to braid her hair because it "was unreasonable to expect a braiding salon in Princeton" (3). Ifemelu is traveling from a culturally white space, with all the privileges it entails, into a Black, feminized space, with all the difficulties it entails.

The journey recounted is reminiscent of Cherríe Moraga's Preface to *This Bridge Called My Back – Writings of Radical Women of Power*, a profoundly influential anthology on so-called Third World Feminism that inaugurated a crucial and ongoing paradigm shift in Anglo-American feminist theory. While Adichie has repeatedly stated that she has never read feminist theory, she might have read this text. As Ifemelu transitions from a platform where everyone is "white and lean, in short, flimsy clothes," to a platform where most are "black people, many of them fat, in short flimsy clothes," the reader is introduced to the *"irreverent, hectoring, funny and thought-provoking"* voice of her blog, a metonymic stand in for Ifemelu's coming to race consciousness in the US (4–5). Similarly, Moraga describes the journey from "the white suburbs of Watertown, Massachusetts," to "Black Roxbury" as her own coming-to-terms with privilege, with female and feminist desire (1981: xiii). Encapsulated in these complex realizations is the demand for a "movement that helps me make some sense of the trip from Waterford to Roxbury, from white to Black. I love women the entire way, beyond a doubt" (Moraga 1981: xiv). Anticipated, at the end of Moraga's journey are the contours of a hard-won, consciously established kind of sisterhood or feminist solidarity.

Ifemelu's own feminist journey does not end with her arrival in the Trenton hair salon. While her social mobility has allowed her to transcend the barriers of racialized urban space, once she finds herself among this involuntary community of predominantly Black women, Ifemelu faces other, less tangible boundaries of class, ethnicity, and nationality. During the course of her stay, Ifemelu manages to move from class condescendence to emphatic, ethical solidarity without collapsing these borders through what Chandra Mohanty criticizes as "vague assumptions of sisterhood or images of complete identification with the other" (2004: 3).

Instead, the hair salon solidarity is forged despite and through vast differences, highlighting how the "most expansive and inclusive visions of feminism need to be attentive to borders while learning to transcend them" (Mohanty 2004: 2). In this, the salon becomes something of a test card for a particular Afro-feminist utopia, or, in the sense of Michel Foucault's heterotopia, an "effectively enacted utopia" (Foucault 1986: 24). It is the kind of real and concrete space that is curiously linked to all sorts of other spaces and times while retaining a somewhat mythical timelessness and placelessness. This deceptively generic African hair salon in Trenton, New Jersey, miraculously bundles the multiple locations and temporalities of the Black Diaspora – including the current contradictions and contestations that mark the moment of Afropolitanism.

The multilocality of the salon in *Americanah* is self-evidenced by the way it links the various routes and roots of the people inhabiting it. It also transpires through the fact that – in countless cosmopolitan cities around the world – there are spaces just like it, mapping the coordinates of the diaspora as what it truly is: "the shape of the globe" (Wright 2013: 15). It also, crucially, reveals the historicity of transnational Black culture, linking what is thought of as "traditionally African" styles with modern fashions, and rendering Afropolitanism a constellation through which both the effects of 1960s 'Black is Beautiful' movements and contemporary African migration become visible. While these salons aren't new phenomena, they do bear a heightened significance in their relation to the contemporary 'Natural Hair movement,' as an expression of transnational Black culture. As Julie Iromuanya writes:

> Because the movement and its associated industry have been disseminated globally in fashion magazines, television, film, and other forms of commercial media, the Natural Hair movement is as much a political orientation and industry as it is a representation of the preeminence of global black popular culture." (2017: 168)[73]

---

[73] In her discussion of the hair braiding salon in *Americanah*, Iromuanya notes that the contemporary "Natural Hair movement, and the dot-com-era celebration of Africentric aesthetics" (2017: 167), rely heavily on the tropes of self-reliance and autonomy and therefore threaten the livelihood of these kinds of salons. However, she also concedes that the hair salon in *Americanah* successfully bridges the movement's by and large middle-class lifeworld with that of the working-class African immigrant.

As a subplot framing the novel's primary narrative, the hair braiding salon takes on a distinct metadiegetic significance. Whilst Ifemelu's and Obinze's life stories unfold over decades and continents, the chronotope of the salon remains more or less unchanged, a spatiotemporal constant. The salon is described as a fairly dilapidated, crowded little shop, confirming nearly all of Ifemelu's preconceptions:

> [I]t would look, she was sure, like all the other African hair braiding salons she had known: they were in a part of the city that had graffiti, dank buildings and no white people, they displayed bright signboards with names like Aisha and Fatima African Hair Braiding, they had radiators that were too hot in the winter and air conditioners that did not cool in the summer, and they were full of Francophone West African women braiders, one of whom would be the owner and speak the best English and be deferred to by the others. (9)

In fact, the salon is so badly ventilated – the air sticky and thick and "seething with heat" (103) – that time itself appears to congeal and move more slowly and Ifemelu's six-hour stay frays into a delirious, dreamlike haze. While Ifemelu's mind wanders in and out of her memories, the literal weaving of strands converges with the weaving of narrative strands, signified in the distinctly gendered metaphor of hair. Launching the temporal porosity of the salon chronotope, hair is the Proustian madeleine that triggers Ifemelu's memory of her mother's hair and her Nigerian childhood. Where, before, Ifemelu had been vaguely pondering her future in Nigeria, anxiously interpreting any positive projection of Nigeria as "an augury of her return home" (13), her braider Aisha's comment on her supposedly hard, unrelaxed hair strikes a delicate nerve and fully transports Ifemelu back to Lagos, where she "had grown up in the shadow of her mother's hair[...], black-black, so thick it drank two containers of relaxer at the salon" (41).

Merging different "slices in time" (Foucault 1986: 26), the hair salon is open to the kind of narrative heterochrony that links the future, past, and present of Ifemelu's life in particular, and the African or Black Diaspora in general. As a heterotopic space fusing the private and the public, the hair salon is also fully permeated by the "hidden presence of the sacred" (Foucault 1986: 23). Here, Ifemelu remembers how her mother, caught up in fundamentalist religious fervor, had one day cut her bounteous hair off and burned it "where she burned her used sanitary pads" (41). When Ifemelu later describes how she and other Black women involved with the online natural hair movement talk about hair in quasi-religious terms, admitting that she "had never talked about God so much," the link between femininity, religion, Blackness, and hair is further established (213).[74]

Hair is the common denominator bringing together women from all rungs of society in a way that confronts Ifemelu with the oftentimes stifling yet cozy expectations of "shared Africanness" and her own admission of the "perverse pleasure" gained from classist self-exaltation (103). The hair salon also stages the somewhat stereotypical tensions between African American and African women, as well as the prejudices prevailing amongst different African nationalities and ethnicities, and the power imbalance behind the one white middle class customer's "aggressively friendly" confidence and the shop owner's submissive, immigrant eagerness (189). The same character lectures Ifemelu on the quaintness of *Things Fall Apart* and the aptness of Naipaul's *A Bend in the River* in showing "how modern Africa works" (ibid.). Ifemelu is particularly irritated by her purported belief "that she was miraculously neutral in how she read books, while others read emotionally," drawing up well-established battle lines between 'Africa' and the 'West.' In many ways, the hair braiding salon contains a space of conflict and contradictions, where the contours of each individual strand remain visible despite and through the ostensive harmony of the braid.

The salon is also the space that allows us to glimpse diasporic pasts, presents, and futures and where, magically, a moment of true solidarity seems possible. Immediately after Ifemelu leaves the salon, she learns about Dike's attempted suicide. While this may appear as the novel's most tragic incident, I would argue that the preceding scene is much more emotionally rendered, and perhaps infinitely more tragic. In the beginning, Aisha hadn't been more much more to Ifemelu than blog fodder for an imagined post on "How the Pressures of Immigrant Life Can Make You Act Crazy" (18). Aisha is rendered strange, irrevocably different and a little repulsive even with her flaming skin condition. While Ifemelu does not want to be "dragged further into Aisha's morass," toward the end of the braiding session she is moved to feel with and acknowledge Aisha's plight (354).

On an intellectual level, Ifemelu already understands the very concrete differences between them, including the fact that she owns a green card and financial independence whereas Aisha does not. But her overall "irritation

---

[74] From an equally gendered and racialized, albeit male, perspective, the African American barbershop has drawn extensive scholarly attention and is often theorized as a pronouncedly political, public space. Likewise, the religious or spiritual connotations of its particular privileging of orality and testimony must not be overlooked. See Mills 2013 or Harris-Lacewell 2004. For an extensive cultural discussion of Black hair, see Byrd and Tharps 2001.

dissolve[s]" into "a gossamered sense of kinship," and she emotionally connects with Aisha's fear of never seeing her sick mother again (363). Ifemelu promises to help by speaking to the Igbo boyfriend with green card papers who refuses to marry Aisha. For a moment, we are led to believe that Ifemelu will wield her personal influence in favor of a stranger. Then, however, Aunty Uju calls with the bad news about Dike, and Aisha is permanently forgotten. This fragile moment – marked by one woman's silent collapse "into despair" and another's inability to "get up and leave" – limns the shape of a Pan-African feminist solidarity that is yet to come (364). It remains limited to the minor cosmopolitan or Afropolitan space of the hair salon, similar to Farouq's internet café in *Open City*. The novel's rendering of the hair salon as a somewhat surreal, effectively utopian space works toward experiencing this stunted plotline as neither particularly jarring, or dissatisfying, nor morally reprehensible on Ifemelu's part. Depending on the angle, Ifemelu has either woken from a utopian dream or awoken into the nightmare of a racist reality.

The communality circumscribed in the utopian diasporic space of the hair salon also serves as a buffer to Ifemelu's individualized success story, which could easily lend itself to the post-racial and post-feminist claims of the neoliberal subject. Already, these claims are frequently projected onto the lives of the Afropolitan, metropolitan, or "Nigerpolitan" – as *Americanah* dubs them – elites of post-Independence African nations. Despite the arguably fantastic element to Ifemelu's economic success, *Americanah* does offer a nuanced investigation of gendered labor and the heightened, systemic vulnerability of certain bodies, particularly female and particularly Black or of color. At the same time, this vulnerability can become a condition for feminist solidarity. As a testing ground for the limits of empathy, the hair braiding salon has already provided Ifemelu with the bitter realization that some subject positions are rarely challenged in their assumptions of objective normativity, a character trait that is particularly noteworthy because Obinze had once ascribed it to Ifemelu herself. Given her propensity for "thinki[ng] everyone is like [her]," Ifemelu's experience in racially stratified and relentlessly racializing American society is all the more insulting to her sense of selfhood (92). In her review of the novel, Ruth Franklin notes the novel's foregrounding of Ifemelu's potential to be "a privileged white woman who does not notice another's agony" (2013: 42). Yet through the novel's privileging of race and the analogy of racialization and Americanization, Ifemelu is never quite allowed that kind of ethical lapse. Without neglecting class, this view complicates the assumption made in the very first chapter, where she meets a white dreadlocked man who tells her that "black people need to get over themselves, it's all about class now" (4). Put blandly, this view reiterates the permeability of class boundaries and the fixity of race, but it also advances this kind of truism

7 "Shared Space of Africanness": The Hair Salon as Afropolitan Heterotopia

by highlighting the mutual imbrications of race and class, their global dimension and local specificity.

While it might be difficult to argue for the fact that this subtle sense of solidarity also mirrors a concretely realized sense of unity and collectivity in the present, the novel's diasporic desire clearly anticipates this. Its generic status as both romance with and love letter to Africa speaks to its Pan-African or diasporic sensibilities, but in a way that is unmistakably gendered and anchors itself more in the present or future rather than the Black Diaspora's painful pasts. Recalling Jameson's contentious notion of the third world novel's natural inclination toward national allegory, *Americanah* projects "a political dimension" by being not only "seemingly private and invested with a properly libidinal dynamic," but empathically so (Jameson 1986: 69). Not only is the private political, but clearly a love story is not apolitical if the object of the love object is both a political unit and the projected antidote. In this sense, the hair braiding salon conveys Adichie's, and by extension Afropolitanism's, commitment to representing the ordinary, the day-to-day, the particular normalcy of the present moment. It revisits not the exceptional historical moments of Pan-Africanism, but the quotidian encounters of humans on different historical trajectories, whose paths routinely converge and ought to affect our understanding of diaspora and Blackness.

In conclusion, I want to suggest that the stark contrast between the novel's depiction of race realism and its happy-go-lucky love story is balanced by its posing as quest romance – in which American racialization is presented as the one obstacle, the dragon Ifemelu needs to slay – and, at the same time, appears somewhat unreal, even fanciful. Positing the fallacy of race, Ifemelu's escape from a dangerously regressive America to a race-less, futuristic Nigeria reflects the kind of Pan-African wish fulfilment that nevertheless draws attention to the very real nightmare of racialization. An only slightly different reading, however, would draw entirely different conclusions from this kind of estrangement, wielding the fictitiousness of race as proof of post-racialism or a refutation of Blackness. Moreover, the view that race and 'politically correct' race talk are archaic residues of the past that need to be surpassed easily obscures the fundamental role racism plays in capital accumulation. In this sense, the novel's ambiguity could actually be read as a compromise, in keeping with what Moretti considers the "deepest vocation" of not only 19th-century novels, but literature as a whole: "forging *compromises between different ideological systems*" (2007: 93).

Indeed, *Americanah* is as much an indictment of racism as it is a diasporic auto-critique. Be it Obinze's faded infatuation with Black American culture or Ifemelu's ill-fated romance with Obama, *Americanah*'s gradual "f[alling] out of love" with America suggests not only a reckoning with the pathology of racism but also with the epistemic hegemony of the Middle Passage (434). Where earlier diasporic texts, most notably Gilroy's *Black Atlantic*, were able to extract a soothing balm of cultural identity from the pressures of slavery and the Middle Passage, *Americanah* exposes this particular Euro-Atlantic notion of tradition as a very limited model for a global Black identity. Understanding the narrative wish fulfillment of her novel as romantic, basically utopian fantasy also allows us to interpret the somewhat naïve, and perhaps even problematic notion of ending or transcending race as Adichie's insistence that slavery is not the only coordinate en route to becoming Black. In *Americanah*, the most tangible legacy of slavery emerges as a system of labor, one that marks certain bodies as viable for expropriation rather than exploitation, but a system of labor nevertheless, not an epistemology, not an axiom.

While the novel indeed navigates the rifts and misunderstandings between old and new diasporas, I wouldn't go so far as to see "black Americans merely lurk in the background like expectant ghosts or persons displaced from a narrative of race they used to own," as Chude-Sokei suggests in his reading of *Americanah* and other new diasporic novels (2014: 68). Instead, the novel again performs a twofold labor: On the one hand, it highlights the differences between these two groups, or at least showcases the distinctness of the African or Nigerian immigrant experience. At the same time, it also offers the kind of Pan-African historical awareness that may generate bonds beyond the limited national framework of an American Blackness. This historical awareness can also serve as a bulwark against external divisions. At one point, for example, Ifemelu counters the "simplistic comparison" behind the proposition that Africans are the better American Blacks because they don't have all these "issues" with the simple historical fact that "[m]aybe when the African American's father was not allowed to vote because he was black, the Ugandan's father was running for parliament or studying at Oxford" (168). Acknowledging the difficult feat of satirizing race or provincializing the Middle Passage without trivializing their effects, the novel's diasporic desire engenders a notion of Pan-African solidarity built to contain the Black Diaspora's contradictions. While Adichie has recently admitted to not yet having the language to write about the deadly way racism renders people subhuman in the US, she has also stressed how Black culture began in Africa, not on the slave ship (Adichie 2017a: 00:37:50).[75] *Americanah*'s romantic return and Pan-African utopia implies that there is much to gain from an at least meta-

---

[75] Cf. Gilroy's assertion that "[c]ulture doesn't just sort of go on hold when you get on a slave ship and then resume when you get to the other side" (Shelby 2008: 121).

phorical return to Africa that does not repeatedly stage the pain of separation nor freeze in a mythical limbo but allows its contemporary voices to intervene into a hegemonic race discourse.

Chapter IV
A Painful Notion of Time – Conveying Black Temporality in Yaa Gyasi's *Homegoing*

> "History clings to our skin. Somehow we must remember that we remember differently."
> Jennifer Nansubuga Makumbi

> "One must return to the site. Detour is not a useful ploy unless it is nourished by return: not a return to the dream of origin [...] but a return to the point of entanglement [*point d'intrication*], from which one was forcefully turned away."
> Édouard Glissant

1 Introduction: Writing Diaspora Across the Middle Passage

In "The Time of Slavery," an analysis of US-American 'roots tourism' in Ghana, Saidiya Hartman notes that "the origin identified is the site of rupture and, ironically, the fort and castles built by Europeans come to approximate home" (2002: 766). Hartman takes issue with the "facile representations of the horrors of the slave trade" that are offered by heritage tourism. She particularly faults the assumed redemption and closure facilitated by the tourist "who acts as a vessel for the ancestor" and questions that curious conflation on behalf of African Americans visiting the west coast of Africa, who act "as if the location of the wound was itself the cure, or as if the weight of dead generations could alone ensure our progress" (2002: 767–768). The metaphor of return becomes for her not only a convenient vehicle for economy-boosting 'roots tourism,' but also a fundamentally doomed concept, a mere placeholder for the irreconcilable desire to "mend the irreparable" (759). Hartman does not exempt herself from this impossible desire, neither in this article nor in its extended examination in *Lose Your Mother*. Regarding the inscription of a memorial plaque at Elmina castle, its call for remembering the dead by mending "ruptured lines of descent and filiation," Hartman argues that "*grief* is a central term in the political vocabulary of the diaspora" (2002: 758). Yet she also concedes that, from a perspective where the "the identification with Africa is always already after the break," Africa is seen, if at all, then only "through the backward glance or hindsight (763). By asking "to what end," then, the ghost of slavery is conjured up, Hartman highlights the epistemic interstice that Yaa Gyasi's *Homegoing* (2016) aims to fill.

Homegoing also mobilizes the tropes of displacement and return as both organizing principles and fundamental problems to diasporic identity. The novel traces eight generations of a family separated through the transatlantic slave

---

 OpenAccess. © 2021 Dominique Haensell, published by De Gruyter. [CC BY-NC-ND] This work is licensed under the Creative Commons Attribution-NonCommercial-NoDerivatives 4.0 International License.
https://doi.org/10.1515/9783110722093-005

trade and their disparate positions within it, episodically juxtaposing US-American and Ghanaian Black lives. In part, *Homegoing* follows what Ferguson has called "the hegemonic mode of plotting African American racial formations," from "transatlantic slavery, to Jim Crow, to civil rights, Black Power, and on to integration" (2011: 114). The vital difference to these forms of historical plotting, however, lies in the novel's bifocal perspective. In that sense, *Homegoing* performs the same Afropolitan gesture as *Americanah*, lateralizing the Black Atlantic by foregrounding Africa. Rather than highlighting diasporic alienation or promising the transcendence of race, it offers a sense of kinship, solidarity, and historical redemption.

The novel's positive or redemptive tone, however, is not achieved through the usual means, including those criticized by Hartman. The novel does not develop a soothing notion of African continuity or conjure the Gold Coast's rich history as a simple antidote to the damaging effects of slavery. Neither is it primarily animated by the Afrocentric fantasy of return, culminating in a sense of closure, even though it emphasizes the importance of thinking through the Black Diaspora's points of entanglement. Through its parallel structure, the novel emphasizes rather than mends the fracturing of kinship, detailing "ruptured lines of descent and filiation" and framing separation and betrayal as the diaspora's original sin. In its detailing of by and large tragic life stories it also appears to be, in keeping with Hartman's proposition, mobilized by a certain sense of grief. At the same time, it abounds with momentary or minor redemptive moments that bespeak its overarching diasporic desire to "reckon with the fullness of slavery," as Gyasi candidly writes in a *New York Times* opinion piece titled "I'm Ghanaian-American. Am I Black?" Growing up as a Ghanaian American, Gyasi writes, she struggled to make sense of her identity in relation to Black Americans. Only after visiting Cape Coast Castle in Ghana – and learning about the conspicuous lacuna of slavery in Ghana's national memory – did she develop a way to broach the subject:

> I knew I wanted to write about everything I was feeling, to write about diaspora and reckon with the fullness of slavery, not just as it was centuries ago, but what it has left us, Ghanaians and Americans alike, today. I started writing with a vague but important question that I put at the top of my blank screen: What does it mean to be black in America? (Gyasi 2016b: para. 15)

Answering Hartman's question in the moment of Afropolitanism, the novel conjures the ghost of slavery in order to (re-)install an active African role in the making of the Black Diaspora, one that reckons with the guilt of betrayal without being paralyzed by it. As such, the novel not only inquires into Black American identity, plotted through the disastrous route of the Middle Passage, but it strives to create a sense of diasporic Black identity that re-inscribes the mutual historical imbrications between West African and American Black subjects. Gyasi's investigation of Black identity seems to resonate with Hall's definition of diasporic identifications as "the names we give to the different ways we are positioned by, and position ourselves within, the narratives of the past" (1994: 394). It also resonates with Clifford's definition of diasporic traditions as "a network of partially connected histories, a persistently displaced and reinvented time/space of crossings" (1994: 321). Accordingly, the questions motivating this historical novel are not exhausted by the complex node of 'how to write about slavery?' but also include 'how to write the diaspora,' meaning: 'how to write a historical novel about a transnational and ever evolving structure?'

In the context of this book, the novel is not only the latest, but also the most obvious intervention into the bleak assessment of Afropolitanism's inability to reckon "with the agency of Africans in the dispersion of diaspora: the betrayal at the heart of the symbol 'Black'" (Balakrishnan 2018: 581). Rather than indicating the repudiation of racial solidarity that Chude-Sokei identifies with newly Black American fictions, the novel is written from a position that aims to bridge the abyss of the transatlantic slave trade *and* adequately represent the rippling effect of this traumatic process. It signals an engagement with these themes not merely as truce but as a sign of active solidarity. As such, *Homegoing* is firmly grounded within contemporary diasporic discourses. In its emphasis on a particular 'feeling' toward history, it offers a very interesting riff on what Best has called an "axiom" of contemporary writing about slavery, fictional and historiographical. In *Homegoing*, too, the past is not really past but continues to haunt future generations by way of a family curse. As an investigation into 21st-century US-American Blackness, Gyasi's novel appears to trade in that very same melancholic historicism that Best argues against, Hartman employs, and Morrison has either perfected or abandoned (depending on who you ask).

On the other hand, the novel clearly defies at least some of the representational conventions that Afro-pessimist-leaning scholars like Markus Nehl declare the litmus test of writing about slavery. For Nehl, proper accounts of slavery refuse "to offer a reconciliatory interpretation of the past" (2016: 194) and instead help to "deconstruct the naïve idea of history as progress" (2016: 12). Narratives that present some form of positive closure or merely emphasize the "liberating power of the act of narration," he posits, ultimately run "the risk of playing down and trivializing the true implications and the horrors of American chattel slavery" (2016: 36). Yet *Homegoing*'s diasporic desire operates on a different level. Rather than merely revolving around the question of trivializing or foregrounding the devastating effects of slavery, the novel shifts the singular burden of 'appropriately' representing this history and focuses instead on the "liberating power" of narrating diaspora, of finding new stories and pushing toward new ways of writing in the African Atlantic.

In doing so, the novel finds itself in the forcefield of various discourses, skillfully engaging the contents of various forms. As a sprawling family saga that projects a sense of hope and solidarity with and through the destruction of traditional kinship ties, *Homegoing* negotiates the narrative strategies of the Afro-pessimist neo-slave narrative, as well as the conventions of the 'classical' historical novel à la Lukács. Signaling also the self-referentiality of postmodern metafiction or the postcolonial historical novel, *Homegoing* also foregrounds the limits of this genre, particularly the ways in which the historical novel relates to the nationalist, totalizing, and teleological demands intrinsic to the project of history and the nation state. In order to provide the history of an imagined community that is not only transnational, but also outside or adjacent to linear progressive temporalities, the novel relies less on the established narrative conventions of historical fiction than on the mediation of temporality. Consequently, *Homegoing* is a historical novel that aims to provide not merely the feeling for a time, but the feeling for a feeling *of* time. This specific sense of Black temporality is primarily conveyed through a distinctly discontinuous structure imparting a distinctly continuous reading experience. On that view, the novel's sense of linear historical progression – provided by the through-line of a literal genealogy – is compromised by what Édouard Glissant calls a "painful notion of time and its full projection into the future" (1996: 64).

Each of the novel's fourteen chapters opens and ends *in medias res* and somewhat impressionistically indicates its respective historical canvas. Hence, in its progression through over two centuries, the general effect is one of fragmentation and disjuncture. Moreover, the absence of central and recurring characters not only limits its potential for readerly empathy but actually evokes a sense of what Dominick LaCapra, in *Writing History, Writing Trauma*, has described as "empathic unsettlement" (2001: 41). Rather than fueling a sense of intimacy with a cast of familiarized characters, the chapters provide only that level of identification that is responsive to the traumatic experiences of others, without entirely appropriating their experience for the sake of narrative continuity. Regarding the novel's specifically traumatic historical subject matter, this kind of unsettlement then "poses a barrier to closure"; it doesn't reconcile the past as distinct and distant and "places in jeopardy harmonizing or spiritually uplifting accounts of extreme events from which we attempt to derive reassurance" (LaCapra 2011: 41–42).

The narrative nevertheless operates with elements of continuity. The urgency and temporal suspension derived from the novel's method of fragmentation accentuates this carefully crafted continuity as the constant interplay of stasis and event. Every chapter is set apart from the preceding one by a radical jump in either time or place. At the same time, the sense of historical and narrative progression is not entirely suspended. Time, on the contrary, is relentlessly moving forward. As each character and period recedes, nothing lasts while everything still remains the same. *Homegoing*'s unusual structure is certainly noteworthy if one contextualizes it as one of the widely popular fictions emerging in the moment of Afropolitanism. As scholar John Murillo III. notes, both critics and lay audiences have perceived the lack of constant narrative threads and characters as the novel's major weakness, describing its effect as "distancing" (2017: para.3). However, he claims, these readings are unable to "grasp the essential genius of what Gyasi has accomplished here" (para. 4). For Murillo, it is precisely her "suturing of the dispersed fragments of Black life scattered across time and space into the single, if necessarily disjointed, 'whole' of *Homegoing* that makes this work so profound" (ibid.). Indeed, if one interprets the novel as an affective meditation on Blackness and temporality, its formal constrains align with what it wants to accomplish: a dizzying sense of progression counteracted by a tragic sense of temporality, recursiveness, and gridlock.

In this sense, the novel's retrospective long view of history resembles that of Benjamin's angel of history: history as a single catastrophe that keeps piling wreckage upon wreckage. While the novel's historical gaze is turned toward the past and its amassing of tragedy, the narrative cannot stay with the dead because the pronounced prolepsis of its episodic structure hurls it forward, or backward, in the simulation of progress that we have come to know as Black history. At the same time, and in keeping with Benjamin, the novel insists on redemptive openings, enabled by this very same tragic sense of history. Only by recognizing the way in which an oppressive history implicates all, in this case a reckoning with the fullness of slavery, can the desire to "blast open the continuum of history" transmute into agency (Benjamin 2003: 396).

The next section of this chapter contextualizes the novel within its particular moment, asking how the historical novel appears particularly pertinent to the 21st-century Black Diaspora. The subsequent section will examine the multifaceted "Problem of History,'" from notions of literariness and 19th-century imperialist plotting illustrated by 20th-century theorists like Hayden White and Georg Lukács, to the representation of traumatic limit events as problematized by Dominick LaCapra and Saidiya Hartman. I then explore how the novel foregrounds its own epistemological status in relation to diasporic history, followed by a more detailed discussion of how diasporic notions of temporality are laid out. The last section will try to integrate the problems of history and disjunctive temporality in a discussion of the novel's transmission of agency and redemption.

2 Historical Fiction Is "Having a Moment"

Listing Yaa Gyasi, Yvonne Owuor, Colson Whitehead, Chimamanda Adichie, and Peter Kimani as examples, historian Dan Magaziner notes in an article on *Africa Is a Country* that historical fiction "has been having a bit of a moment recently, especially among authors from the African continent and its diaspora" (2017: para. 1). Confirming this, Lizzy Attree asks in the *Los Angeles Review of Books*: "Are we on the cusp of a new age of African literature? If so, the key to new novels from African writers seems to be the fresh use of historical fiction to articulate a new future" (2018: para. 1–2).

Homegoing indeed seems to be part of a distinct literary trend, and not only in Afro-diasporic literatures. *The Guardian*, for example, points to the success of Hilary Mantel as proof that the historical novel has finally lost its genre stigma, noting that both escapism and contemporary crises may account for its huge appeal (2017: para. 1–4). But, of course, historical fiction has never really gone out of fashion. What these cultural commentators are observing is rather the rise – and simultaneous decline – of different forms of historical fiction. Academically, there seems to be a consensus about the fact that certain forms of historical fiction have lost their purchase, while other styles have taken over. Linda Hutcheon, who in the late 1980s famously developed the notion of 'historiographic metafiction' in order to classify a distinct postmodernist way of writing, has since labeled postmodernism, and with it the self-reflexive historical novel, "a thing of the past" (2002: 2). After the heydays of historiographic metafiction, as Amy Elias observes, came "a distinctive move toward [...] what is now a realist historiographical perspective" (2005: 163).

The editors of *The Return of the Historical Novel? Thinking about Fiction and History after Historiographic Metafiction* likewise propose a departure from Georg Lukács's and Linda Hutcheon's theoretical paradigms, asserting that we have entered "a new phase" in discussing historical fiction (2017: 14). This new phase, the editors proclaim, is "becoming more inclusive, more tolerant and, above all, more diverse" (ibid.). On the cover, the editors affirm their conviction that a certain "desire for a literary experience of historical otherness has recently increased in urgency." That said, the volume manages to include only a single discussion of a postcolonial or non-white author (M.J. Vassanji).

The "urgency" that the editors of *The Return of the Historical Novel?* make out in the current moment is certainly germane to postcolonial and Afro-diasporic historical fictions, which have long since expressed the importance of understanding "temporal difference as a fundamental category of cultural experience" (ibid. 14). If one follows the established genealogy of the African novel, already the most canonical instance illustrates this. Achebe's *Things Fall Apart* is fundamentally invested in exposing the epistemic violence of the historical archive by imagining what appears to have been erased by a work like *The Pacification of the Primitive Tribes of the Lower Niger* – the fictional historiographic account that concludes the novel, written by the figure of the District Commissioner and threatening to reduce Okonkwo's tragic suicide to "a reasonable paragraph, at any rate," if not a mere footnote in history (*Things Fall Apart* 183). The historicist tropes adopted by Achebe are those of unearthing and countering, his fictional alternative to the colonial archive conveying what Richard Begam terms "adversarial history" (1997: 397).[76] It expresses the kind of metahistorical stance that is embodied in a proverb used by Achebe in a 1994 interview with the *Paris Review* and also taken up by Zimbabwean author J. Nozipo Maraire in her epistolary novel *Zenzele* (1996): "Until the lion learns to write, tales of hunting will always glorify the hunter'" (78). *Zenzele*, written as a fictionalized letter from a Zimbabwean mother to her daughter who is studying at Harvard, also employs the metahistorical frame of intergenerational exchange, striking a tone that is at once affectionate and advisory:

> So it is with us, too. History is simply the events as seen by a particular group, usually the ones with the mightiest pens and the most indelible ink. [...] Do not be fooled by the whitewashed apparent objectivity of the ivory tower. Until the ivory turns to a rainbow with all countries represented, you would do well to be suspicious of the so-called "facts." (78)

This adversarial view of history, suspicious as it is of 'official' historical records and dedicated to unearthing alternative histories, is still a powerfully productive metahistoricist position that hugely impacts on African or postcolonial literatures. In the Afropolitan moment of the 21st century, this backward glance appears to chafe at the simultaneous emphasis on contemporaneity and futurity. Pushing against post-independence Afropessimism and the politicization of African literature, some commentators in the African literary community have urged writers to abandon "Black and African history, with its tragedies, injustices

---

[76] Even though the "unearthed" past of *Things Fall Apart* cannot be read as the conjuring of an authentic, pre-colonial idyll, the long literary shadow cast by this canonical novel may have also led to some reservation concerning the subject matter, resulting instead in a push towards capturing the ordinary complexities of African (urban) contemporaneity. In a portrait of Adichie in *The New Yorker*, her Nigerian writing workshops are described as such: "She encouraged them to write ordinary stories. [...]. Others were still writing 'loincloth fiction': stories of a noble man caught between the white devils and tradition. 'The Nigerian style has always been to bloviate, to put some isms,' Imasuen says. [...] People still think that to tell an important story they must engage colonialism, or the dictatorship of the nineties'" (MacFarquhar 2018: para. 29).

and wars," in favor of lighter, less monothematic and supposedly more "literary" topics (Okri 2014: para. 6).[77]

In the US, a very similar discourse answered the alleged post-racial turn and its demands on all forms of Black cultural expression, including literature. A particularly pertinent example of this is Charles Johnson's "The End of the Black American Narrative" from 2008. Bluntly subtitled with the assertion that "a new century calls for new stories grounded in the present, leaving behind the painful history of slavery and its consequences," the article wields Obama-infused optimism and the demographic diversity amongst Black Americans not only as proof of progress but as an obligation to abandon the "traditional black narrative of victimization" (2008: 36). Johnson advocates that 21st-century Black narratives should be "based not on the past but on the dangerous, exciting, and unexplored present" (ibid. 42).

As evidenced by the unbroken currency of historical fiction in post-colonial, African and Black American literature, and notably also in the writing of newly Black Americans like Gyasi, the 21st century certainly rejects Johnson's counsel. If anything, and in the US-American context especially, metahistorical positionalities have become an even more crucial touchstone for Black cultural production. Most of these debates have also revealed themselves as being only superficially about abandoning the past in favor of the contemporary, but actually about the ways that past and present relate – particularly regarding the significance of past atrocities. Following Kenneth Warren's polemic that the "retrospective" view of contemporary Black American fiction bespeaks its uselessness as literary category, as well as Stephen Best's critique of melancholic historicism, the question is often not only whether but more importantly what *kind* of historicism adequately captures 'the Black experience.'

In the context of African literature, the current moment is perhaps best characterized by what Lizzy Attree describes as a "fresh use" of historical fiction. This new approach does not entirely abandon Achebe's subject matter but nevertheless differs from this ur-moment of African or postcolonial fiction. Like Gyasi's *Homegoing*, contemporary novels like Jennifer Makumbi's *Kintu*, Novuyo Tshuma's *House of Stone*, or Namwali Serpell's *The Old Drift* do not shy away from depicting a pre-colonial past or detailing the contact zone between colonizer and colonized. Yet these novels trace these historical trajectories into the (near) present, strongly indicating the presence of the past in the present. Most importantly, however, they are foregrounding historical continuities and

---

[77] For a similar gist, see Helon Habila's review of Bulawayo's *We Need New Names* (Habila 2013).

counter suppressive historiographies and also reflect on the discursive impact and effects of adversarial, postcolonial, or melancholic historicisms. Both *Kintu* and *Homegoing* employ the manifest destiny of a curse that continues to traumatize and wreak havoc on the members of a family line. In *The Old Drift*, a protean swarm of mosquitos grants a long historical view on the Zambesi basin. One of its human characters thinks of history as "the annals of the bully on the playground" (98), while the narrator of *House of Stone* distinguishes between history and a more personal, "murky hi-story" (7). *House of Stone*'s author Tshuma also advocates a creative and emotional engagement with colonial history rather than a self-legitimizing or purely falsifying approach. Problematizing the project of excavation itself, the Zimbabwean author warns that you cannot excavate a true history – "because every history has an agenda" (Tshuma 2019). Self-knowing and ethically engaged, these novels open up a space to explore different historicist epistemologies beyond the binary of authentic truthfulness or contingent play. In *Homegoing*, the question of how the past bears on the present often extends from the way it makes itself known – through archival traces, notions of spectrality, looping, or echoing – to the very condition of it being written.

3 The Problem of History: Historiography's Imperial Legacies

Two-thirds into Gyasi's debut novel, a middle-aged history teacher named Yaw finds himself questioned by a class of schoolboys. The young boys, hailing from rural parts of what is still called the Gold Coast, have already heard of this teacher and his heavily scarred face. The teacher, who is working on a manuscript titled *Let the Africans Own Africa* and eagerly awaits his country's independence, turns their natural curiosity into a teachable moment. Under the header "History is Storytelling," the teacher urges his students to present their hearsay version of how he got his scar, only to conclude:

> This is the problem of history. We cannot know that which we were not there to see and hear and experience for ourselves. We must rely upon the words of others. Those who were there in the olden days, they told stories to the children. And so on, and so on. But now we come upon the problem of conflicting stories. [...] We believe the one who has the power. He is the one who gets to write the story. So when you study history, you must always ask yourself, Whose story am I missing? Whose voice was suppressed so that this choice could come forth? Once you have figured that out, you must find that story too. From there, you begin to get a clearer, yet still imperfect, picture. (226–227)

3 The Problem of History: Historiography's Imperial Legacies — 159

The chapter on Yaw, and in particularly this passage on the narrative constructedness of history, is crucial for understanding the novel's metahistorical stance toward the diaspora. Yaw's chapter plays on the various notions of historicity exercised in the novel, particularly the way that fiction and historiography intersect in the historical novel. The chapter reads patently metafictional, but it is also very much emplotted within the particular temporal structure of the novel, as well as its redemptive arc. It is noteworthy that, in his classroom, Yaw uses personal anecdote to arrive at a metahistorical commentary on historiography, while at the same struggling to write a proto-national history of a people. In the beginning, we are told how he is close to scrapping his manuscript, an obvious reference to the Pan-Africanist phrase *Africa for Africans*, coined by Martin Robison Delany.[78] Unable to catalyze what he identifies and admires as the "academic rage" of the contemporaneous US-American Civil Rights Movement, Yaw's book project stalls as he feels unable to muster anything but "a long-winded whine" (228). When Yaw, in conversation with his politically active friend, notes how he believes that the revolution "start[s] with ourselves" (223), the sentiment anticipates another canonical text, *Decolonising the Mind* by Ngũgĩ wa Thiong'o (1986). It is also, quite literally, in keeping with the novel's theme of personal family history, as Yaw is able to write his book only once he has confronted his mother and revisited the "evil" in his own home (241). In a way, Yaw exemplifies a metahistoricist position in which various forms of representing history are vying for attention. Yaw references the orality of "the olden days" as something not only unmistakably lost, but also reliant on a romanticized notion of unified meaning or mimetic imminence. As soon as we "come upon the problem of conflicting stories," the discursive influence of power reveals itself. Yet even if one remains attentive to the stories suppressed by "the one who has the power," this still creates only a "clearer" and never a perfect picture. Apart from conceding to these limitations on historiography, Yaw is also unable to write a revolutionary counterhistory of the Gold Coast. He is struggling with simply adopting the content of a form that not only imposes a nationalist narrative but also thrives on a notion of history in which Africa has no place.

Both the historical novel and historiography itself pose a particular set of problems to non-Western writers. Many of Yaw's concerns can be traced to 19th-century European thought, as well as important 20th-century discussions of this period that, unwittingly, reproduce the epistemological lacunae of that

---

[78] See Delany 1861. The phrase was further popularized by other Black Nationalists like Edward Blyden and Marcus Garvey.

Imperial age even as they attempt to show the fictitiousness of historiography or the historical novel's alignment with ordinary agents of history. One example of the latter is the fusing of personal with

national history, signposting "The Classical Form of the Historical Novel" as laid out by Georg Lukács in the eponymous chapter from *The Historical Novel* (1962). Positively gushing over the novels of Sir Walter Scott, particularly his *Waverly* from 1814, Lukács writes: "Scott's greatness lies in his capacity to give human embodiment to historical-social types. The typically human terms in which great historical trends become tangible" (1969: 34). For Lukács, the historical novel's verisimilitude lies not in thick or picturesque description, but in the complex way that the underlying current of historical progress – the "historical factor" – is folded back into personal, human lives (ibid. 42). In Scott's historical novels, it is indeed the realm of the personal and the familial where the political drama of history is played out. Here, "certain crises in the personal destinies of a number of human beings coincide and interweave within the determining context of an historical crisis," and thus "the split of the nation into warring parties always runs through the centre of the closest human relationships" (ibid.). In many ways, *Homegoing* also expounds the kind of "dramatic concentration of the epic framework" that characterizes the historical novel for Lukács, where the central crisis "is never a matter of one single catastrophe, but of a chain of catastrophes," bound together by people "connected and involved with one another" (ibid.).

However, the major difference between *Homegoing* and *Waverly* lies in the historical and ideological contexts of the 19th and 21st centuries, respectively, as well as the different genres and literary chronotopes from which they evolve. Lukács notes how, prior to Scott's figure of Waverly, there had never been a "mediocre, prosaic hero at the central figure" (1996: 34) and that Scott thus departs from the "Romantic hero-worshippers" who explain "the age from the position of the great representatives" (40). As the founding text on Scottish Highland culture, *Waverly* is arguably romantic in terms of its mythologized subject matter. Yet what distinguishes this "historical romance," as Amy Elias notes, is that it ultimately shows how "the mythicized Highland cultures were doomed in the face of an epistemic shift to rationalist modernity" (2005: 164). Lukács also sees the inevitability of historical progress, the way that "historical necessity asserts itself" as the defining feature of Scott's classical historical novel (1969: 64). For Lukács, as an historical materialist, this is clearly a matter of "class timbre," but the notion that the representation of historical progress is brought into productive tension with literary realism is not limited to one ideology of history alone (50). With a quote by the 19th-century German poet Heinrich Heine, Lukács draws attention to the cultural context of Scott's historical novels and points toward their astonishing contemporaneous success: "Strange whim of the people! They demand their history from the hand of the poet and not from the hand of the historian" (Lukács 1969: 61).

This "strange whim," as well as the intricate link between historiographic and fictional writing, has more or less been at the center of Hayden White's entire oeuvre. His most well know publication *Metahistory: The Historical Imagination in Nineteenth-century Europe* (1973) and his later article "The Discourse of History" (1979) trace this link to the 19th century, where the rise of the realist novel coincides with the institutionalization of history as a discipline. For White, 19th-century historiography is fundamentally troubled by literary realism. In becoming more "realistic," literature "fatally undermined" the claims of historians "to deal in a discourse that was realistic, transparent, concrete, and illuminative of events by virtue of the stories it told about them" (2010: 192). Because narrative fiction was not only problematizing of language itself, but also traded in the same "rhetorical mode that conventional historiography relied on to convey authority," historiographers engaged in a more and more frantic effort to distance itself from it – a tendency White traces through to the positivist debates of the 1950s and onwards (ibid. 190). Yet it is particularly against the backdrop of the 19th century that the reciprocal relation between historiography and fiction becomes most legible.

Only a few years after the proclamation of the German Empire in 1871, Friedrich Nietzsche diagnosed that the young nation "was suffering from the consuming fever of history" (1997: 60). Scholars have extensively discussed why historiography would matter in an age that was also the intellectual and political cradle of nationalism, to the point where the mention alone might even seem superfluous. However, the fact that it is also the cradle of imperial colonialism is more easily overlooked. While both Lukács and White presuppose the central role of nationalism in their analyses, neither of them accounts for its imperializing tendencies. For Lukács, it is no surprise that the appeal to national independence and national character is "necessarily connected with a re-awakening of national history" (1969: 23), and he links this to the rippling effect of the French Revolution – an event that "for the first time made history a *mass experience*" (ibid. 20). What he lauds in Scott's novels is indeed the way that Hegel's "national character" is embodied by social types realizing themselves as active agents of historical change (36).

Yet where Lukács limits this historical consciousness to "a European scale" (1969: 20), he overlooks the significance of the Haitian revolution, the paradoxical relation between the Enlightenment concepts of freedom and bondage, and the particular manner that Hegel's notion of Universal History is predicated on these lived contradictions. Hayden White, on the other hand, while noting the

Eurocentric implications behind the burgeoning concept of "proper history," supplements his analyses with universalisms of another kind. Identifying the 19th century as a time of political and epistemic crisis, White notes how the historiography of this period is affected not only by the unresolved "truth claims" of realist writing, but also by the all-encompassing teleological arc provided by "the philosophy of history." White cites Hegel's eponymous lectures merely as an example of philosophy's push toward subjecting history to some form of master narrative. It is interesting that White's observations are finely attuned to what he describes as a "profound cultural anxiety" expressed by the 19th-century historians, a "cultural malaise" arising from the "social pressures" of industrialization that takes the form of an almost pathological obsession with history (2010: 188). For White, this obsession exceeds what he naturalizes as the fundamental desire to develop "[c]onsciousness of the past and awareness of a possible future" in order to "distinguish human beings from their animal prototypes" (ibid.). He identifies the denial of historical discourse's "literariness" as an enduring symptom of this malaise, while remaining conspicuously silent about the racializing discourse not merely supplementing but structuring and mobilizing a founding liberal text like Hegel's *Lectures on the Philosophy of History*. While almost parenthetically asserting humanity's universal desire to distinguish the human from the non-human, White's silence is certainly telling, if not even equally symptomatic. From a postcolonial perspective that admittedly supersedes these writers, the oversights in White's metahistorical and Lukács historical materialist accounts of the 19th century simply reproduce the institutionalized silence, or disavowal, as Sybille Fischer would argue, around the violent and contradictory condition of Western liberalism. A postcolonial reading would first historicize the category of the human and the universal in order to recognize their epistemic and illocutionary ramifications. As Lisa Lowe asserts in *The Intimacies of Four Continents*, the "modern distinction between definitions of the human and those to whom such definitions do not extend is the condition of possibility for Western liberalism" (2015: 3).

Hegel's lectures, notoriously prefaced with the advice to "give up" the "category of Universality" when thinking about the "African character" (2011: 110), have since been subjected to much critical scholarship, yet these repercussions have played out in more or less isolated disciplines, leaving the *grand récits* of philosophy and history mostly intact. Scholars such as Michel-Rolph Trouillot, Sibylle Fisher, Susan Buck-Morss, and others have noted how particularly the Haitian Revolution has been systematically overlooked in historical and philosophical scholarship, pointing toward an institutionalized silence around the flagrant incongruity between the discourse of freedom and the utter thingification of slavery.[79]

In some cases, as in Hayden White's constructivist view of history, certain historiographic absences are indeed acknowledged and accredited to the limited viewpoint of Eurocentrism. Yet this justification alone fails to consider the vital role these "absent causes" might have played in the construction of (capital H) History itself. There is a mutually constitutive tension between Hegel's notion of Africa having no history and his assertion that the Spirit of History unfolds within the laws of the European nation state. The paradox that a thinker like Hegel could develop the concept of mutual recognition in the master-slave dialectic, and at the same time dismiss "the Negro" as being "capable of no development or culture" and thus fit for enslavement, fundamentally destabilizes the image Western thought holds of itself (2011: 98). This "glaring discrepancy between thought and practice" marked the large-scale transformation of global capitalism, ushering in the social context of the 19th century (Buck-Morss 2009: 22). If, as C.L.R. James observed in *The Black Jacobins*, the wealth generated by the slave societies of the Americas specifically fattened the French bourgeoisie – and with it the discourse of the 'rights of man' – then the burgeoning nation states and expanding empires of the 19th century relied even more heavily on the revenue of plunder and primitive accumulation. A certain academic unwillingness or agnotological inhibition to reckon with what Buck-Morss calls simply "a certain constellation of facts," can thus be read as the avoidance of "an awkward truth" that threatens "not only the venerable narratives, but also the entrenched academic disciplines that (re)produce them" (Buck-Morss 2009: 22–23).

Yet not only the example of James's eighty-year-old publication shows that these historical entanglements have long since been exposed and critiqued. Particularly Hegel's remarks on Africa and "the Negro" have been impossible to overlook, contrary to dominant Hegel scholarship, but instead have spawned a long and often productive tradition of intellectual engagement. Indeed, many of the most influential Black intellectual writers of the 20th century explicitly or implicitly take on Hegelian concepts, such as W.E.B. Du Bois, Frantz Fanon, and Aimé Césaire.[80] Considering the sheer ubiquity of Hegel's historicist theo-

---

79 Trouillot 1995; Fischer 2004; Buck-Morss 2009.
80 Du Bois, for example, referred to himself as a world historical man and extensively references Hegel's "national character" in "Conservation of the Races." Gilroy notes the following about Du Bois's Hegelianism: "Du Bois was clearly more comfortable with Hegel's view of the history of the world as 'none other than the progress of the consciousness of Freedom' than with his Eurocentrism and identification of history's theatre as 'the temperate zone,' let alone his collapsing of historical progress into the practical achievements of the Prussian state machine. It is sig-

ries, their quick absorption first into 19th-century dominant German, European, and finally US-American schools of thought, it might be fair to say that whenever a 20th-century person of African descent addressed issues of history, progress, or even freedom, the spirit of Hegel haunted their endeavors.

One reason for the tenacity of these traces was the fact that Hegel's contribution to History, what Glissant calls "a highly functional fantasy of the West," was so fundamentally tied up with the idea of the nation (*Caribbean Discourse* 64). In "The Subject in the Plot," Herman Bennett identifies the conflation of historical progress and the nation state as a particularly pervasive 19th-century plot, in which the 20th-century Black subject struggled to insert itself – often through ill-directed Black Nationalist efforts (2000: 101–124). Indeed, as Michelle M. Wright notes, the major pitfall of 20th-century Black intellectual counterdiscourses was the fact that they functioned just like other "nationalist narratives in the West" (2004: 12). Constructing a world "in which men possess the power to give birth (to other men of course!)," Black Nationalist narratives project a "linear progression of time and space that starts and stops when they want" (ibid.).[81]

Homegoing nonetheless avoids the masculinist rhetoric of (Black) national liberation, especially in its detailing of a nascent independent Ghana. Despite projecting gender balance in terms of characters, its overall emphasis on female agency manifests not only in its matrilineal structure. Read thus, Yaw's inability to produce a Black Nationalist narrative is even more significant, as are the gendered terms in which this inability is represented. Unable to channel what he identifies as an "academic rage," he is only able to produce, in his ears, "a long-winded whine" (228). Generally, it is striking how the popular Pan-African plot around Nkrumah and Ghanaian independence is hinted at yet remains

---

nificant that Du Bois's autobiographies are candid about the extent to which his admiration for German nationalism and the achievements of the Prussian state in particular preceded his visit to Germany. It might be worth speculating whether these dreams of order appealed to him precisely because he was an American. Certainly, the conception of freedom that guided him was deeply influenced by this body of work. Blacks are continually invited to discover the forms of freedom consequent upon yielding to the organic power of a resolute racial collectivity assured of the historicality (Geschichtlichkeit) of its political and philosophical aspirations" (Gilroy 2002: 135).

81 However, the influence of Hegelian historicism did not implicate male philosophers only. Writing about the work of African American novelist Pauline Hopkins, William Moddelmog asserts: "Hegel's historiography constituted a force against which much of Hopkins's work – and that of other Black historians and novelists – struggled. Celebrating the nineteenth-century European nation-state, Hegel's philosophy affirmed a political and cultural model of nationhood to which most African 'nations' did not conform and in which African Americans were denied full participation." (2002: 99).

largely inconsequential to Yaw's personal liberation story. This kind of plotting corresponds with the novel's overall method of unfolding intimate family stories against the background of specific historical events like the War of the Golden Stool on the Gold Coast or the Fugitive Slave Act under US-President Taylor. Yet by avoiding the oftentimes-glorified Independence narrative, the novel foregrounds a particular kind of historicism. Despite its iconic Pan-African status, the legacy of Ghana is not idealized, neither in the period of the slave trade nor later. Instead, the notion of linear progress, and most certainly the idea of the nation as its principal carrier, is put into question. This does not mean that the very concrete and symbolical significance of the first independent African nation are invalidated, but the event itself is not brandished as proof that Hegel's "Spirit of History" or Marxist "Historical Necessity" finally unfold on the African continent. Moreover, *Homegoing* seems to reject what Sidney Lemelle and Robin D.G. Kelley have identified as "the gendered iconography of Pan-Africanism – Black men coming to redeem the soil of a 'Mother Country' 'raped' by Europe" (1994: 6).

Historicizing historiography means reckoning with the limitations of nationalist narratives and rejecting the kind plotting that accompanies the classical form of the (historical) novel. These considerations are also at the heart of Glissant's *Caribbean Discourse* from 1989. Glissant identifies this discourse as not simply adversarial or melancholically attached to the past, but also as an inherently creative and innovative response to the project of capital H history. For Glissant, it is indeed the role of the writer to fill in the void of a "ruined history" and counter the notion of linear progression proper to the national ideal (1996: 244). According to Glissant, the totalizing historical systems of the West have not only run their course and confronted their own limitations but have also been forcefully undermined through the eruption of subaltern histories focused on a poetics of relation rather than diachronic ascension. He writes:

> If Hegel relegated African peoples to the ahistorical, Amerindian peoples to the prehistorical, in order to reserve History for European peoples exclusively, it appears that it is not because these African or American peoples "have entered History" that we can conclude today that such a hierarchical conception of "the march of History" is no longer relevant. (64)

Fighting not only for food and freedom, but also struggling against "the double hegemony of History with a capital H and a Literature consecrated by the absolute power of the written word," the people inhabiting the "hidden side of the earth" have developed other modes of narrating their past (Glissant 1996: 76).

Homegoing also provides a literary image of the African Diaspora that, as in Glissant's vision, contains not the hierarchical chronology of empires or nation states, but the "histories and voice of peoples" (Glissant 1997: 77). Notably, *Homegoing*'s account of the Gold Coast is one of mutual entanglements and messy histories that do not necessarily unravel into discreet periods and genealogies. As a character notes early on: "Everyone is part of this. Asante, Fante, Ga, British, Dutch, and American" (*Homegoing* 98). Accordingly, the novel doesn't construct the myth of a pure ancestral homeland or singular origin but presents the Gold Coast as a synchronic assemblage of collective histories, a complexly flavored "pot of groundnut soup," stirred up by the British and others before them, and already intrinsically diverse, cosmopolitan, modern (98). Even though the scope and thrust of the novel could be read as epic and thus easily reduced to a mythologized quest for origin, there is no harmonious state of innocence to return to and, crucially, also no 'classical' sense of historical or national progress.

4 The Other Problem of History: What Cannot Be Represented

As Dalley states in his study of the postcolonial historical novel, "just as contests over the meaning of history forced historians to reconceptualize their discipline as a form of interpretative realism, so the contested nature of postcolonial pasts prompts novelists to frame their work vis-à-vis norms of plausibility, verifiability, and the dialogue with archives and alternative accounts" (2004: 8). While the metafictional and metahistorical assertion that "History is Storytelling" forms one axis of Yaw's chapter, the other is the knowledge "that sometimes you cannot see that the evil in the world began as the evil in your own home" at the end of the chapter (241). Encouraged by his future wife Esther, Yaw realizes that the political anger he is unable to transfer onto the page conflates with the anger transferred onto his mother – the woman who scarred his face – and that he first has to confront the history of these scars before he can ever progress as a character *and* historiographer. On the one hand, this storyline represents *Homegoing*'s reckoning with the "fullness of slavery" that starts with acknowledging the "evil" in one's own home, but it also indicates the notion of an alternative diasporic historiography, a history of scars that registers on the body as well as in the minds of the people implicated by it. Crucially, as these scars serve as a constant reminder, their traumatic effects do not necessarily ease or cease with time. While, at one point, Yaw reflects on how "you could not inherit a scar. Now [...] [he] no longer knew if he believed this was true" (228).

In this sense, the story of Yaw's scar in *Homegoing* is exemplary for a particular aporia of diasporic and postcolonial counterhistories. The events over which these accounts compete with 'truth claims' are usually violent, traumatic incidences that pose specific problems to narrative representation. There are in fact two notions of violence that bear on these forms of historical writing. One is the actual violence of the event, as well as its rippling traumatic effect. But there is also the epistemic violence that often structures the way it is represented, or suppressed, by 'official' records like the colonial archive or the archive of slavery. This presents a particular problem to narrative representation. As Hartman asks: "How does one revisit the scene of subjection without replicating the grammar of violence?" (2008: 4). The archive of slavery, she notes, often amounts to scattered scraps indicating not more than "a death sentence, a tomb, a display of the violated body, an inventory of property, a medical treatise on gonorrhea, a few lines about a whore's life, an asterisk in the grand narrative of history" (ibid. 2).

In the heavily symbolic system of *Homegoing*, Yaw's scars signify the violent event that mobilizes the emplotment and temporal logic of the novel. At this point in the narrative, the reader knows how these scars came to be and that they result from his mother acting out the family trauma: the curse of two family branches ripped apart by the 'original sin' of the slave trade. In his chapter, Yaw is both grappling with the fact that he cannot remember and thus "doesn't know" – that there might be, in fact, no way of "knowing" but only telling – and that this crisis of representation may either result in an endless play or the dominance of a victor's story. Similar to Hayden White's diagnosis of historiography's 19th-century malaise, he is aware that all these narratives are only ever approximations of the truth. The scars, as embodied knowledge of this trauma, indicate not only an alternative form of history but also serve as the constant reminder of a painful past that is difficult to voice without re-traumatizing or perpetuating violence.

Yaw is not the only character physically bearing witness to the past; in several instances of the novel, scars speak their own language. Subjected to a vicious cycle of domestic violence, Effia can "recite a history of the scars on her body" (4) before the age of 11; by the time we reach Ness, the first descendant born into American chattel slavery, her scarred skin is already "like another body in and of itself" (74). Ness's skin, the reader is told, "was no longer skin really, more like the ghost of her past made seeable, physical. She didn't mind the reminder" (74). Yet what serves as a potent reminder of unspeakable pain also seals her fate when her master suspects her of hurting his son: "Ness was sure that he could see clear as day what had happened, but it was the memory of her scars that made him doubt" (79). In this sense, scars are violent reminders that often beget even more violence. They do not only indicate traumatic pasts but are potentially traumatic in and of themselves. Similarly, encountering "the scraps of the archive," as Hartman muses, cannot fully undo these traumas but may cause its own sense of pain (Hartman 2008: 4).

The crisis of narrative representation, while haunting the status of historiography at large, is particularly evident if one understands the transatlantic slave trade and American chattel slavery as limit events that ultimately defy or at least severely challenge representation. The particular 'unrepresentability' pertaining to the horrors of the Middle Passage and slavery is indeed a kind of truism, already informing their earliest literary incarnations. In his antislavery tract from 1787, Ottobah Cugoano provides only the scarcest description of a British slave hold, repeatedly conceding that these horrors "cannot be well described" (1825: 123), that there is indeed "no language" to describe it and that no ear, except that of "Jehovah Sabaoth," may truly understand the "deep-sounding groans of thousands" (125). Frederick Douglass, too, speaks of his inability to "commit to paper" what he feels apropos the "terrible spectacle" of the whipping of Aunt Hester, symbolizing his "entrance to the hell of slavery" (1845: 28). And William Wells Brown, who published his slave narrative in 1847, famously asserted: "Slavery has never been represented; Slavery never can be represented" (1969: 82). Apart from the impossibility of rendering its horrific spectacles intelligible, there are other aspects to a limit event that further complicate its representation in historical and fiction writing.

Simone Gigliotti defines the term "limit event," as it is applied in scholarly writing about the Holocaust, as variably "the manifestation of the potential barbarism of modernity, as an extreme event of such uniqueness and incomparability that renders it incomprehensible to 'those who were not there', and of contested representational possibility in historical discourse, literary and visual culture, and in testimonial narratives" (2003: 166). The 'limiting' attributes of limit events are thus manifold; for one, they appear as ultimate limits of the social imaginary, and they also impose limits on language and representation. Yet this also means that the particular demands of a limit event problematize the very notion of relativity inherent in a radically constructivist view of history. What White elsewhere terms "imperatives of the real" will necessarily condition the range of possible responses (1987: 4). Precisely because it is so unintelligibly violent and so momentous, and because it can therefore never be contained or neatly periodized, the stakes in representing it aptly or even 'truthfully' are exceedingly high.

In his work on the relation between history and trauma, Dominick LaCapra asserts the particular significance of limit events in Hayden White's thinking. The notion of an unproblematic closure, for example, as well as other rhetoric modes of storytelling that would relativize the crimes of the Holocaust thus present the historian with the difficult task of finding a morally appropriate mode of historiography that doesn't denounce its own "literariness." LaCapra's concern also lies with the notion of narrativization as fictionalization that may depart from or distort traumatic historical events by providing unproblematic closure (2001: 16). LaCapra notes: "The study of traumatic events poses especially difficult problems in representation and writing both for research and for any dialogic exchange with the past which acknowledges the claims it makes on people and relates it to the present and future" (2001: 41). The fictionalization of history writing notwithstanding, he points to what he calls an "irreducible aboutness" of historiography that, while not necessarily being reducible to the ultimate transparency of a documentary or self-sufficient research model, nevertheless distinguishes the "truth claims" of professional history writing from endlessly self-referential play (2001: 4). However, and this is significant in the context of diasporic literature, this kind of referentiality is not limited to historiography but also informs fiction writing and other works of art dealing with historical events. Rather than only thinking about the fictionalization of history – often conflated with narrativization in Hayden White's earlier work – LaCapra is also interested in assessing the way historiography informs fiction writing. On the one hand, this approach would influence the manner in which works of art are critiqued and measured on behalf of their veracity or referentiality. LaCapra stresses "that truth claims coming from historiography […] may be employed in the discussion and critique of art in a manner that is especially pressing with respect to extreme events that still particularly concern people at present" (2001: 14). This approach, however, also entails an extended understanding of the "truthfulness" of literary methods. As LaCapra writes, one could "argue that narratives in fiction may also involve truth claims on a structural or general level by providing insight into phenomena such as slavery or the Holocaust […] or by giving at least a plausible 'feel' for experience and emotion which may be difficult to arrive through restricted documentary methods" (2001: 13).

The fact that the documentary methods of historiography pose certain limitations on diasporic fiction adds an important aspect to the idea of a limit event. Reading diasporic fictions as a form of counterhistory allows one to identify a more or less pronounced critique of so-called official records in many of these texts. This particular stance, the questioning of established historical narratives, may play out very differently but always signposts the notion of metahistoricity in diasporic or postcolonial fiction. The quasi-historiographical ending of *Things Fall Apart* is such an example, as is Yaw's history lesson in *Homegoing*. Other texts introduce critical metahistoricism more formally.[82]

---

[82] For example, as LaCapra notes, one of the quintessential elements of professional historiog-

In their attempt to "truthfully" represent the limit events of slavery and colonialism, writers are confronted with limited archives marked not only by gaps and silences on behalf of the few witnesses, but also with cold and calculating historical records reproducing the very violence they seek to unsettle. Unsurprisingly, therefore, both fiction writers and historians have adopted speculative methods that self-consciously foreground these limitations. M. NourbeSe Philip's long poem *Zong!*, for example, represents the erasure of enslaved subjectivities through disorienting fragmentation and literal blank spaces. Novelists like Fred D'Aguiar, David Daybdeen, or Caryl Phillips, as Abygail Ward argues, expose the "difficulty of representing slavery and the ethics involved in doing so" (2011: 7) through techniques like "contrapuntal montage" (2011: 27).

Yet another formalized response to these issues is Saidiya Hartman's notion of critical fabulation. This method, coined in "Venus in Two Acts," but already employed in Hartman's earlier works *Lose Your Mother* and *Scenes of Subjection*, combines rigorous historical research with critical theory and fiction writing. Born from a double gesture of wishing to represent and narrate, and thus "save," the life of the captive from yet another form of erasure, while at the same time acknowledging the impossibility of this endeavor, critical fabulation is "a history written with and against the archive" (2008: 12). The story of Venus first appears in the chapter "The Dead Book" from *Lose Your Mother*, Hartman's part-autobiographical, part-historiographical account of the Atlantic slave trade. Here, Hartman uses what little traces she can find about the fate of a captive girl in order to imagine her life and thus save her "from oblivion" (2007: 137). While this chapter already concedes the impossibility of reconstructing a life from a mere footnote in history (a court record stating "*the supposed murder*

---

raphy is the referential footnote. In order to be "truthful" and "objective," or at least approximate this ideal, a historical text must have references. Of course, however, "notes may be used in both history and fiction in a manner that questions or even parodies a documentary or self-sufficient research paradigm" (2001: 6). We can witness this effect for example in Junot Díaz's *Oscar Wao*, where extensive footnotes both supplement and question the main narrative, as well as Dominican, Antillean, and world history. Notably, *Oscar Wao* also introduces the particular historical lens of the *fukú*, as a stand in for both family curse and violent world history not unlike the family curse in *Homegoing*, but as with the use of footnotes, the overall effect of these metaliterary and metahistorical elements can be read as simultaneously playful and disturbing. *Oscar Wao* exemplifies how these critical historical metafictions seldom collapse into the utter playfulness of the "self-referential note," that device which, according to LaCapra, announces the "limit of history and the beginning of fiction" (2001: 7). Rather, in addition to introducing alternative temporal frameworks like curses, haunting, and spectrality, theirs is an attempt to destabilize the notion of capital H History without undermining their own critical and counterhistorical thrust.

of a Negro girl"), her later essay restages what Hartman had begun in *Lose Your Mother* but more fully examines her own desire to make whole, reckoning with the necessity of its failure and further restraining her desire to give narrative closure.

For Hartman, the violent omissions of these and other sources, as well as the paradigmatic status of the limit event they circumscribe, place certain demands on the methods of narration. This results in what Hartman describes as a "'recombinant narrative'" that "loops the strands" of incommensurate accounts and "weaves present, past, and future in retelling the girl's story and in narrating the time of slavery as our present" (2008: 12). Hartman, who coined the notion of the "afterlife of slavery," pushes against reconciling a painful history through apt representation because the racializing legacy of said history "is yet to be undone" (2007: 6). Rather than being melancholically attached to the past, she claims, her project is invested in a utopian vision of the future by repeatedly problematizing the archive's "founding violence" and its limiting effect on the present (2008: 10). She writes:

> For me, narrating counter-histories of slavery has always been inseparable from writing a history of the present, by which I mean the incomplete project of freedom, and the precarious life of the ex-slave, a condition defined by the vulnerability to premature death and to gratuitous acts of violence. As I understand it, a history of the present strives to illuminate the intimacy of our experience with the lives of the dead, to write our now as it is interrupted by this past, and to imagine a *free state*, not as the time before captivity or slavery, but rather as the anticipated future of this writing. (2008: 4)

In terms of working with and against the historical archive in Hartman's sense, as well as asserting the historiographical claim of 'truthfulness' in LaCapra's understanding, *Homegoing* provides a range of interesting examples.

Gyasi lists in her "Acknowledgements" section not only the names of family, friends, and mentors, but also a selection of scholarly publications on transatlantic slavery, such as *The Door of No Return* by William St. Clair and *The Fante and the Transatlantic Slave Trade* by Rebecca Shumway. In its detailing of historical events, if only as background to the unfolding of personal stories, the novel utilizes archival sources, for example in the figures of Quey and Cudjo, the inspiration for whom most likely stems from the historical Philip Quaque, son of a wealthy Gold Coast slave trader, and his cousin William Cudjo.[83] In light of these references and considering the novel's more or less ostensive dis-

---

[83] Saidiya Hartman too, uses the archival traces of these figures to speculate on their historical reality (2007: 125–129).

plays of historical verisimilitude, or at least aspirations to a verifiable historical narrative, could one interpret *Homegoing* as a claim to 'truthfully' represent a history of slavery and colonialism? Only, I would argue, if the entire semiotic range of a violent limit event is taken into account. As a traumatic event, which, following both Hartman and LaCapra, continues to affect the present, the notion of representing the past 'the way it really was,' and thus fetishizing it as a totalized object, becomes questionable at best. LaCapra notes that "the historical text becomes a substitute for the absent past only when it is construed as a totalized object that pretends to closure and is fetishized as such" (2001: 10–11). This does not mean that historical facts or accuracies do not matter, but that the extreme violence of this event, or chain of events, troubles the kind of historicist representation that aspires to transparency or totality or strives to situate historical events in an arc of linear progress.

Counterhistories of slavery and colonialism cannot 'prove' how terrible these events were, at least not through 'accurate' description alone. For one, the 'reality' of this violence needn't be disclosed and discovered, but is and was, if anything, hidden in plain sight. Both its ideology and effect weren't felt in the periphery alone but conceived and documented at the heart of empire itself. That is why, already in the 18th century, Ottobah Cugoano found it "needless" to describe the "horrible scenes" of the slave trade "as the similar cases of thousands, which suffer by this infernal traffic, are well known" (1825: 124–125). A similar documentary fatigue affects today's spectacles of anti-Black violence, the exasperated assertion that Black lives matter and, in the case of fiction, a particular mode of representing historical violence. In the case of Colson Whitehead's *The Underground Railroad*, for example, a contemporaneous novel often associated with *Homegoing*, scenes of extreme violence may cause some readers to doubt the novel's historical accuracy. But the question of whether a particularly graphic scene of torture actually took place or not becomes irrelevant if one has only minimally familiarized oneself with the historical archive of slavery, for example, the gruesomely detailed journals of Thomas Thistlewood.[84]

Furthermore, in its allegorized representations of historical events and periods, *The Underground Railroad* already questions the effects of historical realism. While the historical inaccuracies behind a neo-slave narrative like *Roots* could still compromise the claims of its author Alex Haley, Colson Whitehead acknowl-

---

[84] See Hall 1989. For a recent historical assessment, see Baptist, who identifies the coercive techniques of chattel slavery as modern forms of torture: "sexual humiliation, mutilation, electric shocks, solitary confinement in 'stress positions,' burning, even waterboarding" (2014: 141).

edges that he is interested in "the truth of things, not the facts" (Purcell 2017: para. 11). Thus, the novel provides a representation of slavery that centers not (merely) on historical detail. Rather, through its extended metaphor, the introduction of historical and historiographical text types, such as fugitive notes or almanacs, as well as the blending of historical and fictional events, renders historicism itself a subject matter. As Jesse McCarthy observes, Whitehead's "novel doesn't seek to reenact history, but rather to imagine and represent simultaneously the many hydra heads of a system designed to perpetuate the enclosure and domination of human beings" (2016: para. 26). In registering and commenting upon the violence of the archive, both Whitehead's and Gyasi's novels appear to reiterate Hartman's question of why, despite our better knowledge, we still attend to those who were murdered by the "play of power" that is inseparable from the archives, why "at this late date we still want to write stories about them" (Hartman 2008: 11). If it is not 'counter-knowledge' in the strictly documentary sense of the term, these fictional counterhistories aim to do something more imaginative in their oppositional stance. In *Homegoing*, for example, history is imagined as a fold, with layers touching each other, where, as Gyasi describes it in reference to a quote attributed to Mark Twain, historical periods speak to each other "in a way that rhymes" (Bausells 2017: para. 4). This manner of folding and echoing can produce a sense of haunting, a claustrophobic tautology that is used to an effect, particularly in relation to how the violent histories of slavery and colonialism bear upon the present.

In the context of memorializing the transatlantic slave trade, an effort that unfolds, as Angela Davis notes, against the "historical tendency toward willed forgetfulness regarding slavery" (1999: 199), even some of the most pronounced anti-representational stances are tied up with a resistance, not only against cultural amnesia, but also against the legacy of those historical traces and forms of remembering that were complicit with these violent events. With regards to representing the Holocaust, Hayden White has called the most extreme response not the position of the so-called revisionists, but the assumption that no language or medium is ever able to adequately represent or explain it, least of all a historical account. Yet as Andreas Huyssen asserts, by the 1980s the public debate had generally morphed from *whether* to *how* to represent the Holocaust (2000: 65). Faced with the problem of memorializing an ever further receding historical event, debates over whether *Schindler's List*, *Shoah*, or *Maus* are adequate Holocaust representations seemed pressing. However, prioritizing the appropriate form of remembering often loses sight of that aspect of Adorno's often-quoted sentiment – that no poetry could be written after Auschwitz – which points toward the ongoing and unresolved crisis of modernity.[85]

The ossified historical traces – or scars – born by contemporary society still indicate the pulsating wound of absolute barbarism. It was the integral violence of racial capitalism that sanctified the decision of the slave ship *Zong*'s captain to throw more than 140 people over board in a bid to claim insurance money, and this rational violence also sustains the legal documentation of the event. Therefore, even the disintegration of meaning and representability espoused by Philip's *Zong!* is framed by a reworking of this legal document that engenders to confront modernity with its repressed legacies, resulting in what Philip describes as a "hauntological pedagogy" (Watkins para. 10). While not all contemporary representations of slavery are as experimental as Philip's, the wider implications of this kind of memorial culture – as a fundamental critique of modernity – is prevalent in many of today's artistic and theoretical responses. However, even though the metahistorical critique of these contemporary counter-histories is warranted, if not crucial, this mode of representation may also produce its own kind of limitations.

For example, Nehl's study on the "second generation neo-slave narrative" in the 21st century not only focuses exclusively on the issue of slavery in diasporic novels, thus privileging the 'Middle Passage Epistemology,' but also reiterates the morally charged dichotomy of good and bad accounts of slavery – or proper and improper historiography for that matter – from a decidedly Afro-pessimist perspective.[86] Nehl identifies "loss, dispossession and grief as defining features of the African diaspora" and charges contemporary diasporic novels with the task of representing, or at least not misrepresenting, the "true implications and the horrors" of slavery (2016: 12). Considering the representational challenges of this limit event, this is surely an enormous demand and unsurprisingly excludes quite a number of imaginative responses. Despite being anchored in a political critique of the present, this demand may also run the risk of unwittingly aestheticizing racial slavery and converting "trauma into the occasion for sub-

---

[85] Modernity, here, is conterminous with the social, technological, and economic transformations initialed by the French and the Industrial Revolution. For a comparative study of the term 'crisis of modernity,' see Ossewaarde 2018.

[86] Nehl concedes that both the genre of the neo-slave narrative and his distinction of generations is not uncontested or unproblematic. For a wider discussion of the genre, see Rushdy 2004; Beaulieu 1999; Dubey 2010.

limity" – a tendency LaCapra observes in a memorial culture's heightened fidelity to trauma (2001: 23).[87]

5 "An Accumulation of Time": Writing Time as History

Homegoing is not primarily invested in aptly conveying the horrors of chattel slavery. Instead, the novel aims to capture a fuller image of the transatlantic slave trade and its resultant diaspora, tracing its ruptured lines of kinship and its forgone responsibilities, fateful entanglements, and temporal consequences. In doing this, the novel also self-referentially foregrounds its poetic potential, highlighting the ways in which only literature may be able to *make* this kind of history. In line with the Aristotelian dictum that "poetry is more philosophical and more elevated than history, since poetry relates more of the universal, while history relates particulars" (Aristoteles 1995: 59), *Homegoing* contrasts several modes of writing history, subtly favoring the poetic world making of literature.

The difficulty of writing diasporic or Black history is embodied by the figures of Yaw and Marcus, who are struggling to write a book in the book, as well as the figure of Marjorie, who writes the kind of poem which unwittingly 'gets it right,' by exposing not only the 'open wound' of her family's history, but also her desire 'to make whole.' Socially isolated and confused about her cultural identity, Yaw's US-born daughter Marjorie finds solace in the books she receives from her teacher Mrs. Pinkston, who not only tells her that "in this country [...] black is black is black" but is also the only person she knows who has read her father's publication (273). It is Mrs. Pinkston who encourages Marjorie to write and perform at her school's Black cultural event. The end result is a poem that clairvoyantly alludes to various aspects of her family's history and moves from the notion of two sisters being "split" and separate to being "kin" and "same" despite their vastly different experiences (282).

---

87 This process of sublimation, which LaCapra sees occurring when "the excess of trauma becomes an uncanny source of elation or ecstasy" (2001: 23), can, of course, also be related to Paul Gilroy's notion of the slave sublime. However, in my reading of Gilroy, Hartman, and other theorists focusing on the 'founding trauma' of racial slavery, the sublime is not merely an opportunity for a group to "transvalue" trauma into a test of endurance, allowing an "entry into the extraordinary" (LaCapra 2001: 23). Because this event is so tied up with the fabric of modern society, it is never singular but always social and political, even through its negation of social reality and orientation toward "the power of the phatic and the ineffable" (Gilroy 2002: 131). Nevertheless, I agree with critics of the slave sublime that these approaches run the risk of being not only morbid, both in the sense of social and physical death, but are also often unspecific and reifying of slavery. For these discussions, see Goyal 2003; Chrisman 1997.

Yaw's book, on the other hand, his vexed and vexing project, may at first glance represent the *mise en abyme* of the novel. His historical book project is finally completed after many years, either right before or after he and his wife Esther move to the United States. In the chapter on Marjorie, the reader is told that his "lifework" is now titled *The Ruin of a Nation Begins in the Homes of Its People:* "He'd taken the title from an old Asante proverb and used it to discuss slavery and colonialism" (270). The parallels to the novel itself are fairly obvious. While the title, *Homegoing,* alludes to the African American belief that a person's spirit will return home after death, its epigraph is an Akan proverb: "The family is like the forest: if you are outside it is dense; if you are inside you see that each tree has its own position." In terms of scope and subject matter, *Homegoing* strives to accomplish what Yaw's historical work has done, at least for himself and the Pan-Africanist teacher who has read it. Initially wrestling to articulate or represent the unrepresentable, Yaw's turning point most likely occurs when he starts investigating the source of his personal anguish and, most importantly, makes peace with his mother. When his daughter Marjorie admits that she doesn't understand his complex historical treatise, he points toward another factor: time. Marjorie remembers her father telling her "that it was something she wouldn't understand until she was much older. He said that people need time in order to see things clearly" (270).

Time is precisely the crux of the other book project depicted in *Homegoing,* the completion of which remains unsure. Marcus, Marjorie's African American contemporary, has grown up in the shadow of his absent mother's lifelong and his father's precariously contained heroin addiction, yet he has also received the critical consciousness of his father Sonny's "alternative history lessons," himself a former NAACP member and activist of the 1960s (284). Around the year 2000, Marcus is in his 20s and on the way to obtain a PhD in sociology, but his research is stalling. Marcus is painfully aware of historical injustices, the complex workings of racism, and the complicity of his nation's prime institutions, embodied also by the "beautiful but deadly silent" reading room of a Stanford library (289). The anger he feels marks him as an outsider and makes it impossible to subject his book project to the neat periodization and progressive arc of mainstream historiography or the methodical structure of a self-sufficient research paradigm:

> How could he talk about Great-Grandpa H's story without also talking about his grandma Willie and the millions of other black people who had migrated north, fleeing Jim Crow? And if he mentioned the Great Migration, he'd have to talk about the cities that took that flock in. He'd have to talk about Harlem [...]. And if he started talking about the war on drugs, he's be talking about how nearly half of the black men he grew up with were on their way either into or out of what had become the harshest prison system in

the world [...] he'd get so angry that he'd slam his research book on the table of the beautiful but deadly silent Lane Reading Room of Green Library of Stanford University. And if he slammed the book down, then everyone in the room would stare and all they would see would be his skin and his anger, and they'd think they knew something about him, and it would be the same something that had justified putting his great-grandpa H in prison, only it would be different too, less obvious than it once was. When Marcus started to think this way, he couldn't get himself to open even one book. (289–290)

In a way, Marcus is so deeply 'inside' the US-American forest that all he sees is the way that racism has positioned himself and his family. At the same time, the formal constraints of his dissertation do not allow him to draw out the universal, the bigger picture of racism, but rather force him to "[relate] particulars" (Aristoteles 1995: 59). Because *Homegoing* is a contemporary novel about race that, like the other novels discussed in this study, is always at risk to be read (only) sociologically, Marcus's book project performs quite a few things. For one, it allows Gyasi to indeed comment on the history of US-American race relations in a 'realistic' or 'factual' manner. On the other hand, and not unlike Ifemelu's blog in *Americanah* or Julius's historical digressions in *Open City*, these insights are qualified by their intradiegetic function within the novel, if not in content then in form. Marcus is unable to express the "'true implications and the horrors" of the Black experience in a sociological text (Nehl 2016: 12), just as Yaw was unable to write his history book about the Gold Coast in the masculinist rhetoric of Black Nationalism. What finally enabled Yaw – introspection, recognizance, expansion, and, above all, time – is either not applicable or as yet unavailable to Marcus.

Particularly in the context of the US, Marcus cannot insert his experience into what Bhabha, following Bakhtin, describes as the "representative authority" of a national narrative unfolding in the "*fullness of time*" (2004: 206). Marcus's experience is instead marked by an impossible split, a disjunctive temporality that not only troubles "the homogeneous and horizontal view associated with the nation's imagined community" (Bhabha 2004: 206) but also fundamentally motivates this inquiry, this "posing of a question, rather than imitation of a form of being" that Jared Sexton describes as the epitome of Black study (2011: 9). Because *Homegoing* is precisely such an inquiry, motivated by the "vague but important" question "What does it mean to be black in America?" (Gyasi 2016: para. 15), the following passage about Marcus's desire to represent the unspeakable discloses the novel's own modus operandi and fundamental conflict:

How could he explain to Marjorie that what he wanted to capture with his project was the *feeling of time*, of having been part of something that stretched so far back, was so impossibly large, that it was easy to forget that she, and he, and everyone else, existed in it – not apart from it, but inside of it. How could he explain to Marjorie that he wasn't supposed to be here? Alive. Free. (295–296, emphasis added)

Homegoing's fictionalization of the intertwined histories of slavery, colonialism, and institutionalized racism is not necessarily about telling but rather about showing a different kind of history and about adopting a distinctly metahistoricist 'feel' for history. And it claims to do so, as the reflection on failed or complicated book projects suggests, ultimately more successfully than either the historical treatise or the sociological dissertation. While emphasizing the general value of literary imagination, the novel also distinguishes between its own labor and that of poetry. While Marjorie's poem is shown to capture the essence of this story in both vivid and transient imagery, *Homegoing* is able to provide more than the elevated world making of metaphor and mimesis. In its narrative progression, it also provides a sense of this world in its unfolding over time. In its effort to capture the feeling for a feeling of time, *Homegoing* draws on the crucial significance of temporality in the making of the Black Diaspora.

In "Afro-Modernity," Michael Hanchard affirms the central role of Afro-Modern counterhistories, distinguishing between the metahistorical positionalities of *tabula rasa* and *tabula blanca*. For the former, African history simply needed to be unearthed and reconstructed, often in accordance with the Herskovitzean model. The latter approach conceived the history of African-New World peoples as fundamentally severed from Africa and instead often systematized around issues of resistance and mobilization.[88] The reconstruction of a usable past often formed the "first pedagogical project" undertaken by Afro-Modern thinkers and activists, yet even those suggesting a more radical epistemological break with Africa had to reckon with a shared notion of temporal disjuncture imposed by the twin histories of slavery and imperialism (Hanchard 1999: 251–252). The reason behind this, Hanchard writes, was the fact that the "temporal consequences of racial inequality were to be experienced and felt across African and Afro-diasporic contexts wherever a person defined by their phenotypic proximity to

---

[88] Stressing the notion of African continuity and survival in the New World, Melville Herskovits's *The Myth of the Negro Past* (1941) represents one the most important paradigms in diaspora studies. His work intervened into scholarship that had disputed the existence of African survivals, such as E. Franklin Frazier's *The Negro Family in the United States* (1939) or Charles S. Johnson's *Shadow of the Plantation* (1934). Later contestations were rather leveled against romanticizing and essentializing views of African continuity and survival, thus stressing the notion of cultural hybridity and the severing yet also transformative effect of the Middle Passage, such as Gilroy's *The Black Atlantic*.

the indigenous peoples of sub-Saharan Africa inhabited the same territorial realm with whites" (ibid. 252).

Adopting an analytical lens that allows one to view racial politics outside of essentializing or phenotypic terms, Hanchard therefore suggest the notion of racial time, because time, "when linked to relations of dominance and subordination, is another social construct that marks inequality between various social groups" (1999: 253). Hanchard lists several instances of racial time that mark the imposed time structures experienced by the slave or the disparate colonial time relations affecting African nation states, and that also apply to the temporal configurations in *Homegoing*.[89]

There is, for example, the notion of sameness and repetition that overrides the temporal experiences of numerous characters in the novel and that Hanchard links to the temporal constraints of slave labor in the Americas. Because, theoretically, "no time belonged solely to the slave," time becomes utterly devoid of meaning, locking protagonists in feelings of eternal stasis, repetition, or endless waiting (Hanchard 1999: 256). The sentiment of Ness, the first family member born into slavery who, when asked how her day went, rhetorically replies, "Ain't all days the same?" (*Homegoing* 71), is echoed by the Harlem jazz singer and future mother to Marcus, Amani, who answers Sonny's "Long day?" with: "Ain't all days long?" (250). Sonny, in turn, quits his job with the NAACP housing team after the futility of his work is exposed by a young boy who, after reporting his family's dire living conditions, confronts him with another rhetorical question: "You can't do a single thing, can you?" (246). The realization that this boy and his family might wait forever, that in the most 'advanced' and 'progressive' city of the world they would receive decent housing "only *after* those same services were provided for whites" (Hanchard 1999: 263), accentuates Sonny's prior doubts that even if his political work will ever affect any change in America, this change might not be much different but "mostly the same" (*Homegoing* 244).

Several passages in the novel refer to this paradoxical experience of time – the return of the ever same – and signal Hartman's notion of the "incomplete project of freedom," where each ostensibly progressive historical event fails to undo the afterlife of slavery (2008: 4). One character in *Homegoing* also speaks

---

[89] Hanchard's essay is used exemplarily for a variety of theorizations of racial, colonial, or Black time. Similar discussions of these themes can be found in Gikandi, where he describes the "history of the African self as a struggle with the problem of modern time" (2011b: 86). They also appear in Gilroy, particularly in the chapter "Not a Story to Pass On: Living Memory and the Slave Sublime" (2002). See also the concept of distinctly racialized political time in the US in both Reed 2014, and English 2013, or the notion of disjunct temporalities in Bhabha 2004.

of the Civil War as a war that "may be over but it ain't ended" (158); a father contemplates his young daughter's night terrors, fighting in her sleep against "Intangible evil. Unspeakable unfairness" and has a sense of "where it started, but when, where, did it end" (210). Here, the continuity of racism appears to be the 'changing same' that affects Black people's lives right until the (more or less) contemporary moment.[90] Despite being born in the post-Civil Rights era, it is Marcus who still feels like he is nothing but "an accumulation of these times" (286).

In a political sense, the notion of futility, of ineffectual or insufficient change, translates into what Martin Luther King, criticizing the political doctrine of gradualism, described as the "pain of progress" (qtd. in Hanchard 265). Knowing well that the time spent and lost in waiting for freedom could never be regained, King nevertheless suggested that Black people should receive some form of compensation, similar to military veterans, for lost time (ibid.). The most literal instance of lost time in *Homegoing* is experienced by the character of H, who is "doing time" in a chapter detailing one of novel's lesser known episodes of American history – the convict leasing system in Alabama. Around the 1880s, H is sentenced to 10 years of grueling work in the coalmines for an offense as petty as it is fictitious. While H nevertheless manages to somewhat 'make up' for his lost time by finally reconnecting with his girlfriend, starting a family and working the mines on his own accord, it is not only his ultimately fatal case of the black lung that reveals how deeply this unjust experience has been etched into his body.

The chapter on H is an interesting meditation on materiality and embodiment that could be related to Fanon's Black intervention into a purportedly universal model of subjectivity, such as his observation that the "Negro suffers in his body quite differently from the white man" (2008: 106).[91] For Fanon, the process of racialization substitutes Merleau-Ponty's corporeal schema with a "racial epidermal schema" and prevents the Black man from suffering in and as a lived

---

90 Amiri Baraka (LeRoi Jones) wrote about "The Changing Same" in reference to a distinctly Black cultural tradition, most noticeable in music. Gilroy picks up this phrase extensively, for example, when he writes: "The syncretic complexity of black expressive cultures alone supplies powerful reasons for resisting the idea that an untouched, pristine Africanity resides inside these forms, working a powerful magic of alterity in order to trigger repeatedly the perception of absolute identity. Following the lead established long ago by Leroi [sic] Jones, I believe it is possible to approach the music as a changing rather than an unchanging same" (2002: 101).
91 Fanon counters Sartre's existentialist notion of the body as a form of "suffered" imprisonment that nevertheless provides the facticity of our "being in the world" – as a body belonging "with the 'lived'" (Sartre 1965: 339).

body, because awareness of his body is only ever gained in a third, objectifying perspective that conflates his identity, "at the same time," with his body, race, and ancestors (2008: 84). However, this emphasis on collective identity should not obscure Fanon's explicitly gendered position, who self-admittedly "[knew] nothing about" the "woman of color" (2008: 138).[92] In this sense, the literal imprisonment of *H* also signifies the metaphorical imprisonment of the racially objectified *and* gendered body, and this intersectional position severely affects the way H not only suffers but perceives (in) his body.

Exemplifying the ways in which the social discourses of race, gender, and time intersect and affect the Black male body, the story of H highlights the particular vulnerability of Black American masculinity. This vulnerability becomes especially evident if we relate this character to his ancestor Sam and his descendant Marcus. Exceptionally strong and huge, H has unwittingly inherited the genetic disposition of his grandfather and the gendered stereotypes that conscript Kojo from the very moment he is brought into the symbolic system of racial slavery: "He is the large, muscular body of the African beast, and he refuses to be caged" (80). Coming "straight from the Continent," Sam is commanded to "marry" Ness and, railing against his circumstances, his rage turns him into "the animal he's been told that he is" (ibid.). In the historico-biological system of racism, H does not simply resemble his grandfather in stature. He also bears the mark of the 'Black Buck' stereotype. Predictably, H is falsely accused for "studyin' a white woman" (158).

An extremely strong and tireless worker, H accomplishes almost superhuman feats in the mines, earning him the nickname Two-Shovel H. But of course, as he two-handedly shovels his and another man's quota of coal, the shovels extending from his body only make it more apparent that despite his exceptional gift for mining, he is far from being superhuman, or human for that matter, but a mere tool and thus both exploitable and fungible. After that experience, H has his first emotional break down because he cannot "feel his arms" (163). This sense of thingification and alienation, blurring the boundaries between the organic and the inorganic, also extends to the way H imagines his body in relation to others: "Sometimes as he slept the chains would rub against his ankles in such a way that he would remember the feeling of Ethe's hands there, which always surprised him since metal was nothing like skin" (162). When H is released, he showers and tries to scrub away the 'mark' of his experience,

---

[92] See "The Woman of Color and the White Man" in *Black Skins White Masks*. For in-depth discussions of Fanon's gendered position and relation to women, see, for example, Chow 2010; Sharpley-Whiting 1998.

but it has already seeped into his skin, determining not only how the world perceives him but affecting his own perception of the world. Soon, H realizes that he will never be able to "go back to the free world, marked as he was" (167). Because he has only known sharecropping and coal mining in his life, he is unable to conceive of his Blackness outside of the material conditions that have produced it. Remembering Ethe, all "he could think was that her skin was the color of cotton stems. And he missed that blackness, having only known the true blackness of coal for nearly ten years" (166). When H finally reconnects with Ethe, embracing the "full weight of her body" that was "not the same weight as coal," the fact that Ethe's body reacts differently to the material he has "spent nearly a third of his life lifting," anticipates his return to a world populated by bodies not things, as precarious and momentary as this family idyll may be (176).

Deprived of a decade of his life, his body irreparably damaged and his future as an ex-con narrowly predetermined, H nevertheless experiences a brief moment of temporal contingency following his release. He muses on how "easy it was for a life to go one way instead of another" (171) and wonders whether he could now become "a new kind of black man altogether, one who got to use his mind" (168). Referenced, here, is the notion of the "New Negro," an expression that, as Hanchard points out, circulated within the Harlem Renaissance and constitutes a temporal discourse adopted by the political vanguard of almost every Black post-emancipation movement in the New World. This discourse centered on the desire "to rid themselves and their communities of any vestiges of enslavement" (Hanchard 1999: 260).

While H, after being rendered pure material and ruined for any other professional path, will never lead a "life of the mind," *Homegoing*'s particular mode of "rhyming" historical periods gives a fairly definitive answer as to whether newness may also signify freedom. The hopeful notion attached to the passing of time is countered by H's great-grandson Marcus, whose life chances, despite being a Ph.D. student at Stanford, are still predetermined by a racial imaginary manifesting itself as "legends, stories, history, and above all *historicity*" (Fanon 2008: 84). The same deadly fiction that put H in jail for "studyin' a white woman" (158) can still decide over his fate if he, studying the injustices of the convict leasing system, expresses his anger in a public outburst. Despite being admitted into the highest ranks of that which constitutes the public sphere, Marcus is always precariously perched on the margins of it – like a distinguished Harvard professor who, perching on his own front porch, is arrested for attempted burglary.⁹³ As Marcus muses, the fact of "his skin and his anger" would lead "everyone in the room" to "think they knew something about him," and that "something" would be the same "that had justified putting his great-grandpa H in prison" (290). Obviously, the through-line connecting H and Marcus is more than their genetic makeup. It is that makeup's very real vulnerability toward what Claudia Rankine has described as the paranoia, rage, and violence of the white imagination.⁹⁴

Despite his disadvantaged childhood, Marcus may have escaped the school-to-prison-pipeline but, *qua* skin color and just like "nearly half of the black men he grew up with," he could still be conscripted into the prison-industrial complex (189). Marcus is struggling to fully describe the future repercussions of the convict leasing system – his family history and the object of his study. But he is fully aware that the history of "what had become the harshest prison system in the world" is rooted in slavery (289). As H is drawn into the early beginnings of the prison industrial complex, his sentence is only a barely disguised attempt at further extracting slave labor under Jim Crow laws. In exposing these historical links, *Homegoing* reiterates what scholars like Angela Davis, Ruth Wilson Gilmore, and Michelle Alexander have extensively documented and critiqued, and what Ava DuVernay's Oscar-nominated documentary *The 13ᵗʰ* (2016) has brought to the big screen.⁹⁵ Named after the constitutional amendment that abolished slavery "*except as a punishment for a crime*," the film details the enormous legal, cultural, political, and economic efforts that went into maintaining and even exacerbating the fact that certain human beings are continuously made into exceptions. It is noteworthy that DuVernay, who is most known for the historical drama *Selma* (2014), departs from a historicist position that views American history, and particularly the latter half of the 20ᵗʰ century, as marked by some form of teleological progress. Instead, her more recent documentary seems to emphasize how many cards are indeed stacked against this progress, both collectively as a nation and individually, as an inheritor of that nation's history. When DuVernay poses in a T-shirt inscribed with the words "I am my ancestor's wildest dream," one can hear this sentiment echoed by *Homegoing*'s final chapter on Marcus, who wonders "how [he] could explain to Marjorie that he wasn't supposed to be here. Alive. Free" (296).⁹⁶ If, following

---

93 Of course, I am referring to the infamous arrest of Professor Henry Louis Gates in 2009.
94 See Thrasher 2016: para. 22. Also, as Rankine writes in *Citizen: An American Lyric:* "Because white men can't/police their imagination/black men are dying" (2014: 135).
95 See Davis 2003; Wilson Gilmore 2007; Alexander 2012.
96 It also alludes to the final lines of Maya Angelou's poem "Still I Rise" (1978): "Bringing the gifts that my ancestors gave/ I am the dream and the hope of the slave/ I rise /I rise /I rise."

Hayden White's reading of Auerbach, all history is an act of redemption, emplotted through reverse causation, what happens to a people who, in the words of Audre Lorde, "were never meant to survive" (1995: 109)? Or to frame the question differently: If, as White asserts elsewhere, "in choosing our past, we choose a present," what kind of past would a people claim to arrive at what many Black Americans see as a catastrophic present? And how, to reiterate Marcus's question, could one ever explain how that feels?

6 "The Gnarled Fingers of Fate": Curse Temporalities and the Question of Agency

In 1913, W.E.B. Du Bois commissioned the artist Meta Fuller to produce a sculpture in celebration of the 50th anniversary of the abolition of slavery. The sculpture, today located on Harriet Tubman Square in Boston, carries the title *Emancipation* and is inscribed with the following sentence: "Humanity weeping over her suddenly freed children, who, beneath the gnarled fingers of Fate, step forth into the world, unafraid." Fuller elaborated on the idea behind her sculpture:

> I presented the race by a male and female figure standing under a tree, the branches of which are the fingers of Fate grasping at them to draw them back into the fateful clutches of hatred [...]. The Negro has been emancipated from slavery but not from the curse of race hatred and prejudice. (qtd. in Rubinstein 1990: 202)

Reading the stories of sharecropper H or Harlem heroin addict Sonny, familiar in their typicality, readers are confronted simultaneously with what was and what shall be, each event foretold and anticipated by the course of history. While the techniques of flashbacks and foreshadowing aren't particularly noteworthy for a historical novel per se, it is important to read the novel in the context of African and diasporic notions of temporality, particularly those affected by today's bleak political assessment. The historicism employed by *Homegoing* depicts Black lives as ruinously doomed by "the curse of race hatred and prejudice," their destinies unfolding under the shadow cast by this fate. Moreover, diasporic narratives have always indicated alternative temporalities – out of necessity. Writing about the rise of what he calls the "recent historical novel," Manshel notes how this current genre "suggests that recent history is a period defined by insistent states of emergency. World-historical catastrophe punctuates both narrative time and historical time: a particularly useful function in an age of forever wars and 'slow death' threats like climate change" (2017: para. 12). As a transatlantic history of slavery and colonialism, *Homegoing* is necessarily positioned within a temporality in which the catastrophe has always already happened, investing in characters long since subjected to various forms of slow death. Therefore, the notion of history as curse or fate often translates into a somewhat post-apocalyptic temporality that is not exclusive to diasporic New World narratives, but as the following passage will briefly address, is also an important feature of the African novel.

We can find this post-apocalyptic temporality in the tragic ending of *Things Fall Apart*, framing not only Okonkwo's death but also *The Pacification of the Primitive Tribes of the Lower Niger* as mere footnotes in capital H history (Achebe 1958: 183). It also appears in the so-called petro-magic-fiction of contemporary Nigeria, portraying the insidious effect of what Rob Nixon has called "slow other vioviolence" – meaning "a violence that occurs gradually and out of sight, a violence of delayed destruction that is dispersed across time and space" (2011: 2).[97] Another striking example would be Jennifer Makumbi's *Kintu*, a contemporary Ugandan novel with an interestingly bifurcated publication history and an ever growing, enthusiastic readership.[98] Similar to *Homegoing*, the novel follows several generations of one family and employs curse temporality as a historiographic device.

Kintu is often singled out for providing a rich historical panorama of Uganda that bypasses the history of colonialism. As the "great Ugandan novel" it is often praised, *Kintu* stretches far back into the history of the Buganda kingdom and connects it, by way of a family curse resulting from a father accidentally murdering his foster son, to contemporary post-Idi-Amin-Uganda. Yet even though the colonial period is skipped, the temporality of colonialism cannot be undone. This is apparent in the epigraph taken from the writings of colonial explorer John Hanning Speke (1827–1864). Speke professes "accurately to describe naked Africa" in a passage reminiscent of Achebe's District Commissioner, but not only non-fictional, but ultimately more mythical than the Commissioner's of-

---

97 See Jennifer Wenzel's "Petro-Magic-Realism: Toward a Political Ecology of Nigerian Literature," where she lists writings by Ben Okri and Karen King-Aribisala. A more recent exemplar of this theme can be found in Chinelo Okparanta's short story "America" from *Happiness Like Water*, where the lesbian protagonist, instead of moving toward the progressive promise of liberal America, decides to stay and submit herself to the murky and obfuscated futures generated both by the heavily polluted Niger delta and her homophobic environment.

98 After winning the Kwani? Manuscript prize in 2013, *Kintu* was first published by Kwani Trust in Kenya the following year. Only after it had become a huge success was it picked up by American and subsequently British publishers. The novel is a striking exemption of what Akinwumi Adesokan has bemoaned as the process of "reversed extraversion" characterizing African fiction that only gains traction in the author's "historical contexts" after it has become successful in "the West" (2012: 2).

ficial prose (Speke 1863: xiii).[99] This epigraph is followed by the novel's prologue, set in 2004 and detailing the brutal, and coincidental, public execution of Kamu Kintu, who is mistaken for a thief and kicked to death by an angry mob. The scene, eerily reminiscent of the one detailed in Teju Cole's *Every Day Is for the Thief*, sets the stage for the novel's epic, multigenerational sprawl. The murder, it suggests, is just another instance of the curse haunting every descendant of the mythical ancestor Kintu Kidda. At the end of the prologue, as market vendors discuss the significance of Kamu's murder, linking it to other violent incidents and peddling both "fate" and "the curse" as explanations, one woman adds another dimension (*Kintu* 7). Regardless of a family line being cursed, she concludes, "that is what happens to a race that fails to raise its value on the market" (ibid.). The notion of reification and commodification inherent in this comment reiterates the actual horror unfolding in Kamu Kintu's execution, who, in becoming a thief, ceases to be human:

> The word *thief* started to bounce from here to there, first as a question than as a fact. It repeated itself over and over like an echo calling. The crowd grew [...]. Angry men just arriving asked, "Is *it* a thief?", because Kintu had ceased to be human.
> The word *thief* summed up the common enemy. Why there was no supper the previous night; why their children were not on their way to school. *Thief* was the president who arrived two and a half decades ago waving "democracy" at them [...]. *Thief* was God poised with a can of aerosol *Africancide*, his fingers pressing hard on the button. (4–5)

The always-precarious distinction between the human and the non-human is a core theme of the novel, not only because *kintu* is also the Bantu word for 'thing,' but also because Makumbi is certainly aware of how, as Mbembe describes it, "discourse on Africa is almost always deployed in the framework (or on the fringes) of a meta-text about the *animal* – to be exact, about the *beast*" (2001: 1). Reading the prologue in conversation with the epigraph conveys this distinction also in terms of temporality. What the angry crowd in contemporary Kampala feels robbed of is a functioning future, the notion of freedom and agency that appears to be awarded to full humanity. All they can hope for, as racialized and unchanging objects, is to raise their global market value. At the same time, the market woman's deadpan commentary implies that today's squalor provides the retrospective rationalization of yesterday's curse, as "that is

---

99 It goes: "I profess accurately to describe naked Africa [...]. If the picture be a dark one, we should, when contemplating these sons of Noah, try and carry our mind back to that time when our poor elder brother Ham was cursed by his father, and condemned to be the slave of both Shem and Japheth; for as they were then, so they appear to be now – a striking existing proof of the Holy Scriptures."

what happens." The novel's epigraph by Speke suggests a similar sense of predetermination through the biblical hermeneutics of figura and fulfillment. Referencing the myth of Ham and naturalizing a state of enslavement for Africans, Speke asserts that "for as they were then, so they appear to be now – a striking existing proof of the Holy Scriptures" (Speke 1863: xiii).

Utilizing Speke's travelogue and the Hamitic myth as an ironic intertext, *Kintu*'s pre- and post-colonial history of Uganda nevertheless problematizes the lasting effects of these kinds of quasi-theological, 'scientific' writings. As Patrick Wolfe notes in relation to the secularization of the theological discourse during the Enlightenment period, the naturalized discourse of race functioned as a key component to this process. Wolfe writes that, whereas "the Rousseauan vision of improvability through education recast the Christian possibility of grace (in the case of Jews, of conversion), race could also endow debasement with the fixity of a curse" (2015: 9). The problem, then, is not so much that Africa and Africans have been written *out* of History, but that they have also been produced and enveloped by it in a manner that nullifies agency: Blackness as curse or fate. The logic of figuration as racialization imposes not only a scripted past, present, and future, but it does so, most importantly, by inscribing this fate on the body.

As Wolfe observes, besides functioning as a stratifying element that installs hierarchy by (de)valuing difference, race is a classificatory concept that links material and immaterial spheres, rendering it "not a negotiable condition but a destiny, one whose principal outward sign is the body" (2015: 7). As metahistorical device in Afro-diasporic fictions, curse temporalities are thus slightly distinct from haunting and spectrality because they open up questions of relationally, futurity, and agency. Who inherits the curse? What is the difference between a curse and the course of history? And can it be undone? For Benjamin's historical materialist, turning toward the past holds the most promise for exploding the linear time of progress – a progress that continues the subjugation of the marginalized and that holds past, present, and future hostage. In that sense, Benjamin inverts the teleology of messianism, which thrives on the notion of future redemption. Rather than abandoning the concept entirely, however, he proposes a messianism without the singular savior provided by the course of history, where instead each moment, when viewed through the lens of an historical constellation, may reveal its "*weak* messianic power" (Benjamin 2003: 390).

As one literary critic observes, Gyasi expertly utilizes the novel's particular temporal structure to summon "the fantasy of retreat into love and family, and then to show how history will, inevitably, trample that dream" (Miller 2016: para. 10). And indeed, repeatedly, Black life is represented apart from loss, dispossession, and grief – particularly in the chapters set on the Gold Coast. Yet ultimately, these moments are enveloped by the deterministic force of race in/as history. In spite of this ambiguity, however, *Homegoing*'s affective bedrock engenders a sense of potential redemption that does not function as mere gimmick or narrative device, made sweeter by its deferral, but represents a weak messianic possibility. Because, as Gyasi has noted in an interview, "a great way" to think of the novel's chapters is to understand them as "love stories," the romance of redemption is indeed built into these individual snap shots in time, rather than an all-encompassing, grand historical arc (Owens 2016: para. 82).

Within *Homegoing*'s temporal framework, the promise of redemption is not plotted as progressive history but becomes a question of personal agency and introspection lying dormant within each historical moment. At the same time, the generally tragic plotting of its historicism questions a certain "pat liberal notion of human rights" which, according to Walter Johnson, underlies most scholarship on slavery and that tends to emphasize "'independent will and volition' against the possibility of 'dehumanization'" (2018: para. 8). It is therefore insufficient to read the novel as either "fulfillment" or "effect," as Julien outlines it in "The Extroverted African Novel": "If the African novel is construed as a site of fulfillment, it is linked to human agency and self-fashioning. If it is an effect, it is part of a necessary trajectory, merely a product of historical forces beyond writers' control" (2007: 668). *Homegoing* indeed employs and critiques simultaneously, by straining at the limits of both metahistoricist perspectives.

One example of this is the way in which the novel constantly evokes and revokes universalized notions of agency and historical change. In "What is a Historical System," a lecture given to an audience of biologists, Hayden White describes a people's historical past as a fiction that is ultimately more malleable than genetics yet is often interpreted in a similarly deterministic sense. For White, the difference between biological and historical systems lies in the latter's "choosing capacities" (2010: 132). He states that "historical systems differ from biological systems by their capacity to act *as if they could choose their own ancestors*" (ibid.). Most importantly, this act will determine the future behavior of a group, allowing for something of a historic opening with every generation that either chooses or does not choose to accept the transpired fiction of origin. The novel's chapter on James, for example, allows for such an opening to occur. James is already the product of complex cultural entanglements on the Gold Coast. Named after his grandfather James, the Governor of Cape Coast Castle, he is the son of Asante princess Nana Yaa Yeboah and Quey, the only child of Effia the Beauty, the cursed Fante girl who was married to the Governor. Born 1807, the year the slave trade was officially abolished, James nevertheless grows up as heir to the illegal, yet unceasing business of the trade. However, the signs point toward a power shift on the Gold Coast that – as James has

6 "Gnarled Fingers of Fate": Curse Temporalities and the Question of Agency — 189

come to realize – will replace the physical shackles of slavery with the new "invisible ones that wrapped around the mind" (93).

James is unable to fully fathom the role provided to him by his social position and ancestral history until the structures he takes for granted are questioned by Akosua, leading to his very own sense of crisis. Due to the episodic structure of the novel, the chapter on James provides only a short glimpse into a particular historical period, the Gold Coast on the brink of large-scale colonization, which threatens to engulf his personal story. As Europe enters into industrialization, James's cards will be drawn by the markets' invisible hand. His thoughts anticipate the shift from mercantilism and its trading post system to the new set of global relations determined by industrial economies. This new system, as Wolfe notes in *Traces of History*, will soon have "dispensed with the Native middleman and introduced the logic of production into the heart of Native societies, requiring either their removal or their transformation" (2015: 8).

This interplay between historical structure and individual agency arising from personal crisis is precisely the node that White identifies as the breeding ground for new historical systems. White asserts that in the same way in which sociocultural systems do not "die," but are "simply abandoned," new sociocultural systems are in fact "constituted by living men [sic] who have decided to structure their orientation in new ways" (2010: 131). When James first meets Akosua at the funeral of his grandfather, the Asantehene, their encounter is determined by their vastly different social positions. As part of the royal family, James is seated in "a single-file line of people beg[inning] at James's grandfather's first wife and [going] all the way into the middle town square" (*Homegoing* 96). Even though James has never lived in Asanteland and barely knew his maternal grandfather, power and lineage set him apart from the villagers, who are excepted to condole with the royal family by shaking each and every person's hand. The girl Akosua, once she reaches James, politely refuses to "shake the hand of a slaver" (96). Knowing about the Asante's role in the slave trade, James is astonished by her answer: "If the girl could not shake his hand, then surely she could never touch her own" (96) Intrigued, he later sets out to find her, allowing her to elaborate: "It is how we are all taught to think. But I do not want to think this way. When my brothers and the other people were taken, my village mourned them as we redoubled our military efforts. And what does that say? We avenge lost lives by taking more? It doesn't make sense to me" (98). James is deeply impressed with Akosua and her conviction to break the mold and become her "own nation" (98). He decides to become a small-scale farmer with Akosua, sacrificing the privilege of "family name and power," a privilege built in large parts on his father's and grandfather's work in the slave trade. War, the other great historical mechanism, presents him with a chance to opt out of the future provided for him. It is the "roving eye" of Mampanyin the "witch doctor" that sees James in Efutu, where the "never-ending Asante-British-War" (105–106) will be waged and where James will stage his own death in order to emerge on the same social footing as Akosua: "She had nothing, and she came from nothing" (99).

Notably, Hayden White's consistently male agent of change is made female in James's chapter. Not only Akosua, but also Mampanyin and his grandmother Effia, bearer of the original curse, encourage him to try "to make a new way" (107). Effia places hope in learning to be a different person, one that invents "new ways" and does not merely continue "with the old," yet she describes this as a mere possibility (ibid.). The further course of the novel continues to challenge this possibility, as the story of James and Akosua, while allowing them a humble degree of personal happiness, fails to break the tragic and violent "cycle" of the curse that is said to haunt the family "for as long as the line continued" (3). The ideology of race runs contrary to other ideological shifts, which White or Lukács would describe as the result of a crisis leading to a break with a theretofore-naturalized order. In its mediating of what Mbembe calls that "*opaque and murky domain of power*" that operates on human/non-human distinctions and plunges "human beings into a never-ending *process of brutalization*," the ideology of race does not dramatize or merely exacerbate, but actually overdetermine this family drama (2001: 14). While acts of betrayal, violence, and separation brought on by the ethnic conflicts of the Gold Coast create the necessary conditions for the curse, it is the different yet entangled roles in the institution of slavery that connect the bloodlines of the two half-sisters begotten by Maame – who can easily be interpreted as another figure for Mama Africa. The fact that this shared family history of slavery and colonialism has transmuted from simple acts of wrongdoing into a many-headed system fatefully shapes the destinies of all of Maame's children. At the same time, the fact that the imagined community of *Homegoing* is a community brought together by fate also creates the conditions for unity and the possibility for redemption.

7 Forgive Your Mother? Memory, Redemption, and the Sense of an Ending

Homegoing exemplifies how the history of institutionalized racism scripts Black American lives like a preordained fate similar, but also crucially different, from a religious narrative structured around collective enslavement, emancipation, and redemption.¹⁰⁰ Yet its structural emplotment is impossible to undo through an individual liberation narrative, as in Kojo's successful flight to the North, H's release from prison, or Sonny's battle against addiction. In line with many critical race theorists and political commentators, the novel proposes that historical change is cursory and futile as long as it unfolds under the same social symbolic. As Hortense Spillers writes in "Mama's Baby, Papa's Maybe":

> Even though the captive flesh/body has been "liberated", and no one need pretend that even the quotation marks do not *matter*, dominant symbolic activity, the ruling episteme that releases the dynamics of naming and valuation, remains grounded in the originating metaphors of captivity and mutilation so that it is as if neither tie nor history, nor historiography and its topics, show movement, as the human subject is "murdered" over and over again, by the passions of a bloodless and anonymous archaism, showing itself in endless disguise. (2003: 208)

Through its painful notion of time, *Homegoing* effectively conveys the afterlife of that limit event that unmistakably shaped the modern world, but it doesn't paint an entirely glum or hopeless scenario. The fact that Zadie Smith, for example, can endorse the novel as a "beautiful and healing read" speaks to the fact that Gyasi's novel somehow defies the "unflinching paradigmatic analysis" of US-American Afro-pessimism and its deep-seated mistrust of the reparative or recuperative as a mere lifeline of the dominant order.¹⁰¹ While the notion of linear historical progress is questioned, if not thwarted, by the novel's temporal representations of Black history's *longue durée* as marked by predetermination, belatedness, waiting, or erasure, it still manages to generate future-oriented moments of hope and potentiality.

Homegoing represents history as a painfully realist form of tragedy, and it also utilizes the epistemological possibilities behind a genre like romance. As Goyal notes, romance "as a form that can harmonize seemingly irreconcilable opposites – helps black Atlantic writers collapse distances of time and space

---

100 Analyzing the counterhistorical thrust of what he calls "race struggle" in *Society Must Be Defended,* Foucault notes: "And the history – or counterhistory – that is born of the story of the race struggle will of course speak from the side that is in darkness, from within the shadows. It will be, the discourse of those who have no glory, or of those who have lost it and who now find themselves, perhaps for a time – but probably for a long time – in darkness and silence [...]. This also means that this new discourse is similar to a certain number of epic, religious, or mythical forms which, rather than telling of the untarnished and uneclipsed glory of the sovereign, endeavor to formulate the misfortune of ancestors, exiles, and servitude" (2003: 70–71).
101 Frank Wilderson uses the term "unflinching paradigmatic analysis" on several occasions (e.g. 2010: 54).

to imagine a simultaneity of experience" (2010: 9). By connecting two family lines not merely though naturalized essence and genealogy but supernaturally through a curse that is of course also a bond, the novel's parallel focus enables a sense of Black diasporic simultaneity not unlike the "meanwhile" of Benedict Anderson's imagined community. Yet where, as in Anderson's model, this community adheres to the delimitations and assumed sovereignty of the nation, *Homegoing's* temporal configurations are better defined by a sense of historical heteronomy, temporal haunting, or the "prefiguring and fulfillment" inherent in Benjamin's notion of Messianic time, than by the kind of simultaneity that is "transverse, cross-time [...] and measured by clock and calendar" (Anderson 1991: 24). Rather than realizing the imagined community of Africa and its diaspora in a narrative that, "in keeping with the scale and diversity of the modern nation, works like the plot of a realist novel," *Homegoing* engenders to create continuity and unity with and through a fragmented, alternative temporality (Bhabha 2004: 226). It is precisely the impossible desire for unequivocal belonging and rootedness that motivates and connects the narrative strands. By querying the correlation between its imagined community and the teleological narratives of national history, the novel projects a sense of hope and redemption outside of those dominant temporal and narrative frameworks. Unlike the temporal and spatial confinement of Anderson's "meanwhile" and somewhat analogous to Gilroy's notion of the slave sublime, *Homegoing's* hopeful openings are atopical, atemporal, and ateleological.

As Gilroy writes in *The Black Atlantic*, the slave sublime is marked both by the desire to express the "unsayable" truths of slavery (2002: 37) and the eschatological or revolutionary concept of the Jubilee, which emerges "in black Atlantic culture to mark a special break or rupture in the conception of time defined and enforced by the regimes that sanctioned bondage" (ibid. 212). Like Gilroy's tentatively utopian notion of the politics of transformation, these moments abandon the representational constrains of "occidental rationality" that characterizes the demands of the "politics of fulfillment." The utopian promise of a politics of transformation is instead "magically" made audible through music, song, and dance, revealing "the hidden fissures of the concept of modernity" by conjuring and enacting "the new modes of friendship, happiness, and solidarity that are consequent on the overcoming of the racial oppression on which modernity and its antinomy of rational, western progress as excessive barbarity relied" (2002: 37–38). Some of *Homegoing's* minor redemptive moments likewise occur through music, explicitly imagined as both antidote to and result of racial oppression and indexing a vision of liberated Black life after the Jubilee. Yet the distinctly otherworldly nature of this vision not only unfolds in a theological context. It is also imagined as potentially enacted, concrete utopia. While arguably carrying an element of the eschatological, the non-directedness of these openings in *Homegoing* also occurs through what in Benjaminian terms could be described as the messianic pull toward a profane order "erected on the idea of happiness" (2003: 305).

Willie's voice, for example, is described as "one of the wonders of the world," stirring in her grandson Marcus "all the hope and love and faith that he would ever possess" (290). Willie's attempts at becoming a jazz singer in 1920s Harlem remain unsuccessful. After a series of tragic events, she dares to sing again only in the context of her local church, channeling the happy memory of her father "coming home every night" (221). After her husband Robert decides to pass for white and deserts her and Sonny, Willie eventually meets the poet Eli, who fathers her second child, writes poems called "Jazz" or "Flight," and, as a partner, is just as volatile and restless. In the final scene of her chapter, the profane and ever evanescent notion of home and belonging is juxtaposed with the novel's recurring tropes of disjunctiveness, instability, and fugitivity, highlighting the precarity of these momentary recourses into the homely against the backdrop of what Orlando Patterson has described as "natal alienation" (1982: 5). The "hope and love and faith" of Willie's voice, however, derives both from memory and a promised utopian elsewhere, and it is also described as the kind of beauty that is extracted from pressure. As a child, singing at her father H's union meetings, she imagines "that the sound came from a cave at the very bottom of her gut, that like her father and all the men in front of her, she was a miner reaching deep down inside of her to pull something valuable out" (201). Further marking the secularism inherent in that indexical utopian relation, Willie's son Sonny later states that "his mother didn't have to wait for Heaven for her reward. He could see it; she was already wearing her crown" (251).

Here, *Homegoing* employs familiar tropes of American Black life defined by social death and an aesthetic of sublimity conditioned by unimaginable hardship – most popularly embodied by the mythical "vibranium" in Ryan Coogler's *Black Panther* and described by Teju Cole as "that obdurate and versatile substance formed by tremendous pressure," an "embodied riposte to anti-blackness, a quintessence of mystery, resilience, self-containedness, and irreducibility" (2018: para. 51). A somewhat similar notion can be found in the writings of Fred Moten, a theorist who equally examines Black aesthetics in and through the legacies of slavery. Moten's Black Optimist stance is therefore often cast, not necessarily as an antagonist to Afro-pessimist theories, but as something of a middle ground between a guileless celebration of Black culture and an Afro-pessimist avowal of Black culture's ontological relation to slavery and social death. Moten examines this contradictory stance in "The Case of Blackness," where he asks: "How can we fathom a social life that tends toward death, that enacts a kind of being-toward-death, and which, because of such tendency and enactment, maintains a terribly beautiful vitality?" (2008: 188). Like Gilroy's notion of the revolutionary potential of the slave sublime, the knowledge of freedom is thus derived from the condition of absolute unfreedom. Or, as Moten writes, it becomes intelligible only through this condition: "This is the knowledge of freedom that is not only before wage-labor but before slavery as well, though the forms it takes are possible only by way of the crucible of the experience of slavery (as forced and stolen labor and sexuality, as wounded kinship and imposed exile)" (2003: 227).

This dual concept of a freedom both anticipated and remembered may also be conveyed in the temporal and spatial coordinates locating Africa in the diasporic imaginary. Reviewing the prevalent notion of death and suicide in Black literature, Gilroy notes how the "turn towards an African home [...] may also be a turn towards death" (2002: 208). This aspect speaks to the forced dislocations of Black Atlantic modernity and fundamentally affects its notions of temporality and futurity, as Simon Gikandi observes in *Slavery and The Culture of Taste*. While, for "philosophers of modernity from Hegel to Habermas, modernity has been conceptualized as an 'an epochal concept', one that marks a break with a previous period and thus privileges the future as the site of fulfillment," the "African slave's trajectory in the temporality of modernity and the forms of social identity associated with it" were "dominated by fear of the future [...] an acute sense of regressive time" (2011b: 87). The "slaves' notion of the future," Gikandi writes, "was that of a space of death" (ibid.). In this particular epistemic coupling, Black Atlantic temporalities do not only frame the future as unsure or fatally scripted, but Africa itself comes to signify either the realm of a lost past or a future after death.

Homegoing clearly strains at this narrow mapping of the Black Atlantic. Despite the mythical content of its title, Africa is imagined and historicized as an active presence instead of a living memory. In its mobilizing of a return narrative however, the novel comes dangerously close to reiterating the romanticized redemption narrative that diaspora theorists such as Gilroy and Hartman have argued against, and that has also been repudiated by literary responses such as Caryl Phillips's *Crossing the River*. Drawing on the analogous framing of Africa as static and archetypal and its irrevocable abandonment as the diaspora's originary moment in both Gilroy's *Black Atlantic* and Philips' novel, Goyal observes how those influential diasporic discourses that center hybrid and anti-essentialist models of diaspora often tend to reify and essentialize the African continent in turn (2003: 5–38). While *Homegoing* obviously differs from these models by providing rich insights into the history of the Gold Coast, a crucial difference also lies in its particular vantage point regarding notions of redemption and agency. Whereas both Gilroy's slave sublime and the story line of *Crossing the River* allocate the possibility for redemption in the New World, *Homegoing* allows for a much more balanced and indeed more complicated view. Both narrative threads, in the US and on the Gold Coast, incorporate the above-mentioned openings for historical and personal change. If anything, the Gold Coast provides a less tragically fated notion of futurity. This sense of a redeemed past and future, however, does not simply occur through the familiar tropes of a return narrative that casts Africa in the role of a lost and regained homeland. There are three scenes in the novel that most notably employ the theme of redemption, and it is worth considering them in more detail.

The first is the scene of forgiveness between Yaw and his mother Akua that may in an exemplary way stand in for the larger notion of guilt and forgiveness in the African diaspora. Akua suffers from the family curse through Maame's vivid nightmares but also most violently acts out this trauma by somnambulantly setting fire to her hut, killing two of her children and scarring Yaw. The pain and pent-up rage characterizing Yaw's estranged relationship to his mother can be framed in the familiar diasporic narrative of Africa and her diaspora and its addressing of Africa's historical guilt and complicity in the slave trade. In this sense, Akua's words spoken to Yaw are clearly directed to another context and another time:

> "There is evil in our lineage. There are people who have done wrong because they could not see the result of the wrong. They did not have these burned hands as warning."
>
> She held her hand out to him, and he looked at them carefully. He recognized her skin in his own. "What I know now, my son: Evil begets evil. It grows. It transmutes, so that sometimes you cannot see that the evil in the world began as the evil in your own home. I'm sorry you have suffered. I'm sorry for the way your suffering casts a shadow over your life, over the woman you have yet to marry, the children you have yet to have [...]. When someone does wrong, whether it is you or me, whether it is mother or father, whether it is the Golf Coast or the white man [...]. No one forgets they were once captive, even if they are now free. But still, Yaw, you have to let yourself be free." (241)

While there is a certain universalized notion of guilt established here, a tendency Goyal also detects in the multiple perspectives of *Crossing the River*, it does make a difference that Akua is represented not only as repenting. Her recognition of guilt, her reckoning with the past and its consequences, also renders her an active agent of change and enabler of a radically different future. Right before Yaw meets his mother, he begrudgingly considers the danger of exacting forgiveness without the recognition of guilt, here in relation to the colonial instrumentalization of Christianity:

> Esther had been the one to encourage his homecoming. She said it had something to do with forgiveness, but Yaw wasn't certain that he believed in forgiveness. He heard the word most on the few days he went to the white man's church [...] and so it had begun to seem to him like a word the white men brought with them when they first came to Africa. A trick their Christians had learned and spoke loudly and freely about to the people of the Gold Coast. Forgiveness, they shouted, all the while committing their wrongs. [...] Forgiveness was an act done after the fact, a piece of the bad deed's future. And if you point the people's eye to the future, they might not see what is being done to hurt them in the present. (237–238)

It matters that the novel's most explicit moment of redemption, or at least its signaled willingness to work through historical trauma, occurs in the context of the Gold Coast and between the descendants of former slavers. Even if one were to frame the exchange as the more traditional one between Africa and her enslaved children – a reading surely possible considering its pronounced anachronisms – it differs from those accounts in the active role it provides for Akua. It is she who initiates the redemptive moment, "running her fingers along the ruined skin that [Yaw] alone had touched for nearly half a century." Undeterred "by the anger in his voice," she touches "all of it," fully taking in the consequences of her acting out the family trauma (239). In Phillips's novel, the voice of the African father who has sold his children into slavery remains fixed and unchanging, such that the "novel cannot imagine a productive or dynamic role for Africa beyond that of celebrating the determined survival of its descendants in the New World" (Goyal 2003: 22). Instead, the novel presumes "the never-ending guilt of the African father and his one and only role as passive witness" (ibid.).

Homegoing's focus on the moral entanglements between Africa and her diasporas marks a distinct discursive position in the moment of Afropolitanism. While the novel's efforts may be read as continuation of the cultural work of Ama Ata Aidoo's *Dilemma of a Ghost* and *Anowa*, it is also a significant intervention into those contemporary diasporic discourses unfolding under the sign of Afropolitanism that are engaged in disentangling Blackness and Africanity. If anything, *Homegoing* can be credited with reckoning with the question of unity and kinship in a way that does not bypass the question of guilt. In fact, as an inquiry into 'what it means to be Black,' the novel suggests that – even though the racial category of Blackness does not apply or at least unfolds differently on the continent – Africa cannot or should not disavow its role in the genesis of racial slavery and thus divest itself from historical and contemporary agency. Regardless of whether one reads the novel as an Afropolitan intervention or a Pan-African continuation, it highlights the crucial significance of African voices in the ongoing and globalized construction of racial formations.

In the diasporic model centered by Philips or Gilroy, Africa must recede into a monolithic and mythical past in order to make sense of Black modernity and double consciousness. But *Homegoing* not only places an African history teacher at the core of the narrative. It also renders Yaw and Marjorie the characters who, through different modes, shoulder the responsibility of writing a joint history of slavery and colonialism and who can even begin to imagine it. Marcus, in contrast, is so overdetermined by the particular emplotment of Black Western modernity and overwhelmed with surviving and thriving in a racist society that he does not even know where to begin.

The telling of global and American Black history through an African point of view – in the manner of a self-inscribing, participating observer of the Afropolitan moment – corresponds with a larger epistemological shift within the Black Diaspora. More than 70 years after its completion, Zora Neale Hurston's ethnographic account *Barracoon: The Story of the Last "Black Cargo"* was published in May 2018. In the late 1920s, Hurston conducted a series of interviews with the last known person to have been brought to the US from Africa, Cudjo Lewis. The fascinating and, as Alice Walker writes in the foreword, often "harrowing" account is mostly told in his own vernacular and details Cudjo's memories of West Africa, the Middle Passage, the few years he spent on a plantation in Alabama, and his long life after Emancipation (Hurston 2018: x). Walker's foreword alludes to the reasons why Hurston's book could not be published at the time. Through his longing and painful memories of "the Afficy soil" and his unflinching account of the atrocities he had suffered at the hands of other Africans, Walker notes, "[w]e are being shown the wound," something that may have sat badly with the romanticized notion of Africa espoused by Black Nationalist intellectuals (ibid. x). In a way, and despite its archival discovery being a mere coincidence, the text's contemporary release thus appears serendipitously timed, as if the present age were better equipped to reckon with the historical complexity of diasporic entanglements told from the perspective of an African in America.

Those "who love us never leave us alone with our grief," Walker writes. "At the moment they show us our wound, they reveal they have the medicine" (ibid. ix). And the healing balm, in the case of Cudjo's eventful life, is that "though the heart is breaking, happiness can exist in a moment, also. And because the moment in which we live is all the time there really is, we can keep going" (xxii). *Homegoing*'s examination of guilt, love, and kinship in the Black Diaspora works in a similar way. In facing the moral and systemic repercussions of historical wrongs, it details the painful course of a story foretold, but it counters this fatal script by providing momentary openings of profane happiness, exploding the continuum of history. The medicine it offers may also be found in the rich and detailed history of the Gold Coast, not because it is embellished for mythical effect, but because it ascribes agency – then and now. The novel is particularly hopeful in its rendering of strong female characters like Akua or Akosua, who repeatedly want to "make new," regardless of the tenacious structures into which they are thrust. In fact, every chapter includes at least one moment in which a central character is faced with the possibility of defying the heteronomous burden of history, despite being unable to actively undo it. The tension that arises from these opposing forces corresponds with what Tina Campt in *Listening to Images* calls the "quotidian practice of refusal":

> The quotidian practice of refusal I am describing is defined less by opposition or "resistance," and more by a refusal of the very premises that have reduced the lived experience of blackness to pathology and irreconcilability in the logic of white supremacy. Like the concept of fugitivity, *practicing* refusal highlights the tense relations between *acts* of flight and escape, and creative *practices of refusal* – nimble and strategic practices that undermine the categories of the dominant. (2017: 32)

Homegoing's history of Africa and the diaspora is viewed in constellation with today's bleak assessment of the future, structures of feeling that cannot but maintain their pessimism regarding the state of the world. But *Homegoing's* ability to "heal" and "make whole" springs from illustrating a historical moment with that very same pessimist yet hopeful urgency. Tragically fated as these characters ambitions might be, they are rooted in the desire to "make new," to change the reified structures of oppression and with them the tragic course of history. This view is in line with the melancholic yet defiant position of Benjamin's historian. As Sami Kathib describes it in "The Messianic Without Messianism": "The paradoxical hope of the hopeless ones is derived and discontinuously transferred from the past. And it is only this openness to the past that can give rise to a future, which is not the mere continuation of the past" (2013: 3). By turning toward these historical moments of weak messianic potentiality, *Homegoing* limns possibilities for new futures, but it also highlights the limits of its own imaginary.

Hence, the most traditional narrative of redemption in the novel, the story of Marcus's visit to the slave dungeons, does not provide its anticipated sense of closure and forgiveness. In this scene, the problematic sense of emotional transference noted by Hartman and LaCapra does not occur. Despite the sense of fulfilled family destiny that it evokes, an identification with the dead is hindered in the same way in which Marcus's return itself is not framed as a progress narrative per se, at least not one that culminates in the visit to the dungeons. Instead of identifying Elmina castle as the site of healing, the final chapter of the novel represents this locale through a set of troubling, unresolved questions, particularly for Ghanaians themselves. Marjorie reluctantly takes Marcus to the dungeons, telling him that this is "what the black tourists do when they come here" (297). While this highlights their different positions, it also points toward the lack of Ghanaian memory culture regarding the slave trade. The chapter is told from Marcus's point of view, but he can sense Marjorie's uneasiness about the "dirty skeleton of a long-past shame" they encounter in the dungeons of the Castle (298). When the guide tells them about the fact that British soldiers often married local women who then lived above the enslaved – an image Gyasi credits for sparking the idea for the novel – Marjorie shifts uncomfortably and Marcus avoids her gaze: "It was the way most people lived their lives, on upper levels, not stopping to peer underneath" (298). Referencing the heavily classed reality of contemporary Ghana, its colonial origins, and the role that elites played in the slave trade, the dungeons seem to take on a larger significance for Marjorie than they do for Marcus. Similar to Aidoo's play *Anowa*, the novel's addressing of Ghanaian amnesia around the slave trade is also a critique of the social stratification that made both the trade and the ignorance surrounding it possible.

Querying notions of kinship, moral debt, and tradition becomes particularly significant in a novel that largely operates in a genealogical logic. Its underlying critique of national memorial culture on both sides of the Atlantic also translates into a subtle critique of the national imaginary in general – as an inherited and unquestioned structure of norms and traditions.[102] Akosua, the girl who initially refuses to "shake the hand of a slaver" and who pledges that she "will be her own nation," most notably wants to transcend the traditions of a society that renders her either complicit or one of the "expendable and defeated" that made up the historical fodder for the trade (Hartman 2007: 2). Akosua wants to undo the nightmare of the ancestral order, not only because she is someone who, in James's eyes, "had nothing, and [...] came from nothing," but because she decides that imagining beyond nations is the only way to end the cycle of violence (99). The fact that James reiterates and then acts upon her notion of becoming "one's own nation" – that together they cultivate their own "small-small" version of happiness (104) – highlights the performativity and fictitiousness be-

---

[102] The question of memorializing national guilt is surely central to all the writers discussed here. While Adichie explores this most explicitly in *Half of a Yellow Sun*, both *Homegoing* and *Open City* address this question rather explicitly. It might also be of no small significance that both novels include German characters, most obvious in the Julius's German mother, but also through Marjorie's boyfriend Graham, who grew up in Germany but "didn't wear the country on his sleeve the same way she wore Ghana on hers" (277).

hind any notion of kinship. As Ruha Benjamin writes in "Black AfterLives Matter":

> All kinship, in the end, is imaginary. Not faux, false, or inferior, but [...] a creative process of fashioning care and reciprocity. Is it any wonder that black people, whose meta-kinship threatens the biological myth of white supremacy, have had to innovate bonds that can withstand the many forms of bondage that attempt to suffocate black life? Cultivating kinfulness is cultivating life. (2018: para. 51)

Homegoing, despite its focus on family ties and genealogy, equally develops a notion of extended or meta-kinship across space and time – or what Dimock calls "an alchemical overcoming of distance" (2007: 144) – and subtly questions the limitations of biological or national lineages as vehicles for diasporic imagining. The novel thus creatively mobilizes the "racial myth," what Mitchell calls the "temporal dimension of the racial medium" (2012: 25) or what I call race in/as history. Plying the strands of racial myth as "a real force in history" (Mitchell 2012: 22), the novel also provides an understanding of how bloodlines "are not drawn with syringes but with stories, portraits, and family trees" (ibid. 26). That being said, the ambivalent project of transposing the novel's major symbols – two lineages, two nations – into the image of one family and its shared destiny is also encapsulated by how the novel strains against the conventions of a historical novel, nationally emplotted as it is, by writing about the history of a transnational community characterized by a reciprocal and ongoing process.

The novel chooses to look at the past in order to redeem or undo the conventions of national time standing in for a dubious sense of progress. Its narrative progression into the near present nevertheless poses a problem for its sense of an ending and further confronts it with the national emplotment of History. While, particularly from an Afro-pessimist viewpoint, it might be easier to envision the end of the (nationally ordered) world than the end of anti-Blackness, the difficulty to plot history outside of the nation affects all kinds of diasporic narratives. As Bennett contends, the study of the African Diaspora, via its focus on mobility, transnationalism, and dispersal, may offer an attractive "new lexicon," but it should not delude itself concerning the pervasiveness of the established historiographical script (2000: 106).

The final scene of the novel thus reiterates the notion of feeling beyond the nation and envisions a redemptive moment as atopical as it is atemporal. No sense of healing occurs as Marjorie and Marcus are touring the dungeon. Marcus feels sick and realizes that he does not want to be there, that the dead remain inaccessible for identification – not least because "[n]o one called them by name" (*Homegoing* 299). What he feels, instead, is the desire "to be somewhere else, anywhere else" (ibid.). Pushing through the *Door of No Return*, Marcus faces his lifelong fear of open water:

> Marcus started running to the beach. Outside were hundreds of fishermen tending their bright turquoise nets. There were long handcrafted rowboats as far as the eye could see. Each boat had a flag of no nationality, of every nationality. There was a purple polka dotted one beside a British one, a blood-orange one beside a French one, a Ghanaian one next to an American one. (299)

In a final scene both exuberant and profane, the novel's sense of closing and its anticipated sense of redemption occur on the shores of a possible cosmopolitan future, a literally colorful diaspora, with an image of ships as beacons of transnational diasporic difference, connected through an ocean bed littered with Black bodies. By somewhat redeeming the barred sense of healing evoked by the dungeons as a "site of injury," one could certainly put the novel to task for intimating a rather sickly-sweet sense of closure in the Atlantic Ocean (Hartman 2002: 767). Apart from seeking the reasons behind this in the "embarrassment of plot" that haunts all historical narrative, there is of course much to be read into the symbolic significance of the Atlantic (Onega 1999: 282).

Similar to what Dimock notes in *Through Other Continents*, oceanic kinship is imagined as "anything but straightforward," but instead as "oblique, centrifugal, laterally extended, taking the form of arcs, loops, curves of various sorts," and revealing that it is in fact non-adjacency that provides an "unexpected ground for kinship" (2007: 145). What Dimock asserts in reference to creolization also befits the ending of *Homegoing*. Here, the novel finally abandons even its own abandonment of patrilineal clanship in the form of matrilineal cultural transmission across a transnational imaginary, in favor of something even less landlocked and genealogical. As Dimock writes:

> Since it is these far-flung arcs that integrate the globe, that turn distant populations into distant cousins, we might want to rethink the meaning of "ancestry" itself. Rather than being land-based, patrilineal, and clannish, it is here oceanic, flotational, a large-scale and largely exogenous process of "drifting." [...] Ancestry here has less to do with origins than with processes. (2007: 145).

Yet instead of proposing this diasporic image as an entirely rootless, free-floating model of atomized becoming, one could also interpret the novel's ending as a move similar to Glissant's notion of transversality that renders diasporic history a "subterranean site of convergence" (1996: 66). Here, the legacies of this fateful ocean render its depths "not only the abyss of neurosis but primarily the site of multiple converging paths" (ibid.). Responding to E. Kamau Brathwaite's assertion that "The unity is submarine," Glissant writes:

> To my mind, this expression can only evoke all those Africans weighed down with ball and chain and thrown overboard whenever a slave ship was pursued by enemy vessels and felt too weak to put up a fight. *They sowed in the depths the seeds of an invisible presence.* And so transversality, and not the universal transcendence of the sublime, has come to light. It took us a long time to learn this. We are the roots of a cross-cultural relationship. (1996: 66–67)

Glissant proposes a sense of diversion – in his case via the *métissage* of the Caribbean – and conversion that allows a rhizomatic understanding of diaspora constantly creating its own point of origin. Similarly, instead of centering the slave hold as the only site of origin, thus irrevocably cutting ties and eclipsing African agency and history, *Homegoing*'s ending proposes a diasporic imaginary sustained by "[s]ubmarine roots, that is floating free, not fixed in one position in some primordial spot, but extending in all directions of our world through its network of branches" (1996: 67).

In Glissant's theorizing of a poetics of relation, the singular linearity of filiation is replaced by a multiplicity of rhizomatically arranged roots. With reference to Deleuze and Guattari's concept of the rhizome, Glissant writes: "The notion of the rhizome maintains, therefore, the idea of rootedness but challenges that of a totalitarian root. Rhizomatic thought is the principle behind what I call the Poetics of Relation, in which each and every identity is extended through a relationship with the Other" (2010: 11). This play on, or alteration of, the concept of 'roots' or rooted identity is not quite analogous to Gilroy's, and subsequently to Clifford's, supplementing the term with "routes" as a move away from monolithic genealogies and fixed origins toward a more fluid, active mode of movement and becoming. In her reading of Glissant, Goyal describes the notion of free-floating roots as a "fitting alternative to the rootlessness advocated by Gilroy and others insofar as Glissant's image retains subterranean connections even as it eschews fixed origins" (2003: 29). Goyal also emphasizes the concretely political, material dimension of Glissant's image. For Glissant, the subaltern "struggle against a single History" is not only mobilized by the desire to understand itself and its own history, but also by an acute awareness that this struggle proposes "in an unprecedented way a reevaluation of power" (1996: 93).

Like race, history literally matters; it may be a fantasy, yet one that is "highly functional" (1996: 64). In many ways, *Homegoing* is the kind of historical fiction that provides an anchor in what British-Ghanaian artist and director John Akomfrah has called the "sea of amnesia" that constantly surrounds us. In an interview about his 2015 film *Vertigo Sea*, he explores why history indeed matters, as the very ballast that prevents the mental slippage of a dangerous surplus of fiction:

> I was compelled [...] to make *Vertigo Sea* because you're sitting there, listening to someone referring to quote/unquote migrants as cockroaches. [...] How do people migrate from being human beings to cockroaches? What do you have to forget? What's the process of amnesia that allows the kinds of forgetting that builds into hierarchies in which there are beings and non-beings? (00:06:07–00:06:44 min)

In many ways, the struggle against race in/as history counters its fatal myth-making powers by composing other myths and writing other stories. Yet, in grappling with that legacy, this endeavor often expresses itself in the paradoxical desire to render both real and transient, constantly writing that into existence what it wants to surpass. Like Glissant's notion of transversality as the kind of multiplicity that supplants hegemonic or totalitarian roots by cutting across linear routes with a rhizomatic structure, *Homegoing*'s ending proposes 'no nationality' through the sign of 'every nationality.' While the novel may anticipate or promise transcendence, what it really provides is a (renewed) sense of cross-cultural communication, a model for diaspora that focuses on points of entanglement rather than rifts and fissures. In its juxtaposing of Ghanaian and US-American history, *Homegoing* endeavors to not only understand, but also to enrich and expand the meaning of Blackness and the diasporic imaginary in the 21st century. Similar to what Akomfrah describes as his search for a third meaning through the techniques of fragmentation and montage, the novel explores this dialectic exchange as a form of movement. It is precisely that friction conducted through nodal points of connection, or *décalage*, that allows the diaspora to move forward.

Chapter V
Conclusion – The Past Is Always Tense, the Future Perfect

> To survive,
> Know the past.
> Let it touch you.
> Then let
> The past
> Go.
> *Octavia Butler*

"Now More Than Ever," a short story by Zadie Smith that was published in *The New Yorker* in 2018, is an off-center, surrealist satire about academia, paranoia, popular and call-out-culture. It also features some of Smith's favorite themes: beauty, postmodern temporality, Black history, and old-fashioned Hollywood movies. All are explored simultaneously when the narrator, an unnamed, elderly, (maybe) female philosophy professor, visits a screening of *A Place in the Sun* from 1952, whispering improvised dialogues for the mostly silent, servile Black character in her companion's ear: "Yes, Miss, I'll bring the dessert out now. I mean, my brother was lynched not long ago, down in Arkansas, but I can see you've got bigger fish to fry – I'll get right on it." Framing the narrative is the impending scandal and expulsion of a colleague, a character that the professor secretly identifies with but denounces like the rest of the department:

> How Eastman still has a job we really don't know. Not only does he not believe the past is the present, but he has gone further and argued that the present, in the future, will be just as crazy-looking to us, in the present, as the past is, presently, to us, right now! For Eastman, surely, it's only a matter of time. (Smith 2018 para. 5)

In the end, that character blurs into that of a poet endorsed by the department who had "said that philosophy makes nothing happen and also that he happened to quite like the Devil" – most likely a reference to Kanye West's endorsing of Donald Trump (Smith is an avowed fan) – and as he is soon "cancelled," so is the story's first-person narrator. At one point, the ageing professor engages in an email exchange with a high school student, discussing the merits of subtlety or explicitness of metaphor, based on a recent article published in *Philosophy Today* but exemplified with a clear reference to Childish Gambino's *This Is America*:

Chapter V Conclusion – The Past Is Always Tense, the Future Perfect

> Dear High-School Student,
> Have you seen that video? It's a little like that. Some things are so obvious that subtle metaphor is impossible. In that video, for example, there was no point in being subtle about the state-funded violence inflicted on black people in this country: the only way was to show it explicitly. And when we saw all those people dancing in the foreground that was again the most obvious metaphor possible – i.e., while you're watching these black people dance and entertain you, other black people are dying. (para. 14)

Throughout the exchange, the professor tries to maintain dignified authority but in reality is not so sure about the aesthetic sublimation of suffering. When the professor dubs the mute servant in *A Place in the Sun*, it is done for grimly comic relief, yet in the full knowledge that

> nothing I could do in the present could ameliorate or change this fictional fact; no, all I could do was remember it, and tell myself I was remembering it – so that it wasn't forgotten, although with the mental proviso that suffering has no purpose in reality. To the suffering person suffering is solely suffering. It is only for others, as a symbol, that suffering takes on any meaning or purpose. No one ever got lynched and thought, Well, at least this will lead inexorably to the civil-rights movement. They just shook, suffered, screamed, and died. Pain is the least symbolic thing there is. (para. 10)

Besides its social commentary, Smith's short story may be a self-knowing allusion to her own work, particularly her 2016 novel *Swing Time*. Here, Smith is equally interested in exploring the complex node of temporality, race, and history and also guilty of trading in fairly obvious metaphors. While the uneven distribution of time or futurity along the gradients of class and race is symbolized by the recurrent image of watches – one an ostentatiously large Swatch wall clock decorating a middle class home and drawing the envy of the protagonist, the other a defunct wristwatch on the arm of an abject poor in an unnamed African country – the history in and as race is also explored through racial tropes of cinematic history and a reference to the West African Sankofa myth, told by the narrator's fervently activist mother: "'It's a bird, it looks back over itself, like this.' She bent her beautiful head round as far as it could go. 'From Africa. It looks backwards, at the past, and it learns from what's gone before. Some people never learn'" (*Swing Time* 30).

The concept of Sankofa, quite widely known in diasporic contexts, transports a specific Afro-diasporic notion of temporality. Linking to, yet also distinguishing, the Sankofa concept from Benjamin's Angel of History and his focus on a past appropriated by *Jetztzeit*, the time of the now, Susan Arndt writes[103]:

---

[103] The article seeks to develop the notion of "FutureS" as an analytical category through

> Reading the beak as the symbol of both communication and nourishment, the picking backward represents an active decision-making about which memories (as narrations about the past) to choose [...]. Whereas the Angel of History and Benjamin's interpretation thereof feature the power that the past holds over the present with hardly any concern about access to futureS, here, the present holds power over the past being selective on behalf of dream*hoped futureS. Thus, rather than Benjamin's continuing the past and its present, the bird's bridging of the past, present and futureS is all about agency, which gives space to discontinuity even in the heart of continuities. (2017: 10)

Metahistory as the conscious process of glancing backward may signal an equally ambiguous object for Smith, who has quipped that "the past is always tense, the future perfect."[104] For one, she harbors no romantic notions of a past not designed for her. In an acceptance speech published as "On Optimism and Despair" in her essay collection *Feel Free*, Smith expounds:

> I find these days that a wistful form of time travel has become a persistent political theme, both on the right and on the left. On 10 November *The New York Times* reported that nearly seven in ten Republicans prefer America as it was in the fifties, a nostalgia of course entirely unavailable to a person like me, for in that period I could not vote, marry my husband, have my children, work in the university I work in, or live in my neighborhood. Time travel is a discretionary art: a pleasure trip for some and a horror story for others. (2018: 37)

Indeed, contemporary public discourse is often characterized by a strange nostalgia, expressed not only in dangerously retrograde politics but also in what Simon Reynolds defines as pop culture's addiction to its own past (2012), or what Zygmunt Bauman, in his posthumous publication *Retrotopia* (2017), described as contemporary societies' inability to imagine anything but the return to an idealized past. But the very concept of a better past can only be maintained if one conveniently ignores the majority of people on this planet, for whom the

---

somewhat confusing neologisms: "The capitalized "S" in both FutureS and futureS suggests that 'future' does not exist in the (simplicity of any) singular, and this is largely due to three reasons: First, the 'S' refers to the fact that futureS are causally intersected with both the past and the present. Second, it draws attention to the fact that futureS are intersected and molded by complexities and coexistences of glocal encounters of conflicting, competing, and complementary agencies, interests, contingencies, possibilities and options in the un/making and (not) sharing of futureS. Consequently, and third, futureS are made (as guided by agencies in power) and can be un*made (through resistance)" (3).

104 In fact, the narrator in Smith's *White Teeth* actually warns about buying into this "wicked lie" (2001: 541).

'good old days' were anything but that.[105] Smith's observation that for "a black woman the expanse of livable history is so much shorter" (2018: 38) probably also fuels historian Olivette Otele's uninterest in time travel. In an interview conducted in March 2018, months before she would become the UK's first (!) Black woman history professor, Otele gave a simple and straightforward answer to a history journal's question which moment in time she would like to go back to: "Now is a good place for me as a scholar and a black woman" (2018: para. 5).

Despite its complications, history, and particularly Black history, remains an important resource for diasporic writers like Smith – or Cole, Adichie, and Gyasi. Consequently, Blackness often becomes something to be learned, studied, or immerse oneself in. For example, when Ifemelu reads "every James Baldwin title on the shelf" (*Americanah* 135), Sonny constantly rereads *The Souls of Black Folk* (*Homegoing* 243), and when Cole, in his essay "Black Body," not only revisits the Swiss town where Baldwin wrote "Stranger in the Village" but actually runs a bath and lies "neck-deep in the water" with his "old paperback copy" of *Notes of a Native Son*, the sound of Bessie Smith playing on his laptop (2016: 4). Generally, all of these authors insist on the value of reading. This shows in the abundant references to books as material objects, but also in plain descriptions of the power of reading. Contrary to the self-referential play of historiographic metafictions, there is really nothing cynical about this kind of intertextuality, no irony, no hint of self-deprecation or self-adulation, just an earnest, and oftentimes urgent admiration for the mental sanctuary provided by literature.

This reverence of reading does not suggest a certain naiveté concerning the political dimension of literature. On the contrary, books are selected and read with purpose and meaning, even if this occurs unconsciously. Ifemelu, for example, reminds an unsuspecting reader that no one is "miraculously neutral in how [they] read books" (190). *Open City* often exhibits explorations of Yoruba culture and other subaltern histories, markedly juxtaposed with what Baldwin had described as "these white centuries" – a received Western cultural canon, boldly appropriated rather than harmonically fused (1968: 4). The church scene in Brussels allegorizes this notion of disharmonic and contrapuntal histories, disrupting the complacent self-image of a liberal multiculturalism that renders alternative claims and traumatic histories unpalatable – even when they morph into the aestheticized commodity of jazz. Julius recognizes this, but he is unable to become a vessel, translator, or ambassador for these claims – he is unwilling to em-

---

[105] Unwitting proof of this may be the proliferation of 'colorblind casting' in pop culture, such as Lin-Manuel Miranda's *Hamilton* (2015) or Shondaland's Netflix series *Bridgerton* (2020).

body a bridge. Part of his reluctance springs from this very same recognition: that doing so will be perceived, at best, as self-exoticizing or commercially viable, if not disrupting and petulant.

When Cole in "Black Body" claims that he does not need to surrender the "intimidating beauty of Yoruba-language for, say, Shakespeare" because he is "happy to own all of it," he is explicitly engaged in the kind of Afropolitan world-making that fuels these novels' utopian subtext (2016: 10). There is, he writes, "no world in which" he would do so, embodying the confident poise of the Afropolitan who needn't write back nor employ a victim's narrative to be part of this world. Opposing what Cole describes as Baldwin's "self-abnegation" about what he perceived as both the paragon of art and a heritage that excluded him, could be mapped onto earlier responses to Baldwin that function as subtle diasporic critique of an African American primacy regarding Black experiences (Cole 2016: 11). As Nadia Ellis notes in *Territories of the Soul*, George Lamming also chastised Baldwin for his feelings of "inferiority, both personal and racial," contrasting Baldwin's tormented attitude toward white Western culture with the "certain leisure" gained from living in a majority Black country (qtd. in Ellis 2015: 74). But Lamming's assertion that "No black West Indian in his own native environment would have this highly oppressive sense of being Negro" not only belies the complexities of colonialism, but, as Ellis notes, also reveals Lamming's own ambiguous positioning as a minority Black writer in majority-white exile (ibid.). Likewise, Ifemelu's claim of a racism-free Nigeria is not only interpretable as a utopian antidote to a racism-ridden US but must be refracted through the lens of a writer who knows and claims both experiences – and thus challenges hegemony through lateralization. This awareness that the Afropolitan world, to be truly that, does not end at the coastline of Africa, but of course encompasses all, sustains these authors' negotiations and explorations of Blackness, particular those triggered by African American struggles and experiences. As such, the novels actively grapple with these legacies, and, while emphasizing the historicity of Blackness, also inquire into the ways in which race in/as history continues to evolve and adapt, curiously posing as timelessness.

How do you inherit a scar? This question, posed most overtly by *Homegoing*, also mobilizes the other novels' investigation of unresolved and perhaps unresolvable trauma. After being confronted with Moji's rape accusation, Julius muses: "I had been ever-present in her life, like a stain or a scar" (*OC* 244). And yet, as Moji concedes, her confrontation alone will not change the course of history: "It only needs to happen once" (245). While this could also be related to the painful histories of the Black Diaspora, structurally unacknowledged despite the evidence, countlessly retold yet not generally felt, one need not even extrapolate so far. Whose memories matter? In a post-#MeToo age, Moji's contention that she is "just another woman whose story of sexual abuse will not be believed" rings eerily familiar (ibid.). Or does it ring familiar precisely because a temporal marker like 'post' will not affect the timelessness of this tale? Somewhat resignedly, *Open City* suggests that it may not even matter if the subaltern is heard or believed because no response formed by the axioms of today can alter the past and change the course of history. And yet, as Kimberlé Crenshaw asks, what if America had believed Anita Hill? What fateful chain of political developments could have been prevented by this simple act of trust?[106]

Still, there may also be merit in Julius's reticence, his unwillingness or inability to actively respond to someone else's trauma. Already with Moji's revelation, Julius highlights the impulse to convert the scene into an aestheticized spectacle. Traumatic accounts, this suggests, may be all too easily sublimated, packaged and sold as easily consumable testaments of other people's pain, and read as reports of distant tragedies. Deifying the conscience-pricking victim narrative of what Robert Eaglestone describes as "African trauma literature," all the authors discussed here address the conundrum of nevertheless narrating the traumatic repercussions of history. In these novels, abstract notions of trauma and public recognition make way for introspective and personal reckonings and explorations of quotidian experience that forgo the merely didactical or engaged, as well as the grand narrative of counterhistory. Sometimes, this occurs within the novels, as in Ifemelu blogging the *The Small Redemptions of Lagos*, or via the libidinal dynamic of *Homegoing's* episodic "love stories." Sometimes, this point is made elsewhere, as in Cole's Twitter series "Small Fates."[107] On Twitter, too, Cole has provided his own commentary on the usage of this literary form, the *fait divers:* "The small fates are tragicomic at a distance. Closer to home they are of necessity more tragic. There's a tension between the two." It is this tension, the interplay between an earnest dedication to tragic fates and the unwillingness to perform these tragedies as spectacles of fated peoples – that also characterizes these novel's treatment of race in/as history. Dedicated to detailing

---

[106] Crenshaw, who famously developed the concept of intersectionality, was also part of Anita Hill's legal team during the sexual harassment case against Supreme Court Justice nominee Clarence Thomas. In a speech in April 2019, she illuminated the historical continuity and possibly disastrous political repercussion of the Kavanaugh case. She also made a strong case for the value of intersectional practice by pointing to the deep-seated sexism that caused large parts of the African American population to question Hill on account of protecting a respectable "Race Man" like Thomas.

[107] Depicting curious snapshots of contemporary life in Nigeria, they read, for example, like this: "With a razor blade, Sikiru, of Ijebu Ode, who was tired of life, separated himself from his male organ. But death eluded him."

the normalcy of Black life on both sides of the Atlantic, Cole's "small fates," Adichie's "small redemptions," and Gyasi's "love stories" are not superfluous or adjacent investigations of race in/as history. In many ways, their epistemological stance resembles that of Foucault's *petit récits*, as the kind of "imperceptible events" which, following Bhabha, encrypt the value of modernity "in signs apparently *without* meaning and value – empty and eccentric – in events that are outside the 'great events of history" (2004: 348).

But the history of race and Blackness, then, is not only something to be read and revisited. It is also something to be written and rewritten. These novels, among many other things, endeavor to make time palpable, for example, when *Open City*'s Julius muses over "time [becoming] material in a strange new way" (219) or Marcus in *Homegoing*, thinking about how his racialized self intersects with the "accumulation of these times," wants nothing else for his book project than to capture the "feeling of time" (295). Probing the confines of a "race-time-continuum" (Stallings 2013: 194), they provide an answer to what it feels like to be *raced:* It's a particular way of being timed, as 'not yet,' as waiting, as accumulation, as embodied history, as memories of tom-toms, as too-late, as offbeat, as fated or fallen out of time. While the revisiting and rewriting of race in/as history has of course been done before, this does not make these accounts any less significant. These things cannot be 'overdone' or overstated. The fact of race is infinitely startling, its histories infinitely troubling, particularly because the confrontation with, and uncovering of, historical violence continues to take place under the sign of this violence. Regardless of the familiarity of the narrative, Hortense Spillers reminds us, "every writing as revision makes the discovery again" (2003: 209).

In probing, navigating, and negotiating Blackness, these authors are consciously inscribing themselves into a tradition that often tends to neglect contemporary African voices. By historicizing Blackness, they avoid the pitfalls of claiming an experience that is not theirs while positioning themselves within an entangled history. As such, they easily identify the "simplistic comparison" behind attempts at pitting the new against the old diaspora (Adichie, *Americanah* 168). By they also identify it behind the reproach that they're not feeling what they're writing because they're "writing from the outside" (ibid. 336). Countering this, these novels can be read as a call "to understand a bit more history" (ibid. 168). Expanding the narrow frame of Blackness, they are not only able to insert themselves, but also acknowledge their own responsibility and position. The Black Diaspora, then, is the "forest" of *Homegoing's* epigraph: "if you are inside you see that each tree has its own position." Foregrounding their formal distinctness from the kind of "strict historical record" that stifles Julius's patient V.

(*OC* 27), these novels are able to provide a long view of history *and* contain the melancholy that always threatens to cloud that vision.

In the current political climate, as the noose continues to tighten, those who have no time to mourn a past they never owned and who have nowhere else to go but the future, have, for some, begun to signal the last glimmer of hope. This becomes apparent in the more general idea that Black Americans are the perfecters of democracy. Examples are the *New York Time*'s hugely successful "1619 Project" and the much-evoked notion that Black (women) voters 'saved us' during the crucial elections of 2020 and 2021 – with "Thank Black Voters" op-eds often illustrating the kind of hollow liberal gratitude that barely conceals its solipsism. Yet the recent years have also seen more substantial public interest in the hard-won insights gained by Black thinkers and activists – for example the abolitionist movements pushing for a reevaluation of common safety amidst the relentless militarization of the American public. As George Lipsitz writes in "The Changing Same":

> New social movements are emerging in this conjuncture. They are often race based but rarely race bound. They recognize racism as a technology of power, as a justification and excuse for unfair gains and unjust enrichments. They see racism as innately intersectional, as ever present, but never present in isolation from sexism, homophobia, imperial conquest and class subordination. These movements acknowledge the long fetch of history, the depressing collective, cumulative and continuing consequences of slavery unwilling to die, yet they also perceive new possibilities for the present and for the future. They challenge the logics of color blindness and balanced budget conservatism by drawing on the enduring and viable repressed radicalisms of previous eras. (2018: 17)

Simultaneously, Black America's popular culture has emerged from its so-called "category crisis" with a newfound, defiantly (post-post-) racial aesthetics, exploring the contemporary complexities of race and racism through absolutely stellar cultural productions. Donald Glover's aka Childish Gambino's *This Is America* is one of them, and so is his FX series *Atlanta*. This new wave of Black cultural production is also host to a choir of different Black voices, from British-Ugandan actor Daniel Kaluuya, who stars in Jordan Peele's sensational *Get Out*, to Senegalese-American Issa Rae, who, with the series *Insecure* and *Awkward Black Girl*, has created two of the most refreshing representations of contemporary Black America. The visibility of these newly Black Americans, however, does not presuppose a mere subsuming under an African American rubric of Blackness. On the contrary, these processes are often accompanied by the valuation and reevaluation of the "African" signifier that defines the Afropolitan moment. This process has never been limited to a howsoever defined "apolitical" aesthetic but has of course always encompassed both. While many commentators rightly observe how African immigrant groups in the US have largely clustered into national and ethnic groups that reject the generalizing term "African," signaling the dynamic of diaspora nationalism, it appears as though "African" – this highly synthetic and indeterminate category – is also (re-)emerging as a politics. Simon Gikandi observes: "As African communities encounter racism, they want to develop connections, political movements, solidarity, and one way of unifying them is by invoking that term 'African.' So, in times of crisis African becomes a conceptual category with more force than it has in everyday life" (2016: 44).

This strategic employment of Africanity is not limited to the US. Indeed, as movements like the South African #RhodesMustFall intersect with similar concerns in Europe and the US, as racist statures topple globally, questions of reparations become concrete again and looted artifacts are beginning to embarrass museums across the Northern hemisphere, "Africa" becomes yet again a political sign around which to coalesce. It is indeed the urgency of African migrations, turning the Mediterranean into an open wound "where the Third World grates against the first and bleeds," that most crassly belies he advent of Black cosmopolitanism but at the same time helps to establish this newly forged and long forgotten web of political solidarity (Anzaldúa 1999: 25). Acknowledging the globality of anti-Blackness, as many scholars and activists have,[108] means theorizing history as a violent continuity discernible through uncanny echoes, for example, when Christina Sharpe identifies in the precarious vessels drifting on the Mediterranean a continuation of "the semiotics of the slave ship," highlighting not only the entanglement of slavery and contemporary "forced movements of the migrant and the refugee" (2016: 21) but also their larger embeddedness in what she calls the "crisis of capital and the wreckage from the continuation of military and other colonial projects of US/European wealth extraction and immiseration" (ibid. 59).

In many ways, the moment of Afropolitanism gives rise to this rediscovered vocabulary of a shared political imaginary sustained by historical continuities, but just as Sharpe also endeavors to imagine "new ways to live in the afterlife of slavery" (2016: 18), so does the African signifier undergo change and renewal

---

108 The global nature of anti-Blackness is not only an avowed tenet of Afro-pessimism – what Wilderson calls the "global common denominator" of the "White and non-Black position" (2010: 51) – but is also a prerequisite for #BlackLivesMatter's international chapters and a key concern of the movement's co-founder, Opal Tometi. It has been theorized widely, for example, in relation to Western immigration laws, as a necessary condition for the expansion of capital, or, more generally, as constitutive to global white supremacy and condition for Western modernity. See Wynter 2003; Bashi 2004; Mills 2014; Gordon 2017; Bledsoe and Wright 2019.

in what Mbembe calls the Afropolitan "worlds-in-movement" (2005: 28). Sometimes, this shared imaginary might also mean at least temporarily abandoning the abstract plane of theorizing anti-Blackness as principally and immediately operative, and acknowledging that, as Gikandi notes, "there are many parts of the world in which race is quite low on the totem pole of terror and as a cause of social death" (1996: 607). What would it mean, for example, to fuse the historical sensitivity demanded by the case for reparations with the notion of climate debt, as droughts and floods continue to wreak havoc on those regions underdeveloped by Europe? Far from denouncing the validity of Blackness as a socio-political identity or signaling an end to Black diasporic solidarity, realizing how Blackness intersects differently with the time and space of its articulation is a vital tool for disrupting the permanence of race in/as history, countering racial essentialism and building an antiracist future.

However, while these novels do not 'make Black(ness) history' as a form of socio-political organizing, there is a distinct polysemy to the phrase that nevertheless retains a utopian dimension, not unlike Paul Gilroy's position in *Postcolonial Melancholia*. Hope, here, is intimately tied to notions of conviviality that transcend the intradiasporic communications that are primarily examined in *Making Black History*. In this distant cosmopolitan vision, the often painful and violent stories of Blackness may indeed be made history. Even as these texts detail the contemporary implications and long-lasting effects of race in/as history, one should, in the words of Gilroy, perhaps not interpret the "ancient invocation of the color line as a suggestion that 'race' is a fatal, unchanging principle of political cultures that stretches unbroken and infinite into a future that is defined, just as the past was, precisely by the violent force of racial divisions" (2005: 38).

While Cole's "On the Blackness of the Panther" illuminates how "those who have to learn black also expand what black can be," it also resonates the predicament of dreaming beyond the nation state while attending to the complexity of the diaspora, and particularly the African continent. "African countries have always been in conversation with the world," he writes, "[a]n isolationist blackness is incoherent and impossible: we already *been* cosmopolitan." Against this mutual imbrication of Africa and the world, he reminds us to be "particular about being particular about what we are talking about when we talk about Africa." The novels investigated are constantly giving shape and complexity to whatever "Africa" may signify in the diasporic and global imaginary. How may Afropolitan fictions maintain and develop the utopian 'extranationality' of diasporic writing in the 21st century? As a testing ground for a solidarity built on difference, these novels' literary world-making really functions as an anteroom for Black cosmopolitanism, that is, the building of a world in which Black humanity and belonging is given, not merely by proudly proclaiming cosmopolitanism, but also by negating this kind of belonging and thus indicating other and better worlds.

Considering the extraordinary nuance and richness of cultural, intellectual, and political Black discourse, it is perhaps unsurprising that Black culture and thought symbolizes yet again a path through the mired present and into the future. As such, so-called 'diverse' stories and representations are utilized to quicken the dwindling flow of the mainstream, particularly in Hollywood, where remakes and sequels have replaced novel ideas, often substituting innovation with surface level diversity. It is perhaps not surprising that the vocabulary and semiotics of counterculture have become once again sources of rejuvenation. Yet this issue highlights the problems of co-optation or representation versus redistribution as much as the question, posed by Smith's professor in "Now More Than Ever," whether particularly Black suffering has become a mere cypher, a citable index of a perpetually violent history that neither saves and makes whole the suffering of the past nor alters the present. This is a complicated issue, questioning the extent to which the representations of (historical) violence reproduce rather than undo the violence of lived experience, and there is surely no definitive answer. Besides an acknowledgement of the political urgency of these issues and a celebration of heightened visibility, there is also a pronounced push back against the appropriation of this work and the logics of tokenization.

In late 2017, I visited an extensive event series named "The Milieu of the Dead," organized by the Berliner Humboldt Forum, the highly contested institution set to host Prussia's ethnological collection in the nostalgic nightmare that is the reconstructed Berliner Schloss. In what can only be described as a preemptive move, the Humboldt Forum, as a self-described "platform for debate," had invited scholars Saidiya Hartman and Christina Sharpe to investigate the "Afterlife of Slavery and the Gaps of the Archive." The event, in short, was an awkward, over-produced disaster. Sharpe and Hartman, it turned out, had been flown in as a mere gesture toward, or indeed index of, their work. This signaled the co-optation or incorporation of an uncomfortable critique that literally never left the realm of representation as both theorists were sat on pedestals, asked to read, and then seated in the audience and excluded from the subsequent discussion about the future of the Humboldt Forum. Sat thus, they were forced to witness an agonizing and futile exchange between predominantly white German curators and historians, oscillating between PR damage control and theoretical abstraction. As this was a two-day event, Sharpe and Hartman had picked up on this dynamic on the first night. For Sharpe's reading on the second night, in which she built on the very concrete questions of repair and social justice that Hartman had put forth the night before, they had prepared a response.

Chapter V Conclusion – The Past Is Always Tense, the Future Perfect

First, Sharpe read from *In the Wake*, choosing the harrowing account of the "left-to-die-boat," the boat that had left Tripoli with 72 Africans in March 2011 and reached the coast of Libya two weeks later with only 9 left alive. Then, she read out their joint statement:

> Last night Saidiya Hartman began with a question: How do we attend to Black Death? A question we must return to again and again, since our suffering to the degree that it is recognized, is exploited in the service of rehabilitating anti-Black and colonial institutions. The vampires continue to feed on us. Our deaths are not the prequel to a discussion about reforming institutions that were and remain instruments of colonial violence. Our work, each and every word we have ever written is a critique of this project and of the world built on stolen land, stolen lives, stolen labor, stolen objects, stolen futures.
>
> Saidiya and I reckon with Black Death, with Black life in the wake with the intent of making possible other ways of living/other ways of inhabiting the earth. Don't use our death, our suffering, our lives and our work to regenerate your projects. Don't turn our flesh into gold again. We do not consent to this.

What does it mean if Black suffering becomes a political cypher? What does it mean if intellectual projects appropriate Black critique to appear fresh, cutting edge, or as if their own ideas had not "run out of steam"? What does it mean when capitalist institutions sell diversity as innovation, if Black people become tokens of futurity? What does it, in fact, mean if Africa is declared the future?

As curator Bonaventure Soh Behjeng Ndikung asked at the 2015 African Futures Festival in Johannesburg, an interdisciplinary international project funded by the German Goethe Institute: "What is this sudden interest in futurism and the future [...], what are we trying to skip in not talking about the present, and not talking about the past?" (131) Instead of overdetermining Africa by a disjunctive past or future, it might be time to thoroughly realize its present. As I have argued in relation to the intradiasporic signification of Afropolitanism, it is problematic to mobilize Afropolitan futurity against an allegedly backward African American historicism – not only because of the attendant cultural politics but also because this perspective fails to recognize Afropolitanism's own historicisms.

At the same time, Afropolitanism is indeed decidedly 'of the moment,' inviting the world to realize what Africa contributes to this 'now,' even, or precisely as it is haunted by the ghostly remnants of obstinate histories. As we begin to be more "particular about being particular about what we are talking about when we talk about Africa," Africa may be awarded the kind of specificity that also translates into normalcy. Simon Gikandi has identified a certain "African Exceptionalism," positive or negative, as one of the main challenges for African writers and intellectuals today: "How do you go about conducting African conversations as ordinary conversations?" Positing the African "as ordinary, as a subject, a normal, ordinary human being" must also entail a firm grounding in the present (2016: 58). Surely, the contemporary presence of Africa can only ever be realized in and as the present. As such, one must insist on African modernity as a global modernity in the same way that Gilroy insisted on Black modernity as northern hemispheric modernity.

Contrary to culturalist or nationalist nostalgic projects hoping to resuscitate a romanticized past, Black people and other historically marginalized groups open history's violent chapters first and foremost with the hope of opening up a different, better future. Similar to Ranjana Khanna's notion of a "critical melancholia" that does not serve but undercuts nationalism, so did Stephen Best and Saidiya Hartman once describe their work as being concerned with "the contemporary predicament of freedom, with the melancholy recognition of foreseeable futures still tethered to this past" (2005: 5). Best has since warned of transmuting this historicist perspective into an axiomatic affect. And there are indeed good reasons for abandoning the past "as it falls away, as that which falls away" (Best 2012: 466), and, instead of waiting for the convoluted knots of history to unravel, grasp a hold of the present and realize a future. We will not wait. Now is a good time.

Bibliography

Abani, Chris. 2007. *The Virgin of Flames*. London: Penguin.
Abdur-Rahman, Aliyyah I. 2017. "Black Grotesquerie." *American Literary History* 29(4): 682–703.
Achebe, Chinua. 1958. *Things Fall Apart*. London: Heinemann.
Achebe, Chinua. 1973. *A Man of the People*. London: Heinemann.
Adeleye, Tej. 2016. "Black on All Sides: Five Lessons We Learned from Teju Cole". *Huck Magazine* March 29. <https://www.huckmag.com/art-and-culture/learnt-listening-teju-cole/> [accessed 28 December 2020].
Adesokan, Akinwumi. 2011. *Postcolonial Artists and Global Aesthetics*. Bloomington: Indiana University Press.
Adesokan, Akinwumi. 2012. "New African Writing and the Question of Audience". *Research in African Literatures* 43(3): 1–20.
Adichie, Chimamanda Ngozi. 2003. *Purple Hibiscus*. New York: Alonquin Books.
Adichie, Chimamanda Ngozi. 2006. *Half of a Yellow Sun*. New York: Knopf.
Adichie, Chimamanda Ngozi. 2008. "The Color of an Awkward Conversation". *Washington Post* June. <https://www.washingtonpost.com/wp-dyn/content/article/2008/06/06/AR2008060603141.html> [accessed 28 December 2020].
Adichie, Chimamanda Ngozi. 2009a. "The Danger of a Single Story". TEDtalk recorded July 2009 at *TEDGlobal*, <https://www.ted.com/talks/chimamanda_ngozi_adichie_the_danger_of_a_single_story>[accsessed 28 December 2020].
Adichie, Chimamanda Ngozi. 2009b. *The Thing Around Your Neck*. London: Fourth Estate.
Adichie, Chimamanda Ngozi. 2013. *Americanah*. London: Forth Estate.
Adichie, Chimamanda Ngozi. 2014. *We Should All Be Feminists*. London: Fourth Estate.
Adichie, Chimamanda Ngozi. 2015. Wellesley Commencement Address. 29 May 2015, <https://www.wellesley.edu/events/commencement/archives/2015/commencementaddress> [accessed 28 December 2020].
Adichie, Chimamanda Ngozi. 2017a. *Dear Ijeawele, or A Feminist Manifesto in Fifteen Suggestions*. New York: Knopf.
Adichie, Chimamanda Ngozi. 2017b. "Chimamanda Ngozi Adichie and Trevor Noah". *PEN World Voices Festival*, May 2017, <https://www.youtube.com/watch?v=yiX5XvykVSk> [accessed 28 December 2020].
Adorno, Theodor W. 1999. *Aesthetic Theory*. Edited by Gretel Adorno and Rolf Tiedemann, translated by Robert Hullot-Kentor. London: Athlone Press.
Ahmed, Sara. 2012. *On Being Included: Racism and Diversity in Institutional Life*. Durham: Duke University Press.
Aidoo, Ama Ata. 1977. *Our Sister Killjoy or Reflections from a Black-Eyed Squint*. London: Longman.
Aidoo, Ama Ata. 1987. *The Dilemma of a Ghost & Anowa*. London: Longman.
Aidoo, Ama Ata. 1995. *No Sweetness Here and Other Stories*. New York: The Feminist Press.
Aidoo, Ama Ata. 1998. "The African Woman Today". In: Obioma Nnaemeka (ed.). *Sisterhood, Feminisms and Power*. Trenton: Africa World Press. 39–50.
Aidoo, Ama Ata. 2012. *Diplomatic Pounds and Other Stories*. Banbury: Ayebia Clarke.

Akinbi, Joseph O. 2017. "Contemporary migrations of Nigerians to the United States". In: Toyin Falola and Adebayo Oyebade (eds.). *The New African Diaspora in the United State*. London: Routledge. 98–104.

Alexander, Michelle. 2012. *The New Jim Crow: Mass Incarceration in the Age of Colorblindness*. New York: New Press.

Akomfrah, John. 2015. "Why History Matters". *TateShots*. <https://www.youtube.com/watch?v=jDJYyG7jKV0> [accessed 28 December 2020].

Anderson, Benedict. 1991. *Imagined Communities*. London & New York: Verso.

Angelou, Maya. 2010. "Still I Rise." *Sister Namibia* 22(1): 36.

Anzaldúa, Gloria. 1999. *Borderlands/La Frontera: The New Mestiza*. San Francisco: Aunt Lute Press.

Appiah, Anthony Kwame. 1992. *In My Father's House: Africa in the Philosophy of Culture*. Oxford: Oxford University Press.

Appiah, Anthony Kwame. 2005. *The Ethics of Identity*. Princeton: Princeton University Press.

Appiah, Anthony Kwame. 2006. *Cosmopolitanism: Ethics in a World of Strangers*. New York: Norton.

Aristoteles et al. 1995. *Poetics*. New edition, revised by Donald A. Russell. Cambridge, Mass.: Harvard University Press.

Arndt, Susan. 2017. "Dream-Hoping Memory into Futures: Reading Resistant Narratives about Maafa by Employing Futures as a Category of Analysis." *JALA: Journal of the African Literature Association* 11(1): 3–27.

Armah, Ayi Kwei. 1968. *The Beautyful Ones Are Not Yet Born*. Boston: Houghton Mifflin.

Ashcroft, Bill. 2013. "Menippean Marechera." In: Grant Hamilton (ed.). *Reading Marechera*. Melton: Currey. 76–98.

Ashe, Bertram D. 2010. "Post-Soul President: Dreams from My Father and the Post-Soul Aesthetic." In: Heather E. Harris, Kimberly R. Moffitt, and Catherine R. Squires (eds.). *The Obama Effect: Multidisciplinary Renderings of the 2008 Campaign*, Albany: State University of New York Press. 103–115.

Atta, Sefi. 2013. *A Bit of Difference*. London: Fourth Estate.

Attree, Lizzy. 2018 "Reclaiming Africa's Stolen Histories Through Fiction." *Los Angeles Review of Books* July 11. <https://lareviewofbooks.org/article/reclaiming-africas-stolen-histories-through-fiction/> [accessed: 30 January 2021].

Auden, W.H. 1991. "Musée Des Beaux Arts." *Collected Poems*. New York: Vintage International. 179.

Bady, Aaron. 2013. "Chimamanda Ngozi Adichie: 'Race Doesn't Occur to Me.'" *Salon* July 14. <www.salon.com/2013/07/14/chimamanda_ngozi_adichie_race_doesnt_occur_to_me_partner> [accessed 28 December 2020].

Bady, Aaron. 2015. "Interview with Teju Cole." *Post45* January 19. <www.post45.research.yale.edu> [accessed 28 December 2020].

Balakrishnan, Sarah. 2017. "The Afropolitan Idea: New Perspectives on Cosmopolitanism in African Studies." *History Compass* 15(2): 1–11.

Balakrishnan, Sarah. 2018. "Afropolitanism and the End of Black Nationalism." In: Gerard Delanty (ed.). *Routledge International Handbook of Cosmopolitanism Studies*. 2nd ed. London & New York: Routledge. 575–585.

Bakhtin, Mikail. 1986. *The Dialogic Imagination: Essays*. Austin: University of Texas Press.

Baldwin, James. 1963. *The Fire Next Time*. New York: Dial Press.

Baldwin, James. 1968. *Notes of a Native Son*. New York: Bantam Books.
Baptist, Edward E. 2014. *The Half Has Never Been Told: Slavery and the Making of American Capitalism*. New York: Basic Books.
Baraka, Amiri. 1999. "The Changing Same." In: William J. Harris (ed.) *The LeRoi Jones/Amiri Baraka Reader*. New York: Thunder's Mouth. 186–209.
Barnes, Natasha. 1996. "Black Atlantic-Black America." *Research in African Literatures*, 27(4): 106–107.
Bashi, Vilna. 2004. "Globalized Anti-Blackness: Transnationalizing Western Immigration Law, Policy, and Practice." *Ethnic and Racial Studies* 24(4): 584–606.
Bauman, Zygmunt. 2017. *Retrotopia*. Cambridge: Polity.
Bausells, Marta. 2017. "The Ghanaian-American Novelist Unpacking Slavery, Identity, and Immigration." *VICE* February 20. <www.vice.com/en_us/article/3k8djy/yaa-gyasi-home going-book-interview> [accessed 28 December 2020].
Bayerischer Rundfunk. 2019. "Ich bin nicht schwarz" – Chimamanda Ngozi Adichies "Americanah." *Radio Wissen* May 9. <www.br.de/radio/bayern2/service/manuskripte/ra diowissen/manuskriptradiowissen-2674.html> [accessed 28 December 2020].
Beaulieu, Elizabeth Ann. 1999. *Black Women Writers and the American Neo-Slave Narrative: Femininity Unfettered*. Santa Barbara: Greenwood Press.
Begam, Richard. 1997. "Achebe's Sense of an Ending: History and Tragedy in 'Things Fall Apart.'" *Studies in the Novel* 29(3): 396–411.
Benjamin, Ruha. 2018. "Black After Lives Matter: Cultivating Kinfulness as Reproductive Justice." In: Donna Haraway and Adele Clarke (eds.). *Making Kin Not Population*. Chicago: Prickly Paradigm Press 2018. Excerpted online: <www.bostonreview.net/race/ ruha-benjamin-black-afterlives-matter> [accessed 28 December 2020].
Benjamin, Walter and Rolf Tiedemann. 1999. *The Arcades Project*. Cambridge, Mass.: Harvard University Press.
Benjamin, Walter, 2003. Selected Writings Vol. 1–4, edited by Marcus Bollock and Michael W. Jennings. Cambridge, Mass.: Belknap Press of Harvard University Press.
Bennett, Herman L. 2000. "The Subject in the Plot: National Boundaries and the 'History' of the Black Atlantic." African *Studies Review* 43(1): 101–124.
Bergson, Henri. 1965. *Duration and Simultaneity*. Indianapolis: Bobbs-Merrill.
Bergson, Henri. *Matter and Memory*. 1991. Princeton: Zone Books.
Berlant, Lauren. 2006. "Cruel Optimism." *Differences* 17(3): 20–36.
Bernasconi, Robert. 2002. "The Assumption of Negritude: Aimé Césaire, Frantz Fanon, and the Vicious Circle of Radial Politics." *parallax* 8: 69–83.
Best, Stephen, and Saidiya Hartman. 2005. "Fugitive Justice." *Representations* 92: 1–15.
Best, Stephen and Sharon Marcus. 2009. "Surface Reading: An Introduction." *Representations* 108: 1–21.
Best, Stephen. 2012. "On Failing to Make the Past Present." *Modern Language Quarterly: A Journal of Literary History* 73(3): 453–474.
Bhabha, Homi K. 2004. *The Location of Culture: with a New Preface by the Author*. London: Routledge.
Black Panther.2018. Dir. by Ryan Coogler. Marvel Studios.
Bledsoe, Adam, and Willie Jamaal Wright. 2019. "The Anti-Blackness of Global Capital." *Environment and Planning D: Society and Space* 37(1): 8–26.

Borzaga, Michela. 2012. "Trauma in the Postcolony: Towards a New Theoretical Approach." In: Ewald Mengel and Michela Borzaga (eds.). *Trauma, Memory, and Narrative in the Contemporary South African Novel.* Amsterdam: Rodopi. 65–91.
Bradbury, Malcolm. 1977. *The Novel Today: Contemporary Writers on Modern Fiction.* Manchester: Manchester University Press.
Brah, Avtar. 2005. *Cartographies of Diaspora: Contesting Identities.* London: Routledge.
Brooks, Peter. 1984. *Reading for the Plot: Design and Intention in Narrative.* Oxford: Clarendon Press.
Brooks, Van Wyck. 1918. "On Creating a Usable Past." *The Dial* April 11: 337–341.
Buck-Morss, Susan. 2009. *Hegel, Haiti, and Universal History.* Pittsburgh: University of Pittsburgh Press.
Bulawayo, NoViolet. 2013. *We Need New Names.* New York: Reagan Arthur Books.
Byrd, Ayana D., and Lori L. Tharps. 2001. *Hair Story: Untangling the Roots of Black Hair in America.* New York: St. Martin's.
Campbell, Mary Schmidt. 2007. "African American Art in a Post-Black Era." *Women & Performance: A Journal of Feminist Theory* 17(3): 317–330.
Campt, Tina. 2017. *Listening to Images.* Durham: Duke University Press.
Carby, Hazel V. 1987. *Reconstructing Womanhood: the Emergence of the Afro-American Woman Novelist.* Oxford: Oxford University Press.
Carby, Hazel V.1998. *Race Men.* Cambridge, Mass.: Harvard University Press.
Carretta, Vincent. 1999. "Olaudah Equiano or Gustavus Vassa? New Light on an Eighteenth Century Question of Identity." *Slavery and Abolition* 20(3): 96–105.
Carretta, Vincent. 2005. *Equiano, the African: Biography of a Self Made Man.* Athens: University of Georgia Press.
Caruth, Cathy. 1995. "Trauma and Experience: Introduction." In: Cathy Caruth et al. (eds.). *Trauma: Explorations in Memory.* Baltimore: Johns Hopkins University Press.
Caruth, Cathy. 1996. *Unclaimed Experience: Trauma, Narrative, and History.* Baltimore: Johns Hopkins University Press.
Cheng, Anne Anlin. 2001. *The Melancholy of Race: Psychoanalysis, Assimilation, and Hidden Grief.* Oxford: Oxford University Press.
Chikwawa, Brian. 2009. *Harare North.* London: Jonathan Cape.
Choonoo, R. Neville. 2015. "Parallel Lives: Black Autobiographical Writing in South Africa and the United States." In Benaouda Lebdai (ed.). *Autobiography as a Writing Strategy in Postcolonial Literature.* Newcastle upon Tyne: Cambridge Scholars Publishing.
Chow, Rey. 2010. "The Politics of Admittance: Female Sexual Agency, Miscegenation, and the Formation of Community in Frantz Fanon." *The Rey Chow Reader.* New York: Columbia University Press. 56–75.
Chrisman, Laura. 1997. "Journeying to Death: Gilroy's Black Atlantic." *Race & Class* 39(2): 51–64.
Chude-Sokei, Louis. 2014. "The Newly Black Americans." *Transition: An International Review* 113: 52–71.
Clarke, Becky. 2003. "The African Writers Series – Celebrating Forty Years of Publishing Distinction." *Research in African Literatures* 34: 163–174.
Clifford, James. 1994. "Diasporas." *Cultural Anthropology* 9(3): 302–338.
Coates, Ta-Nehisi. 2017. *We Were Eight Years in Power: An American Tragedy.* London: Hamish Hamilton.

Coetzee, J.M. 2003. *Elizabeth Costello: Eight Lessons*. London: Secker & Warburg.
Coetzee, J.M. *Disgrace*. 1999. London: Secker & Warburg.
Coetzee, J.M. *Waiting for the Barbarians*. 1983. London: Secker & Warburg.
Cole, Teju. 2011a. *Open City*. New York: Random House.
Cole, Teju. 2011b. "The small fates." *Twitter* September 11. <twitter.com/tejucole/status/109317429112475648> [accessed 20 December 2020].
Cole, Teju. 2014a "At Home in Brooklyn." *Kings County Exhibition Catalogue*. <issuu.com/stevensonctandjhb/docs/kings_county_catalogue_issuu> [accessed 20 December 2020].
Cole, Teju. 2014b. *Every Day Is for the Thief*. London: Faber & Faber.
Cole, Teju. 2016. "Black Body." *Known and Strange Things*. London: Faber & Faber.
Cole, Teju. 2017. "Interview with The World Staff." *PRI The World* June 17 2017, www./themillions.com/2017/07/finding-way-new-form-interview-teju-cole.html. [accessed 20 December 2020]
Cole, Teju. 2018. "On the Blackness of the Panther." *Medium* March 6. <medium.com/s/story/on-the-blackness-of-the-panther-f76d771b0e80> [accessed 20 December 2020].
Conti, Paul. 2018. "Trauma, Suicide, Community, and Self-Compassion." *The Peter Attia Drive Podcast* September 17.
Cooper, Frederick. 2015. "African Studies: History." *International Encyclopedia of the Social & Behavioral Sciences*. Elsevier Science & Technology: 286–291.
Cosimini, Seth. 2013. "Review of Americanah." *Fullstop*, June 25. <www.full-stop.net/2013/06/25/reviews/seth-cosimini/Americanah-chimamanda-ngozi-adichie> [accessed 20 December 2020].
Craps, Stef. 2012. *Postcolonial Witnessing: Trauma Out of Bounds*. London: Palgrave Macmillan.
Crawford, Margo Natalie. 2017. "The Twenty-First-Century Black Studies Turn to Melancholy." *American Literary History* 29(4): 799–807.
Crenshaw, Kimberlé. 2019. "Speech given by Kimberlé Crenshaw at the Gala in Her Honor." *Heinrich Böll Institut Berlin* April 28. https://www.intersectionaljustice.org/publication/2019-05-07-speech-given-by-kimberl%C3%A9-crenshaw-at-the-gala-in-her-honor-on-april-28th-2019 [accessed 20 December 2020].
Cugoano, Ottobah. 1825. "Narrative of the Enslavement of Ottobah Cugoano, a Native of Africa; published by himself, in the Year 1787." *The Negro's Memorial, or, Abolitionist's Catechism by an Abolitionist*. London: Hatchard and Co. 120–127.
Cunningham, Vinson. 2018. "The Shifting Perspective in Kehinde Wiley's Portrait of Barack Obama." *The New Yorker* February 13. www.newyorker.com/culture/annals-of-appearances/the-shifting-perspective-in-kehinde-wileys-portrait-of-barack-obama. [accessed 20 December 2020].
Dabiri, Emma. 2014. "Why I'm Not an Afropolitan." *Africa Is a Country* January 21. <africasacountry.com/2014/01/why-im-not-an-afropolitan> [accessed 20 December 2020].
Dalley, Hamish. 2014. *The Postcolonial Historical Novel: Realism, Allegory, and the Representation of Contested Pasts*. London: Palgrave Macmillan.
Dalley, Hamish. 2015. "The Question of 'Solidarity' in Postcolonial Trauma Fiction: Beyond the Recognition Principle." *Humanities* 4(3): 369–392.
Davis, Adrienne. 2002. "Don't Let Nobody Bother Yo' Principle." In: Sharon Harley and the Black Women and Work Collective (eds.). *Sister Circle: Black Women and Work*. New Brunswick: Rutgers University Press. 103–127.

Davis, Angela Y. 1999. "Prison Abolition." In: Walter Mosley et al. (eds.). *Black Genius: African American Solutions to African American Problems,* New York: Norton. 193–215.
Davis, Angela Y. 2003. *Are Prisons Obsolete?* New York: Seven Stories Press.
Dayan, Colin (Joan). 1996. "Paul Gilroy's Slaves, Ships, and Routes: The Middle Passage as Metaphor." *Research in African Literatures* 27(4): 7–14.
De B'Beri, Boulou Ebanda, and P. Eric Louw. 2011. "Afropessimism: a Genealogy of Discourse, Introduction." *Critical Arts-South-North Cultural and Media Studies* 25(3): 335–346.
de Certeau, Michel. 2008. "Walking in the City." *The Practice of Everyday Life.* Berkeley: University of California Press. 91–111.
Delany, M.R. 1861. *Official Report of the Niger Valley Exploring Party.* New York: Thomas Hamilton.
de Man, Paul. 1971. *Blindness & Insight: Essays in the Rhetoric of Contemporary Criticism.* Oxford: Oxford University Press.
de Man, Paul. 1979. "Autobiography as De-Facement." *MLN* 94(5): 919–930.
Díaz, Junot. 2007. *The Brief Wondrous Life of Oscar Wao.* New York: Riverhead Books.
Díaz, Junot. 2014. "MFA vs. POC." *The New Yorker* April 30. <www.newyorker.com/books/page-turner/mfa-vs-poc> [accessed 20 December 2020].
Dickerson, Debra. 2007. "Colorblind." *Salon* January 22. <www.salon.com/2007/01/22/obama_161/> [accessed 20 December 2020].
Dimock, Wai Chee. 2007. *Through Other Continents: American Literature across Deep Time.* Princeton: Princeton University Press.
Douglass, Frederick. 1845. *Narrative of the Life of Frederick Douglass: an American Slave.* Boston: Webb and Chapman.
Dubey, Madhu. 2010. "Neo-Slave Narratives." *A Companion to African American Literature.* In: Gene Andrew Jarrett (ed.). New Jersey: Wiley-Blackwell. 332–333.
Du Bois, W.E.B. 1926. "Criteria of Negro Art." *The Crisis* 32: 290–297.
Du Bois, W.E.B. and Brent Hayes Edwards. 2007. *The Souls of Black Folk.* Oxford: Oxford University Press.
Dyson, Michael Eric. 2016. *The Black Presidency: Barack Obama and the Politics of Race in America.* Boston: Houghton Mifflin Harcourt.
Eaglestone, Robert. 2008. "'You Would Not Add to My Suffering If You Knew What I Have Seen': Holocaust Testimony and Contemporary African Trauma Literature." *Studies in the Novel* 40: 72–85.
Edwards, Brent Hayes. 2003. *The Practice of Diaspora.* Cambridge, Mass.: Harvard University Press.
Edwards, Brent Hayes. 2007. Introduction. In: W.E.B. Du Bois. *The Souls of Black Folk.* Oxford: Oxford University Press: vii-xxiv.
Eggers, Dave. 2006. *What Is the What.* San Francisco: McSweeneys Books.
Eisenberg, Eve. 2013. "'Real Africa'/'Which Africa?': The Critique of Mimetic Realism in Chimamanda Ngozi Adichie's Short Fiction." In: E. Emenyonu (ed.). *Writing Africa in the Short Story.* Woodbridge: Boydell & Brewer. 8–24.
Elias, Amy J. 2005. "Metahistorical Romance, the Historical Sublime, and Dialogic History." *Rethinking History* 9(2): 159–172.
Ellis, Nadia. 2015. *Territories of the Soul: Queered Belonging in the Black Diaspora.* Durham: Duke University Press.
Ellison, Ralph. 1952. *Invisible Man.* New York: Random House.

Emecheta, Buchi. 1994. *In the Ditch.* London: Heinemann, 1994.
Emezi, Akwaeke. 2018. *Freshwater.* New York: Grove Press.
Engler, Sandra. 2004. *"A Career's Wonderful, but Love Is More Wonderful Still": Femininity and Masculinity in the Fiction of Mills & Boon.* Marburg: Francke.
English, Daylanne K. 2013. *Each Hour Redeem: Time and Justice in African American Literature.* Minneapolis: University of Minnesota Press.
Equiano, et al. 1969. *Equiano's Travels: His Autobiography; the Interesting Narrative of the Life of Olaudah Quiano or Gustavus Vassa the African.* London: Heinemann.
Eze, Chielozona. 2014. "Rethinking African Culture and Identity: the Afropolitan Model." *Journal of African Cultural Studies* 26(2): 234–247.
Falola, Toyin. 2011. "African History Writing." In: *The Oxford History of Historical Writing: Volume 5: Historical Writing Since 1945.* Oxford: Oxford University Press. 399–422.
Falola, Toyin et al. (eds.). 2017. *The New African Diaspora in the United States.* London: Routledge.
Fanon, Frantz. 2001. *The Wretched of the Earth.* London: Penguin Books.
Fanon, Frantz. 2008. *Black Skin, White Masks.* London: Pluto.
Faulkner, William. 1951. *Requiem for a Nun.* New York: Random House.
Felski, Rita. 1989. *Beyond Feminist Aesthetics: Feminist Literature and Social Change.* London: Hutchinson Radius.
Felski, Rita. 2011. "Context Stinks." *New Literary History* 42(4): 573–591.
Ferguson, Roderick. 2011. "The Lateral Moves of African American Studies." In: Grace Kyungwon Hong and Roderick Ferguson (eds.). *Strange Affinities: the Gender and Sexual Politics of Comparative Racialization.* Durham: Duke University Press. 113–131.
Fick, Maggie. 2016. "Publisher's Expansion Brings Nigerian Writers to World Stage." *Financial Times* November 27. <www.ft.com/content/8cebd6d6-79b4-11e6-97ae-647294649b28> [accessed 20 December 2020].
Fields, Karen E., and Barbara J. Fields. 2014. *Racecraft: the Soul of Inequality in American Life.* New York: London & New York: Verso.
Fischer, Sibylle. 2004. *Modernity Disavowed: Haiti and the Cultures of Slavery in the Age of Revolution.* Durham: Duke University Press.
Fleissner, Jennifer. 2013. "Historicism Blues." *American Literary History* 25(4): 699–717.
Flood, Alison. 2014. "Junot Díaz Condemns Creative Writing Courses for 'Unbearable too-whiteness.'" *The Guardian.* May 19. <www.theguardian.com/books/2014/may/19/junot-diaz-attack-creative-writing-unbearable-too-whiteness> [accessed 20 December 2020].
Foden, Giles. 2011. "Open City by Teju Cole – Review." *The Guardian* August 17. <www.theguardian.com/books/2011/aug/17/open-city-teju-cole-review> [accessed 20 December 2020].
Foner, Eric. 1994. "The Meaning of Freedom in the Age of Emancipation. Presidential Address, 1994." *Journal of American History* 81(2): 435–460.
Foucault, Michel. 1986. "Of Other Spaces." *Diacritics: A Review of Contemporary Criticism* 16(1): 22–27.
Foucault, Michel. 2003. *"Society Must Be Defended": Lectures at the Collège De France*; 1975–76. London: Picador.
Franklin, Ruth. 2013. "Homeland Truth: A Young Woman from Lagos Upends Her False American Existence." *Book Forum* June.
Fraser, Nancy. 1990. "Rethinking the Public Sphere." *Social Text* 8(3): 56–80.

Fraser, Nancy. 2016. "Expropriation and Exploitation in Racialized Capitalism: A Reply to Michael Dawson." *Critical Historical Studies* Spring: 163–178.
Frazier, Franklin E. 1939. *The Negro Family in the United States*. Chicago: University of Chicago Press.
Freud, Sigmund. 1955. "Beyond the Pleasure Principle." In: *The Standard Edition of the Complete Psychological Works of Sigmund Freud* Vol. 18, translated by James Strachey and Anna Freud. London: Hogarth. 7–64.
Freud, Sigmund. 1989. "Mourning and Melancholia." In: Peter Gay (ed.) *The Freud Reader*. New York: Norton. 584–589.
Frías, María. 2003. "An Interview with Ama Ata Aidoo: 'I Learnt My First Feminist Lessons in Africa.'" *Revista Alicantina De Estudios Ingleses* 16: 317–335.
Frost, Robert. 1923. "Nothing Gold Can Stay." *Complete Poems of Robert Frost*. New York: Holt, Rinheart and Winston, 1923.
Frye, Northrop and Helen Kemp. 1965. *Anatomy of Criticism: Four Essays*. Cambridge, Mass.: Harvard University Press.
Frye, Northrop. 1976. *The Secular Scripture: a Study of the Structure of Romance*. Cambridge, Mass.: Harvard University Press.
Frye, Northrop. 1997. *The Harper Handbook to Literature*. Harlow: Longman.
Fuchs, Barbara. 2004. *Romance*. London: Routledge.
Gates, Henry Louis, Jr. 1988. *The Signifying Monkey: A Theory of Afro-American Literary Criticism*. Oxford: Oxford University Press.
Gehrmann, Susanne. 2015. "Cosmopolitanism with African Roots: Afropolitanism's Ambivalent Mobilities." *Journal of African Cultural Studies* 28(1): 1–12.
Genette, Gérard. 1980. *Narrative Discourse: An Essay in Method*. Ithaca: Cornell University Press.
Gigliotti, Simone. 2003. "Unspeakable Pasts as Limit Events: The Holocaust, Genocide, and the Stolen Generations." *Australian Journal of Politics and History* 49(2): 164–181.
Gikandi, Simon. 1996. "Introduction: Africa, Diaspora, and the Discourse of Modernity." *Research in African Literatures* 27(4): 1–6.
Gikandi, Simon. 2002. "Race and Cosmopolitanism." *American Literary History* 14(3): 593–615.
Gikandi, Simon. 2011a. "On Afropolitanism." In: Jennifer Wawrzinek and J.K.S. Makokha (eds.). *Negotiating Afropolitanism: Essays on Borders and Spaces in Contemporary African Literature and Folklore*. Amsterdam: Rodopi. 9–11.
Gikandi, Simon. 2011b. *Slavery and the Culture of Taste*. Princeton: Princeton University Press.
Gikandi, Simon. 2016. "The Authors in Conversation with Simon Gikandi." In: Eva Rask Knudsen and Ulla Rahbek (eds). *In Search of the Afropolitan*. London: Rowman & Littlefield International. 43–63.
Gilroy, Paul. 2000. *Against Race: Imagining Political Culture beyond the Color Line*. Cambridge, Mass.: Harvard University Press.
Gilroy, Paul. 2005. *Postcolonial Melancholia*. New York: Columbia University Press.
Gilroy, Paul. 2002. *The Black Atlantic: Modernity and Double Consciousness*. 3. impr., reprint. London & New York: Verso.
Gilroy, Paul. 2010. *Darker than Blue: on the Moral Economies of Black Atlantic Culture*. Cambridge, Mass.: Harvard University Press.

Glissant, Édouard. 1996. *Caribbean Discourse: Selected Essays*. Charlottesville: University Press of Virginia.

Glissant, Édouard. 2010. *Poetics of Relation*. Ann Arbor: University of Michigan Press.

Golden, Thelma. 2001. *Freestyle*, exhibition catalogue. New York: Studio Museum in Harlem.

Gordon, Lewis R. 1997. *Her Majesty's Other Children: Sketches of Racism from a Neocolonial Age*. Lanham: Rowman & Littlefield.

Gordon, Lewis R. 2007. "Through the Hellish Zone of Nonbeing: Thinking through Fanon, Disaster, and the Damned of the Earth." *Human Architecture: Journal of the Sociology of Self-Knowledge* 5: 5–11.

Goyal, Yogita. 2003. "Theorizing Africa in Black Diaspora Studies: Caryl Phillips' Crossing the River." *Diaspora* 12(1): 5–38.

Goyal, Yogita. 2010. *Romance, Diaspora, and Black Atlantic Literature*. Cambridge: Cambridge University Press.

Goyal, Yogita. 2014. "Africa and the Black Atlantic." *Research in African Literatures* 45(3): v–xxv.

Goyal, Yogita. 2017a. "The Transnational Turn and Postcolonial Studies." In: Yogita Goyal (ed.). *The Cambridge Companion to Transnational American Literature*. Cambridge: Cambridge University Press: 1–19.

Goyal, Yogita. "We Need New Diasporas." *American Literary History* 29(4): 640–663.

Gyasi, Yaa. 2016a. *Homegoing*. New York: Knopf.

Gyasi, Yaa. 2016b. "I'm Ghanaian-American. Am I Black?" *The New York Times* June 18. <www.nytimes.com/2016/06/19/opinion/sunday/im-ghanaian-american-am-i-black.html> [accessed 20 December 2020].

Gyasi, Yaa. 2019. "Slavery Is on People's Minds. It Affects Us Still." *The Guardian* January 8. <www.theguardian.com/books/2017/jan/08/yaa-gyasi-slavery-is-on-peoples-minds-it-affects-us-still-interview-homegoing-observer-new-review.> [accessed 20 December 2020].

Habila, Helon. 2013. "Review of We Need New Names, by NoViolet Bulawayo." *The Guardian* June 20. <www.theguardian.com/books/2013/jun/20/need-new-names-bulawayo-review> [accessed 20 December 2020]

Hale, Thomas. A. 2006. "Bursting at the Seams: New Dimensions for African Literature in the 21st Century." In: Ernest Emenyonu (ed.). *New Directions in African Literature*. Melton: Currey. 10–22.

Haley, Alex. 1976. *Roots: the Saga of an American Family*. New York: Doubleday.

Hall, Douglas. 1989. *In Miserable Slavery: The Diaries of Thomas Thistlewood in Jamaica 1750–1786*. New York: Macmillan.

Hall, Stuart. 1993. "What Is this 'Black' in Black Popular Culture?" *Social Justice: A Journal of Crime, Conflict and World Order* 20(1): 104–114.

Hall, Stuart. 1994. "Cultural Identity and Diaspora." In: Patrick Williams and Laura Chrisman (eds.). *Colonial Discourse and Post-Colonial Theory. A Reader*. New York: Columbia University Press. 392–403.

Hall, Stuart. 2003. "Maps of Emergency: Fault Lines and Tectonic Plates." In: Gilane Tawadros and Sarah Campbell (eds.). *Fault Lines: Contemporary African Art and Shifting Landscapes*. Institute of International Visual Art in collaboration with the Forum for African Art and the Prince Claus Forum. 32–41.

Hallemeier, Katherine. 2013. "Literary Cosmopolitanisms in Teju Cole's Every Day Is for the Thief and Open City." *ARIEL: A Review of International English Literature* 44(2–3): 239–250.

Hallemeier, Katherine. 2015. "'To Be from the Country of People Who Gave': National Allegory and the United States of Adichie's *Americanah*." *Studies in the Novel* 47(2): 231–245.

Hanchard, Michael. 1999. "Afro-Modernity: Temporality, Politics, and the African Diaspora." *Public Culture* 11(1): 245–268.

Harris, Leonard. 2004. "The Great Debate: W. E. B. du Bois vs. Alain Locke on the Aesthetic." *Philosophia Africana* 7(1): 15–39.

Harris-Lacewell, Melissa Victoria. 2004. *Barbershops, Bibles, and BET: Everyday Talk and Black Political Thought*. Princeton: Princeton University Press.

Hart, William David. 2018. "Constellations: Capitalism, Antiblackness, Afro-Pessimism, and Black Optimism." *American Journal of Theology and Philosophy* 39(1): 5–33.

Hartman, Saidiya. 1996. "Seduction and the Ruses of Power." *Callaloo* 19(2): 537–560.

Hartman, Saidiya. 2002. "The Time of Slavery." *South Atlantic Quarterly* 101(4): 757–777.

Hartman, Saidiya. 2007. *Lose Your Mother: A Journey Along the Atlantic Slave Route*. New York: Farrar, Straus and Giroux.

Hartman, Saidiya. 2008. "Venus in Two Acts." *Small Axe* 26: 1–14.

Hartman, Saidiya. 2019. *Wayward Lives, Beautiful Experiments*. New York: W. W. Norton & Company.

Hartwiger, Alexander. 2016. "The Postcolonial Flaneur: Open City and the Urban Palimpsest." *Postcolonial Text* 11(1): 1–17.

Haselstein, Ulla. 2000. *Die Gabe der Zivilisation: Kultureller Austausch und Literarische Textpraxis in Amerika, 1682–1861*. München: Wilhelm Fink Verlag.

Hayman, Casey. 2015. "'Black Is... Black Ain't': Ralph Ellison's Meta-Black Aesthetic and the 'End' of African American Literature." *American Studies* 54(3): 127–149.

Hegel, Georg Wilhelm Friedrich. 2011. *The Philosophy of History*. Translated by J. Sibree. Ontario: Batoche Books.

Hensher, Philip. 2013. "'Well, That's the End of the Booker Prize, Then.'" *The Guardian* September 18. <www.theguardian.com/books/booksblog/2013/sep/18/booker-prize-us-writers-end> [accessed 20 December 2020].

Herskovits, Melville. 1941. *The Myth of the Negro Past*. New York: Harpers & Brothers.

Hill Collins, Patricia. 2000. *Black Feminist Thought: Knowledge, Consciousness and the Politics of Empowerment*. London & New York: Routledge.

Huggan, Graham. 2001. *The Postcolonial Exotic: Marketing the Margins*. London & New York: Routledge.

Hurston, Zora Neale, et al. 2018. *Barracoon: The Story of the Last 'Black Cargo'*. New York: Harper Collins.

Hutcheon, Linda. 2002. "Postmodern Afterthoughts." *Wascana Review* 37(1): 5–12.

Huyssen, Andreas. 2000. "Of Mice and Mimesis: Reading Spiegelman with Adorno." *New German Critique* 81: 65–82.

Huyssen, Andreas. 2003. *Present Pasts: Urban Palimpsests and the Politics of Memory*. Palo Alto: Stanford University Press.

Ifowodo, Ogaga. 2013. *History, Trauma, and Healing in Postcolonial Narratives: Reconstructing Identities*. London: Palgrave Macmillan.

Irele, Abiola. 2001. *The African Imagination. Literature in Africa & the Black Diaspora.* Oxford: Oxford University Press.

Irele, Abiola. 2009. "Perspectives on the African Novel." In: Abiola Irele (ed.). *The Cambridge Companion to the African Novel.* Cambridge: Cambridge University Press.

Iromuanya, Julie. 2017. "Are We All Feminists?: The Global Black Hair Industry and Marketplace in Chimamanda Ngozi Adichie's Americanah." *Meridians: Feminism, Race, Transnationalism* 16(1): 163–183.

Jahn, Janheinz. 1968. *Neo-African Literature.* Trans. Oliver Coburn and Ursula Lehrburger. New York: Grove.

James, C. L. R. 1938. *The Black Jacobins: Toussaint L'Ouverture and the San Domingo Revolution.* London: Secker & Warburg.

Jameson, Fredric. 1975. "Magical Narratives: Romance as Genre." *New Literary History: A Journal of Theory and Interpretation,* 7(1): 135–63.

Jameson, Fredric. 1986. "Third-World Literature in the Era of Multinational Capitalism." *Social Text* 15: 65–88.

Jarrett, Gene Andrew. 2011. *Deans and Truants.* Philadelphia: University of Pennsylvania Press.

Jean-Baptiste, Cindy Ogalla Tyeastia Green. 2020. "Commentary on COVID-19 and African Americans: The Numbers Are Just a Tip of a Bigger Iceberg." *Social Sciences & Humanities Open* 2(1), 100070. doi: 10.1016/j.ssaho.2020.100070.

Jewsiewicki, Bogumil. 1989. "African Historical Studies Academic Knowledge as 'Usable Past' and Radical Scholarship." *African Studies Review 32*(3): 1–76.

Johnston, Andrew, and Kai Wiegand. (eds.) 2017. *The Return of the Historical Novel? Thinking about Fiction and History after Historiographic Metafiction.* Heidelberg: Universitätsverlag Winter.

Johnson, Charles R. 2008. "The End of the Black American Narrative: A New Century Calls for New Stories Grounded in the Present, Leaving behind the Painful History of Slavery and Its Consequences. (Critical Essay)." *American Scholar* 77(3): 32–42.

Johnson, Charles Spurgeon. 1934. *Shadow of the Plantation.* Chicago: University of Chicago Press.

Johnson, Daryl. 2012. *Right-Wing Resurgence: How a Domestic Terrorist Threat Is Being Ignored.* Lanham: Rowman & Littlefield.

Johnson, Walter. 2018. "To Remake the World: Slavery, Racial Capitalism and Justice." *Boston Review* February 20. <bostonreview.net/forum/walter-johnson-to-remake-the-world> [accessed 20 December 2020].

Joyce, James. 1964. *Ulysses.* London: Bodley Head.

Julien, Eileen. 2006. "The Extroverted African Novel." In: Franco Moretti (ed.). *The Novel. 1, History, Geography, and Culture.* Volume 1: *History, Geography, and Culture.* Princeton and Oxford: Princeton University Press. 667–702.

Julien, Eileen. 2018. "The Extroverted African Novel, Revisited: African Novels at Home, in the World." *Journal of African Cultural Studies* 30(3): 371–381.

Khanna, Ranjana. 2003. *Dark Continents: Psychoanalysis and Colonialism.* Durham: Duke University Press.

Khatib, Sami. 2013. "The Messianic Without Messianism." *Anthropology & Materialism* 1: 1–17.

Knudsen, Eva Rask, and Ulla Rahbek. *In Search of the Afropolitan: Encounters, Conversations, and Contemporary Diasporic African Literature*. Lanham: Rowman & Littlefield International.

Komunyakaa, Yusef. 2000. "Notations in Blue: Interview with Radiclani Clytus." In: Radiclani Clytus (ed.). *Blue Notes: Essays, Interviews and Commentaries*. Ann Arbor: University of Michigan Press. 135–147.

Konadu-Agyemang, Kwadwo, Baffour K. Takyi, and John A. Arthur. 2006. *The New African Diaspora in North America: Trends, Community Building, and Adaptation*. Lanham: Lexington Books.

Krishnan, Madhu. 2014. *Contemporary African Literature in English: Global Locations, Postcolonial Identifications*. London: Palgrave Macmillan.

Krishnan, Madhu. 2015. "Postcoloniality, Spatiality and Cosmopolitanism in the Open City." *Textual Practice* 29(4): 1–22.

Kunzru, Hari. 2011. "Praise for *Open City* by Teju Cole." *PenguinRandomhouse.com*. <www.penguinrandomhouse.com/books/29908/open-city-by-teju-cole/9780812980097> [accessed 20 December 2020].

Law, Robin and Kristin Mann. 1999. "West Africa in the Atlantic Community: The Case of the Slave Coast." *William and Mary Quarterly* 51(2): 307–334.

LaCapra, Dominick. 2001. *Writing History, Writing Trauma*. Baltimore: Johns Hopkins University Press.

Latour, Bruno. 2004. "Why Has Critique Run out of Steam? From Matters of Fact to Matters of Concern." *Critical Inquiry* 30(2): 225–48.

Launius, Roger. 2013. "Public History Wars, the 'One Nation/One People' Consensus, and the Continuing Search for a Usable Past." *Magazine of History* 27(1): 31–36.

Lemelle, Sidney, and Robin D.G. Kelley. 1994. *Imagining Home: Class, Culture, and Nationalism in the African Diaspora*. London & New York: Verso.

Leong, Nancy. 2013. "Racial Capitalism." *Harvard Law Review* 126(8): 2152–226.

Levine, Caroline. 2015. "'The Strange Familiar': Structure, Infrastructure, and Adichie's *Americanah*." *Modern Fiction Studies* 61(4): 587–605.

Li, Stephanie. 2017. "Introduction: What Is Twenty-First-Century African American Literature?" *American Literary History* 29(4): 631–39.

Lipsitz, George. 2018. "The Changing Same." *Social Identities* 24(1): 16–20.

Liu, Max. 2011. "Doctor without Frontiers." *The Independent* July 31. <www.independent.co.uk/arts-entertainment/books/reviews/open-city-by-teju-cole-2329001.html> [accessed 20 December 2020].

Locke, Alain. 1992. *The New Negro: Voices of the Harlem Renaissance*. New York: Macmillan.

Lorde, Audre. 1995. "A Litany for Survival." *Affilia Journal of Women and Social Work* 10 (1): 108–109.

Lovejoy, Paul E. 2006. "Autobiography and Memory: Gustavus Vassa, Alias Olaudah Equiano, the African." *A Journal of Slave and Post-Slave Studies* 27(3): 317–47.

Lowe, Lisa. 2015. *The Intimacies of Four Continents*. Durham: Duke University Press.

Luckhurst, Roger. 2008. *The Trauma Question*. London & New York: Routledge.

Lukács, Georg. 1969. *The Historical Novel*. London: Penguin.

MacFarquhar, Larissa. 2018. "Chimamanda Ngozi Adichie Comes to Terms with Global Fame." *The New Yorker* May 28. <www.newyorker.com/magazine/2018/06/04/chimamanda-ngozi-adichie-comes-to-terms-with-global-fame> [accessed 20 December 2020].

McCarthy, Jesse. 2016. "A Literary Chameleon." *Harvard Magazine* August 2. <harvardmagazine.com/2016/09/a-literary-chameleon> [accessed 20 December 2020].
Magaziner, Dan. 2017. "The Work of Historical Fiction." *Africa is a Country* December 4. <https://www.africasacountry.com/2017/04/the-work-of-historical-fiction> [accessed 28 December 2020].
Makokha, J.K.S., and Jennifer Wawrzinek. 2011. *Negotiating Afropolitanism: Essays on Borders and Spaces in Contemporary African Literature and Folklore*. Amsterdam: Rodopi.
Makumbi, Jennifer Nansubuga. 2017. *Kintu*. Oakland: Transit Books.
Mangold, Ijoma. 2014. "Roman 'Americanah': 'Ich bin nicht schwarz.'" *Die Zeit* May 15. <www.zeit.de/2014/21/chimamanda-ngozi-adichie-americanah> [accessed 20 December 2020].
Manshel, Alexander. 2017. "The Rise of the Recent Historical Novel." *Post45* September 29. <post45.research.yale.edu/2017/09/the-rise-of-the-recent-historical-novel> [accessed 20 December 2020].
Mareira, Noiripo J. 1996. *Zenzele: A Letter for my Daughter*. London: Phoenix.
Marx, Karl. 1976. *Capital. A Critique of Political Economy, Volume 1*. London: Penguin.
M'Baye, Babacar. 2009. "Richard Wright and African Francophone Intellectuals: A Reassessment of the 1956 Congress of Black Writers in Paris." *African and Black Diaspora: An International Journal* 2(1): 29–42.
Mbembe, Achille. 2001. *On the Postcolony*. Berkeley: University of California Press.
Mbembe, Achille and Sarah Nuttall. 2004. "Writing the World from an African Metropolis." *Public Culture* 16(3): 347–372.
Mbembe, Achille. 2005. "Afropolitanism." Translated by Laurent Chauvet. In: Njami Simon and Lucy Durán (eds.). *Africa Remix: Contemporary Art of a Continent*. Hamburg: Hatje Cantz Publishers. 26–30.
Mbembe, Achille and Bregtje van der Haak. 2015. "The Internet Is Afropolitan." *Chimurenga Chronic* March 17. <www.chimurengachronic.co.za/the-internet-is-Afropolitan> [accessed 20 December 2020].
Mbembe, Achille and Sarah Balakrishnan. 2016. "Pan-African Legacies, Afropolitan Futures." *Transition: An International Review* 120: 28–37.
Mbembe, Achille. 2017. *Critique of Black Reason*. Durham: Duke University Press.
Mbembe, Achille. 2018. "The Reason of Unreason: Conversation: Achille Mbembe and David Theo Goldberg on Critique of Black Reason." *Theory, Culture & Society* July. <www.theoryculturesociety.org/conversation-achille-mbembe-and-david-theo-goldberg-on-critique-of-black-reason/#_ftn1> [accessed 20 December 2020].
Mbue, Imbolo. 2017. *Behold the Dreamers: A Novel*. New York: 4th Estate.
McCathy, Jesse. 2016. "A Literary Chameleon." *Harvard Magazine*. September-October 2016, www.harvardmagazine.com/2016/09/a-literary-chameleon.
McClintock, Anne. 1992. "The Angel of Progress: Pitfalls of the Term 'Post-Colonialism.'" *Social Text* 31/32: 84–98.
McGurl, Mark. 2009. *The Program Era: Postwar Fiction and the Rise of Creative Writing*. Cambridge, Mass.: Harvard University Press.
Mengestu, Dinaw. 2007. *The Beautiful Things That Heaven Bears*. New York: Riverhead Books.
Mesure, Susie. 2013. "Chimamanda Adichie: Dark-skinned Girls Are Never the Babes.'" *The Independent* Saturday 13. <www.independent.co.uk/news/people/profiles/chimamanda-

adichie-dark-skinned-girls-are-never-the-babes-8572145.html> [accessed 20 December 2020].
Miller, Laura. 2016. "Descendants – A sprawling Tale of a Family Split between Africa and America." *The New Yorker* May 30. <https://www.newyorker.com/magazine/2016/05/30/yaa-gyasis-homegoing> [accessed 26 April 2021].
Mills, Charles W. 2014. *The Racial Contract.* Ithaca: Cornell University Press.
Mills, Quincy T. 2013. *Cutting along the Color Line: Black Barbers and Barber Shops in America.* Philadelphia: University of Pennsylvania Press.
Mitchell, W.J.T. 2012. *Seeing Through Race.* Cambridge, Mass.: Harvard University Press.
Moddelmog, William E. 2002. *Reconstituting Authority.* Iowa City: University of Iowa Press.
Mohanty, Chandra Talpade. 2004. *Feminism without Borders: Decolonizing Theory, Practicing Solidarity.* Durham: Duke University Press.
Moten, Fred. 2003. *In the Break: the Aesthetics of the Black Radical Tradition.* Minneapolis: University of Minnesota Press.
Moten, Fred. 2008. "The Case of Blackness." *Criticism: A Quarterly for Literature and the Arts* 50(2): 177–218.
Moraga, Cherríe (ed.). 1981. *This Bridge Called My Back: Writings by Radical Women of Color.* London: Persephone Press.
Moretti, Franco. 2013. *The Bourgeois: Between History and Literature.* London & New York: Verso.
Morrison, Toni. 2004. *Beloved.* New York: Vintage Books.
Moya, Paula. 2015. *The Social Imperative.* Palo Alto: Stanford University Press.
Msimang, Sisonke. 2019. "All Your Faves Are Problematic: A Brief History of Chimamanda Ngozi Adichie, Stanning and the Trap of #blackgirlmagic." *Africa Is a Country* April 10. <www.africasacountry.com/2017/04/all-your-faves-are-problematic-a-brief-history-of-chimamanda-ngozi-adichie-stanning-and-the-trap-of-blackgirlmagic> [accessed 20 December 2020].
Mudimbe, Valentin. 1988. *The Invention of Africa.* Bloomington: Indiana University Press.
Mudimbe, Valentin. 1994. *The Idea of Africa.* Bloomington: Indiana University Press.
Mulvey, Laura. 1996. *Fetishism and Curiosity.* Bloomington: Indiana University Press.
Murillo, John III. 2017. "Review of Homegoing." *MAKE Literary Magazine* March 17. <www.makemag.com/homegoing-by-yaa-gyaasi> [accessed 20 December 2020].
Murphy, David. 2000. *Sembène: Imagining Alternatives in Film and Fiction.* Melton: Currey.
Nadiminti, Kalyan. 2018. "The Global Program Era: Contemporary International Fiction in the American Creative Economy." *Novel* 51(3): 375–398.
Nash, Gary B., et al. 2000. *History on Trial: Culture Wars and the Teaching of the Past.* New York: Vintage Books.
Ndikung, Bonaventure Soh Behjeng. 2016. "Statement at African Futures Festival, Johannesburg, 30 October 2015." In: Lien Heidenreich-Seleme and Sean O'Toole (eds.). *African Futures.* Bielefeld & Berlin: Kerber Culture. 131.
Nehl, Markus. 2016. *Transnational Black Dialogues: Re-Imagining Slavery in the Twenty-First Century.* Bielefeld: Transcript Verlag.
Neumann, Birgit, and Yvonne Kappel. 2019. "Music and Latency in Teju Cole's Open City: Presences of the Past." *ARIEL* 50(1): 31–62.
Ngai, Sianne. 2005. *Ugly Feelings.* Cambridge, Mass.: Harvard University Press.

Nietzsche, Friedrich. 1997. "On the Uses and Disadvantages of History for Life." *Untimely Meditations*. Cambridge: Cambridge University Press. 57–124.

Nixon, Rob. 2011. *Slow Violence and the Environmentalism of the Poor*. Cambridge, Mass.: Harvard University Press.

Nnaemeka, Obioma. 1998. *Sisterhood, Feminisms, and Power: From Africa to the Diaspora*. Africa World Press, 1998.

Nnaemeka, Obioma. 2004. "Nego-Feminism: Theorizing, Practicing, and Pruning Africa's Way." *Signs* 29(2): 357–385.

Noel, Melissa. 2016. "Black & Undocumented: Caribbean Immigrant's Long Fight for Citizenship." *NBC News* April 23. <www.nbcnews.com/news/nbcblk/black-undocumented-caribbean-immigrant-s-long-fight-citizenship-n557441> [accessed 20 December 2020].

Norris, Michele. 2014. "Interview with Chimamanda Ngozi Adichie." *Washington Ideas Forum*. <www.youtube.com/watch?v=2ijEqposkyk> [accessed 20 December 2020].

Nwakanma, Obi. 2010. *Christopher Okigbo 1930–67: Thirsting for Sunlight*. Woodbridge: Boydell and Brewer.

Nwankwo, Ifeoma Kiddoe. 2005. *Black Cosmopolitanism: Racial Consciousness and Transnational Identity in the Nineteenth-Century Americas*. Philadelphia: University of Pennsylvania Press.

Nwaubani, Adaobi Tricia. 2017. "Opinion: African Books for Western Eyes." *The New York Times* December 21. <www.nytimes.com/2014/11/30/opinion/sunday/african-books-for-western-eyes.html> [accessed 20 December 2020].

Obama, Barack. 2004. *Dreams from My Father: A Story of Race and Inheritance*. New York: Three Rivers Press.

Obi-Young, Otosirieze. 2017. "Keeping Up With African Writers: Aminatta Forna." *Brittle Paper* June 21. <brittlepaper.com/2017/06/african-literary-gossip-dinaw-mengestu-binyavanga-aminatta-forna-ama-ata-aidoo-victor-ehikhamenor-week> [accessed 20 December 2020].

Odamtten, Victor O. 1994. *The Art of Ama Ata Aidoo*. Gainesville: University Press of Florida.

Oguine, Ike. 2000. *A Squatter's Tale*. London: Heinemann.

Okparanta, Chinelo. 2014. *Happiness, Like Water*. London: Granta.

Okri, Ben. 2014. "A Mental Tyranny Is Keeping Black Writers from Greatness." *The Guardian* December 27.

Onega, Jaén. 1999. *Narratology: and Introduction*. London: Longman.

Ossewaarde, Marinus. 2018. "'Crises of Modernity' Discourses and the Rise of Financial Technologies in a Contested Mechanized World." *Philosophy & Technology* 31(1): 59–76.

Otele, Olivette. 2018. "On the Spot: Olivette Otele." *History Today* 68(1). <www.historytoday.com/history-today/spot-olivette-otele> [accessed 20 December 2020].

O.W. 2007. "Barack – Be Real Black for Me." *Poplicks.Com* February 9. <poplicks.com/2007/02/barack-be-real-black-for-me.html> [accessed 20 December 2020].

Owens, Jill. 2016. "Powell's Interview: Yaa Gyasi, author of 'Homegoing.'" *Medium* September 23.

Owuor, Yvonne Adhiambo. 2014. *Dust*. New York: Vintage Books.

Patterson, Orlando. 1982. *Slavery and Social Death: A Comparative Study*. Cambridge, Mass.: Harvard University Press.

Paul, Heike. 2014. *The Myths That Made America*. Bielefeld: Transcript Verlag.

PBS (Public Broadcasting Service). 2017. "In 'Behold the Dreamers,' the American Dream and Immigrant Reality Collide." *PBS NewsHour* May 5. <www.pbs.org/newshour/show/behold-dreamers-american-dream-immigrant-reality-collide> [accessed 20 December 2020].

Philip, M. NourbeSe. 2008. *Zong!* Middleton: Wesleyan University Press.

Purcell, Andrew. 2017. "Colson Whitehead: 'The truth of Things, not the Facts.'" *The Sidney Morning Herald* May 11. <www.smh.com.au/entertainment/books/colson-whitehead-the-truth-of-things-not-the-facts-20170511-gw2bud.html> [accessed 20 December 2020].

Rabaka, Reiland. 2015. *The Negritude Movement: W.E.B. Du Bois, Leon Damas, Aime Cesaire, Leopold Senghor, Frantz Fanon, and the Evolution of an Insurgent Idea.* Lanham: Lexington Books.

Radway, Janice A. 1984. *Reading the Romance: Women, Patriarchy, and Popular Literature.* Chapel Hill: University of North Carolina Press.

Ranger, Terence. "Toward a Usable African Past." In: C.H. Fyfe (ed.). *African Studies since 1945: A Tribute to Basil Davidson.* London: Longman. 28–39.

Ranger, Terence and Eric Hobsbawm (eds.). 1983. *The Invention of Tradition.* Cambridge: Cambridge University Press.

Rankine, Claudia. 2014. *Citizen: An American Lyric.* Minneapolis: Graywolf Press.

Rankine, Claudia. 2016. "In Our Way: Racism in Creative Writing." Keynote address at the AWP Conference & Bookfair in Los Angeles, California. <www.awpwriter.org/magazine_media/writers_chronicle_view/4120> [accessed 20 December 2020].

Reed, Anthony. 2014. *Freedom Time: the Poetics and Politics of Black Experimental Writing.* Baltimore: Johns Hopkins University Press.

Reising, Russell. 1986. *The Unusable Past: Theory and the Study of American Literature.* London: Methuen.

Reynolds, Simon. 2012. *Retromania: Pop Culture's Addiction to its Own Past.* London: Faber & Faber.

Rippl, Gabriele and Birgit Neumann. 2017. "'Celebrating Afropolitan Identities?' Contemporary African World Literatures in English." *Anglia* 135(1): 159–185.

Rippl, Gabriele. 2018. "Picturing Lagos: Word-Photography Configurations in Teju Cole's Every Day Is for the Thief." *Social Dynamics* 44(3): 472–484.

Robbins, Bruce. 1990. "Telescopic Philanthropy: Professionalism and Responsibility in Bleak House." In: Homi Bhabha (ed.). *Nation and Narration.* London & New York: Routledge. 213–231.

Roberts, Sam. 2005. "More Africans Enter U.S. Than in Days of Slavery." *The New York Times* February 21. <https://www.nytimes.com/2005/02/21/nyregion/more-africans-enter-us-than-in-days-of-slavery.html> [accessed 20 December 2020].

Rosenzweig, et al. 1998. *The Presence of the Past: Popular Uses of History in American Life.* New York: Columbia University Press.

Rothberg, Michael. 2008. "Decolonizing Trauma Studies: A Response." *Studies in the Novel* 40(1/2): 224–234.

Rothberg, Michael. 2000. *Traumatic Realism: The Demands of Holocaust Representation.* Minneapolis: University of Minnesota Press.

Rubinstein, Charlotte Streifer. 1990. *American Women Sculptors.* Boston: G.K. Hall & Co.

Rushdy, Ashraf H.A. 2004. "The Neo-Slave Narrative." In: Maryemma Graham (ed.). *The Cambridge Companion to the African American Novel.* Cambridge: Cambridge University Press. 87–106.

Rutledge Fisher, Rebecka et al. 2014. *Retrieving the Human: Reading Paul Gilroy*. Albany: SUNY Press.
Said, Edward. W. 1994. *Culture and Imperialism*. New York: Vintage Books.
Salami, Minna. 2015. "My Views on Afropolitanism." *MsAfropolitan.Com*. <www.msafropolitan.com/my-views-on-afropolitanism> [accessed 20 December 2020].
Saldívar, Ramón. 2013. "The Second Elevation of the Novel: Race, Form, and the Postrace Aesthetic in Contemporary Narrative." *Narrative* 21(1): 1–18.
Sarte, Jean Paul. 1965. *Being and Nothingness: an Essay in Phenomenological Ontology*. New York: Citadel Press.
Saval, Nikil, and Dayna Tortorici (eds.). 2013. "World Lite: What is Global Literature?" *n+1 Magazine* 17: 1–14.
Scarry, Elaine. 1985. *The Body in Pain: The Making and Unmaking of the World*. Oxford: Oxford University Press.
Schulz, Kathryn. 2013. "Review of Americanah by Chimamanda Ngozi Adichie." *New York Magazine* June 3.
Schur, Richard. 2013. "The Crisis of Authenticity in Contemporary African American Literature." In: Lovalerie King and Shirley Moody-Turner (eds.) *Contemporary African American Literature: The Living Canon*. Bloomington: Indiana University 235–254.
Scott, David. 2004. *Conscripts of Modernity: The Tragedy of Colonial Enlightenment*. Durham: Duke University Press.
Segal, Parul. 2013. "A Conversation with Chimamanda Ngozi Adichie." *Tin House* 56(3). <www.parulsehgal.com/2013/06/09/a-conversation-with-chimamanda-ngozi-adichie> [accessed 20 December 2020].
Selasi, Taiye. 2013. "Bye-Bye Barbar." *Callaloo* 36(3). 528–30.
Selasi, Taiye. 2013. *Ghana Must Go*. New York: Viking.
Selasi, Taiye. 2017. "A Portrait of the Artist as a Young African Immigrant." *The New York Times* May 8. <www.nytimes.com/2017/05/08/t-magazine/yaa-gyasi-toyin-ojih-odutola.html> [accessed 20 December 2020].
Senghor, Léopold Sédar. 1956. "The Spirit of Civilisation, or the Laws of African Negro Culture." *Presence Africaine* 8–10: 51–65.
Sexton, Jared. 2011. "The Social Life of Social Death." *InTensions* 5: 1–47.
Sharpe, Christina. 2016. *In the Wake: On Blackness and Being*. Durham: Duke University Press.
Sharpe, Christina and Saidiya Hartman. 2017. "Response & Statement." Presentation given at *The Milieu of the Dead. Part 2: Absences – The Afterlife of Slavery and the Gaps in the Archive*. December 7, Berlin.
Sharpley-Whiting, Tracy Denean. 1998. "Fanon and Capécia." *Frantz Fanon: Conflicts and Feminism*. Lanham: Rowman & Littlefield. 31–52.
Shaw-Taylor, et al. 2007. *The Other African Americans: Contemporary African and Caribbean Immigrants in the United States*. Lanham: Rowman & Littlefield.
Shelby, Tommie. 2008. "Cosmopolitanism, Blackness, and Utopia: A Conversation with Paul Gilroy." *Transitions* 98: 116–135.
Shohat, Ella. 1992. "Notes on the 'Post-Colonial.'" *Social Text* 10(2): 99–113.
Shumway, Rebecca. 2011. *The Fante and the Transatlantic Slave Trade*. Rochester: University of Rochester Press.

Singh, Nikhil Pal. 2004. *Black Is a Country: Race and the Unfinished Struggle for Democracy.* Cambridge, Mass.: Harvard University Press.

Singleton, Jermaine. 2015. *Cultural Melancholy: Readings of Race, Impossible Mourning, and African American Ritual.* Champaign: University of Illinois Press.

Skinner, Ryan Thomas. 2017. "Why Afropolitanism Matters." *Africa Today* 64(2): 3–21.

Smith, Zadie. 2001. *White Teeth.* Penguin Books.

Smith, Zadie. 2014. "Between the Lines: Chimamanda Adichie with Zadie Smith." *New York Public Library* March 19. <www.youtube.com/watch?v=LkeCun9aljY> [accessed 20 December 2020].

Smith, Zadie. 2016. *Feel Free. Essays.* London: Penguin.

Smith, Zadie. 2016. *Swing Time.* London: Penguin Press.

Smith, Zadie. 2018. "Now More Than Ever." *The New Yorker* July 23.

Sollors, Werner. 2018. "Cosmopolitan Curiosity in an Open City: Notes on Reading Teju Cole by Way of Kwame Anthony Appiah." *New Literary History* 49(2): 227–48.

Sontag, Deborah. 1992. "Canonizing a Slave: Saint or Uncle Tom?" *The New York Times* February 23. <https://www.nytimes.com/1992/02/23/nyregion/canonizing-a-slave-saint-or-uncle-tom.html> [accessed 24 April 2021].

Soyinka, Wole. 1967. "The Writer in an African State." *Transition* 31: 11–13.

Speke, John Hanning. 1863. *Journal of the Discovery of the Source of the Nile.* Edinburgh: William Blackwood and Sons.

Spiegel, Hubert. 2014. "Exilanten-Epos 'Americanah': Dieser Roman markiert eine Zäsur." *Frankfurter Allgemeine Zeitung* May 9. <www.faz.net/1.2932011> [accessed 20 December 2020].

Spillers, Hortense. 2003. *Black, White, and in Color: Essays on American Literature and Culture.* Chicago: University of Chicago Press.

St. Clair, William. 2007. *The Door of No Return: The History of Cape Coast Castle and the Atlantic Slave Trade.* New York: BlueBridge.

Stallings, L.H. 2013. "Sampling the Sonics of Sex (Funk) in Paul Beatty's *Slumberland*." In: Lovalerie King (ed.). *Contemporary African American Literature: The Living Canon.* Bloomington: Indiana University Press. 189–213.

Sterling, Cheryl. 2010. "Can You Really See through a Squint? Theoretical Underpinnings in Ama Ata Aidoo's Our Sister Killjoy." *The Journal of Commonwealth Literature* 45(1): 131–150.

Sterling, Cheryl. 2015. "Race Matters: Cosmopolitanism, Afropolitanism, and Pan-Africanism via Edward Wilmot Blyden." *Journal of Pan African Studies* 8(1): 119–127.

Stuelke, Patricia. 2017. "Trayvon Martin, *Topdog/Underdog*, and the Tragedy Trap." *American Literary History* 29(4): 753–778.

Susman, Warren. 1964. "History and the American Intellectual: Uses of a Usable Past." *American Quarterly* 16(2): 243–263.

Taylor, Keeanga-Yamahtta. 2016. *From #Blacklivesmatter to Black Liberation.* Chicago: Haymarket Books.

Thrasher, Steven W. 2016. "Claudia Rankine: Why I'm Spending $625,000 to Study Whiteness." *The Guardian* October 19. <www.theguardian.com/books/2016/oct/19/claudia-rankine-macarthur-genius-grant-exploring-whiteness> [accessed 20 December 2020].

The Economist (Editorial). 2011. "Bird's Eye View – New Fiction." *The Economist* July 30 <www.economist.com/books-and-arts/2011/07/30/birds-eye-view>[accessed 20 December 2020].
The Guardian (Editorial). 2017. "The Guardian View on Historical Fiction: Reimagining, not Reproducing." *The Guardian* July 21. <www.theguardian.com/commentisfree/2017/jul/21/the-guardian-view-on-historical-fiction-reimagining-not-reproducing> [accessed 20 December 2020].
Touré. 2011. *Who's Afraid of Post-Blackness?: What It Means to Be Black Now.* New York: Free Press.
Trouillot, Michel-Rolph. 1995. *Silencing the Past: Power and the Production of History.* Boston: Beacon Press.
Tshuma, Novuyo Rosa. 2018. *House of Stone.* London: Atlantic Books.
Tshuma, Novuyo Rosa. 2019. "Writing Beyond History." *African Book Festival* May 4, Babylon Mitte, Berlin.
Unigwe, Chika. 2009. *On Black Sisters' Street.* Athens: Ohio University Press.
Vermeulen, Pieter. 2013. "Flights of Memory: Teju Cole's Open City and the Limits of Aesthetic Cosmopolitanism." *Journal of Modern Literature* 37(1): 40–57.
Visser, Irene. 2011. "Trauma Theory and Postcolonial Literary Studies." *Journal of Postcolonial Writing* 47(3): 270–282.
wa Ngũgĩ, Mukoma. 2018. *The Rise of the African Novel: Politics of Language, Identity, and Ownership.* Ann Arbor: University of Michigan Press.
wa Thiong'o, Ngũgĩ, Taban Lo Liyong, and Henry Owuor-Anyumba. 1972. "On the Abolition of the English Department." In: Ngũgĩ wa Thiong'o (ed.). *Homecomings: Essays on African and Caribbean Literature, Culture and Politics,* London: Heinemann. 145–150.
wa Thiong'o, Ngũgĩ. 1982. *Devil on the Cross.* London: Heinemann.
wa Thiong'o, Ngũgĩ. 1986. *Decolonising the Mind: The Politics of Language in African Literature.* Melton: Currey.
wa Thiong'o, Ngũgĩ. 1993. *Moving the Centre: The Struggle for Cultural Freedoms.* Melton: Currey.
wa Thiong'o, Ngũgĩ. 2012. *Globalectics: Theory and the Politics of Knowing.* New York: Columbia University Press.
wa Thiong'o, Ngũgĩ. 2016. "A Globalectic Heterotopia: Writing a Novel from a Liminal Space." *Novel* 49(1): 5–9.
Walker, Alice. 2018. "Those Who Love Us Never Leave Us Alone with Our Grief: Reading Barracoon: The Story of the Last 'Black Cargo.'" In: Zora Neale Hurston. *Barracoon.* New York: HarperCollins.
Walters, Wendy W. 2013. *Archives of the Black Atlantic: Reading Between Literature and History.* London & New York: Routledge.
Ware, Owen. 2004. "Dialectic of the Past / Disjuncture of the Future: Derrida and Benjamin on the Concept of Messianism." *Journal for Cultural and Religious Theory* 5(2): 99–114.
Ward, Abigail. 2011. *Caryl Phillips, David Dabydeen and Fred D'Aguiar: Representations of Slavery.* Manchester: Manchester University Press.
Warren, Kenneth W. 2011. *What Was African American Literature?* Cambridge, Mass.: Harvard University Press.

Watkins, Paul. 2014. "'We Can Never Tell the Entire Story of Slavery': In Conversation with M. NourbeSe Philip." *The Toronto Review of Books* April 30. <www.torontoreviewofbooks.com/2014/04/in-conversation-with-m-nourbese-philip> [accessed 20 December 2020].

Wells Brown, William. 1969. "A Lecture Delivered Before the Female Anti-Slavery Society of Salem at Lyceum Hall, Nov. 14, 1847." In: Larry Gara et al. (eds.). *Four Fugitive Slave Narratives*. Boston: Addison-Wesley. 81–82.

Wenzel, Jennifer. 2006. "Petro-magic-realism: Toward a Political Ecology of Nigerian Literature." *Postcolonial Studies* 9(4): 449–464.

White, Hayden V. 1973. *Metahistory: The Historical Imagination in Nineteenth-century Europe*. Baltimore: Johns Hopkins University Press.

White, Hayden V. 1987. *The Content of the Form: Narrative Discourse and Historical Representation*. Baltimore: Johns Hopkins University Press.

White, Hayden V. 1996. "The Modernist Event." In: Vivian Sobchack (ed.). *The Persistence of History: Cinema, Television, and the Modern Event*. London & New York: Routledge. 17–38.

White, Hayden V. 2010. "What Is a Historical System." In: Robert Doran (ed.). *The Fiction of Narrative: Essays on History, Literature, and Theory, 1957–2007*. Baltimore: Johns Hopkins University Press. 126–136.

White, Hayden V. 2014. "'We're Trying to Destroy the World' – Anti-Blackness & Police Violence After Ferguson, an Interview with Frank B. Wilderson." *ILL WILL EDITIONS* November 2014. 1–23.

White, Hayden V. 2015. *Incognegro: a Memoir of Exile & Apartheid*. Durham: Duke University Press.

White, Hayden V. 2016. Samira Spatzek, and Paula von Gleich. "'The Inside-Outside of Civil Society': An Interview with Frank B. Wilderson, III." *Black Studies Papers* 2(1): 4–22.

Whitehead, Colson. 2016. *The Underground Railroad: a Novel*. New York: Doubleday

Wilderson, Frank B. III. 2010. *Red, White & Black: Cinema and the Structure of US Antagonisms*. Durham: Duke University Press.

Williams, Aaron. 2018. "Hate Crimes Rose the Day after Trump Was Elected, FBI Data Show." *The Washington Post* March 23. <www.washingtonpost.com/news/post-nation/wp/2018/03/23/hate-crimes-rose-the-day-after-trump-was-elected-fbi-data-show/?utm_term=.098f85dd087c> [accessed 20 December 2020].

Williams, William Carlos. 1962 "Landscape with the Fall of Icarus." *Pictures from Brueghel and Other Poems: Collected Poems 1950–1962*. Cambridge, Mass.: New Directions.

Williams, Raymond. 2001. *The Long Revolution*. Peterborough: Broadview Press.

Wilson Gilmore, Ruth. 2007. *Golden Gulag*. Berkeley: University of California Press.

Winters, Joseph Richard. 2016. *Hope Draped in Black: Race, Melancholy, and the Agony of Progress*. Durham: Duke University Press.

Wolfe, Patrick. 2015. *Traces of History: Elementary Structures of Race*. London & New York: Verso.

Wood, James. 2011. "The Arrival of Enigmas." Review of *Open City*, by Teju Cole. *New Yorker* February 20. <www.newyorker.com/magazine/2011/02/28/the-arrival-of-enigmas> [accessed 20 December 2020].

Wright, Michelle M. 2004. *Becoming Black: Creating Identity in the African Diaspora*. Durham: Duke University Press.

Wright, Michelle M. 2013. "Can I Call You Black? The Limits of Authentic Heteronormativity in African Diasporic Discourse." *African and Black Diaspora* 6(1): 3–16.

Wright, Michelle M. 2015. *Physics of Blackness: Beyond the Middle Passage Epistemology*. Minneapolis: University of Minnesota Press.

Wright, Richard. 1940. *Native Son*. New York: Random House.

Wright, Richard. 1995. *White Man, Listen! Lectures in Europe*, 1950–1956. New Yorker: Harper Perennial.

Wynter, Sylvia. 2003. "Unsettling the Coloniality of Being/Power/Truth/Freedom: Towards the Human, After Man, Its Overrepresentation – An Argument." *The New Centennial Review* 3(3): 257–337.

Zeleza, Paul Tiyambe. 2009. "Diaspora Dialogues." In: Ididore Okpewho et al. (eds.). *The New African Diaspora*. Bloomington: Indiana University Press. 31–58.

Zeleza, Paul Tiyambe. 2011. "Pan-Africanism in the Age of Obama: Challenges and Prospects." *The Black Scholar* 41(2): 34–44.

Index

Abdur-Rahman, Aliyyah 14, 70
A Bend in the River 145
A Bit of Difference 4, 47
Achebe, Chinua 48, 102, 106, 118, 155–157, 185
Adichie, Chimamanda Ngozi 3, 5–7, 13, 25, 36, 39, 47, 51, 55f., 100–106, 108, 114, 116–118, 120, 122, 125f., 130–136, 139, 142, 147f., 155f., 199, 207, 210
Adorno, Theodor W. 94, 173
Africa 1–8, 10, 13, 15–21, 23–39, 42f., 45–48, 53f., 56, 58, 60f., 65, 68–70, 74, 77–79, 83, 85f., 90, 94, 100, 102, 104–109, 112, 115–118, 121–125, 129, 131–141, 143–153, 155–159, 162–165, 176, 178f., 181, 184–187, 190, 192, 194–198, 202, 205, 208–213, 215f.
– Africa for Africans 159
– *Africa Is a Country* 155
– African Americans 12, 15, 26, 34f., 56, 104, 125f., 150, 164
– African American subjectivity 7
– African American writing 6, 70
– African artists 3, 12, 17
– African complexity 4
– African consciousness 8
– African continent 1, 8, 30f., 86, 139, 155, 165, 194, 213
– African descent 13, 53, 164
– African Diaspora 2, 6, 12, 19, 32f., 47, 51, 102, 137, 165, 174, 195, 200
– African emigration 2
– African globality 8
– African identities 1
– African identity 11, 17, 37
– Africanity 10, 180, 196, 212
– africanization 6, 19
– African Literature 5, 14, 18–21, 24, 155–157
– African modernity 30, 216
– Africanness 2, 10, 15, 105, 124, 142, 145
– African novel 6, 18f., 21, 103, 155, 185, 188

– African publisher 6
– Africans 1, 3, 16, 26, 34–36, 38, 46, 53, 61, 83, 124, 136, 138, 148, 152, 158, 187, 197, 202, 215
– African signifier 3, 6, 11, 32, 106, 212
– African subject 11
Afro 3, 27f., 31f., 34–37, 53f., 56, 70, 122, 136, 141, 143, 152f., 155, 174, 178, 187, 193, 200, 205
– Afrocentric 30, 33, 139, 151
– Afro-cosmopolitans 10
– Afrofuturistic 3
– Afro-Modernity 26, 178
– Afro-pessimism 26f., 31f., 35, 191, 212
– Afropolitan 1f., 6f., 10–12, 14, 16, 20f., 26, 33–35, 37–40, 42f., 45, 48, 53f., 56, 60, 87, 99, 103, 106, 125, 142, 146, 151, 196, 208, 213, 215
– Afropolitanism 1–3, 6f., 9–12, 16f., 26f., 31, 35–40, 43f., 46–48, 52–56, 58, 60, 69, 97, 102f., 105f., 126, 143, 147, 151f., 154, 196, 212, 215
– Afropolitan literature 4–6, 13, 16, 18, 21, 37, 44f., 47
– Afropolitan moment 3–7, 9, 12, 21, 27, 35f., 38, 53, 59, 98, 101, 156, 197, 211
– Afropolitan novels 2, 4, 17, 51
– Afropolitans 3, 16
– Afropolitan writing 7
Against Race 9, 203
Ahmed, Sara 24f.
Aidoo, Ama Ata 6, 135–137, 139–141, 196, 199
Akomfrah, John 202f.
A Man of the People 48
A Mercy 44
Americanah 5, 13, 25, 34, 43, 47f., 51, 55, 100f., 103–118, 122f., 125, 127–137, 139, 141–143, 146–148, 151, 177, 207, 210
American Literary History 6, 29
Anderson, Benedict 134, 192
Angel of History 73f., 89, 154, 205f.

Index

Angelou, Maya 183
Anowa 136, 140, 196, 199
anti-Blackness 6, 32, 53–55, 200, 212 f.
anti-Black racism 8, 15, 54
Apartheid 33–35
A Place in the Sun 204 f.
Appiah, Anthony Kwame 9, 69
Arcades Project 73, 75
Aristotele 175, 177
Armah, Ayi Kwei 48
A Squatter's Tale 5
Atlanta 211
Atta, Sefi 4, 10, 47
Attree, Lizzy 155, 157
Auden, W.H. 72
Awkward Black Girl 211

Bakhtin, Mikhail 43, 60, 66 f., 96 f., 177
Balakrishnan, Sarah 2 f., 11, 37 f., 47, 152
Baldwin, James 13, 15, 104, 207 f.
Bandung-solidarity 4
Barracoon: The Story of the Last "Black Cargo" 197
Barthes, Roland 72
Baudelaire, Charles 72–74
Bauman, Zygmunt 30, 206
Beatty, Paul 40
Behold the Dreamers 47
Beloved 29, 37, 42
Benjamin, Walter 52, 65, 72–75, 77 f., 80, 82, 89 f., 93, 154, 187, 192, 198, 200, 205 f.
Bennett, Herman 164, 200
Best, Stephen 4 f., 21, 29 f., 70 f., 74 f., 77, 80, 89, 92, 95, 98, 100 f., 115, 117, 121, 125, 144, 152, 157, 172, 208, 216
Beyoncé 3, 101
Bhabha, Homi K. 40–42, 60, 111, 124, 134, 177, 179, 192, 210
biracial 11, 13
Black 2–4, 6–18, 21, 23–44, 47, 50–54, 56, 58, 60, 70, 77, 79, 81, 83 f., 87 f., 90, 95, 100, 102–105, 109, 111, 113 f., 116–118, 120–123, 125 f., 128–131, 134–136, 141–146, 148, 150–154, 156 f., 159, 163–165, 172, 175–184, 187, 190–194, 196 f., 199–201, 204 f., 207 f., 210–216
– Black African writers 21
– Black American authors 10
– Black American culture 13, 29, 147
– Black Atlantic studies 28 f., 74
– Black body 28, 207 f.
– black citizenship 8
– Black Cosmopolitanism 44, 58, 212 f.
– Black Diaspora 6 f., 11, 14, 16, 36, 38 f., 43, 45, 52 f., 55, 59, 87, 100, 106, 108, 143 f., 147 f., 151, 154, 178, 197, 208, 210
– Black fugitivity 99
– Black identity 7, 40, 105, 117, 148, 152
– Black Internationalism 23, 44
– Black liberation 14
– Black literature 23, 194
– Black Lives Matter 9, 14 f., 172
– Black male body 181
– Black Nationalism 177
– Black Nationalist 47, 164, 197
– Black neighborhood 4
– Blackness 3–7, 10–17, 25 f., 29–42, 51–56, 58, 69, 81, 88, 95, 97, 103–105, 111, 117, 122, 124, 126, 128, 142, 145, 147 f., 152, 154, 182, 187, 193, 196, 198, 200, 203, 207 f., 210–213
– Black Panther 3 f., 193
– Black Power 34, 44, 47, 151
– Black signification 11
– Black subjectivity 7, 123
– Black womanhood 120
– Black woman writers 103
– Black writer 21, 24, 37, 208
#BlackGirlMagic 100, 102 f.
Bleak House 115
Blyden, Edward 159
Blyton, Enid 118
Bonaparte, Napoleon 84
Boukman, Dutty 84
Brah, Avtar 17, 48
Brewster, John 93
Bridgerton 207
Brooks, Peter 45, 100, 127
Brown, Michael 14
Brown, William Wells 168
Bruegel, Pieter 72

Buck-Morss, Susan   162f.
Bulawayo, NoViolet   4, 37, 124, 157
Butler, Octavia   13, 20

Camera Lucida   72
Capital Vol. 1   90
Carby, Hazel   15, 118, 121
Caruth, Cathy   50, 57
Certeau, Michel de   61–63, 67, 72
Césaire, Aimé   23, 57, 163
Chikwava, Brian   4
Choonoo, R. Neville   33f.
Christiansë, Yvette   44
Chude-Sokei, Louis   7, 10, 13, 148, 152
Civil Rights movement   15, 33, 70, 159
Civil Rights politics   12
Clifford, James   17, 30f., 152, 202
Coetzee, J.M.   46, 72
Cole, Teju   4–6, 10, 13, 15f., 38f., 55–58, 63f., 68, 74, 85f., 88, 92, 118, 186, 193, 207–210, 213
colonialism   16, 18f., 27, 33, 38, 44, 48, 50, 60, 79, 116, 123, 134, 137, 156, 161, 170, 172f., 176, 178, 184f., 190, 197, 208
Conti, Paul   49
Coogler, Ryan   3, 193
Crawford, Margo Natalie   29, 36
Crossing the River   194f.
Cudjo, William   171, 197
Cugoano, Ottobah   95, 168, 172

D'Aguiar, Fred   170
Dalley, Hamish   50–52, 166
Das Lied von der Erde   62, 93
Davis, Angela   121, 173, 183
Daybdeen, David   170
Dear Ijeawele, or A Feminist Manifesto in Fifteen Suggestions   135
dehumanization   120, 188
Delany, Martin   29, 159
Devil on the Cross   48
diaspora   1, 4–6, 8, 10, 12, 17f., 26, 28, 32, 37–40, 44, 48, 56, 60, 81f., 85, 105f., 117, 134, 137f., 141–143, 147, 150–153, 155, 159, 175, 178, 192, 194–196, 198, 201–203, 210, 212f.

– diasporic Blackness   6, 16
– diasporic communities   6, 33, 37
– diasporic conversation   7, 140
– diasporic epistemologies   7
– diasporic historicism   44, 52
– diasporic imaginary   2–4, 6–8, 34, 37, 48, 56, 99, 113, 194, 202f.
– diasporic perspectives   98
– diasporic trajectories   6
Díaz, Junot   22, 170
Dickens, Charles   115
Die Zeit   103
Dilemma of a Ghost   136, 140, 196
Dimock, Wai Chee   43, 200f.
Diop, Alioune   23
Diplomatic Pounds   136
Disgrace   72
Douglass, Frederick   29, 168
Dreams from My Father   12
Du Bois, W.E.B.   1, 12, 14f., 23, 28f., 34, 54, 126f., 163f., 184
Dust   48
DuVernay, Ava   183

Edugyan, Esi   48
Edwards, Brent Hayes   23, 44, 127
Eggers, Dave   86
Elias, Amy   155, 160
Eliot, George   115
Elizabeth Costello   72
Ellison, Ralph   124
Emancipation   36, 54, 70, 88, 182, 184, 190, 197
Emecheta, Buchi   6
Emezi, Akwaeke   47
Entertainment Weekly   101
Every Day Is for the Thief   38, 74, 97, 186

Fanon, Frantz   18f., 23f., 32, 41f., 51, 111, 123f., 163, 180–182
Felski, Rita   71, 129
Ferguson, Roderick A.   14f., 27, 36, 151
flâneur   59f., 62, 72f., 78, 93, 97
Fleissner, Jennifer   71, 77, 80
Floyd, George   8
Foreign Gods, Inc.   51
Forna, Aminatta   22, 38f., 100

Foucault, Michel   54, 134, 143f., 191, 210
Frankfurter Allgemeine   103
Fraser, Nancy   123, 129
Freshwater   47
Freud, Sigmund   49, 70, 76, 78, 90
Frost, Robert   125
Fuchs, Barbara   127f.
fugueur   95, 97
Fuller, Meta   175, 184

Gambino, Childish   204, 211
Garner, Eric   14, 86, 108
Garvey, Marcus   159
Gates, Henry Louis   8, 60, 183
Get Out   211
Ghana Must Go   4, 10, 17, 53
Gikandi, Simon   1f., 10, 27, 30, 108, 110, 179, 194, 212f., 215
Gilroy, Paul   9, 17, 26, 29–31, 34–37, 40, 52, 60, 111f., 130, 148, 163f., 175, 178–180, 192, 194f., 197, 202, 213, 216
Glissant, Édouard   150, 153, 164–166, 201–203
Glover, Donald   211
Golden, Thelma   12, 136, 165
Goyal, Yogita   7, 26, 30f., 37, 49, 80, 82, 85, 87, 89, 91, 103, 106, 108f., 117, 125, 137–139, 141, 175, 191, 194–196, 202
Granta   101
Gyasi, Yaa   5, 16f., 38f., 55f., 150–152, 154, 157f., 171, 173, 177, 187f., 191, 199, 207, 210

Haley, Alex   172
Half of a Yellow Sun   101, 106, 120, 199
Half-Blood Blues   48
Hallemeier, Katherine   59, 68, 97, 133
Hall, Stuart   6, 45, 62, 105, 152, 172
Hamilton   207
Hanchard, Michael   26, 40, 178–180, 182
Happiness, Like Water   2, 4, 74, 185, 190, 192f., 197, 199
Harare North   4
Harlem Renaissance   23, 37, 182
Hartman, Saidiya   14, 28, 32, 52, 95, 120f., 150–152, 154, 167f., 170–173, 175, 179, 194, 198f., 201, 214–216

Hegel, George Wilhelm Friedrich   54, 68, 161–165, 194
Heine, Heinrich   160
Hill, Anita   13, 120, 209
Historiography   7, 44–47, 52, 61f., 71, 98, 158–162, 164–170, 174, 176, 191
Holocaust   50, 168f., 173
Homegoing   5, 38, 43, 48, 55, 150–155, 157f., 160, 164–167, 169–173, 175–180, 182–185, 188–203, 207–210
Hopkins, Pauline   164
House of Stone   48, 157f.
Huggan, Graham   21f.
Hurston, Zora Neale   118, 197
Huyssen, Andreas   91, 173

In A Station of the Metro   93
Incidents in the Life of a Slave Girl   121
Incognegro   35
independent woman   102
Insecure   211
In the Ditch   6
Invisible Man   124
Irele, Abiola   19, 37

Jacobs, Harriet   118, 124
James, C.L.R.   163, 199
James, Marlon   44
Jameson, Frederic   18f., 71, 108, 127–129, 147
Jim Crow   16, 23, 36, 123, 151, 176, 183
Johnson, Charles   157, 178
Johnson, Daryl   113
Johnson, Walter   188
Joyce, James   74
Julien, Eileen   18, 21, 188
"Jumping Monkey Hill"   120

Kaluuya, Daniel   211
Katrina-Ferguson Conjuncture   14f.
Khanna, Ranjana   80, 216
Kimani, Peter   155
King-Aribisala, Karen   185
King Jr., Martin Luther   48
Kingston, Maxine Hong   122
Kintu   48, 157f., 185–187
Klee, Paul   73

Knudsen, Eva Rask   2, 43, 48, 105 f.
Komunyakaa, Yusef   108
Kunzru, Hari   58
Kwani Trust   5, 185

LaCapra, Dominick   153 f., 168–172, 175, 198
Lamar, Kendrick   3
Landscape with Falling Icarus   72
Levine, Caroline   114–116
Ligon, Glenn   12
Lipsitz, George   14 f., 211
Li, Stephanie   1, 6, 14, 29, 76, 91 f., 97, 101, 108, 114, 132, 151, 160, 169, 188, 194, 206 f.
Locke, Alain   23, 109
Los Angeles Review of Books   155
Lose Your Mother   150, 170 f.
Lukács, Georg   153–155, 160–162, 190

Mahler, Gustav   62, 93
Makumbi, Jennifer Nansubuga   48, 150, 157, 185 f.
Man, Paul de   86 f., 91
Manshel, Alexander   112 f., 184
Mantel, Hilary   155
Maraire, J. Nozipo   156
Marvel   3
Marx, Karl   90
matrix of domination   120
Maus   173
Mbembe, Achille   1 f., 24, 31–33, 43, 48, 186, 190, 213
Mbue, Imbolo   47
melancholic historicism   29, 52, 70 f., 74, 77, 89, 113, 152, 157 f.
melancholy   29, 69, 75, 77, 122, 124, 211, 216
Mengestu, Dinaw   4, 37
Middlemarch   115
Middle Passage   26–31, 35–39, 55, 85 f., 105, 124, 148, 150 f., 168, 174, 178, 197
Miranda, Lin-Manuel   207
Mitchell, W.J.T.   8, 11, 25, 33, 40, 200
Moddelmog, William   164
Moraga, Cherríe   142
Moretti, Franco   110, 147

Morrison, Toni   29, 37, 42, 44, 118, 122, 152
Moten, Fred   90, 95, 193 f.
Movement   9, 14 f., 18, 27, 33 f., 37, 43, 47, 54, 57–62, 66–74, 78, 81–83, 85–88, 92 f., 95, 97, 99, 113, 124, 127, 136, 142 f., 159, 182, 191, 202 f., 205, 211–213
Msimang, Sisonke   102, 116

Nadiminti, Kalyan   21 f.
Naipaul, V.S.   145
Nationality   7, 29, 124, 142, 201, 203
Native Son   124
Natural hair movement   143 f.
Ndibe, Okey   51
Ndikung, Bonaventure Soh Behjeng   215
Négritude   24, 37, 136, 139
Nehl, Markus   44, 152, 174, 177
Neo-slave narrative *see* slave narrative
New diaspora   7, 12, 148
Newly Black   7, 10, 16, 39, 152, 157, 211
New Negro   23, 26, 56, 182
Newsday   101
New York Magazine   114
New York Times   2, 108, 151, 206
New York Times Book Review   101
New York Times Magazine   101
Nietzsche, Friedrich   161
Nigerpolitan   146
Non-American Black   7, 100, 105, 114, 117
non-white foreignness   110 f.
No Sweetness Here   136
Notes of a Native Son   207
Nothing Gold Can Stay   125
Nyong'o, Lupita   101

Obama, Barack   8 f., 12–15, 37, 48, 101, 110, 112–114, 116, 147, 157
Odamtten, Victor   136 f.
Odutola, Toyin Ojih   16 f.
Oguine, Ike   5, 13
Okparanta, Chinelo   4, 185
Okri, Ben   157, 185
On Black Sisters' Street   4
Open City   5, 13, 43, 48, 55, 57–64, 66, 68 f., 71–74, 78, 80–82, 85, 87–89,

91–93, 95–98, 100, 146, 177, 199, 207, 209f.
Orwell, George 107
Oscar Wao 170
Otele, Olivette 207
Our Sister Killjoy 6, 136–141
Owour, Yvonne Adhiambo 48
Oyelowo, David 101

Pan-African 8, 10, 15, 23, 25, 34, 56, 100f., 104f., 116f., 125, 136–142, 146–148, 164f., 196
Pan-Africanism 8, 33, 38, 44, 106, 127, 147, 165
Pan-Africanist 2, 28, 134–136, 159, 176
Paris Review 156
Patterson, Orlando 28, 32, 193
Peele, Jordan 211
Philip, M. NourbeSe 170, 174, 194, 197
Phillips, Caryl 170, 194, 196
Philosophy Today 204
Pitt, Brad 101
pop-feminism 102
Poplicks 13
post- 9, 37, 39, 42, 48, 100, 102, 211
– post-Black 10, 12f., 99
– post-Blackness 11–13
– Postcolonialism 51
– post-Emancipation America 14
– post-feminism 102
– post-independence era 19, 139
– post-#MeToo 208
– post-racial 7–10, 12, 14, 25, 28, 37, 39, 56, 69, 87, 103, 112, 126, 146, 157
– post-racialism 9f., 26, 103, 147
Pound, Ezra 74, 93
Purple Hibiscus 101, 106

Quaque, Philip 171

race 1, 6–11, 13, 15–17, 22–26, 29, 33f., 37, 39–43, 49f., 52–56, 58, 69f., 73, 81, 88, 93, 99, 101–111, 113f., 116, 120, 122f., 126–132, 134, 137, 142, 146–149, 151, 163, 177, 181, 184, 186f., 190f., 200, 202, 205, 208–211, 213
– Racial Imaginary Institute 25

– racialization 11, 24, 49, 51f., 98, 101, 110f., 116f., 122f., 126f., 137, 146f., 180, 187
– racialized discourse 9
– Racial Trauma 49, 51
– racism 9, 12, 15f., 22, 34, 54, 58, 69f., 79, 100, 104, 110, 113–117, 121, 126–129, 134f., 137f., 147f., 176–178, 180f., 190, 208, 211f.
– racist violence 8
radioWissen 103
Rae, Issa 211
Rahbeck, Ulla 43, 48, 106
Rankine, Claudia 22f., 25, 183
rape 63–66, 68, 72, 97, 118, 120f., 124, 141, 208
Representations 3, 25, 71, 109, 120, 139, 150, 172–174, 191, 211, 214
#RhodesMustFall 212
Roots 29f., 34, 69, 123, 133, 139, 141, 143, 150, 172, 202f.

Salami, Minna 48
salon.com 103
Sankofa 205
#SayHerName 15
Schindler's List 173
Scott, David 79
Scott, Sir Walter 160f.
Seattle Times 101
Selasi, Taiye 1–4, 10–12, 16f.
Selma 183
Senghor, Léopold 23f., 139
Serpell, Namwali 48, 157
Sexton, Jared 27f., 32, 177
sexual violence 120
Shakespeare, William 208
Shange, Ntozake 118
Sharpe, Christina 212, 214f.
Shoah 173
Skinner, Ryan Thomas 2
slave-descent 13
slave narrative 44, 84f., 87, 95, 153, 168, 172, 174
Slavery 7, 13f., 16, 26–38, 44f., 50, 52, 55f., 74, 80, 84, 90f., 117f., 121–123, 126, 141f., 148, 150–152, 154, 157, 163,

166–176, 178 f., 181, 183 f., 188–190, 192–194, 196 f., 211 f., 214
Slumberland 40
Smith, Bessie 207
Smith, Zadie 107, 131, 204–207, 214
Soyinka, Wole 24 f., 102
Speke, John Hanning 185–187
Spillers, Hortense 32, 41, 54, 121 f., 191, 210
Stallings, L.H. 40, 210
Sterling, Cheryl 9, 137 f.
"Still I Rise" 183
Stormfront 113
Swing Time 205

Taylor, Keeanga-Yamahtta. 2, 15, 165
The 13th 84
The Beautiful Things That Heaven Bears 4, 37
The Beautyful Ones Are Not Yet Born 48
The Black Jacobins 163
The Bluest Eye 122
The Book of Night Women 44
The Bourgeois 110
The Chicago Tribune 101
The Economist 58
The Fire This Time 104
The Guardian 155
The Interesting Narrative of the Life of Olaudah Equiano 85
The LIP 1
The New Yorker 14, 96, 156, 204
The Old Drift 48, 157 f.
The Souls of Black Folk 14, 126 f., 207
The Thing Around Your Neck 101
The Underground Railroad 60, 172
Things Fall Apart 145, 155 f., 169, 185
Thiong'o, Ngũgĩ wa 18, 46, 48, 159
Third World Feminism 142
This Bridge Called My Back – Writings of Radical Women of Power 142
This Is America 204, 211
Thomas, Clarence 20, 172, 209
Tometi, Opal 1, 15, 212
too-whiteness 22
Toussaint, Pierre 84
transnational Black culture 143

trauma 7, 23, 31, 35, 37 f., 49–52, 55, 58, 68 f., 73–75, 78–80, 89, 91, 99, 117, 121, 153, 167 f., 174 f., 195 f., 208 f.
– Trauma Studies 50
Trump, Donald 38, 204
Tshuma, Novuyo Rosa 48, 157 f.

Ulysses 74
Unconfessed 44
Unigwe, Chika 4
US Movement for Black Lives 8

Vassa, Gustavus 85 f.
Vermeulen, Peter 68, 92, 97
Vertigo Sea 202 f.

Walker, Alice 117 f., 136, 197
Ward, Abygail 126, 170
Warren, Kenneth 23, 69 f., 157
Washington Ideas Forum 118
Washington Post 101, 113
Waverly 160
We Need New Names 4, 37, 124, 157
We Should All Be Feminists 101, 135
West 3, 13, 16, 21, 30, 33–35, 42, 137, 139, 141, 144 f., 150, 152, 164 f., 185, 197, 205, 208
– West African slaves 13
– Western 1 f., 5, 22, 24, 30, 46, 54, 61, 87, 134 f., 137 f., 159, 163, 192, 197, 207, 212
– Western influence 18, 20, 135
– Western liberalism 162
West, Kanye 204
What Is the What 86
White, Hayden 8 f., 16, 22 f., 26, 32–35, 41 f., 45, 51, 61, 77, 79, 83, 88, 93, 104 f., 110, 112, 114, 116–119, 121, 125, 129, 142, 144–146, 154–156, 161–163, 167–169, 173, 179–184, 188–190, 193, 195 f., 198, 200, 206–208, 212, 214
Whitehead, Colson 155, 172 f.
White Mythology 25
whiteness 25, 54, 120, 124
white Western culture 208
Whitman, Walt 74

Wilderson, Frank B.   28, 32, 35, 53f., 122, 191, 212
Williams, William Carlos   39f., 72, 74, 113
Winters, Joseph R.   15, 29
Wolfe, Patrick   187, 189
Woman Warrior   122
Wood, James   59, 94, 96f.

Wright, Michelle M.   6, 15, 27, 30, 36, 143, 164, 212
Wright, Richard   23f., 29, 118, 124, 126

Zenzele   156
Zong!   170, 174

www.ingramcontent.com/pod-product-compliance
Lightning Source LLC
Chambersburg PA
CBHW031425150426
43191CB00006B/399